Electoral Engineering

From Kosovo to Kabul, recent decades have witnessed multiple attempts at electoral engineering designed to improve political representation and alter voting behavior. This study compares and evaluates two broad schools of thought about this process, each offering contrasting expectations. Rational-choice institutionalism claims that by changing the incentives offered by electoral rules, reformers have the capacity to alter the behavior of parties, politicians, and citizens, thereby solving multiple social problems, whether by mitigating ethnic conflict, improving turnout, strengthening voter–party bonds, generating democratic accountability, or boosting women's representation. Alternative theories of cultural modernization are more cautious about the capacity of electoral engineering to achieve these goals, suggesting that formal rules adapt to, rather than alter, deeply embedded patterns of human behavior. To examine these accounts, in this study Pippa Norris compares new survey evidence derived from about three-dozen parliamentary and presidential elections in a wide range of established and newer democracies, spanning the globe from the United States to the Ukraine, and from Australia to Peru. The author concludes that formal rules *do* matter, with important implications for the choice of electoral systems.

Norris integrates the extensive literature on electoral systems with studies of voting behavior and political representation; develops a clear theoretical framework supported by original empirical research based on new cross-national data; presents the findings in an accessible, stimulating, and nontechnical manner; covers a broad sweep of nations around the globe; and provides results of interest for political scientists and policymakers in many countries.

Pippa Norris is the McGuire Lecturer in Comparative Politics at the John F. Kennedy School of Government, Harvard University. Her work compares elections and public opinion, gender politics, and political communications. Companion volumes by this author, also published by Cambridge University Press, include *A Virtuous Circle* (2000), *Digital Divide* (2001), *Democratic Phoenix* (2002), and *Rising Tide* (2003, with Ronald Inglehart).

Electoral Engineering

Voting Rules and Political Behavior

PIPPA NORRIS
Harvard University

CAMBRIDGE
UNIVERSITY PRESS

PUBLISHED BY THE PRESS SYNDICATE OF THE UNIVERSITY OF CAMBRIDGE
The Pitt Building, Trumpington Street, Cambridge, United Kingdom

CAMBRIDGE UNIVERSITY PRESS
The Edinburgh Building, Cambridge CB2 2RU, UK
40 West 20th Street, New York, NY 10011-4211, USA
477 Williamstown Road, Port Melbourne, VIC 3207, Australia
Ruiz de Alarcón 13, 28014 Madrid, Spain
Dock House, The Waterfront, Cape Town 8001, South Africa

http://www.cambridge.org

First published 2004

Printed in the United States of America

Typeface Sabon 10/12 pt.   *System* LATEX 2$_\varepsilon$ [TB]

A catalog record for this book is available from the British Library.

Library of Congress Cataloging in Publication data

Norris, Pippa.
Electoral engineering : voting rules and political behavior / Pippa Norris.
   p. cm.
Includes bibliographical references and index.
ISBN 0-521-82977-1 (hardback) – ISBN 0-521-53671-5 (pbk.)
1. Elections.   2. Voting.   3. Party affiliation.   4. Representative government and
representation.   5. Comparative government.   I. Title.
JF1001 N67   2004
324.6'3–dc21   2003055179

ISBN 0 521 82977 1 hardback
ISBN 0 521 53671 5 paperback

Contents

List of Tables and Figures

Tables

Figures

Preface

"It is complicated." With these words, Hans-Dieter Klingemann warned me, with typical German understatement, of what was ahead when I first mentioned plans for this book over a (not very good) dinner in Turin. The words have echoed in my mind on countless occasions since then, sticking rather like an annoying few bars from a television commercial. He did not say impossible. He did not say impractical. He said complicated. "Yes," I said casually, "of course." But I didn't really listen. I had just completed another book that covered 193 nations. The core dataset for this volume covers just more than 30. It was a little puzzling to me that so few others had ever attempted a book comparing voting behavior across many different types of societies, including older and newer democracies. But with the arrogance of ignorance I plunged ahead. After all, courtesy of the hardworking team at the University of Michigan, I had access to the first integrated cross-national dataset bringing together election studies from Australia to the Ukraine. But as I soon discovered, complicated it was, and still is. But it was also, I happily discovered, fascinating, stimulating, and challenging.

This book would not have been possible without the work of all those who contributed toward the Comparative Study of Electoral Systems (CSES), especially Virginia Sapiro, Phil Shively, David Howell, Karen Long, and all the staff who worked on this project at the Center for Political Studies, Institute for Social Research, at the University of Michigan, Ann Arbor. Details are available online at www.umich.edu/~nes/cses. The 1996–2001 Module I Study was carried out by CSES collaborators in more than 30 countries. These collaborators are: Australia (Ian McAllister), Belarus (David Rotman and Larysa Saglaeva), Belgium (in Flanders, Jacques Biliet), Canada (André Blais and Neil Nevitte), Chile (Marta Lagos), Czech Republic (Gabor Toka), Denmark (Ole Borre), Germany (Bernhard Wessels and Hermann Schmitt), Great Britain (Anthony Heath, Roger Jowell, and John Curtice), Hong Kong (Pang Kwong Li and Kwong Ka Shi), Hungary (Gabor Toka), Iceland (Olafur Hardarson), Israel (Michal Shamir), Japan (Yoshitaka Nishizawa),

Korea (Nam Young Lee), Lithuania (Elena Liubsiene), Mexico (Ulises Beltran and Benito Nacif), the Netherlands (Kees Aarts), New Zealand (Jack Vowles), Norway (Bernt Aardal), Peru (Catalina Romero), Poland (Radoslaw Markowski), Romania (Gabriel Badescu), Russia (Timothy Colton and Michael McFaul), Slovenia (Janez Stebe), Spain (Juan Diez-Nicolas), Sweden (Soren Holmberg and Per Hedberg), Switzerland (Sibylle Hardmeier), Taiwan (Hu Fu), Thailand (Robert Albritton), Ukraine (Olga Balakireva), and the United States (Virginia Sapiro). Planning Committee members for Module I were: Rita Bajarunieni (Lithuania), John Curtice (Great Britain), Juan Diez-Nicolas (Spain), Oscar Hernandez (Costa Rica), Soren Holmberg (Sweden), Hans-Dieter Klingemann (Germany), Marta Lagos (Chile), Felipe B. Miranda (Philippines), Yoshitaka Nishizawa (Japan), Steven Rosenstone (United States), Jacques Thomassen (the Netherlands), and Gabor Toka (Hungary). Consultants to the Planning Committee were: Gary Cox (University of California, San Diego), Ekkehard Mochmann (Zentralarchiv fur empirische Sozialforschung), Richard Rockwell (Inter-university Consortium for Political and Social Research), Hermann Schmitt (European Election Study), and W. Phillips Shively (University of Minnesota).

Work on this book gradually developed over the years in conjunction with many other projects. As ever, I am indebted to many. Research on women's election to office, on gender quotas, and on constituency service was developed in collaboration with Joni Lovenduski and in successive surveys of British parliamentary candidates in the British Representation Study 1992–2001, resulting in numerous related publications. A special issue of the *International Political Science Review* that I edited in 1995, originally suggested by Pat Dunleavy, generated my initial interest in the comparative politics of electoral reform. Work with colleagues on the 1997 British Election Study helped clarify my ideas on social and partisan dealignment. An earlier version of Chapter 9 was presented at the International Conference on Institutional Design, Conflict Management and Democracy in the Late Twentieth Century, Kellogg Institute, University of Notre Dame, December 9–11, 1999. I would like to thank Andy Reynolds, Jorgen Elklit, and Giovanni Sartori for many helpful comments at the meeting that stimulated my thinking on this topic. An earlier version of Chapter 10 (on constituency service) was presented at the British Politics Group annual meeting at the American Political Science Association meeting in August 2000. Other chapters were presented as works-in-progress at other professional meetings, including the conference Political Reform in Brazil in Comparative Perspective, in Rio de Janeiro in June 2002; the symposium, Exporting Congress, at Florida International University, Miami, in December 2002; the Center for Social Science Research Seminar at the University of Cape Town in January 2003; the Mid-West Political Science Association meeting in Chicago in April 2003; and the centennial meeting of the American Political Science Association in Philadelphia in

August 2003. Meg Russell, Drude Dahlerup, Swanee Hunt, Julie Ballington, and Judith Squires were particularly helpful in providing information about the use of gender quotas used in Chapter 8. I also appreciate all the encouragement and advice provided as chapters for the book developed gradually, particularly ideas and comments by Roberto D'Alimonte, David Butler, Ivor Crewe, John Curtice, David Denver, Jorge Dominguez, Geoff Evans, David Farrell, Mark Franklin, Elizabeth Gidengil, Peter Hall, Gretchen Helmke, David Howell, Mala Htun, Ron Inglehart, Simon King, Hans-Dieter Klingemann, Karen Long, Steven Levitsky, Arend Lijphart, Joni Lovenduski, Jane Mansbridge, Ian McAllister, Michael Marsh, Neil Nevitte, Joseph Nye, Ben Reilly, David Sanders, Fred Schauer, Gregory Schmidt, Hermann Schmidt, Andy Reynolds, Nigel Roberts, Richard Rose, Jacques Thomassen, Jack Vowles, and Margaret Weir, among others, as well as the research assistance of Roopal Thaker and Eric Lockwood, the constant encouragement of my publisher, Lew Bateman, the efficient team at Cambridge University Press, and all my colleagues and students in the Government Department and the John F. Kennedy School of Government at Harvard University.

Pippa Norris
Cambridge, Massachusetts

Electoral Engineering

Voting Rules and Political Behavior

PART I

INTRODUCTION

I

Do Rules Matter?

Structure versus Culture

From Kosovo to Kabul, the last decade has witnessed growing interest in "electoral engineering." The end of the Cold War, the global spread of democracy, and new thinking about development spurred this process. During the late 1980s and early 1990s the flowering of transitional and consolidating "third wave" democracies around the globe generated a wave of institution building. International agencies such as the World Bank came to understand that good governance was not a luxury that could be delayed while more basic social needs were being met, like the provision of clean water, basic health care, and schooling. Instead the establishment of democracy was understood as an essential pre-condition for effective human development and management of poverty, inequality, and ethnic conflict.[1] The donor community recognized that the downfall of many corrupt dictatorships in Latin America, Central Europe, Asia, and Africa created new opportunities for political development.[2] Subsequent histories show that the process of deepening democracy and good governance has proved to be fraught with many difficulties, with little change to many repressive regimes in the Middle East, only fragile and unstable consolidation in Argentina and Venezuela, and even occasional reversions back to authoritarian rule, exemplified by Zimbabwe and Pakistan.[3]

International agencies have used a triple strategy to promote democracy. Institution building has been one priority, by strengthening independent judiciaries and effective legislatures designed to curb and counterbalance executive powers. Civic society has been another priority, with attempts to nurture grassroots organizations, advocacy nongovernmental organizations (NGOs), and independent media. But among all the strategies, attempts to establish competitive, free, and fair elections have attracted the most attention. Only the ballot box provides regular opportunities for the public to select representatives, to hold governments to account, and to "kick the rascals out," where necessary. Electoral systems are commonly regarded as some of the most basic democratic structures, from which much else flows.

3

Elections are not sufficient by themselves for representative democracy, by any means, but they are a necessary minimal condition. Views differ sharply about the appropriate evaluative criteria, but most agree that, at minimum, elections must meet certain essential conditions to ensure democratic legitimacy. They should be free of violence, intimidation, bribery, vote rigging, irregularities, systematic fraud, and deliberate partisan manipulation. Contests should provide an unrestricted choice of competing parties and candidates, without repression of opposition parties or undue bias in the distribution of campaign resources and media access. Elections should use fair, honest, efficient, and transparent procedures from voter registration to the final vote tally. Parliamentary representatives should reflect the society from which they are drawn and should not systematically exclude any minority group. And campaigns should generate widespread public participation.[4] Where rulers have blocked, derailed, or corrupted the electoral process in attempts to retain power, as in Burma, Zimbabwe, or Iraq, their actions undermined their legitimacy and attracted critical scrutiny.

Until the 1980s, international electoral assistance was fairly exceptional, applied only in special cases, such as in the first transfer of power following decolonization or at the end of civil war. Yet from the early 1990s onward, international observers, technical aid experts, and constitutional advisers have played leading roles as dozens of transitional elections have occurred throughout Central and Eastern Europe, Asia, and Latin America. Attempts to deepen and strengthen good governance have focused on the basic design of electoral systems and, more generally, on issues of electoral administration, voter education, election observing, and party capacity-building.[5] Elections played a particularly important role in attempts to manage ethnic tensions in plural societies such as Bosnia-Herzegovina. Debates about electoral systems have traditionally revolved around the desirability of the major ideal types. Majoritarian electoral systems are designed to promote accountable single-party government by awarding the greatest representation to the two leading parties with the most votes. Proportional electoral systems aim to generate inclusive and consensual power sharing by producing parliaments that reflect the vote shares of multiple parties. During the 1990s debates turned increasingly toward the pros and cons of combined (or mixed) electoral systems, incorporating features of each of the major ideal types.[6]

Interest in electoral engineering has not been confined to third wave democracies. During the postwar era, electoral systems have usually proved to be relatively stable institutions in most established democracies. Nevertheless, occasional modifications to electoral law have occurred, including minor adjustment to voting thresholds, electoral formulas, and suffrage qualifications.[7] Moreover, some long-standing democracies have implemented far more radical reforms of the basic electoral system during the last decade. In the United Kingdom, the Blair government radically overhauled the electoral system of First-Past-the-Post (FPTP), with alternative systems adopted at almost every level except for Westminster and local councils.[8] In New Zealand in 1993, after more than a century of First-Past-the-Post, the nation switched to a mixed-member proportional system, producing a sudden fragmentation of the two-party system.[9] In 1992, Israel introduced direct elections for the prime minister to create a stronger executive capable of counterbalancing party fragmentation in the Knesset and overcoming the problems of frequent government turnover.[10] The following year Italy changed. After prolonged debate about the best way to overcome unstable party governments, and a deep crisis in the parliamentary system, Italy adopted a combined electoral system whereby three-quarters of the parliamentary seats are distributed by plurality vote in single member districts and the remaining one-quarter are distributed proportionally, as compensation for minor parties.[11] Venezuela, one of Latin America's oldest democracies, aiming to strengthen the independence of elected members over the national party leadership, changed in 1993 from a closed-list proportional representation (PR) system for the Chamber of Deputies to a combined system.[12] In March 1994, Japan moved from a Single Non-Transferable Vote (SNTV) to a system combining PR seats with First-Past-the-Post single-member districts, in the attempt to craft a competitive two-party, issue-oriented politics and a cleaner, more efficient government.[13] Beyond the basic electoral formula, many democracies have overhauled electoral procedures by reforming the legal statutes and party rules to facilitate positive action for women, improving the administrative process of electoral registration and voting facilities, and revising the regulation of campaign finance and broadcasting.[14]

During the last decade, therefore, issues of effective democratic design have risen sharply on the policy agenda in many nations. The first "founding" contests held under any revised rules may prove anomalous and unstable, as citizens and parties learn the ropes, but their effects can be assessed more reliably after a decade of elections held under the revised arrangements. Attempts at electoral engineering have commonly sought to achieve a balance between greater democratic accountability through majoritarian systems or wider parliamentary diversity through proportional systems. Underlying the long-standing normative debates are certain important empirical claims about the consequences of electoral engineering for voting choices and for political representation. Electoral reform is founded upon the principle that altering the formal rules matters based on the assumption that certain desirable consequences for social and political engineering can be achieved through the public policy process. There is certainly persuasive evidence that electoral rules have important *mechanical* effects as they help to determine which candidates are elected to parliament and which parties enter government. This is an essential function in representative democracies. Even if electoral rules had no other impact, this still provides ample justification for their study. But do formal rules have important *psychological* effects with the capacity to alter the behavior of political actors and citizens?[15] Far less agreement surrounds this question.

To understand these issues, this book compares and evaluates alternative perspectives offered by *rational-choice institutionalism* and *cultural modernization* theories. These broad schools of thought shape the literature, each with multiple contributors. Each offers contrasting expectations about the impact and the consequences of electoral engineering on human behavior, one more optimistic, the other more cautious. Each also reflects deeper divisions within the social sciences. Both perspectives offer alternative interpretations about how political actors will respond to changes in the formal rules of the game, and both rest ultimately upon contrasting visions of human behavior. Of course, many other perspectives are possible, such as historical institutionalism emphasizing the distinctive process of path-dependency in any nation. There are also general cultural theories, which do not make any assumptions about processes of societal development. The framework chosen as the focus in this book should not be regarded as providing an exhaustive and definitive overview of the arguments. Nevertheless, the two approaches that are the selected focus of this study can be regarded as among the most pervasive and important theories. Essentially, rational-choice institutionalism assumes that formal electoral rules have a substantial impact upon the strategic incentives facing politicians, parties, and citizens, so that changing the formal rules has the capacity to alter political behavior. Yet it remains unclear *how much* formal rules and strategic incentives matter in comparison with deep-rooted cultural "habits of the heart" arising from the process of societal modernization; and we know even less about how structure and culture interact. This, in a nutshell, is the central puzzle to be unraveled at the heart of this book. Rules are thought to have multiple consequences so this study focuses upon understanding their potential impact upon many important dimensions of electoral behavior and political representation. The most important aspects of voting behavior concern patterns of party competition, the strength of social cleavages and party loyalties, and levels of electoral turnout. Political representation is compared by the inclusion of women and ethnic minorities in elected office and by the provision of constituency service.

The aim of this book is, therefore, to reintegrate two strands in the literature. One rich and extensive set of studies has long sought to understand electoral systems through classifying the formal rules, deducing certain consequences, and analyzing the evidence from aggregate election results held under different systems. Another substantial literature has sought to analyze how voters respond to the electoral choices before them, based on the evidence from individual-level national surveys of the electorate and on more occasional experiments or focus groups, often studied within each country or region in isolation from their broader institutional context. What this study seeks to do is to reintegrate some of the core strands in these literatures, so that we can explore how *formal electoral rules* (the independent variable) shape the strategic behavior of *political actors* (both parties and politicians, as the intervening variables) and how, in turn, the behavior of political actors affects *voting choices* (the dependent variable). The study does not claim to be a comprehensive and exhaustive treatment of electoral systems or voting behavior but, rather, it seeks to open new questions and identify new challenges for further research that arise from combining these perspectives. The claim is made that the sum is greater than the parts, and creative synthesis across the subfields of electoral systems and voting behavior, even if difficult, can be a fruitful and illuminating path of inquiry. This introduction first compares and clarifies the key assumptions made within each theoretical perspective, then summarizes the research design, comparative evidence, and overall plan of the book.

Rational-choice Institutionalism and the Calculus of Rewards

The basic idea that formal rules determine political behavior is a popular approach to understanding electoral laws, and it is particularly common in rational-choice institutionalism and game-theoretic models, as well as implicit in the assumptions made within many legal, historical, and structural accounts of electoral systems. The core theoretical claim in rational-choice institutionalism is that formal electoral rules generate important incentives that are capable of shaping and constraining political behavior.[16] *Formal* electoral rules are understood here as the legislative framework governing elections, as embodied in official documents, constitutional conventions, legal statutes, codes of conduct, and administrative procedures authorized by law and enforceable by courts. It is neither necessary nor sufficient for rules to be embodied in the legal system for them to be effective; social norms, informal patterns of behavior, and social sanctions also create shared mutual expectations among political actors. Nevertheless, I focus here upon the formal rules as most attention in the literature on electoral engineering has emphasized these as core instruments of public policy.[17] The key distinction is that formal rules are open to amendment by the political process, whether by legislation, executive order, constitutional revision, judicial judgment, or bureaucratic decree. Although there is a "gray" overlapping area, by contrast, most social norms are altered gradually by informal processes such as social pressures, media campaigns, and cultural value shifts located outside of the formal policy arena.

The account of rational-choice institutionalism explored in this book rests upon a series of claims, illustrated schematically in Figure 1.1:

1. Formal electoral rules shape the *incentives* facing political actors.
2. Political actors are rational vote-maximizers in pursuit of electoral office who respond strategically to electoral incentives.

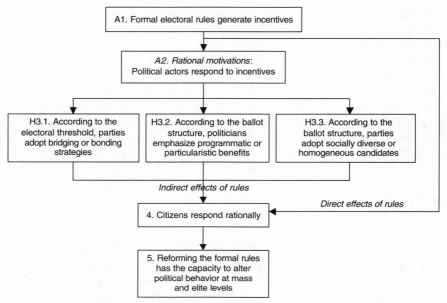

FIGURE 1.1. The rational-choice institutionalism model

3. In particular, based on the formal rules, we hypothesize that:
    3.1. According to the electoral threshold, parties decide whether to follow *bridging or bonding* strategies.
    3.2. According to the ballot structure, politicians calculate whether to offer *particularistic or programmatic* benefits.
    3.3. According to the ballot structure, parties choose whether to select *socially homogeneous or socially diverse* legislative candidates.
4. Citizens respond to the alternative electoral strategies adopted by political actors; they also respond directly to electoral rules affecting their role as citizens, with observable consequences evident in mass behavior.
5. "Electoral engineering" – changing the formal electoral rules – has the capacity to generate major consequences by altering the strategic behavior of politicians, parties, and citizens.

In subsequent chapters I compare systematic survey evidence to test whether formal rules do indeed confirm these expectations, as claimed. Before considering the data, what is the logic of this argument?

Electoral Incentives

Rational-choice institutionalism is founded upon the premise that the rules adopted in any political system have the capacity to shape the electoral rewards and punishments facing political actors. That is to say, the theory assumes that the basic choice of either a proportional or majoritarian electoral system, or more detailed matters such as the average size of electoral districts, the type of ballot structure, or the use of statutory gender quotas, influences the structure of opportunities for parties and individual politicians. To take a simple and uncontroversial illustration, some countries have public financing of election campaigns, free election broadcasting, and, moreover, legislative candidates elected every four or five years on the basis of closed party lists; within this context individual candidates have little incentive for political fund-raising, and, indeed, they may have few opportunities to do this, even if they wanted to, because election financing may be strictly controlled. In other places, there are frequent elections, entrepreneurial candidates raise most funds on an individual basis, there are few or no public subsidies covering the costs of election campaigns, there are limited party resources, political advertising is commercially priced and expensive, and rules controlling campaign expenditure are lax. In such a context, candidates face every electoral incentive to devote much of their time and energies to campaign fund-raising. In this regard, as in many others, formal electoral rules are not neutral in their impact; instead they systematically benefit some while penalizing others.

Vote-Maximizing Political Actors

The second premise of the theory assumes that political actors in representative democracies are essentially vote-maximizers seeking office in the electoral marketplace. The idea that politicians are *only* seeking public popularity is, of course, a drastic simplification given the complex range of motivations driving the pursuit of power. Legislators may fail to follow this logic because of many other priorities. Biographies suggest that politicians come in all shapes and sizes. Elected representatives may prefer the cut-and-thrust drama of parliamentary debate in the public spotlight to less-glamorous behind-the-scenes constituency casework. Ideologues may opt for purity to fundamental principles rather than the "ambulance-chasing" pursuit of public popularity ("better red than dead"). Materialists may want to line their own pockets. Philanthropists may be attracted to serve the public good. Status-seekers may enjoy the seductive aphrodisiac of the ministerial limo. Statespersons may seek to make their mark upon the history books. Yet, in all these cases, the Darwinian theory predicts that politicians who are not vote-maximizers, at least to some degree, will gradually become less common because, in general, they will be less successful in gaining election or re-election. This premise is empty of content: It does not assume *what* particular strategies political actors will pursue to gain power but merely that they will seek votes.

Party Bridging or Bonding Strategies

If we accept these two premises as working assumptions or axioms, they generate a series of testable specific hypotheses about how certain formal electoral rules shape the opportunities for politicians to garner votes.

The first core hypothesis is that the electoral threshold will shape the inducements for parties to campaign collectively using either *bridging* or *bonding* strategies. The theory that parties are "masters of their fate," so that they can actively reinforce or weaken party-voter linkages, was developed by Przeworski and Sprague, and subsequently expanded by Kitschelt.[18] But how does this process relate systematically to electoral rules? Majoritarian electoral systems provide higher electoral hurdles because parties need a simple plurality or a majority of votes in each district to win. Under these rules, we theorize that successful parties will commonly adopt bridging strategies designed to gather votes promiscuously and indiscriminately wherever campaign support can be found among diverse sectors of the electorate.[19] Bridging parties seek to create a broad coalition across diverse social and ideological groups in the electorate, typically by focusing upon uncontroversial middle-of-the-road issues that are widely shared among the public: the benefits of economic growth, the importance of efficient public services, and the need for effective defense. These strategies bring together heterogeneous publics into loose, shifting coalitions, linking different generations, faiths, and ethnic identities, thereby aggregating interests and creating crosscutting allegiances. Bridging parties are highly permeable and open organizations, characterized by easy-entrance, easy-exit among voters rather than by fixed lifetime loyalties. This proposition suggests many important consequences, not least of which is that under majoritarian electoral rules, parties are likely to be centripetal socially and ideologically, with competition clustered in the middle of the political spectrum.[20]

Alternatively, PR electoral systems provide lower hurdles to office, based on a far-smaller share of the electorate. Where there are lower electoral thresholds, this study hypothesizes that parties will typically adopt bonding strategies. These appeals focus upon gaining votes from a narrower home base among particular segmented sectors of the electorate – whether blue-collar workers, rural farmers, environmentalists, trade unionists, ethnic minorities, older women, or Catholic churchgoers. Bonding parties bring together citizens who are homogeneous in certain important respects, whether they share class, faith, or ethnic identities, or they are bound together ideologically by common beliefs about capitalism and socialism, environmentalism, or nationalism. Bonding parties are sticky organizations, promoting the interests of their own members and developing tightly knit social networks and clear "one-of-us" boundaries. Such strategies are usually efficient for parties because it is often easier to mobilize niche sectors with specific social and ideological appeals that are distinctive to each party, rather than to try to attract the mass public on consensual issues advocated by many parties. Party systems under proportional rules are more likely to be centrifugal, with competition dispersed throughout the ideological spectrum and issue space, rather than clustered closely around the center-point.[21] Bonding parties maintain strong ties with social cleavages in the electorate and strengthen enduring party loyalties. They are also more likely to be able to mobilize their supporters through programmatic appeals, thereby maximizing turnout at the ballot box. One-of-us campaigns reinforce party unity among ideologically motivated members, activists, and politicians. This proposition predicts that the type of electoral rules will, therefore, have important results for party campaign strategies and for voting behavior.

Through their bridging or bonding strategies, we assume that parties can either reinforce or weaken the political salience of social and partisan identities. The linkages between parties and citizens should, therefore, differ systematically according to the electoral threshold and, therefore, by the basic type of majoritarian, combined, or proportional electoral system. It is not claimed that politicians have the capacity to *create* social cleavages. But the account assumes that the initial adoption of certain electoral rules (for whatever reason) will generate incentives for parties to maintain, reinforce, and, possibly, exacerbate the political salience of one-of-us bonding, or, alternatively, to modify, downplay, and, possibly, erode group consciousness by encouraging catch-all bridging. This is most important in plural societies divided by deep-rooted ethnic conflict, exemplified by Northern Ireland, Sri Lanka, or Israel/Palestine, if leaders can heighten sectarian consciousness or, alternatively, moderate community divisions. The electoral rules of the game should be regarded as *one* (although only one) of the critical influences shaping the behavior of leaders and their followers.

In practice, this distinction between bridging and bonding parties obviously involves considerable oversimplification, as with any ideal type. Many parties blend both elements as complex organizations composed of different interests among party leaders, parliamentary candidates and elected representatives, paid officers, grassroots members, and more-occasional voters.[22] Case studies such as the British Labour Party or the German Social Democratic Party (SDP) suggest that parties are also capable of shifting type at different points of time, as they alternatively choose to prioritize ideological purity or electoral popularity rather than conforming strictly to fixed categories. Despite these important limitations, some parties can be identified as ideal types at both polar extremes, at least impressionistically. By comparing the strength of social cleavages, party loyalties, and patterns of turnout evident in contests held under majoritarian, combined, and proportional electoral rules, this study tests whether there are significant differences, as predicted theoretically.

Particularistic or Programmatic Benefits

The second core hypothesis suggests that the ballot structure – determining how electors can express their choices – is paramount in campaign strategies designed to secure election.[23] Ballot structures can be classified into the following four categories based on the choices facing citizens when they enter the voting booth:

Candidate-Ballots: In single-member districts, citizens in each constituency cast a single ballot for an individual candidate. The candidate who wins either a plurality or majority of votes in each district is elected. Through casting a ballot, electors indirectly express support for parties, but they have to vote directly for a particular candidate. In this context, politicians have a strong incentive to offer particularistic benefits, exemplified by casework helping individual constituents and by the delivery of local services ("pork") designed to strengthen their personal support within local communities.[24]

Preference-Ballots: In open-list multimember districts, electors cast a ballot for a party, but they can express their preference for a particular candidate or candidates within a party list. Where citizens exercise a preference vote (otherwise known as an open or nonblocked vote), this strengthens the chances that particular candidates will be elected and, therefore, change their rank on the list. Under these rules, politicians have a moderately strong incentive to offer particularistic benefits, to stand out from rivals within their own party.

Dual-Ballots: In combined (or mixed) electoral systems, voters can cast separate ballots in both single- and multimember districts, as exemplified by elections in Italy, Germany, and New Zealand.

Party-Ballots: Last, in closed-list multimember districts, citizens cast a single ballot for a party. Each party ranks the order of the candidates to be elected within its list, based on the decisions of the party selectorate, and the public cannot express a preference for any particular candidate within the list. Closed-list multimember districts, where voters can only "vote the ticket" rather than support a particular candidate, are expected to encourage politicians to offer programmatic benefits, focused on the collective record and program of their party, and to strengthen cohesive and disciplined parliamentary parties.[25]

The ballot structure is, therefore, closely related to the basic type of electoral system, although party-ballots can be used with both majoritarian and proportional systems. Other secondary rules that may influence the incentives for constituency service concern the centralization of the candidate selection processes within parties, the size of any multimember district, and any term limitations on legislators. Politicians have limited time and energies, and in considering multiple demands vying for their attention, they have to prioritize. Where politicians face strong electoral incentives to stand out from other rivals within their own party, they are expected to prioritize particularistic benefits offered through constituency service, allowing elected members to claim credit for dealing with local problems and community concerns. In this context, politicians emphasize the delivery of services and public goods (pork) to their home districts, as well as prioritize contact with local voters and party activists through their mail, community meetings, and doorstep canvassing. By contrast, closed-list PR systems, where voters can only vote the ticket rather than support a particular candidate, generate few electoral incentives that encourage politicians to offer constituency service. In this context, we can hypothesize that politicians rationally focus their efforts upon collective party appeals, typically based on their party's retrospective record in office or their prospective manifesto policies. Given accurate information about the ballot structure, we theorize that successful vote-seeking politicians will rationally adopt whichever particularistic or programmatic strategy is necessary for gaining and maintaining office.

Of course, some politicians may not conform to these expectations. Despite party-ballots, legislators may still engage in constituency service because of tacit social norms, informal rules within parliaments, or because some enjoy the intrinsic philanthropic rewards of helping the public. Despite candidate-ballots, given other personal ambitions, Westminster Members of Parliament (MPs) or Members of the U.S. House of Representatives also may prioritize the cut and thrust of legislative debate about the nation's affairs or the glory and glamour of appearing in TV studios, while neglecting the more prosaic matters of sorting out within dusty government bureaucracies particular housing claims or welfare benefits.[26] Yet the Darwinian logic suggests that, if citizens reward constituency service in candidate-ballots, under these rules politicians who fail to behave strategically will be less likely to be returned to parliament. Natural selection through the ballot box means that, over time, the legislature will gradually become composed of politicians pursuing more successful electoral strategies. These propositions can be examined systematically by testing whether constituency service and voter contact with members do, indeed, vary systematically under different ballot structures.

The Diversity of Parliamentary Representatives
The third hypothesis suggests that the ballot structure also influences the diversity of parliamentary bodies, by shaping the inducements for parties to select a group of socially homogeneous or socially diverse parliamentary candidates. Rational-choice institutionalism assumes that in selecting candidates for parliament, parties will also act collectively in a vote-maximizing manner, seeking popular standard-bearers. Yet when picking candidates, parties possess limited information about public preferences. To minimize electoral risks, as the default position, it is rational for parties to re-select incumbents and to choose new candidates who share characteristics similar to those of representatives who have been elected in the past, thereby preserving the status quo and creating a socially homogeneous parliament. Because many legislative elites are usually disproportionately male, middle-aged professionals, such as lawyers, teachers, and journalists, as well as drawn from the predominant ethnic group in any society, it minimizes electoral risk to select candidates with a similar social profile for future contests.

Yet this process may also be affected by electoral law, including the basic type of ballot structure, as well as by the statutory adoption of gender or ethnic quotas and the use of reserved seats for women and ethnic minorities. Electoral rules can alter the balance of incentives. Most obviously, statutory quotas create legal sanctions if parties fail to select a minimum number of women or minority candidates. The basic type of ballot structure may be important as well. Party-ballots present voters with a collective list of legislative candidates, and parties risk an electoral penalty if they exclude any major social group. By contrast, under candidate-ballots, each local party can pick its own contestant within each constituency, without any collective accountability or electoral penalty for any overall social imbalance across the whole party list. These propositions can be examined by seeing whether electoral rules are consistently associated with the social diversity or homogeneity of parliamentary candidates.

The Direct and Indirect Impact of Rules upon Citizens

How can we test these core hypotheses? This model assumes that formal electoral rules (the independent variable) impact the behavior of rational politicians (the intermediate variable). By shaping the strategies of political actors, we predict that rules exert an *indirect* impact upon citizens (the dependent variable) and also have the capacity to exert a *direct* effect on the electorate. Despite their central importance in many rational-choice theories and although we can make logically plausible deductions, we commonly lack directly observable evidence of the electoral strategies adopted by political actors.[27] Before the contest, party campaign tactics are often cloaked in official secrecy, like the battle plans of generals. Post-hoc accounts of contests provided by party managers and politicians can be heavily colored by self-serving post-hoc rationalizations ("No, we never really tried to win California"). Proxy indicators of campaign strategies can be found through analyzing patterns of campaign spending and advertising, where reliable information is publicly available. Yet, too often, even this is absent, especially where legal regulations are not enforced or where disclosure of public accounts is inadequate.[28] Through surveys or personal interviews it also remains difficult to establish systematic cross-national evidence for patterns of constituency service among legislators ("Sure, I spend thirty hours a week dealing with local casework") or the factors influencing the selection of parliamentary candidates ("We really choose the best candidates, irrespective of their race or gender"). Nevertheless, reliable evidence is widely available allowing us to document, compare, and classify formal electoral rules based on analysis of legal statutes, official electoral guidelines, and written constitutions, as the independent variable. Moreover, we can also analyze cross-national surveys of voting behavior in the electorate and aggregate electoral results, such as the percentage of women in parliament or levels of electoral turnout, to measure the dependent variables. If we can establish certain systematic patterns of electoral behavior and political representation that are consistently associated with the type of electoral rules, then we can infer the linkages between electoral rules, political actors, and voting behavior.

Reforming the Formal Electoral Rules

To recap the argument, given a few simple assumptions about rational motivations, knowledge of the formal rule-based incentives should allow us to predict certain consistent patterns of behavior. It follows that policy reforms that alter the formal rules – or electoral engineering – should have the capacity to generate important consequences for political representation and for voting behavior. As mentioned earlier, the international community has become deeply engaged in attempts to generate free and fair elections in dozens of nations around the globe, exemplified by the transitions following the collapse of the authoritarian regime in Bosnia and Herzegovina, decolonization in East Timor, and the end of civil war in Cambodia.[29] In established democracies, as well, beyond the basic electoral formula, debates also have been common about the best way to overhaul electoral procedures. This includes reforms to the legal statutes and party rules governing party eligibility and candidate nomination, the administrative process of electoral registration and voting facilities, the regulation of campaign finance and political broadcasting, and the process of election management. Established democracies have introduced a range of reforms, whether switching between d'Hondt and Largest Remainder (LR)-Hare formulae, adjusting the effective voting threshold for minor parties to qualify for parliamentary representation, expanding the conditions of electoral suffrage, or altering the size of legislative assemblies.[30] In all these cases, it is assumed that electoral reform has the capacity to overcome certain problems, such as the paucity of women in elected office, the management of ethnic tensions, or civic disengagement. This account is, therefore, worth investigating because it is not only theoretically important in the literature but also policy-relevant to real-world problems.

Rational-choice institutionalism generates certain important propositions, which I test systematically in subsequent chapters. In particular, if the assumptions are correct, and formal electoral rules do indeed shape the behavior of politicians, parties, and citizens, then, all other things being equal, *systematic cross-national contrasts in voting behavior and in political representation should be evident under different electoral rules.* The impact of the basic type of majoritarian, combined, and proportional electoral systems can be compared, along with subsidiary legal rules such as the ballot structure, the use of statutory gender quotas, the regulation of registration and voting facilities, and the employment of compulsory voting laws. In subsequent chapters I examine whether electoral rules are systematically related to many important indicators, especially patterns of party competition, the strength of social cleavages and party loyalties, levels of electoral turnout, the inclusion of women and ethnic minorities in parliaments, and patterns of constituency service.

Cultural Modernization Theory and Habits of the Heart

The logic of rational-choice institutionalism is both powerful and attractive, with a seductive elegance and a parsimonious Ockham's razor capable of cutting through the swathe of complexities in understanding human behavior. Formal legal rules embodied in written constitutions, laws, and regulations can be carefully documented, exhaustively categorized, precisely measured, and, hence, fruitfully compared across many nations. Yet, of course, it is recognized widely that the rational calculus of rewards may have limited impact, for multiple reasons. Deep-seated and habitual patterns of behavior may persist unaltered, frustrating the dreams of electoral reformers. Political actors may be ill informed about, blind to, or unaware of the potential consequences of institutional rules. Legislators may prioritize career goals, such as the achievement of programmatic policy goals or rising up the greasy pole to higher office, over immediate electoral rewards.[31] Rational-choice institutionalism can always be rescued by stretching the notion of career goals to cover many priorities for legislators beyond electoral survival. But, if so, the danger is that any reward becomes equally rational, leading toward empty tautologies with minimal predictive or analytical capacity. In the same way, parties may determine their campaign strategies and tactics due to internal organizational structures, factional power-struggles, and traditional tried-and-tested methods of campaigning, almost irrespective of the calculation of any electoral benefits. And citizens may also fail to respond rationally to the carrots and sticks designed by legal reformers. Strong party loyalists may vote the ticket in open-list PR systems, supporting all party candidates listed on the ballot paper, irrespective of their records of constituency service. Apathetic citizens may stay away from the polls, even if registration and voting procedures are simplified.[32]

Alternative cultural modernization theories differ in their emphasis on the primary motors driving human behavior, their expectations about the pace of change, and also their assumptions about the ability of formal institutional rules to alter, rather than adapt to, deeply embedded and habitual social norms and patterns of human behavior. Although many assume that cultural modernization matters, again it remains unclear how much it matters compared with legal-institutional electoral rules. Cultural modernization theories, representing one of the mainstream perspectives in voting behavior, share four basic claims (see Figure 1.2):

1. The process of *societal modernization* transforms the structure of society in predictable ways. In particular, the shift from industrial to

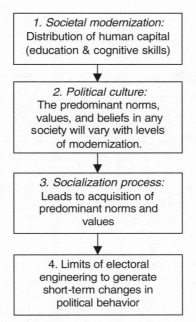

FIGURE 1.2. The cultural modernization model

postindustrial societies is associated with rising levels of human capital (education, literacy, and cognitive skills).

2. Societal modernization has profound consequences for the *political culture*, with new forms of citizen politics arising in post-industrial societies. The theory predicts that there will be marked contrasts in the mass basis of electoral politics evident in industrial and postindustrial societies, notably in the strength of social identities and party loyalties and in patterns of electoral turnout.

3. The political culture is transmitted through the *socialization process* experienced in early childhood and adolescence, including the acquisition of habitual social norms and values. Political elites and citizens are driven primarily by affective motivations and by habitual habits of the heart, rather than by the strategic calculation of rule-based rewards.

4. *Electoral engineering has limited capacity* to generate short-term changes in political behavior, although reforms will probably have a cumulative impact in the longer term as new generations grow up under different rules.

If these assumptions are correct, then systematic differences in political representation and mass electoral behavior should be evident among societies at different levels of development, especially a contrast between industrial and postindustrial nations, even if countries share similar electoral rules.

The Process of Societal Modernization

Cultural modernization theories start from the premise that economic, cultural, and political changes go together in coherent ways, so that industrialization brings about broadly similar trajectories. Even if situation-specific factors make it impossible to predict exactly what will happen in a given society, certain changes become increasingly likely to occur, but the changes are probabilistic, not deterministic.[33] Modernization theories originated in the work of Karl Marx, Max Weber, and Emile Durkheim, and these ideas were revived and popularized in the late 1950s and early 1960s by Seymour Martin Lipset, Daniel Lerner, Walt W. Rostow, Karl W. Deutsch, and Daniel Bell. Theories of cultural modernization were later developed more fully in the work of Ronald Inglehart and Russell Dalton.[34] These accounts emphasize that mass electoral behavior is profoundly influenced by the process of societal development, particularly by rising levels of human capital in the transition from agrarian to industrial to postindustrial societies.

Modernization theories emphasize that traditional agrarian societies are characterized by subsistence livelihoods based largely on farming, fishing, extraction, and unskilled work, with low levels of literacy and education, predominately agrarian populations, minimum standards of living, and restricted social and geographic mobility. Citizens in these societies are strongly rooted to local communities through ties of "blood and belonging," including those of kinship, family, ethnicity, and religion, as well as long-standing cultural bonds. The shift toward industrial production leads toward a range of societal developments – notably growing prosperity and an expanding middle class, higher levels of education and literacy, the growth of the mass media, and urbanization – which in turn are believed to lay the social foundations for democratic participation in the political system.

In the early 1970s, Daniel Bell popularized the view that after a certain period of industrialization a further, distinct stage of development could be distinguished, as a nonlinear process, in the rise of postindustrial societies.[35] For Bell the critical tipping point was reached when the majority of the workforce moved from manufacturing into the service sector, generating profound social and economic shifts. These shifts include the rise of a highly educated, skilled, and specialized workforce; population shifts from urban to suburban neighborhoods and greater geographic mobility, including immigration across national borders; rising living standards and growing leisure time; rapid scientific and technological innovation; the expansion and fragmentation of mass media channels, technologies, and markets; the growth of multilayered governance with power shifting away from the nation-state toward global and local levels, market liberalization, and the expansion of nonprofit social protection schemes; the erosion of the traditional nuclear family; and growing equality of sex roles within the home, family, and workforce.

The Impact of Modernization on Political Culture

The account offered by Ronald Inglehart emphasizes that societal developments have profound consequences for political culture, in particular, that postindustrial societies are characterized by an extensive value shift, with important implications for a new citizen politics.[36] After World War II, postindustrial societies developed unprecedented levels of prosperity and economic security, with rising standards of living fuelled by steady economic growth, despite occasional cyclical downturns. Governments in these societies expanded the role of the welfare state to provide greater social protection for the worst-off citizens; more recently, contracting out services to the nonprofit and private sectors, under state regulation. In conditions of greater security, Inglehart theorizes, public concern about the material issues of unemployment, health care, and housing no longer takes top priority. Instead, in postindustrial societies, the public has given increasingly higher priority to quality-of-life issues, individual autonomy and self-expression, and the need for environmental protection. Dalton theorizes that this process has given rise to a new form of citizen politics, making greater demands for direct participation in the policymaking process through activities such as petitions, protests, and demonstrations.[37]

Most important, the traditional party-voter loyalties, and the social identities upon which these are founded, can be expected to erode in postindustrial societies, to be replaced by more contingent patterns of party support based upon particular leaders, issues, and events. Many studies, discussed fully in Chapters 5 and 6, have documented trends in partisan and social dealignment occurring in many postindustrial societies. Growing levels of education and cognitive skills, and the access this provides to a diverse range of information sources via the mass media, are thought to play a particularly important role in transforming the basis of individual voting behavior, representing a shift from the politics of loyalties toward the politics of choice. Moreover, because the causes are essentially societal factors – exemplified by changes in educational levels, access to the mass media, and the decline of traditional political organizations – these processes are widely assumed to affect all postindustrial societies equally, whether the Netherlands or Britain, the United States or Sweden, irrespective of the particular electoral rules operating in each political system. If processes of societal modernization have, indeed, shaped political cultures and patterns of electoral behavior, then, all other things being equal, this should be evident by *contrasts in voting behavior and political representation among societies at different levels of human development*; in particular, we would expect to find substantial differences between industrial and postindustrial societies.

The Acquisition of Enduring Cultural Values and the Socialization Process
Cultural modernization accounts are based upon traditional theories of
socialization. These assume that social and political values are gradually
acquired during the formative years in childhood and adolescence, due to
early experiences in the home, school, community, and workplace, influenced by family, friends, teachers, neighbors, and colleagues. The formal
rules play a significant role in the acquisition of social norms and values
during the formative years, but in this theory, once established, these stable patterns of human behavior are likely to persist even if the institutions
change. Cultural accounts emphasize that habitual patterns of electoral behavior evolve slowly and incrementally, adapting new laws to existing social
norms, predominant practices, and enduring values. Society is regarded as
the primeval "soup" or base from which the legal system arises as superstructure. In this view, for example, even if exactly the same formal gender quota
policies are implemented to generate positive action policies for women in
parliaments in Buenos Aires, Berlin, and Bogotá, the effect of these rules
are likely to vary in different contexts. In one society these laws may result
in substantial gains for women in elected office, yet in another the same
regulations may exist on paper more than in practice. Similar illustrations
could be drawn concerning the failure of electoral laws governing compulsory voting or party funding. What defeats these attempts at social engineering, skeptics suggest, is the unwillingness of citizens and legal authorities
to implement the statutes in practice, the strength of tacit social norms and
unwritten rules governing patterns of political behavior, and the meaning
and interpretation of any formal laws within a broader culture. Hence, for
example, the Single Transferable Vote (STV) system is used in Australia,
Malta, and Ireland, yet the effects of STV vary substantially in different
countries.[38]

Cultural modernization theorists suggest that the political behavior of
politicians and citizens is shaped by multiple complex factors, especially
by affective orientations toward the predominant values, tacit norms, and
attitudes in a society, rather than by any strategic calculation of electoral rewards. Hence sociopsychological accounts emphasize that leaders
often have diverse motivations for pursuing a political career; some prioritize the need for ideological purity, the public-service role of legislative committee work, or the national interest rather than the simple pursuit of public popularity.[39] Along similar lines, the classic Michigan social
psychological studies of voting behavior, discussed fully in Chapter 5, emphasize that citizens commonly know little about the government's record,
the party leaders, or the policy platforms offered by each party.[40] Nevertheless, many citizens do participate, and in this view, they are guided by
affective partisan identification, ideological shortcuts, and long-standing ties
between parties and social groups, based on class, ethnic, and regional identities. Social psychological studies emphasize that we should avoid generating

post-hoc rationalizations for human behavior that is, at heart, purely habitual and irrational.

The Limits of Electoral Engineering

This account has important implications for understanding the pace of change brought about through electoral engineering. The primary impact of institutional reform is expected to be glacial and cumulative, as enduring social practices gradually adapt to new policies. In many older democracies, for example, when the suffrage qualification was first expanded to women, the initial impact was a sharp fall in the overall level of electoral turnout. This reform only brought women into the voting booths at the same rate as men many decades later, once younger generations of women had gradually acquired the habit of voting.[41] At elite-level, as well, cultural theories suggest that politicians who have acquired their habitual patterns of legislative behavior under one set of rules will respond slowly to new conditions and incentives, with the greatest impact occurring upon the socialization process of younger cohorts of legislators. As a result, institutional reforms may take many years to become fully embedded within parliamentary cultures. For example, although constituency service is strongly entrenched within Anglo-American democracies, cultural modernization theories suggest that the adoption of single-member districts in the Italian Chamber of Deputies or the Russian Duma would not generate similar behavior in these parliaments, as predominant values, ideological beliefs, and institutional customs are deeply rooted and socially determined. Moreover, in democratic systems, successful parties and politicians are largely following social tides and adapting to patterns of mass political behavior in the electorate, rather than attempting to reshape them, still less to determine the strength of linkages between citizens and parties.

Overall, therefore, these accounts suggest serious doubts about the more grandiose claims of rational-choice institutionalism and the capacity of electoral reform for social engineering. During earlier decades it was commonly thought that formal institutions of representative government, like the Westminster parliament, could be uprooted from their embedded institutional context and exported to newly independent countries undergoing decolonization in Sub-Saharan Africa. The attempts usually failed.[42] Hence it has been argued that rational-choice institutionalism has difficulty explaining the complicated, variegated, and fluid patterns of Latin American politics by overemphasizing the electoral and legislative arenas, by overestimating the importance of formal rules and institutions, by failing to explain the origins of political crisis and change, and by neglecting the importance of political beliefs. Moreover, when considering issues of electoral reform, there is considerable evidence that existing institutions matter as the starting point for any modifications, begun in an incremental process rather than started de novo. Institutional imports may fail to flourish in alien soil, such as the introduction of single-member districts designed to change the behavior of representatives in the Italian Chamber of Deputies or the Japanese Diet. For cultural modernization theorists, incentives-based approaches sacrifice too much to the altar of theoretical elegance, naively oversimplifying the multiple and messy reality of complex motivations driving human behavior, as well as failing to recognize the embedded quality of taken-for-granted institutional traditions and cultural norms.[43] Short-term mechanical fixes, while sounding simple and attractive, can flounder on the unintended consequences of institutional reforms.

Comparing Electoral Rules

Therefore, debates in the literature on electoral systems and voting behavior can be divided into alternative schools of thought, the two of which I have summarized providing, perhaps, the most pervasive viewpoints. Scholars differ sharply about the democratic criteria that electoral rules should meet, as well as about the possible consequences that can flow from these choices. What evidence is available to allow us to evaluate these theories? The most extensive body of research on electoral systems, following seminal work by Maurice Duverger (1954) and by Douglas Rae (1967),[44] established systematic typologies of electoral systems and then analyzed their consequences for a variety of macrolevel phenomena, either through formal game-theoretic models or through inductive generalizations.[45] Electoral rules are typically defined, operationalized, and classified, including by their electoral formula, assembly size, and ballot structure. The outcomes of elections conducted under different rules are then compared using multiple indicators, such as patterns of vote-seat disproportionality, electoral turnout, the proportion of women in parliament, or multiparty competition. Most attention has focused on analyzing the results of national elections to a lower house of parliament, although comparisons have also been drawn with many other types of contests, including elections to the European parliament and contrasts among state, regional, or local contests within one nation, as well as differences between presidential and parliamentary systems.

Invaluable insights are derived from pre-post "natural experiments," comparing the outcome in cases when the electoral system changes in one nation. In the early twentieth century, many countries in Western Europe shifted from majoritarian to proportional electoral systems, while in this era, two-dozen American cities experimented with PR then abandoned this project.[46] During the postwar era, France shifted between majoritarian and proportional elections.[47] During the 1990s, major reforms were implemented in New Zealand, the United Kingdom, Israel, Venezuela, Italy, and Japan, allowing pre-post comparisons in each nation, holding many other factors constant.[48] Structural-institutional comparison has many advantages because the basic features of electoral systems can be classified consistently around the world, or in a sequence of elections over time, along with indicators about their consequences.

Yet, at the same time, this approach has serious limitations, as we know more about what Duverger termed the "mechanical" rather than the "psychological" impact of electoral systems.[49] The mechanical focuses on the effects that flow directly from the electoral rules and the structural conditions in which such relationships vary in a consistent manner at macro-level, exemplified by legal electoral thresholds that automatically exclude some minor parties from parliamentary representation. By contrast, far less is known about the psychological effects of how the public, politicians, and parties respond to electoral rules and, hence, the underlying reasons for some of these relationships. For example, it is well established in the literature that more women are usually elected to office under proportional electoral systems than under majoritarian systems, all other things being equal, a generalization confirmed in repeated studies.[50] Yet the precise reasons for this pattern remain a matter of speculation. Many similar generalizations can be drawn from the literature, such as the way that turnout is usually higher in proportional than in majoritarian systems, although exactly why this occurs has never been satisfactorily established. Of course, it could be argued that it is more important to identify this sort of regularity than it is to understand the underlying reasons. Yet, unless the causes are discovered, any attempt at practical electoral engineering may well fail under different conditions. In the well-known but nevertheless true cliché, correlation does not mean causation, no matter its strength or statistical significance. For all these reasons, despite the extensive body of literature, electoral design remains more art than science. To understand how electoral rules constrain social expectations, structural comparisons need supplementing with individual-level survey analysis.

Comparing Electoral Behavior

The main alternative approach in electoral behavior has focused on understanding how social norms, political attitudes, cognitive opinions, and cultural values shape patterns of voting choice and party support. Studies have employed increasingly sophisticated research designs, including cross-sectional postelection surveys representative of electors and parliamentary elites, multiwave campaign panel surveys, experimental methods, and content analysis of the mass media and party platforms.[51] The literature on voting behavior based on single-nation election studies is flourishing and extensive, yet most research focuses upon individual-level attitudes and behaviors, necessarily taking for granted the context of the electoral rules and the broader constitutional arrangements that operate within each country, an approach that has come under increasing challenge in recent decades.[52]

Time-Series Trends

One traditional way to understand the impact of electoral rules would be to collect a series of national election surveys to compare trends over time in countries using proportional, combined, or majoritarian electoral systems. Time-series analysis has been used commonly to compare the strength of cleavage politics and the erosion of partisan loyalties in a wide range of advanced industrial societies.[53] Yet the available survey evidence on voting behavior is limited in the consistency and length of the time-series data, and it is restricted usually in the range of countries where election surveys have been conducted on a regular basis. Most series of national election surveys started in established democracies only in the 1960s or 1970s, with the oldest having begun in the United States (1952), followed by Sweden (1956) and Norway (1957), hindering researchers' ability to examine longer-term trends associated with societal modernization. Surveys repeated over successive elections provide a continuous series of regular observations, sometimes for almost half a century, but, even so, the precise wording and coding of many survey core items often have been slightly amended over time, introducing inconsistencies into the series.[54] Even where similar concepts shape the research traditions in voting behavior and networks of data archives are sharing national election surveys, nevertheless, often there are significant differences among different countries based on matters such as the precise question wording, coding conventions, the order of the survey items within the questionnaire, fieldwork techniques, and sampling procedures. The comparison of trends over time on matters such as partisan identification, issue voting, or leadership popularity using similar but not identical questions within one country often requires heroic assumptions, even more so when comparing a series of independent national election studies conducted using different questionnaires in different nations.[55]

Case Studies of Reform

Another fruitful line of inquiry uses case studies to analyze changes over time in countries where surveys were conducted before and after major electoral reforms were implemented, such as in New Zealand and in the United Kingdom, generating a prolific literature in these nations. Aggregate election results, such as patterns of turnout or the proportion of women in office, also can be compared in countries such as France that have altered their electoral systems back and forth between proportional and majoritarian formulae. The introduction of statutory gender quotas in the selection of parliamentary candidates provides one such "natural experiment," as discussed in Chapter 8. Still, many factors vary over successive elections in these countries beyond changes in the electoral law, including the pattern of party competition, the campaign efforts at voter mobilization, the popularity of the government, the party in government, and the personality of particular party leaders. As a result, it can prove difficult to disentangle these separate effects from the role of the formal rules, per se.[56] Moreover only a handful of established democracies have experienced fundamental electoral reform during the last decade, and even fewer have consistent before-and-after surveys, so it remains difficult to generalize from the available survey evidence in specific countries such as New Zealand. The comparison of the election immediately before and after reforms is also limited because cultural theories suggest any long-term shifts in party competition, in voting behavior, and in the activities of elected representatives may take many years, perhaps even decades, to become established.

The Research Design and Comparative Framework

The research design adopted by this study is, at heart, extremely simple. If rational incentive theories are accurate and electoral rules do indeed have the capacity to shape the behavior of politicians, parties, and citizens, then, all other things being equal, this should become evident in systematic cross-national differences in voting behavior and political representation evident under different rules, notably contrasts among countries using majoritarian, combined, and proportional electoral systems. Alternatively, if processes of societal modernization have shaped the political culture of nations, then, all other things being equal, this should be evident by contrasts in voting behavior and political representation among societies at different levels of human development, in particular between industrial and postindustrial societies. To build upon this approach, in subsequent chapters I explore to what extent electoral systems and societal modernization affect party competition (Chapter 4), the strength of social cleavages and partisan alignments (Chapters 5 and 6), and patterns of voting turnout (Chapter 7). At elite level, I analyze to what extent electoral rules and societal modernization have the capacity to influence political representation, including the gender and ethnic diversity of legislatures (Chapters 8 and 9), as well as patterns of constituency service (Chapter 10).

Data Sources

In this book I use multiple sources of data. The most important source concerns survey research drawn from the Comparative Study of Electoral Systems (CSES). This project is based on an international team of collaborators who have incorporated a special battery of survey questions into national election studies, based on a representative sample of the electorate in each country. Data from each of the separate election studies was coordinated, integrated, and cleaned by the Center for Political Studies, Institute for Social Research, at the University of Michigan.[57] The dataset is designed to facilitate the comparison of macro- and micro-level electoral data. Module I of the CSES (released in July 2002) used in this study allows one to compare surveys of a representative cross-section of the electorate in 37 legislative

TABLE 1.1. *The Elections under Comparison*

Majoritarian Electoral Systems (14 elections)	Combined Electoral Systems (10 elections)	Proportional Electoral Systems (15 elections)
Legislative	Legislative	Legislative
Australia (1996)	Germany (1998) (l,c)	Belgium (1999)
Britain (1997)	Hungary (1998) (l,c)	Czech Republic (1996)
Canada (1997)	Japan (1996) (l,c)	Denmark (1998)
United States (1996)	Korea, Republic of (2000) (c)	Iceland (1999)
	Mexico (1997) (c)	Israel (1996)
Presidential	New Zealand (1996) (l,c)	Netherlands, The (1998)
Belarus (2001)	Russia (1999) (l)	Norway (1997)
Chile (1999)	Taiwan (1996) (c)	Peru (2000)
Israel (1996) (i)	Thailand (2001) (c)	Poland (1997)
Lithuania (1997)	Ukraine (1998) (l)	Portugal (2002)
Mexico (2000)		Romania (1996)
Peru (2000)		Slovenia (1996)
Romania (1996)		Spain (1996, 2000)
Russia (2000)		Sweden (1998)
Taiwan (1996)		Switzerland (1999)
United States (1996)		

Note: The year of the election included in the CSES dataset Module I is listed in parenthesis. Under combined electoral systems, the election study collected either the candidate vote (c), the party-list vote (l), or both (l,c).
(i) The elections in Israel are for the prime minister not president. For the classification of electoral systems see Chapter 2.

and presidential national elections in 32 countries. The geographic coverage includes countries containing in total more than 1.2 billion inhabitants, or one-fifth of the world's population. The focus on voters' choices, the cross-national integration, and, above all, the timing of the data collection (within a year following each election), provide a unique opportunity to compare voting behavior in a way that is not possible through other common sources of comparative data such as the World Values Survey. Throughout the book, the national elections under comparison are those held from 1996–2001 for the lower house of the national parliament and for presidential contests. The definition and typology of electoral systems is discussed in detail in the next chapter, and the main contrasts among nations are illustrated in Table 1.1.

Comparative Framework

Many previous studies have commonly adopted a *most similar* comparative framework, seeking to consider patterns of electoral behavior within Western Europe, or post-Communist Europe, or Latin America, or within the universe of established democracies. This approach helps isolate the effects of different electoral rules from certain common historical traditions, shared cultural values, or political experiences, but, nevertheless, it remains difficult to generalize from any particular regional context, for example, for any lessons derived from new democracies in Latin America that might also hold true in Central and Eastern Europe. This is particularly problematic if one wants to test the effects of societal modernization and electoral rules on voting behavior in both older and newer democracies. For example, Lijphart's theory claims that PR elections lead toward greater long-term democratic stability in deeply divided plural societies, yet this cannot be tested effectively if studies are limited to the comparison of older democracies that have persisted uninterrupted in recent decades rather than examining the characteristics of a wide range of political systems that have, and have not, undergone major regime change.[58]

Given these considerations and the nature of the primary CSES dataset, the comparative framework in this book adopts instead the *most different* comparative framework.[59] The study is focused upon the extent to which certain patterns of voting behavior and political representation are systematically related to either levels of societal modernization (in industrial vs. postindustrial societies) or to types of electoral systems (majoritarian, combined, or proportional). This approach also carries certain well-known difficulties, particularly the familiar problem of too many variables and too few cases. Multiple contrasts can be drawn among the countries under comparison, ranging from Australia, the United States, and Sweden to the Ukraine, Peru, and Taiwan. As a result, it remains difficult to establish whether the outcomes can indeed be attributed to the selected factors under comparison (societal modernization or the type of electoral rules), or if these relationships are spurious due to omitted variables not included in our simple models, such as the role of economic inequality, the history of military coups in Latin America, the legacy of Communism in Central and Eastern Europe, or religious traditions in Asia. The "controls" introduced into the multivariate models can provide only rough proxies for a few of the multiple cross-national differences among political systems around the world. The limited number of elections and countries restricts inevitably the reliability of the generalizations that can be drawn from the study. Survey-based research covering many different nations and cultures encounters also the familiar problems of establishing equivalence and whether responses to questions asked in each country, for example, items monitoring satisfaction with democracy in Belarus, Belgium, and Peru, can be treated as functionally equivalent. Yet the comparison of a diverse range of countries facilitates theory-building and testing in a way that is not possible with regionally based studies.

This approach is particularly well suited to the societies included in the CSES survey ranging from low- or middle-income developing nations, such as Thailand, Mexico, Ukraine, Belarus, and Romania (all with a per capita Purchasing Power Parity (PPP) Gross Domestic Product (GDP) of less than U.S.$5,000 in 1998) to some of the most affluent societies in the world, including Switzerland, the United States, and Japan (with an equivalent per capita GDP of more than U.S.$30,000). The countries under comparison have varied political systems, rates of human development, patterns of democratization, and cultural traditions, all of which can be incorporated into explanations of patterns of electoral behavior. Ethnically homogeneous societies such as Poland, Norway, and Britain are included, as well as plural societies with multiple cleavages, exemplified by Israel and Belgium. The length of time that each country has experienced democratic institutions varies considerably also, which can be expected to have an important impact upon electoral behavior and patterns of party competition. Although Australia and Sweden are long-established democracies, countries such as Spain and Portugal consolidated within recent decades, whereas still others, such as the Ukraine and Belarus, remain in the transitional stage, characterized by unstable and fragmented opposition parties, ineffective legislatures, and limited checks on the executive.[60]

The historical experiences of democracy during the late twentieth century can be compared using the mean score for each nation on the 7-point Gastil Index of democratization, based on an annual assessments of political rights and civil liberties monitored by Freedom House from 1972 to 2000. The Gastil scale is reversed so that a high score represents a more consolidated democracy. Many indices attempt to gauge levels of democratization, each with different strengths and weaknesses, but the measure by Freedom House provides annual benchmarks over three decades.[61] The results of the comparison in Figure 1.3 show that just over half the countries in the CSES dataset had a mean score on this index of 4.0 or above, and all these 17 nations can be classified as "established," "consolidated," or "older" democracies. This includes Spain and Portugal, which were part of the third wave of democratization starting in 1973.[62] The other 15 nations falling clearly well below the overall mean of 4.1 are classified as "newer electoral democracies" still experiencing the transition, at different levels of consolidation. Some such as South Korea, Hungary, the Czech Republic, and Mexico have gone a long way down the road toward establishing stable democratic institutions. Others, including Ukraine and Belarus, ranked at the bottom of the scale, currently lack many political rights and civil liberties commonly taken for granted in older democracies, although they hold competitive elections contested by more than one party. Belarus, in particular, has deeply flawed elections, in which opposition leaders are silenced, intimidated, and even imprisoned by the government of President Lukashenko. The nations in the CSES dataset can be categorized by this classification in almost equal numbers as either older or newer democracies. The sample in the CSES dataset reflects this rough balance, with 53% of respondents drawn from older democracies (28,800) whereas the remaining 47% are living in newer democracies (25,600).

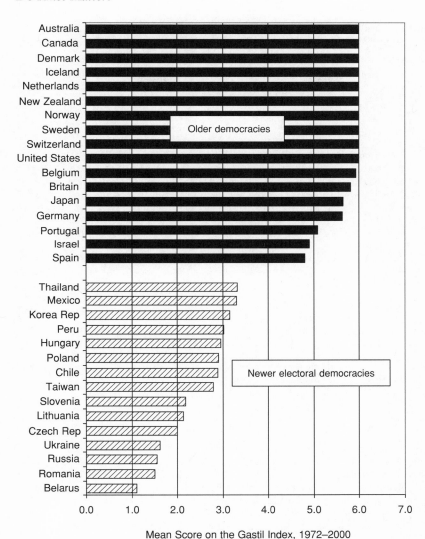

FIGURE 1.3. Societies by length of democratization. *Note:* The mean scores on the 7-point Gastil Index of political rights and civil liberties, 1972–2000, based on annual assessments by Freedom House, with the scores reversed so that 1 = least democratic and 7 = most democratic. *Source:* Calculated from Freedom House, *Freedom in the World.* Available online at www.freedomhouse.org.

TABLE 1.2. *Social Indicators*

Type of Electoral System for Lower House	No. of Nations	HDI	GDP ($)	Education (%)	Urban Pop. (%)	Life Expectancy (years)	% GNP from Services	Total Pop.
Majoritarian	5	.898	18,891	94.6	80.2	75.9	62.4	78
Combined	11	.824	11,791	79.0	71.9	72.0	55.4	59
Proportional	16	.872	19,059	85.1	74.9	75.8	58.4	14
TOTAL	32	.861	16,687	84.6	75.0	74.5	57.6	151

Note: Comparisons among the 32 nations included in the CSES dataset. Electoral system: The countries are classified by the electoral system used for the lower house of parliament. For the classification of electoral systems see Chapter 2. For the list of nations see Table 1.1. HDI: Countries are classified based on the 1998 rankings of the Human Development Index. GDP: Mean per capita Gross Domestic Product measured in Purchasing Power Parity $U.S., 1998. Education: Gross educational enrollment ratio in 1998. % Urban population: 2000. Average life expectancy (years): 1997. % Gross National Product: from the service sector. Total population: (in millions) 1997.
Sources: All the social and economic indicators are derived from the United Nations Development Programme. 2000. *Human Development Report 2000.* New York: Oxford University Press. Available online at www.undp.org.

TABLE 1.3. *Political Indicators*

Type of Electoral System	No. of Nations	Level of Democratization, 1999–2000	Mean Level of Democratization, 1972–2000
Majoritarian	5	5.9	5.0
Combined	11	5.7	3.5
Proportional	16	6.4	4.5
TOTAL	32	6.1	4.2

Levels of democratization: The 32 nations included in the CSES dataset are classified based on the annual ratings provided by Freedom House from 1972 to 2000. Countries are classified according to the 1999–2000 ratings and also to the combined mean score for political rights and civil liberties in Freedom House's annual surveys from 1972–2000. The 7-point Gastil Index is reversed for ease of interpretation so that it ranges from low levels of civil liberties and political rights (coded "1") to high levels of civil liberties and political rights (coded "7"). For details see *Freedom in the World.* Available online at www.freedomhouse.org. Nations: The countries are classified by the electoral system used for the lower house of parliament. For the classification of electoral systems see Chapter 2. For the list of nations see Table 1.1.

The countries using proportional electoral systems have slightly higher levels of per capita GDP and also smaller populations (see Table 1.2) but have similar levels of education, urbanization, or average life expectancy. Countries that utilize PR are rated as slightly more democratic today than are countries using majoritarian systems and as having a stronger record of democratic consolidation during the last thirty years (see Table 1.3).

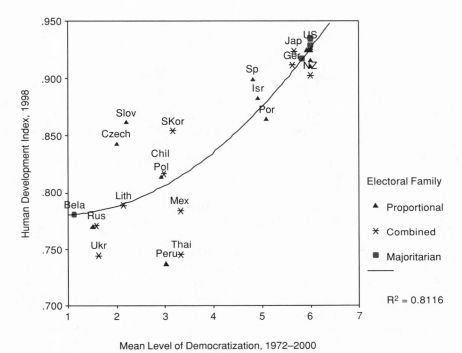

FIGURE 1.4. Societies by level of development. *Notes: Human Development Index 1998*: All countries are classified based on the 1998 rankings of the Human Development Index from the United Nations Development Programme. 2000. *Human Development Report 2000*. New York: Oxford University Press. Available online at www.undp.org. *Mean level of democratization*: Societies are classified based on the annual ratings provided by Freedom House from 1972 to 2000. The Gastil Index is classified according to the combined 7-point mean score for political rights and civil liberties (reversed) from Freedom House's 1972–2000 annual surveys, *Freedom of the World*. Available online at www.freedomhouse.org. For the classification of electoral systems, see Chapter 2.

Some of the main contrasts between nations, and the relationship between economic and political development, are illustrated in Figure 1.4. The level of societal modernization is measured by the United Nations Development Programme (UNDP) 1998 Human Development Index, combining indicators of longevity, educational attainment, and standard of living. The level of democratization is gauged by the mean score on the Gastil Index of political rights and civil liberties from 1972 to 2000, as already discussed. Most of the established democracies are clustered in the top right-hand corner, as are the most developed societies. The newer democracies in Latin America and post-Communist Central Europe, as well as the countries of Ukraine, Belarus, and Russia, are clustered in the lower left-hand corner. The distribution of types of electoral systems used for the lower house of parliament (discussed in detail in the next chapter) shows that these are spread throughout all levels of human and democratic development.

There are a number of important limitations of the dataset for our purposes. The first concerns the range of countries, in particular those using majoritarian electoral systems for *legislative* elections. All these cases are drawn from the Anglo-American democracies, which restricts the direct comparison of how majoritarian systems work in parliamentary elections in developing societies such as India, Jamaica, or Malawi. Nevertheless, comparisons can be drawn with majoritarian electoral systems used for *presidential* elections in developing nations, including Chile, Lithuania, and Peru, which greatly expands the range of societies within this category. In this approach, we assume that there is sufficient similarity between voting in parliamentary and presidential elections, so that the electoral systems can be compared across both types of contest. Now, it is always possible that certain features of the type of office mean that there are important contrasts between these types of elections, for example, if presidential elections generate more personal appeals based on the character and experience of the candidates whereas parliamentary elections encourage more programmatic party campaigns.[63] A simple comparison of the typical election campaigns fought in Western European parliamentary elections and in United States presidential races lends some superficial plausibility to such an argument. Yet it remains unclear whether this assumption is supported by the systematic empirical evidence; in the United States, for example, the national party conventions used for nominating the presidential candidate and for endorsing the party platform may make the presidential races more programmatic, partisan, and nationally issue-oriented than the mid-term congressional elections, which are often fought on the personal record and experience of particular candidates in each district, with little capacity of the presidential candidate or party to exert any national "coattails" influence.[64] In countries such as Brazil, where party politics tend to be personalistic and clientalistic rather than programmatic, with weak national party organizations and minimal party discipline in the legislature, campaigning based on personal appeals may be equally evident in both presidential and congressional elections.[65] From systematic cross-national election research it remains unclear whether any apparent differences in presidential and parliamentary elections are due to the nature of the office per se, or to the type of electoral system used in these contests. Further research, with an expanded range of countries under Module II of the CSES survey, will eventually allow us to test these sorts of propositions more fully, as well as any systematic contrasts between presidential and parliamentary elections. Where there are good reasons to suspect from the literature that the level of office will probably make a significant difference – for example, in the lower levels of electoral turnout common in second-order legislative elections – we can test for this by classifying countries into

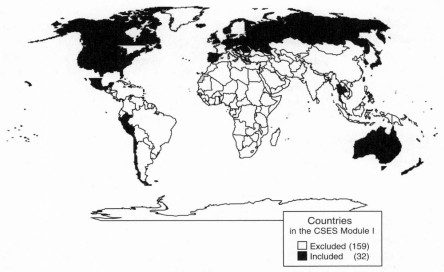

FIGURE 1.5. The countries included in Module I of the CSES dataset

presidential and parliamentary executives and then adding this factor to the analytical models to see whether this does, indeed, matter. But we can only follow this strategy by comparing within our framework both presidential and parliamentary elections.

The comparative framework for the CSES dataset remains limited in another important respect. The countries that collaborated in the project reflect those that regularly fund national election surveys utilizing a network of scholars and experienced market research companies, and their geographical distribution is uneven. Figure 1.5 maps the 32 countries included in Module I of the CSES dataset and highlights the lack of coverage of much of the developing world, especially Africa, Latin America, and Asia. Much existing research on electoral systems and electoral administration is based upon analysis of established democracies with a long tradition of national elections, including the Anglo-American countries, Western Europe, and Scandinavia. Yet it is unclear to what extent generalizations can be drawn from these particular contexts, and during the last decade much has been learned about the impact of electoral systems in newer democracies. The focus on comparative electoral behavior has been spurred by broader intellectual developments, particularly the breakdown of the old-fashioned tripartite Cold War framework that used to divide the globe into advanced industrialized nations, Communist states, and developing societies. A revival of interest in the study of political institutions and the role of the state also has swept through the discipline in recent years.[66] This process also has been encouraged by the globalization of political science and the wider availability of social and political survey data in many developing countries. To compensate for the limited geographic coverage of the CSES and to provide a more systematic worldwide comparison of parliamentary and presidential elections, as in previous work, I also utilize multiple datasets, drawing upon sources provided by the World Bank, the United Nations, International IDEA, and the Inter-Parliamentary Union. Where relevant, I draw upon other suitable public opinion surveys for time-series and cross-national data.[67]

The Plan of the Book

Debates about electoral reform have often produced conflict about means (e.g., what would be the effects on party fortunes of alternative systems?) but even more fundamentally about ends (e.g., what is the primary objective of the electoral system?). To examine these issues, we need to analyze what consequences flow from the adoption of alternative electoral rules.

Chapter 2 goes on to describe the main institutional variations in electoral systems that can be expected to influence voting behavior and political representation. Key terms are defined and the major differences among electoral systems are classified, with illustrations drawn from the nations included in the CSES dataset. A typology is developed classifying the major families of electoral systems worldwide, and tables are presented summarizing the detailed features of the electoral systems used for the elections to the lower house of parliament and for presidential elections in the CSES nations under comparison.

The normative arguments underlying debates about electoral reform are considered in Chapter 3, comparing visions of "adversarial" versus "consensus" democracy. Institutional reform is often regarded as the fix for many endemic problems associated with the process of democratic consolidation and good governance, whether the problem is the lack of accountability of public officials, the failure of an effective opposition in parliament, the splintering of fragmented party systems, the erosion of electoral participation, the conflicts arising from deep-seated ethnic cleavages, the paucity of women in elected office, or the general problems of public confidence in government and the policy process. Argument about these issues produced growing awareness that taken-for-granted electoral rules are not neutral: instead the way that votes translate into seats means that some groups, parties, and representatives are systematically ruled into the policymaking process, whereas some are systematically ruled out. We need to understand and clarify the normative claims and evaluative criteria concerning the consequences that flow from electoral rules for political representation and voting behavior before we can consider the empirical evidence.

The Consequences for Voting Behavior

Chapter 4 considers how electoral rules influence party systems. The starting point for my analysis is Duverger's famous claim that, in a law-like relationship, plurality elections in single-member districts favor a two-party system whereas simple-majority and proportional systems lead toward multipartyism.[68] The accuracy of these claims has attracted considerable debate in the literature.[69] The underlying reasons for this relationship are believed to be partly mechanical, depending upon the hurdles that plurality systems create for minor parties, especially those such as the Greens, with widely dispersed support. Proportional formulae with large district magnitudes and low vote thresholds, exemplified by elections to the Israeli Knesset, lower the barriers faced by minor parties to entry into elected office. There is considerable evidence that this correlation holds in many established democracies, although there are some important exceptions, and debate continues to question the causal direction of the relationship. It is usually assumed that electoral systems are "given" as fairly stable institutions in most established democracies and that party systems are, therefore, constrained by the existing electoral rules, such as the way that third parties are systematically penalized in the United States. Yet the interpretation of the direction of causality may be reversed; historically, countries already highly factionalized by multiple social cleavages may well adopt electoral systems facilitating and perpetuating multipartyism. I examine how far "Duverger's Law" applies in different countries worldwide, comparing the major families and types of electoral systems by measures of the effective number of electoral and parliamentary parties and measures of proportionality.

Chapter 5 analyzes the major traditional social cleavages in the countries under comparison and explores the classic debate in electoral behavior about how much class and religious cleavages continue to predict patterns of voting behavior. Modernization theories suggest that in many postindustrial societies, class and religious identities – the traditional foundations of the mass basis of party politics in the postwar era – are no longer capable of generating stable affective party loyalties.[70] If traditional voter–party bonds are fraying in these societies, this could have important political consequences by boosting electoral volatility, the proportion of late-deciders, split-ticket voting, and potential support for minor parties and protest parties.[71] If theories are correct in linking processes of societal modernization to social and partisan dealignment, then social class and religion should play a less important role in structuring voting behavior in affluent postindustrial societies than in less-developed, industrialized nations. Given different cultural legacies, historical traditions, and social structures, we also expect to find considerable differences in the role of class and religion in structuring voting behavior in post-Communist and developing societies. By contrast, rational-choice institutionalism suggests that the strength of cleavage politics is related closely to the type of electoral system, particularly levels of electoral thresholds, so that the ties of class and religion will prove a stronger predictor of voting choices in proportional systems with lower thresholds. The topics examined in Chapter 5 are, therefore, (1) the influence of social class, religiosity, and other social cleavages on voting choice in the range of countries under comparison; (2) how much this pattern is systematically related to levels of societal modernization; and (3) how far these relationships vary according to the type of electoral system.

Building upon this foundation, Chapter 6 considers the impact of party loyalties upon voting choice, contrasting institutional and cultural modernization explanations for patterns of party identification in the electorate. Classic Michigan theories of electoral behavior suggest that most citizens in Western democracies were anchored over successive elections and, sometimes, for their lifetimes, by long-standing affective party loyalties. Theories of cultural modernization suggest that, over time, rising levels of education and cognitive skills have reduced gradually dependence upon these long-standing party attachments, replacing the politics of loyalties with the politics of choice. If modernization theories are essentially correct, then party and social identities can be expected to prove to be strong influences upon voting behavior in industrialized societies, while these attachments would have faded somewhat in affluent postindustrial nations. By contrast, rational incentive-based accounts suggest that the institutional environment determines the rewards for adopting bridging or bonding campaign appeals. In particular, rational-choice institutionalism suggests that electoral thresholds shape the behavior of parties and candidates directly, and, therefore, all other things being equal, the strength of partisan identification in the electorate.

Chapter 7 proceeds to consider the reasons why levels of electoral turnout vary among the countries under comparison and how much this is influenced by the institutional or cultural context. Previous studies have commonly found that the type of electoral formula shapes participation, with proportional representation systems generating higher voter participation than majoritarian or plurality elections.[72] This pattern seems well supported by the evidence in established democracies, although the exact reasons for this relationship remain unclear.[73] Strategic explanations focus on the differential rewards facing citizens under alternative electoral arrangements. Under majoritarian systems, such as FPTP used for the House of Commons in Westminster and for the United States Congress, supporters of minor and fringe parties with geographic support dispersed widely but thinly across the country, such as the Greens, may believe that casting their votes will make no difference to who wins in their constituency, still less to the overall composition of government and the policy agenda. The "wasted votes" argument is strongest in safe seats where the incumbent party is unlikely to be defeated. In contrast, PR elections with low vote thresholds and large district magnitudes, such as the Party Lists system used in the Netherlands, increase the opportunities for minor parties with dispersed support to enter parliament even with a relatively modest share of the vote and, therefore, increase the incentives for their supporters to participate. Cultural theories offer alternative reasons for differential patterns of turnout, emphasizing the role of rising levels of education and cognitive skills. Building on my previous book, *Democratic Phoenix*, this chapter seeks to understand the reasons for differential patterns of electoral turnout in more depth.

The Consequences for Political Representation

Beyond the mass electorate, the selection of electoral rules also is believed to have important consequences for political representation. Chapter 8 considers the classic issue of the barriers to women in elected office and how much this process is influenced by cultural traditions and by electoral rules. These factors are not, by any means, the only ones that influence opportunities for elected office, but a substantial literature suggests that these are among the most important at the national level. It is well known that usually more women win office under party-ballots than under candidate-ballots, despite some important exceptions to this rule.[74] Moreover, in recent years many positive action policies have been used to boost the number of women in office, including the use of reserved seats and statutory gender quotas applying by law to all parties in a country, as well as voluntary gender quotas implemented in rule books within particular parties. In some cases, positive action policies have had a decisive effect on women's representation, whereas elsewhere, they have generated only meager gains. This chapter analyzes the reasons for this phenomenon, and to what extent formal rules interact with the political culture, especially in societies where traditional attitudes toward sex roles prevail so that women are still perceived as fulfilling their primary roles only as wives and mothers.

Chapter 9 then outlines and presents evidence for how electoral systems influence the election of ethnic minority representatives and parties. One of the most influential accounts in the literature has been provided by the theory of "consociational" or "consensus" democracy, developed by Arend Lijphart, which suggests that nations can maintain stable governments despite being deeply divided into distinct ethnic, linguistic, religious, or cultural communities.[75] Majoritarian electoral systems, such as FPTP, systematically exaggerate the parliamentary lead for the party in first place, with the aim of securing a decisive outcome and government accountability, thereby excluding smaller parties from the division of spoils. By contrast, proportional electoral systems lower the hurdles for smaller parties, maximizing their inclusion into the legislature and, ultimately, into coalition governments. Consociational theories suggest that proportional electoral systems are, therefore, most likely to facilitate accommodation between diverse ethnic parties and groups, making them more suitable for new democracies struggling to achieve legitimacy and stability in plural societies. These are important claims that, if true, have significant consequences for agencies seeking to promote democratic development and peacekeeping. Yet critics suggest that by appealing only to a small ethnic base, PR systems can actually reinforce ethnic cleavages, so that majoritarian systems are preferable because they provide incentives for politicians to appeal across ethnic lines.[76]

The chapter breaks down the predominant ethnic majority and minority populations in the countries under comparison and tests the central propositions about the effects of electoral systems on differences in minority–majority support for the political system.

Chapter 10 analyzes the impact of constituency service. Rational-choice institutionalism suggests that elected representatives are more likely to be responsive and accountable to electors, offering particularistic benefits to cultivate a personal vote, where they are elected directly using candidate-ballots. One classic argument for First-Past-the-Post is that single-member territorial districts allow citizens to hold individual representatives, not just parties, to account for their actions (or inactions). It is argued that this provides an incentive for constituency service, maintains the representative's independence from the party leadership, and ensures that representatives serve the needs and concerns of all their local constituents, not just party stalwarts. Candidates can also be expected to emphasize personalistic appeals under preference-ballots. These are used in multimember constituencies where candidates compete with others within their own party for votes, exemplified by the Single Transferable Vote in Ireland, the Single Non-Transferable Vote used for two-thirds of the districts in Taiwan, and the use of open-list PR where voters can prioritize candidates within each party, such as in Belgium, Peru, and Denmark.[77] By contrast, party labels and programmatic benefits are likely to be given greater emphasis in campaigns where there are party-ballots, such as in Israel or Portugal, because all candidates on the party ticket sink or swim together. This chapter examines whether there is good evidence supporting the claim that citizens living under candidate-ballot and preference-ballot systems generally know more about parliamentary candidates and have more contact with elected representatives – and can, therefore, hold them to account more effectively – than those living under party-ballot systems.

Finally, Chapter 11 recapitulates the theoretical arguments and summarizes the major findings documented throughout the book. The conclusion considers the implications for understanding the impact of electoral rules on voting choices and political representation, the lessons for the process of electoral engineering, and the consequences for the democratization process worldwide.

2

Classifying Electoral Systems

Before we can examine the impact of rules on voting behavior and political representation, I first need to outline a typology of the main families of electoral systems and classify their subtypes. The most important institutions influencing electoral rules can be divided into three nested components, ranging from the most diffuse to the most specific levels.

- The *constitutional structure* represents the broadest institutional context, denoted, most importantly, by whether the executive is presidential or parliamentary, whether the national legislature is bicameral or unicameral, and whether power is centralized in unitary government or more widely dispersed through federal arrangements.
- The *electoral system* concerns multiple aspects of electoral law, and the most basic features involve the *ballot structure*, determining how voters can express their choices, the *electoral threshold*, or the minimum votes needed by a party to secure representation, the *electoral formula*, determining how votes are counted to allocate seats, and the *district magnitude*, referring to the number of seats per district. Electoral systems are categorized in this study into three primary families: majoritarian, combined, and proportional, each with many subsidiary types.
- Last, *electoral procedures* concern more detailed rules, codes of conduct, and official guidelines, including practical and technical issues that can also prove important to the outcome, such as the distribution of polling places, rules governing the nomination procedure for candidates, the qualifications for citizenship, facilities for voter registration and for casting a ballot, the design of the ballot paper, procedures for scrutiny of the election results, the use of compulsory voting, the process of boundary revisions, and regulations governing campaign finance and election broadcasting.

The constitutional structure is important obviously because it sets the institutional context for many aspects of political behavior, but systematic comparison of all these features is also well beyond the scope of this limited study.[1] I focus instead upon classifying electoral systems used in all independent nation-states around the globe, to examine their distribution worldwide. In subsequent chapters I consider specific electoral procedures and legal rules in more detail, such as the use of statutory gender quotas on women's representation or the impact of voting facilities on turnout. The way that electoral rules work is illustrated by examples from the countries under comparison in the CSES study. Electoral systems can be compared at every level of office – presidential, parliamentary, supranational and subnational – but to compare like with like, I focus here on national elections, including systems used for parliamentary elections for the lower house and for presidential contests.

The Classification of Electoral Systems

Ever since the seminal work of Maurice Duverger (1954) and Douglas Rae (1967), a flourishing literature has classified the main types of electoral systems and sought to analyze their consequences.[2] Any classification needs to strike a difficult balance, being detailed enough to reflect subtle and nuanced differences between systems, which can be almost infinitely varied, while also being sufficiently parsimonious and clear so as to distinguish the major types that are actually used around the globe. Worldwide, excluding dependent territories, we can compare the electoral systems for the lower house of parliament in 191 independent nation-states. Of these nations, seven authoritarian regimes currently lack a working, directly elected parliament, including Saudi Arabia, Brunei, and Libya. Electoral systems in the remaining countries are classified into three major families (see Figure 2.1), each including a number of subcategories: *majoritarian* formulae (including First-Past-the-Post, Second Ballot, the Bloc Vote, Single Non-Transferable Vote, and the Alternative Vote systems);[3] *combined* systems (incorporating both majoritarian and proportional formulae); and *proportional* formulae (including the Party Lists system as well as the Single Transferable Vote system).

The comparison in Figure 2.1 shows that in elections to the lower house, about half of all countries worldwide use majoritarian formulae, whereas one-third use proportional formulae and the remainder employ combined systems. As discussed earlier, electoral systems vary according to a number of key dimensions; the most important concern the electoral formula, ballot structure, effective threshold, district magnitude, malapportionment, assembly size, and the use of open/closed lists. Within the family of proportional systems, for example, in Israel the combination of a single national constituency and a low minimum vote threshold allows the election of far more parties than in Poland, which has a 7% threshold and small electoral districts. Moreover, electoral laws and administrative procedures, broadly defined, regulate campaigns in numerous ways beyond the basic electoral formulae, from the administration of voting facilities to the provision of

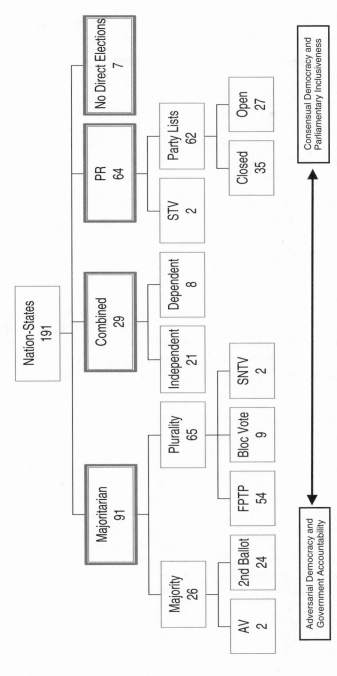

FIGURE 2.1. Electoral systems used worldwide for the lower house of parliament, 1997. *Notes:* FPTP = First-Past-the-Post; 2nd Ballot; Bloc Vote; AV = Alternative Vote; SNTV = Single Non-Transferable Vote; STV = Single Transferable Vote. Systems were classified in May 1997 based on Appendix A in Andrew Reynolds and Ben Reilly. Eds. *The International IDEA Handbook of Electoral System Design.* Stockholm: International IDEA. For more details see http://www.aceproject.org/.

political broadcasts, the rules of campaign funding, the drawing of constituency boundaries, the citizenship qualifications for the franchise, and the
legal requirements for candidate nomination.

Majoritarian Formulae

Worldwide, in total, 91 out of 191 countries use majoritarian formulae in
national election to the lower house of parliament. The aim of majoritarian electoral systems is to create a "natural" or a "manufactured" majority,
that is, to produce an effective one-party government with a working parliamentary majority while simultaneously penalizing minor parties, especially
those with spatially dispersed support. In "winner-takes-all" elections, the
leading party boosts its legislative base, while the trailing parties get meager
rewards. The design aims to concentrate legislative power in the hands of
a single-party government, not to generate parliamentary representation of
all minority views. This category of electoral systems can be subdivided into
those where the winner needs to achieve a simple plurality of votes or those
where they need to gain an absolute majority of votes (50%+).

Plurality Elections
The system of First-Past-the-Post or single-member plurality elections is used
for election to the lower chamber in fifty-four countries worldwide, including
the United Kingdom, Canada, India, the United States, and many Commonwealth states. This is the oldest electoral system, dating back at least to the
twelfth century, and it is also the simplest. Plurality electoral systems can
also use multimember constituencies; for example, some dual-member seats
persisted in Britain until 1948. As discussed later, the Bloc Vote continues to
be employed in nine nations, such as Bermuda and Laos, using multimember districts with plurality thresholds. But today First-Past-the-Post elections
for the lower house at Westminster are all based on single-member districts
with candidate-ballots. The basic system of how FPTP works in parliamentary general elections is widely familiar: countries are divided into territorial
single-member constituencies; voters within each constituency cast a single
ballot (marked by an "X") for one candidate (see Figure 2.2); the candidate
with the largest share of the vote in each seat is elected; and, in turn, the
party with the largest number of parliamentary seats forms the government.
Under First-Past-the-Post candidates usually do not need to pass a minimum
threshold of votes to be elected,[4] nor do they require an absolute majority
of votes to be elected. Instead, all they need is a simple plurality, that is,
one more vote than their closest rivals. Hence, in seats where the vote splits
almost equally three ways, the winning candidate may have only 35% of
the vote, while the other contestants fail with 34% and 32%, respectively.
Although two-thirds of all voters supported other candidates, the plurality
of votes is decisive.

VOTE FOR ONE CANDIDATE ONLY

1	**COTTIER** Barbara Elizabeth Cottier, 11 Twines Close, Sparkford, Yeovil, Somerset. BA22 7JW Conservative Party Candidate	
2	**GRAHAM** Leona Alice-Mae Graham, The Coach House, Hornblotton House, Hornblotton, Nr. Shepton Mallet, Somerset. BA4 6SB Green Party	
3	**MAYER** Theodor Mayer, Forty Acres Farm, Soth Barrow, Yeovil, Somerset. BA22 7LE Independent	
4	**WINCHILSEA** Shirley Winchilsea, South Cadbury House, Nr. Yeovil, Somerset. BA22 7HA Liberal Democrat	

FIGURE 2.2. An example of the First-Past-the-Post (FPTP) ballot in the U.K. general election

Under this system, the party share of parliamentary seats, not their share of the popular vote, counts for the formation of government. Government may also be elected without a plurality of votes, so long as it has a parliamentary majority. In 1951, for instance, the British Conservative Party was returned to power with a 16-seat majority in parliament based on 48.0% of the popular vote, although Labour won slightly more (48.8%) of the vote. In February 1974 the reverse pattern occurred: the Conservatives gained a slightly higher share of the national vote, but Labour won more seats and formed the government. Another example is the 2000 U.S. presidential contest, where, across the whole country, out of more than 100 million votes cast, the result gave Gore a lead of 357,852 in the popular vote, or 0.4%, but Bush beat Gore by 271 to 267 votes in the Electoral College. Moreover, under FPTP, governments are commonly returned without a *majority* of votes. No governing party in the United Kingdom has won as much as half the popular vote since 1935. For instance, in 1983 Mrs. Thatcher was returned with a landslide of seats, producing a substantial parliamentary majority of 144, yet with the support of less than a third of the total electorate (30.8%).

One of the best-known features of winner-takes-all elections is that they create high thresholds for minor parties with support that is spatially dispersed across many constituencies. In single-member seats, if the candidates standing for the minor parties frequently place second, third, or fourth, then even though these parties may obtain substantial support across the whole country, nevertheless, they will fail to win a share of seats that in any way reflects their share of the national vote. This characteristic is the basis of Maurice Duverger's well-known assertion that the "simple-majority single ballot system favors the two party system" whereas "both the simple-majority system with second ballot and proportional representation favor multi-partyism."[5] As discussed fully in the next chapter, the accuracy of these claims has attracted much debate in the literature.[6] One important qualification to these generalizations is the recognition that FPTP is based on territorial constituencies, and the geographical distribution of votes is critical to the outcome for minor parties and for minority social groups.[7] Green parties, for example, which usually have shallow support spread evenly across multiple constituencies, do far less well under FPTP than do nationalist parties with support concentrated in a few areas. Hence, for example, in the 1993 Canadian elections the Progressive Conservatives won 16.1% of the vote but suffered a chronic meltdown that reduced their parliamentary representation to only 2 MPs. In contrast, the Bloc Québécois, concentrated in one region, won 18.1% of the vote but returned a solid phalanx of fifty-four MPs. In the same election, the New Democratic Party won even fewer votes (6.6%), but they emerged with nine MPs, far more than the Progressive Conservatives.[8] In a similar way, in the United States, ethnic groups with concentrated support, such as African-American or Latino voters in inner-city urban areas, can get more representatives into the U.S. Congress than do groups such as Korean-Americans, who are widely dispersed across multiple legislative districts.[9]

Malapportionment (producing constituencies containing differently sized electorates) and gerrymandering (the intentional drawing of electoral boundaries for partisan advantage) can both exacerbate partisan biases in constituency boundaries, but electoral geography is also a large part of the cause. Single-member constituencies usually contain roughly equal numbers of the electorate; for example, the United States is divided into 435 congressional districts, each including roughly equal populations, with one House representative per district. Boundaries are reviewed at periodic intervals, based on the census, to equalize the electorate. Yet the number of electors per constituency can vary substantially within nations, where boundary commissions take account of "natural" communities, where census information is incomplete or flawed, or where periodic boundary reviews fail to keep up with periods of rapid migration. There are also substantial differences cross-nationally: India, for example, has 545 representatives for a population of 898 million, so that each MP serves about 1.6 million people. By contrast, Ireland has 166 members in the Dial for a population of 3.5 million, or one seat per 21,000 people. The geographic size of constituencies also varies a great deal within countries, from small, densely packed inner-city seats to sprawling and more remote rural areas.

The way that FPTP systems work in practice can be understood most clearly with illustrations from the elections compared in the CSES surveys, including the 1997 British general election, the 1997 Canadian election, and the 1996 United States presidential and congressional elections.[10] Although all Anglo-American democracies, important differences in how these systems operate include variations in the number of parties contesting elections, the size of the legislatures, the number of electors per district, the dominant types of social cleavages in the electorate, the geographic distribution of voters, the regulations governing campaign finance and party election broadcasts, and the maximum number of years between elections.

The system of FPTP used for Westminster elections to the British House of Commons generally produces a manufactured "winner's bonus," exaggerating the proportion of seats won by the party in first place compared with their proportion of votes. For proponents of plurality elections, this bias is a virtue because it can guarantee a decisive outcome at Westminster, and a workable parliamentary majority, even in a close contest in the electorate.[11] One simple and intuitive way to capture the size of the winner's bonus produced by any electoral system is to divide the proportion of votes into the proportion of seats. A ratio of 1:1 would suggest no bias at all. But in contrast, the size of the bias in the winner's bonus at Westminster has fluctuated over time but has also gradually risen since the 1950s until the 1997 election, when the winner's bonus was the second highest ever recorded in the postwar era (only surpassed by the 2001 election). This phenomenon is the product of three factors: the geographical spread of party support in Britain, the effects of anti-Conservative tactical voting, and disparities in the size of constituency electorates.[12] The 1997 British general election witnessed one of the most dramatic results in British postwar history, where eighteen years of Conservative government under Margaret Thatcher and then John Major were replaced by the Labour landslide of seats under the prime ministerial leadership of Tony Blair. The United Kingdom is divided into 659 single-member parliamentary constituencies where voters cast a single ballot and MPs are elected on a simple plurality of votes. At Westminster, the party share of parliamentary seats, not their share of the popular vote, counts for the formation of the government. Under FPTP, British governments are commonly elected with less than a majority of votes; in 1997 Tony Blair was returned with almost two-thirds of the House of Commons, and a massive parliamentary majority of 179 out of 659 seats, based on 43.3% of the U.K. vote. As the party in first place, Labour enjoyed a seats-to-votes ratio of 1.47 whereas in contrast, with 30.7% of the vote, the Conservatives gained only 25% of all seats, producing a seats-to-votes ratio of 0.81.

The U.S. system is also based on FPTP in single-member districts for multiple offices including congressional races for the House and Senate, and the system of the Electoral College used for presidential contests. The ballot paper presents the voter with more complex choices than in Britain due to multi-level elections, as shown by Figure 2.3, as well as due to the use of referenda and initiatives in many states and the sheer frequency of primary, congressional, and presidential elections. The winner's bonus under majoritarian systems is also exemplified by the outcome of the 1996 U.S. presidential election pitting the incumbent, President Bill Clinton, against the Republican nominee, Senator Bob Dole; in this contest President Clinton was returned with 70.4% of the Electoral College vote, mainly by winning the largest states, but this substantial lead was based on only 50.1% of the popular vote across the whole country. In 1996 the congressional results for the 435-seat House of Representatives was highly proportional, however, because FPTP leads to proportional results in two-party systems when the vote totals of the two parties are fairly close. Roughly in accordance with the "cube" law, disproportionality increases as the vote totals diverge.

The 1997 Canadian federal election saw at least a partial consolidation of the multiparty system that had developed so dramatically with the emergence of two new parties, the Bloc Québécois and Reform, during the 1993 contest. The result of the 1997 Canadian election saw the return of the Liberals under the leadership of Jean Chrétien, although with a sharply reduced majority of only four seats and with 38% of the popular vote.[13] The Bloc Québécois lost its status as the official opposition, dropping from fifty-four to forty-four seats after a sharp decline in support. By contrast, the Reform party moved into second place in the House of Commons, with sixty seats, although with its strongest base in the West. Both the Progressive Conservatives and the New Democratic Party improved their positions after their disastrous results in 1993. The level of proportionality in the Canadian system was similar to that found in the British general election, with the Liberal Party and the Bloc Québécois enjoying the highest votes-to-seats bonus, and both countries had far lower proportionality than the United States. The existence of a multiparty system within plurality elections could be expected to lead to stronger calls for electoral reform by moving toward a proportional or combined formula, but the regional basis of party competition allows minor parties to be elected to parliament despite the hurdles created by the Canadian electoral system.[14]

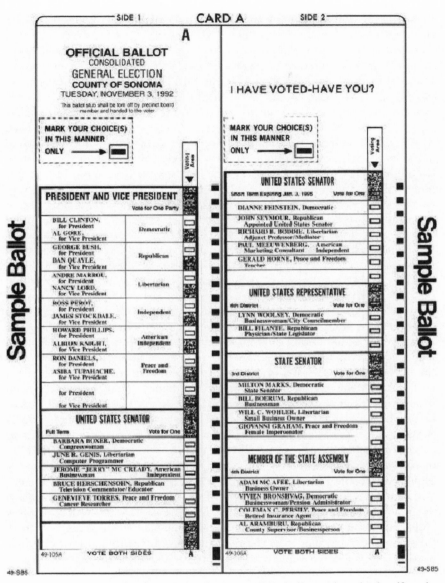

FIGURE 2.3. An example of First-Past-the-Post (FPTP) ballot with multiple offices for the U.S. General Election: Sonoma County, California

The Single Non-Transferable Vote, the Cumulative Vote, the Limited Vote, and the Bloc Vote

Many other variants on the majoritarian formula are available. From 1948 to 1993, Japanese voters used the Single Non-Transferable Vote for the lower house of the Diet, where each citizen casts a single vote in small multimember districts. Multiple candidates from the same party compete with each other for support within each district. Those candidates with the highest vote totals (a simple plurality) are elected. Under these rules, parties need to consider how many candidates to nominate strategically in each district, and how to make sure that their supporters spread their votes across all their candidates. The system has been classified as "semi-proportional" (Reynolds and Reilly), or even "proportional" (Sartori), but it seems preferable to regard this as a variation of the majoritarian family because candidates need a simple plurality of votes in their districts to be elected, and there is no quota or requirement for proportionality across districts. The system continues to be employed for parliamentary elections in Jordan and Vanuatu, as well as for two-thirds of the legislators in the Taiwanese elections under comparison (see the "Combined Systems" section in this chapter).[15] Other alternatives that fall within the majoritarian category, although not employed at national level for the lower house, include the Cumulative Vote, where citizens are given as many votes as representatives and where votes can be cumulated on a single candidate (used in dual-member seats in nineteenth-century Britain, where voters could "plump" both votes for one candidate, and in the state of Illinois in the United States until 1980). The Limited Vote system is similar, but citizens are given fewer votes than the number of members to be elected (used in elections to the Spanish Senate). The Bloc Vote system is similar to FPTP but with multimember districts. Each elector is given as many votes as there are seats to be filled, and they are usually free to vote for individual candidates regardless of party. The candidates winning a simple plurality of votes in each constituency win office. This system has been used for national parliamentary elections in nine countries, including Laos, Thailand, and Mauritius. Such contests allow citizens to prioritize particular candidates within parties, as well as maintain the link between representatives and local communities. On the other hand, where electors cast all their votes for a single party rather than distinguishing among candidates for different parties, this can exaggerate the disproportionality of the results and give an overwhelming parliamentary majority to the leading party.

Second Ballot Elections

Other systems use alternative mechanisms to ensure that the winning candidate gets an overall majority of votes. Second Ballot systems (also known as runoff elections) are used in two-dozen nations worldwide for election to the lower house. In these, any candidate obtaining an absolute majority of votes (50% or more) in the first round is declared elected. If no candidate reaches a majority in this stage of the process, a second round of elections is held between the two candidates with the highest share of the vote. The traditional way that this process is understood is that the first vote is regarded as largely expressive or sincere (voting with the heart), whereas the second is regarded as the more decisive ballot between the major contenders, where strategic considerations and alliances among left and right party blocs come into stronger play (voting "with the head"). In the countries under comparison, the Second Ballot system was employed for two-thirds of the seats in the Lithuanian combined system, as well as in seven of the presidential elections. Runoff elections are most common in presidential elections, but they are also used for elections to the lower house in France, in eleven ex-French colonies (including Chad, Haiti, Mali, and Gabon), in seven authoritarian ex-Soviet Eastern European states (such as Belarus, Kyrgyzstan, Moldova, Uzbekistan, Kazakhstan), and in some unreconstructed Communist states (Cuba and North Korea), as well as in the U.S. state of Louisiana. This system can be seen as encouraging centrist party competition, as well as bolstering the legitimacy of the eventual winner by ensuring that they receive the support of at least half the public. On the other hand, the rules harshly penalize minor parties, and the need for citizens to go to the polls on at least two occasions in rapid succession can induce voter fatigue, thereby depressing turnout. This phenomenon was exemplified by the May–June 2002 French elections where voters were called to the polls four times following nonconcurrent presidential and parliamentary elections.

Alternative Vote

The Alternative Vote, used in elections to the Australian House of Representatives and in Ireland for presidential elections and by-elections, is also majoritarian. This system, or "preferential voting" as it is commonly known in Australia, was introduced for Australian federal elections in 1919 and is now employed in all states except Tasmania, which uses STV.[16] Australia is divided into 148 single-member constituencies. Instead of a simple "X" on the ballot paper, voters rank their preferences among candidate (1,2,3 . . .) (see Figure 2.4). To win, candidates need an absolute majority of votes. Where no one candidate wins more than 50% after first preferences are counted, then the candidate with the least votes is eliminated, and his or her votes are redistributed among the other candidates. The process continues until an absolute majority is secured. In the 1996 Australian federal elections under comparison, for example, the victory of the conservative Liberal–National coalition ended the longest period of Labour Party government in Australia's history. The contest saw an extremely close call on the first preferences, with the Australian Labour Party (ALP) and the Liberal Party receiving identical shares of the vote (38.7%). In the final preferences, however, the ALP won 46.4% compared with 53.6% for non-ALP candidates. As a result, the Liberal–National government won ninety-three seats, and a substantial

FIGURE 2.4. An example of the Alternative Vote ballot for the Australian House of Representatives

majority, while Labour won only forty-nine.[17] This process worked as intended by translating an extremely close result in the first preference vote into a decisive majority of parliamentary seats for the leading party elected to government. This process systematically discriminates against those parties and candidates at the bottom of the poll to promote single-party government for the winner. The Alternative Vote functions similarly in many ways as the Second Ballot system, with the important distinction being that there is no opportunity for citizens to re-vote or for parties to create new alliances, in the light of the outcome of the first preference ballots. The balloting and counting process is also more efficient, avoiding repeated trips to the polling station and possible reductions in turnout due to voter fatigue.

Proportional Representation Formulae

Adversarial democracies and majoritarian electoral systems emphasize popular control by the party in government. By contrast, consensus democracies and PR electoral systems focus on the inclusion of all voices, emphasizing the need for bargaining and compromise within parliament, government, and the policymaking process. The basic principle of PR is that parliamentary seats are allocated according to the proportion of votes cast for each party. The main variations concern the use of open or closed lists of candidates, the formula for translating votes into seats, the level of the electoral threshold, and the size of the district magnitude. The Party Lists system exemplifies the proportional formula but the Single Transferable Vote system should also be included in this category because it allocates seats based on quotas.

Party Lists Systems

Proportional electoral systems based on party lists in multimember constituencies are widespread throughout Western Europe. Worldwide, 62 out of 191 countries use party list PR (see Figure 2.1). Party lists may be open as in Norway, Finland, the Netherlands, and Italy, in which case voters can express preferences for particular candidates within the list. Or they may be closed, as in Israel, Portugal, Spain, and Germany, in which case voters can only select which party to support, and each party decides the ranking of their candidates on the list. The rank order of candidates on the party list determines who is elected to parliament. In Israel, all the country is one constituency divided into 120 seats; but, often, lists are regional, as in the Czech Republic, where 200 total members are elected from eight regional lists. Proportional Party Lists systems are used in fifteen of the countries under comparison in the CSES dataset.[18] A typical party list ballot paper from South Africa is illustrated in Figure 2.5.

The electoral formula for the lower-house legislative elections varies among proportional systems (see Table 2.1). Votes can be allocated to seats based on the *highest averages* method. This requires the number of votes for each party to be divided successively by a series of divisors, and seats are allocated to parties that secure the highest resulting quotient, up to the total number of seats available. The most widely used is the *d'Hondt* formula, using divisors (such as 1,2,3, etc.), employed in Poland, Romania, Spain, and Israel. The "pure" *Sainte-Laguë* method, used in New Zealand, divides the votes with odd numbers (1,3,5,7, etc.). The "modified" *Sainte-Laguë* method replaces the first divisor by 1.4 but is otherwise identical to the pure version. An alternative is the *largest remainder* method, which uses a minimum quota, which can be calculated in a number of ways. In the simplest, the *Hare* quota, used in Denmark and Costa Rica, and, for the list constituencies in Taiwan, Ukraine, and Lithuania, the total number of valid votes in each constituency is divided by the total number of seats to be allocated. The *Droop* quota, used in South Africa, the Czech Republic, and Greece, raises the divisor by the number of seats plus one, producing a slightly less proportional result.

Other important differences in countries under comparison within the PR category include the formal threshold that parties must pass to qualify for seats. It should be noted that the formal threshold set by statute or specified in constitutional requirements is distinct from the effective vote threshold, which is the actual minimum share of the vote that leads to gaining at least one seat. The formal threshold ranges from the lowest level of 0.67% of the national vote, used in the Netherlands, to up to 7% of the vote, used in Poland. Worldwide, one of the highest vote thresholds is in Turkey, with a 10% hurdle, whereas there is no formal threshold in some countries such as South Africa, where less than 0.25% of the national vote is necessary for election. The formal threshold can have an important impact upon

TABLE 2.1. *Electoral Systems for the Lower House of Parliament, Selected Elections under Comparison, 1996–2002*

Type of Districts	Year of Election	Electoral System	Party List	Formula	Formal Vote Threshhold (%)	Total No. of MPs	No. of SMD MPs	No. of List MPs	Total No. of Districts for Lists	Voting Age Population (VAP)	Average VAP per Member	Mean District Mag. List Seats	Prop.	ENPP	Max. Years between Elections
Majoritarian															
Australia	1996	AV	None	Majority	None	148	148	0	0	13,547,900	91,500	1	84	2.61	3
Canada	1997	FPTP	None	Plurality	None	301	301	0	0	23,088,800	78,300	1	83	2.98	5
UK	1997	FPTP	None	Plurality	None	659	659	0	0	45,093,500	68,400	1	80	2.11	5
USA	1996	FPTP	None	Plurality	None	435	435	0	0	196,511,000	436,700	1	94	1.99	2
Combined-Independent															
Japan	1996	FPTP+PR	Closed	d'Hondt		500	300	200	11	96,672,700	193,400	18	86	2.93	4
Korea, Rep.	2000	FPTP+PR	Closed	LR-Hare	5	299	253	46	1	34,364,700	114,900	46	84	2.36	4
Russia	1999	FPTP+PR	Closed	LR-Hare	5	450	225	225	1	109,212,000	242,700	225	89	5.40	4
Taiwan	1996	SNTV+PR	Closed	LR-Hare	5	334	234/27	100	2	14,340,600	42,900	50	95	2.46	4
Ukraine	1998	FPTP+PR	Closed	LR-Hare	4	450	225	225	1	38,939,100	86,500	225	86	5.98	5
Combined-Dependent															
Germany	1998	FPTP+PR	Closed	LR-Hare	5	656	328	328	1	65,942,100	100,000	328	94	3.30	4
Hungary	1998	2nd Ballot+PR	Closed	d'Hondt	5	386	176	210	20	7,742,900	20,000	8	86	3.45	4
New Zealand	1996	FPTP+PR	Closed	St.-Laguë	5	120	65	55	1	2,571,800	21,400	55	96	3.78	3
Mexico	1997	FPTP+PR	Closed	LR-Hare	2	500	300	200	5	55,406,900	110,800	40	92	2.86	3
Thailand	2001	FPTP+PR	Closed	d'Hondt	5	500	400	100	1	42,663,000	85,000	100	88	2.92	4
Proportional															
Belgium	1999	PR Lists	Open	d'Hondt	0	150	0	150	20	8,000,000	53,300	8	96	9.05	4
Czech Republic	1996	PR Lists	Open	LR-Droop	5	200	0	200	8	7,859,200	39,300	25	89	4.15	4
Denmark	1998	PR Lists	Open	LR-Hare	2	179	0	179	17	4,129,000	23,000	8	98	4.92	4
Iceland	1999	PR Lists	Closed	LR-Hare		63	0	63	9	196,604	3,120	6	98	3.45	4
Israel	1996	PR Lists	Closed	d'Hondt	1.5	120	0	120	1	3,684,900	30,700	120	96	5.63	5
Netherlands	1998	PR Lists	Closed	d'Hondt	0.67	150	0	150	1	11,996,400	80,000	150	95	4.81	4
Norway	1997	PR Lists	Closed	St.-Laguë	4	165	0	165	19	3,360,100	20,000	9	95	4.36	4

Peru	2000	PR Lists	Open	d'Hondt	0	120	120	0	1	15,187,000	127,000	120	98	3.81	4
Poland	1997	PR Lists	Open	d'Hondt	7	460	460	0	52	27,901,700	60,700	9	82	2.95	4
Portugal	2002	PR Lists	Closed	d'Hondt	0	230	230	0	22	8,882,561	38,619	10	93	2.61	4
Romania	1996	PR Lists	Closed	d'Hondt	3	343	343	0	42	16,737,300	48,800	8	82	3.37	4
Slovenia	1996	PR Lists	Open	LR-Hare	3	90	90	0	8	1,543,000	17,000	11	84	5.52	4
Spain	1996	PR Lists	Closed	d'Hondt	3	350	350	0	52	31,013,030	88,600	7	93	2.73	4
Sweden	1998	PR Lists	Open	St.-Laguë	4	349	349	0	29	6,915,000	19,800	11	97	4.29	4
Switzerland	1999	PR Lists	Panachage	d'Hondt	0	200	200	0	26	5,736,300	28,700	8	93	5.08	4

Notes: PR, Proportional Representation; FPTP, First-Past-the-Post; AV, Alternative Vote; SMD, Single-member Districts; List, Party List; ENPP, Effective Number of Parliamentary Parties; Prop., Proportionality. ENPP is calculated following the method of Laakso and Taagepera (1979). The Index of Proportionality is calculated as the difference between a party's share of the vote and its share of the total seats in parliament, summed, divided by two, and subtracted from 100. Theoretically, it can range from 0 to 100. This is a standardized version of the Loosemore-Hanby Index. For details see Rose, Munro, and Mackie (1998). The formal vote threshold is the minimum share of the vote (in the district or nation) required by law to qualify for a seat, and this is distinct from the informal threshold or the actual minimum share of the vote required to win a seat. Note that the classification distinguishes between combined dependent systems, where the outcome depends upon the proportion of votes cast in the party lists, and independent combined systems used in Japan, Russia, and Korea, where the single-member districts and party lists operate in parallel. It should be noted that Belgium subsequently introduced a 5% formal vote threshold for the May 2003 general elections.

Sources: Voting Age Population: IDEA Voter Turnout from 1945 to 1997. Available online at www.idea.int; Successive volumes of *Electoral Studies;* Richard Rose, Neil Munro, and Tom Mackie. 1998. *Elections in Central and Eastern Europe Since 1990.* Strathclyde, U.K.: Center for the Study of Public Policy; Richard Rose. Ed. *International Encyclopedia of Elections.* Washington, D.C.: Congressional Quarterly Press 2000; http://www.aceproject.org/; Lawrence LeDuc, Richard G. Niemi, and Pippa Norris. Eds. 2002. *Comparing Democracies 2: New Challenges in the Study of Elections and Voting.* London: Sage; Table 1.2; CSES Macro-Level Dataset.

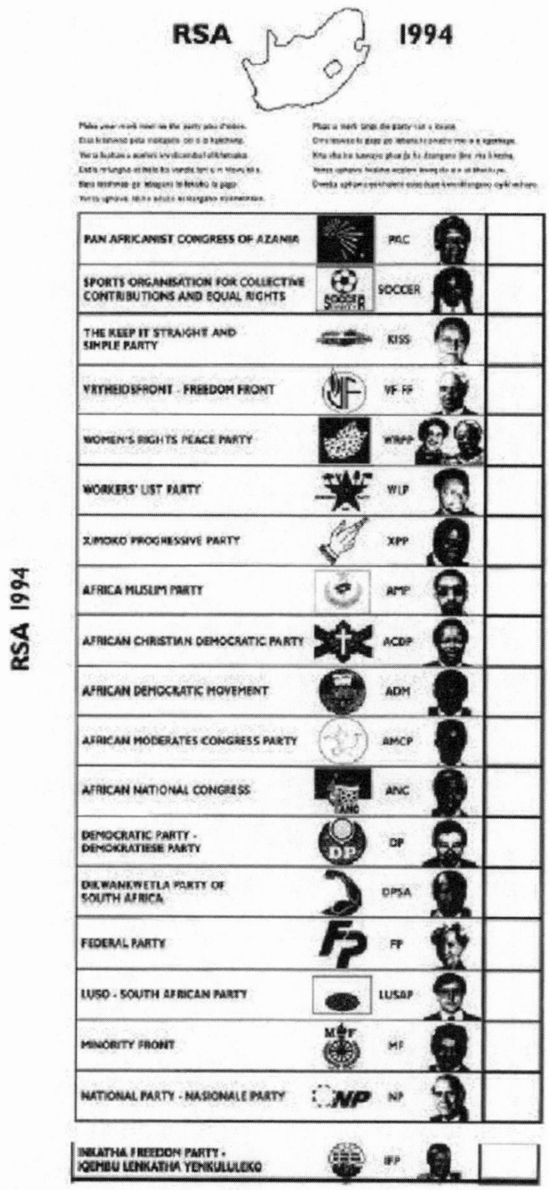

FIGURE 2.5. An example of a Party List ballot for the South African Parliament

proportionality and the opportunities for minor parties. District magnitude, or the mean number of seats per constituency, also varies substantially. In Israel, for example, all 120 members of the Knesset run in one nationwide constituency. By contrast, in Spain, the 350 members are elected in fifty list districts, each district electing 7 members on average. Generally, under PR systems, the larger the district magnitude the more proportional the outcome, and the lower the hurdles facing smaller parties.

Single Transferable Vote

The other alternative system in the proportional category is the STV, currently employed in legislative elections in Ireland, Malta, and for the Australian Senate.[19] The system can be classified as proportional because of the use of the quota for election. Under this system, each country is divided into multimember constituencies that each have about four or five representatives. Parties put forward as many candidates as they think could win in each constituency. Voters rank their preferences among candidates in an ordinal fashion (1st, 2nd, 3rd, . . .). The total number of votes is counted, and then the number of seats divides this vote total in the constituency to produce a quota. To be elected, candidates must reach the minimum quota. When the first preferences are counted, if no candidates reach the quota, then the candidate with the least votes is eliminated, and his or her votes are redistributed according to second preferences. This process continues until all seats are filled. Proponents argue that by allowing citizens to identify a rank order for their preferences within parties, or by ballot-splitting their votes across different parties, STV provides greater freedom of choice than do other systems.[20] Moreover, by retaining proportionality, these rules also generate a fair outcome in terms of the votes-to-seats ratio.

Combined Systems

An increasing number of countries, including Italy, New Zealand, and Russia, use combined systems, employing different electoral formulae in the same contest, although with a variety of alternative designs. In this regard, we follow Massicotte and Blais in classifying combined systems (otherwise known as mixed, hybrid, or side-by-side systems) according to their mechanics, not by their outcome.[21] If we followed the latter strategy, such as defining or labeling electoral systems based on their levels of proportionality, then this approach could create circular arguments. There is an important distinction within this category, which is overlooked in some discussions, between *combined-dependent* systems, where both parts are interrelated, and *combined-independent* systems, where two electoral formulae operate in parallel toward each other.

Combined-Dependent Systems

Combined-dependent systems, exemplified by the German and New Zealand parliamentary elections, include both single-member and party-list constituencies, but the distribution of seats is proportional to the share of the vote cast in the party list. As a result, the outcome of combined-dependent systems is closer to the proportional than the majoritarian end of the spectrum, although the logic of voter choice in these systems means that they still remain different from pure PR. The best-known application is in Germany, where electors can each cast two votes (see Figure 2.6). Half the members of the Bundestag (328) are elected in single-member constituencies based on a simple plurality of votes. The remaining MPs are elected from closed party lists in each region (Land). Parties that receive less than a specified minimum threshold of list votes (5%) are not be entitled to any seats. The total number of seats that a party receives in Germany is based on the *Niemeyer* method, which ensures that seats are proportional to second votes cast for party lists. Smaller parties that received, say, 10% of the list vote, but that did not win any single-member seats outright, are topped up until they have 10% of all the seats in parliament. It is possible for a party to be allocated "surplus" seats when it wins more district seats in the single-member district vote than it is entitled to under the result of the list vote.

New Zealand is also classified as a combined-dependent system because the outcome is proportional to the party-list share of the vote. The Mixed Member Proportion (MMP) system (as it is known in New Zealand) gives each elector two votes, one for the district candidate in single-member seats and one for the party list.[22] As in Germany, the list PR seats compensate for any disproportionality produced by the single-member districts. In total, 65 of the 120 members of the House of Representatives are elected in single-member constituencies based on a simple plurality of votes in single-member districts. The remainder is elected from closed national party lists. Parties receiving less than 5% of list votes fall below the minimal threshold to qualify for any seats. All other parties are allocated seats based on the Sainte-Laguë method, which ensures that the total allocation of seats is highly proportional to the share of votes cast for party lists. Smaller parties that received, say, 10% of the list vote but that did not win any single-member seats outright are topped up until they have 10% of all the seats in the House of Representatives. The 1996 New Zealand election saw the entry of six parties into parliament and produced a National–New Zealand First coalition government.

Combined-Independent Systems

Other electoral systems under comparison can be classified as combined-independent systems, following the Massicotte and Blais distinction, with two electoral systems used in parallel, exemplified by the Ukraine and Taiwan.[23] In these systems, the votes are counted separately in both types

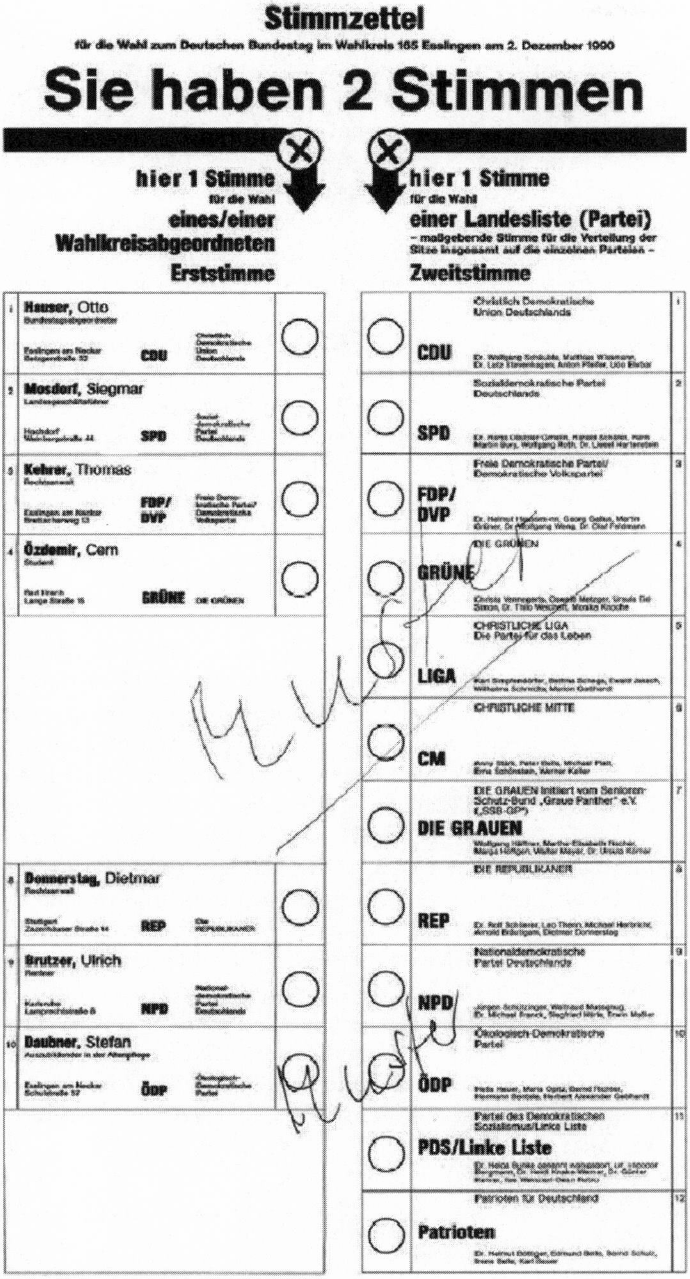

FIGURE 2.6. An example of a Combined or Mixed-Member ballot used for the German Bundestag

of seat so that the share of the vote cast for each party on the party lists is unrelated to the distribution of seats in the single-member districts. As a result, combined-independent systems are closer to the majoritarian than to the proportional end of the spectrum.

The March 1996 elections to the National Assembly in Taiwan exemplify this system. The Taiwanese National Assembly is composed of 334 seats, of which 234 are filled by the single non-transferable vote. Voters cast a single vote in one of fifty-eight multimember districts, each having 5 to 10 seats. The votes of all candidates belonging to the same party in all districts are aggregated into party votes, and the list PR seats are allocated among those parties meeting the 5% threshold. There are 80 PR list seats on a nationwide constituency and 20 PR list seats reserved for the overseas Chinese community. Taiwan has a three-party system, with the Nationalist Party (KMT) being dominant since 1945; the Democratic Progressive Party, founded in 1986, providing the main opposition; and the New Party, founded in 1993, having the smallest support. The major cleavage in Taiwanese party politics is the issue of national identity, dividing those who identify themselves as mainlanders who favor re-unification with China and those native Taiwanese who favor independence. The New Party is commonly considered most pro-unification and the Democratic Progressive Party the most pro-independence.[24]

The Ukrainian elections also illustrate how combined-independent systems work. The March 29, 1998 parliamentary contests were the second elections held since Ukrainian independence. Ukrainian voters could each cast two ballots. Half the deputies were elected by First-Past-the-Post in single-member districts, and others were elected from nationwide party lists, with a 4% threshold. Unlike the system in New Zealand and Germany, the two systems operated separately so that many smaller parties were elected from the single-member districts. The 1998 elections were contested by thirty parties and party blocs, although only ten of these groups could be said to have a clear programmatic profile and organizational base.[25] The Ukrainian result produced both an extremely fragmented and unstable party system: eight parties were elected via party lists and seventeen won seats via the single-member districts, along with 116 Independents. The election produced the highest Effective Number of Parliamentary Parties (ENPP) (5.98) in the countries under comparison, and it also generated fairly disproportional votes-to-seats ratios that benefited the larger parties. Ethnicity was reflected in the appeal of particular parties, including the Russophile Social Liberal Union, the Party of Regional Revival, and the Soyuz (Union) Party, and also in the way that ethnic Russians were twice as likely to support the Communist Party as were ethnic Ukrainians.[26]

For the comparison of the consequences of electoral systems, such as the link between different types of formula and patterns of party competition or electoral turnout, in this study I compare the broadest range of countries

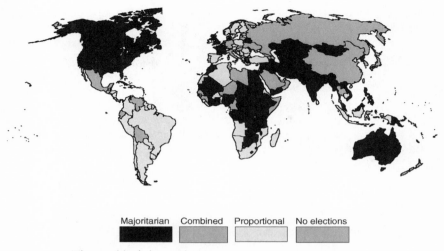

Majoritarian   Combined   Proportional   No elections

FIGURE 2.7. The world of electoral systems, 1997

worldwide that is possible from available sources of international data. For the survey analysis, however, I compare a more limited range of legislative and presidential elections. For parliamentary elections for the lower house, in the countries under comparison in Module I of the CSES dataset, fifteen elections were held from 1996 to 2002 using proportional electoral systems. Ten nations held parliamentary elections using combined electoral systems, including independent and dependent subtypes. Last, four countries held parliamentary elections for the lower house under majoritarian rules. There are also many important differences in electoral systems within each category, summarized in Table 2.1, for example, in the ballot structure of FPTP in the United Kingdom and the Alternative Vote in Australia, in the proportion of members elected in single-member and proportional districts in combined systems, as well as in the level of electoral thresholds facing minor parties.

The distribution of electoral systems around the world, illustrated in Table 2.2 and in Figure 2.7, confirms the regional patterns and the residual legacy stamped upon constitutions by their colonial histories. Three-quarters of the former British colonies continue to use a majoritarian electoral system today, as do two-thirds of the ex-French colonies. By contrast, three-quarters of the former Portuguese colonies, two-thirds of the ex-Spanish colonies, and all the former Dutch colonies use proportional electoral systems today. The post-Communist states freed from rule by the Soviet Union divided almost evenly among the three major electoral families, although slightly more countries (37%) have adopted proportional systems. Although Eastern Europe leans toward majoritarian arrangements, Central Europe adopted more proportional systems.

TABLE 2.2. *Type of Electoral System in Use by Past Colonial History (by percentage)*

	Britain	France	Portugal	Spain	The Netherlands	Belgium	Soviet Union	Other	None	All
Majoritarian										
FPTP	62.7	10.7				66.7	3.7	42.9	26.3	29.3
Second Ballot	5.1	39.3		4.8			25.9		10.5	13.0
Bloc Vote	6.8	10.7		4.8				7.1		4.9
Alternative Vote	3.4									1.1
Single Non-Transferable Vote	1.7	3.6								1.1
Combined										
Combined-Independent	3.4	14.3	14.3	14.3			29.6	14.3	5.3	11.4
Combined-Dependent	1.7			14.3			3.7		15.8	4.3
Proportional										
Party List PR	11.9	21.4	85.7	61.9	100.0	33.3	37.0	35.7	42.1	33.7
Single Transferable Vote	3.4									1.1
TOTAL NUMBER OF STATES	59	28	7	21	4	3	27	16	19	184

Note: The percentage of each colonial group using different types of electoral systems. Countries were classified by electoral system using the typology and sources in Figure 2.1 and by their predominant colonial history from the *CIA World Fact Book, 2002*. Available online at www.cia.org. The comparison covers 191 nation-states worldwide, excluding the seven states without direct elections during this period.

Presidential Electoral Systems

The countries under comparison in Module I of the CSES dataset also allow comparison of ten presidential elections (illustrated in Table 2.3), all held under majoritarian or plurality rules.[27] The simple plurality FPTP was used in Mexico and Taiwan. The Second Ballot "majority-runoff" system (also known as the double ballot) is used worldwide in fifteen of the twenty-five countries with direct presidential elections, including in Austria, Colombia, Finland, France, Belarus, and Russia, and in seven of the nations under comparison in the CSES dataset. In these elections, if no candidate gets at least 50% of the vote in the first round, then the top two candidates face each other in a second round to insure a majority of votes for the leading candidate. This system is exemplified by the 1996 Russian presidential election, where seventy-eight candidates registered to run for election, of which seventeen qualified for nomination. In the first round, Boris Yeltsin won 35.3% of the vote, with Gennadii Zyuganov, the Communist candidate, close behind with 32% and Alexander Lebed third, with 14.5% of the vote. After the other candidates dropped out, and Lebed swung his supporters behind Yeltsin, the final result of the second election was a decisive 53.8% of the vote for Yeltsin against 40.3% for Zyuganov.[28] Runoff elections aim to consolidate support behind the major contenders and to encourage broad cross-party coalition building in the final stages of the campaign.

The United States uses the unique device of the Electoral College. The president is not decided directly by popular vote, instead popular votes are collected within each state and, since 1964, the District of Columbia. Each state casts all of its electoral votes for the candidate receiving a plurality of votes within each state (the unit rule). Each state is allowed as many electoral votes as it has senators and representatives in Congress. This means that even sparsely populated states such as Alaska have at least three electoral votes. Nevertheless, the most populous states each cast by far the greatest number of electoral votes, and, therefore, presidential contenders devote most attention and strategic resources (spending, political ads, and visits) during the campaign to states such as New York, California, New Jersey, Pennsylvania, Ohio, Florida, Illinois, Michigan, and Texas, especially when polls suggest that the race is close in these areas. The importance of these rules is exemplified by the outcome of the 2000 election, where Republican George W. Bush won a 271–266 majority in the electoral college despite the fact that his opponent, Al Gore, won about half a million more popular votes. The results called attention to the need to alter the Electoral College, which has not experienced major reform since 1804, despite the fact that critics have regarded the system as archaic, outmoded, and essentially flawed.[29] Other important variations among the presidential electoral systems under comparison include length of time in office (ranging from four to six years) and whether presidential elections are held in conjunction

TABLE 2.3. *Direct Elections for President/Prime Minister, Selected Elections under Comparison, 1996–2001*

	Type	Year of Election	Electoral System	In Conjunction with Legislative Elections	Voting Age Population (VAP)	Vote/VAP	Max. Years between Elections
Belarus	Majoritarian	2001	2nd Ballot	Yes	7,585,000	81.3	5
Chile	Majoritarian	1999	2nd Ballot	No	10,066,000	72.8	6
Israel (i)	Majoritarian	1996	2nd Ballot	Yes	3,995,000	84.5	4
Lithuania	Majoritarian	1997	2nd Ballot	No	2,740,000	70.7	5
Mexico	Plurality	2000	FPTP	Yes	62,685,000	60.0	6
Peru	Majoritarian	2000	2nd Ballot	Yes	15,430,000	78.6	5
Romania	Majoritarian	1996	2nd Ballot	Yes	16,737,000	78.1	4
Russia	Majoritarian	2000	2nd Ballot	No	109,037,000	68.8	5
Taiwan	Plurality	1996	FPTP	Yes	14,154,000	76.9	4
USA	Majoritarian	1996	Electoral College	Yes	196,511,000	49.3	4

Note: (i) In Israel, direct elections for the prime minister, not the president.

Sources: See Table 2.1.

TABLE 2.4. *The Parliamentary and Presidential Elections under Comparison*

	Presidential Vote		Lower House of Parliament		
	1st	2nd	District Vote	Party List Vote	Party List Candidate Preferential Vote
Australia	✗		✓	✗	✗
Belarus	✓	✓	✗	✗	✗
Belgium	✗		✗	✓	✓
Canada	✗		✓	✗	✗
Chile	✓	✓	✗	✗	✗
Czech Republic	✗		✗	✓	✗
Denmark	✗		✗	✓	✓
Germany	✗		✓	✓	✗
Hungary	✗		✓	✓	✗
Iceland	✗		✗	✓	
Israel (i)	✓	✓	✗	✓	✗
Japan	✗		✓	✓	✗
Korea, Rep. of	✗		✓	✓	✗
Lithuania	✓	✓	✗	✗	✗
Mexico	✓		✓	✓	✗
Netherlands	✗		✗	✓	✗
New Zealand	✗		✓	✓	✗
Norway	✗		✗	✓	✗
Peru	✓	✓	✗	✓	✓
Poland	✗		✗	✓	✓
Portugal	✗		✗	✓	
Romania	✓	✓	✗	✓	✗
Russia	✓	✓	✓	✓	✗
Slovenia	✗		✗	✓	✗
Spain	✗		✗	✓	✗
Sweden	✗		✗	✓	✓
Switzerland	✗		✗	✓	✓
Taiwan	✓		✓	✓	✗
Thailand	✗		✓	✓	✗
UK	✗		✓	✗	✗
Ukraine	✗		✓	✓	✗
USA	✓		✓	✗	✗

Note: This does not count other electoral options on the ballot, such as for local, regional, state-level, upper house/senate, European, or other elected office, or any referenda issues.
(i) Note Israel includes direct elections for the prime minister, not president.
✗ = Not applicable in the election under comparison.
✓ = Applicable.

with legislative contests (which could be expected to strengthen the party coattails of presidential candidates and, therefore, create stronger legislative–executive links) or whether they are held separately, which reinforces the separation of powers.

The consequences of different arrangements also generate different electoral decisions by citizens, including how often they are called to the ballot box and what choices they face. Table 2.4 illustrates the major variations in the countries and national elections under comparison. The least demands are in parliamentary democracies such as Australia and Britain where citizens only cast one ballot at national level, although there are many other types of contest such as Australian state and local elections, and British elections to the European parliament, as well as to the Scottish Parliament and Welsh Assembly and to local government. By contrast, at national level Russian citizens are called to the polls twice for the second ballot presidential elections, as well as to cast two votes for the Duma. The other nations present different demands upon citizens ranging between these extremes. Obviously, greater options for voting provide citizens with more opportunity for political expression, for example, with split-ticket voting between levels, but at the same time, frequent demands from successive elections at multiple levels of office carry the danger of voter fatigue.

Conclusion: The Consequences of Electoral Systems

Often the choice of electoral system seems mechanistic, abstract, and highly technical, with constitutional engineering designed to bring about certain objectives. But the issue of how the electoral system should function reflects essentially contested normative concepts of representative government. For advocates of adversarial democracy, the most important considerations for electoral systems are that the votes cast in elections (not the subsequent process of coalition building) should determine the party or parties in government. The government should be empowered to implement its program during its full term of office, without depending upon the support of minority parties. The government should remain accountable for its actions to parliament, and ultimately to the public. And, at periodic intervals, the electorate should be allowed to judge the government's record, evaluate prospective policy platforms offered by the opposition parties, and cast their votes accordingly. Minor parties in third or fourth place are discriminated against by majoritarian elections for the sake of governability. From this perspective, proportional elections are ineffective because they can produce indecisive outcomes, unstable regimes, disproportionate power for minor parties in "kingmaker" roles, and a lack of clear-cut accountability and transparency in decision-making.

By contrast, proponents of consensual democracy argue that majoritarian systems place too much faith in the winning party, especially in plural societies divided by ethnic conflict, with too few constraints on government during its term of office. For the vision of consensual democracy, the electoral system should promote a process of conciliation, consultation, and coalition-building within parliaments. Parties above a minimum threshold should be included in the legislature in rough proportion to their level of electoral support. The party or parties in government should craft policies based on a consensus among their coalition partners. Moreover, the composition of parliament should reflect the main divisions in society and the electorate, so that all citizens have spokespersons articulating their interests, perspectives, and concerns in national debates. In this view, majoritarian systems over-reward the winner, producing "an elected dictatorship" where a government based on a plurality can steamroller its policies and implement its programs, without the need for consultation and compromise with other parties in parliament or other groups in society. The unfairness and disproportionate results of plurality electoral systems, outside of two-party contests, means that some voices in the electorate are systematically excluded from public debate.

We can conclude, agnostically, that there is no single best electoral system: the central arguments between adversarial and consensual democratic theorists represent irresolvable value conflicts. For societies that are divided by deep-rooted ethnic or religious conflict, such as Rwanda, Bosnia, or Israel, proportional electoral systems may prove more inclusive, as Lijphart argues. But, as others warn, PR elections may also reinforce, rather than ameliorate, such cleavages.[30] For states that are highly centralized, such as Britain or New Zealand, majoritarian systems can insulate the government from the need for broader consultation and for democratic checks and balances. In constitutional design it appears that, despite the widespread appeal of the rhetoric of "electoral engineering" for optimal decision-making, in practice there are no easy choices. A wide range of alternative rules can potentially influence the impact of these electoral systems on both patterns of voting behavior and political representation. The mechanical effects of electoral rules are easier to predict than the psychological ones, and, in both cases, many effects are highly contingent because they are embedded within many other institutional, political, cultural, and social contexts. In the next chapters I discuss the normative debates about electoral systems in more detail and then consider some of the most important consequences of electoral rules for voting behavior, including party competition, the strength of social cleavages and partisan identification, and patterns of electoral turnout.

3

Evaluating Electoral Systems

In recent decades, debate about electoral engineering has moved from margin to mainstream on the policy agenda in many nations. Political discussions about electoral reform have revolved largely around the practical options, the sometimes bewildering combination of trade-off choices, and the consequences of particular reforms to the status quo within each state. Underlying these pragmatic arguments are contested normative visions about the basic principles of representative government.[1] The most fundamental debate raises questions about the ultimate ends as well as means of elections.[2] The general consensus in the literature emphasizes that no "perfect" bespoke electoral system fits every society. Instead, arrangements have to be tailored to different contexts, and choices require trade-offs among competing public goods.[3] The most common argument today revolves around the pros and cons claimed for majoritarian, combined, and proportional types of electoral systems, for example, which is best for maximizing electoral participation or for containing ethnic conflict. Major questions underlying these empirical claims concern what forms of representative democracy are more desirable, and what functions electoral systems *should* perform. Some studies of electoral systems fail to deal explicitly with the normative assumptions, preferring to focus exclusively upon the factual claims. Others present lengthy shopping lists of the alternative values that electoral systems are supposed to meet, emphasizing the desirability of, say, the inclusion of women, the management of ethnic conflict, or the importance of governability, agnostically letting readers pick and choose whatever values they regard as most important.[4] A comprehensive list has the advantages of identifying all the possible claims that people can and often do make about electoral systems. Many practical arguments about reform are conducted at this level. But from this procedure it remains unclear why we should prioritize one value over another or how values are logically connected to form part of a broader framework. What reasonable person could not want, say, both social inclusiveness in parliamentary representation and also effective governance, in a win-win situation, even if these values may conflict or contradict each other in practice.

A preferable strategy seeks to locate the normative values underlying the choice of electoral systems within coherent theories of representative democracy.[5] In one of the most familiar frameworks of ideal types used in comparative politics, Lijphart contrasts *consensus* (or consociational) democracies based upon proportional representation electoral systems with *majoritarian* (or Westminster) democracies based upon majoritarian and plurality electoral systems.[6] Consensus democracies are defined as those aiming at power sharing among multiple political actors to maximize deliberation, bargaining, and compromise. Majoritarian political systems are envisaged as those concentrating power in the hands of the largest parliamentary party to maximize governability. This dichotomy represents an important typology, commonly used in the comparative literature. Yet the term majoritarian can become confusing when used to refer simultaneously to the type of democracy as well as to the type of electoral system that bear these names. The term Westminster democracy is equally inadequate, referring as it does to a form of parliamentary government exported from the United Kingdom to many Commonwealth nations decades ago, yet a system that can find few recognizable exemplars today, even in its original home.[7] The term is also potentially misleading given that the Westminster House of Commons uses FPTP, a plurality not a simple-majority electoral system, whereas the House of Lords currently remains an unelected body, an anomaly in the modern democratic world. The traditional terminology also seems to weight the deck by disingenuously framing the choice as one between either consensual ("a kinder, gentler") democracy or effective majoritarian government, rather than understanding the central choice as between competing visions of the best form of representative democracy.

In a recent comprehensive study, G. Bingham Powell, Jr., proposes that the alternative ideal types can be conceptualized as *majoritarian* or *proportional* visions of democracy. Yet this strategy extends the term proportional, which originally referred to the PR type of electoral formula, to many other aspects of the basic political system or constitution that are conceptually distinct from the type of proportional formula per se, such as the distribution of power within the legislature. Moreover, Powell does not classify some systems with PR electoral formulae as proportional democracies (such as Greece, which is classified as majoritarian, or Ireland, which is classified as mixed). As a result, it seems best to maintain a clear conceptual distinction to avoid any confusing slippage between proportional representation electoral formulae per se and any notion of a "proportional" democracy.[8] Matthew Soberg Shugart and John M. Carey, focusing upon two dimensions of political systems, develop another alternative typology used to understand presidentialism. The authors distinguish between *efficient* political systems designed to maximize government accountability, disciplined programmatic parties, and identifiable policy mandates and *inefficient* systems that maximize the provision of particularistic local concerns and personal votes. They also distinguish the *representative* dimension, with systems reflecting either local or group interests. Although the central typology is useful, the term efficiency, originally drawn from Walter Bagehot's *The English Constitution*, seems potentially misleading because efficiency is conventionally understood to concern the most appropriate means to an end, rather than any specific end goal per se. Hence, there can be an efficient or inefficient delivery of particularistic pork and patronage.[9]

For all these reasons, I will draw upon an older conceptualization suggested by the noted constitutional expert, Samuel Finer.[10] In this study the central normative debate about the fundamental ideals that electoral systems should meet is conceptualized as one between either *adversarial* or *consensual* visions of representative democracy. This distinction captures the central features of the argument more closely than many of the current alternatives in the literature. (See Table 3.1 and Figure 3.1.)

The Arguments For and Against Adversarial Democracy

Advocates of adversarial democracy believe that democratic political systems should promote government accountability, transparency, and responsiveness, through the generation of single-party executives, responsible programmatic parties, and vigorous parliamentary opposition. Electoral systems designed to give the leading party the majority of parliamentary seats, through the use of majoritarian and plurality electoral formulae, are an essential, although not sufficient, component of adversarial democracy by connecting voters' preferences directly to a representative in parliament and, indirectly, to the party that enters government. The purported virtues of these electoral systems, advocates claim, are that they maximize democratic accountability, strengthen citizen–member linkages, facilitate governability, generate decisive electoral outcomes, and encourage political responsiveness.

Democratic Accountability
Proponents of adversarial democracy envisage elections primarily as a critical link in the chain designed to insure that parties in government remain collectively accountable to parliament (on a day-to-day basis) and to the electorate (at regular intervals). This vision suggests that electoral systems that systematically reduce the multiple contenders for office to the leading parties that win power both simplifies electoral choices and clarifies responsibility for government decisions. In this ideal, the "In" and the "Out" parties compete for popular support by presenting alternative programmatic platforms, leadership teams, and candidates for elected office. In the words of Walter Lippmann: *"To support the Ins when things are going well; to support the Outs when things seem to be going badly, this, in spite of all that has been said about*

TABLE 3.1. *The Ideal Functions of Electoral Institutions*

	Adversarial Democracy	Consensual Democracy
Ideal Function of the Political System	Should promote government accountability, transparency of decision-making, and responsible parties through single-party executives, effective opposition parties, vigorous parliamentary debate, and decisive elections.	Should promote consensual decision-making, bargaining, and compromise among multiple parliamentary parties, each with a stake in power, and dispersed decision-making processes.
Ideal Function of the Electoral System	Should maximize electoral decisiveness by directly linking the votes cast to the parties and members elected to parliament, thereby providing an indirect link from voters to the party in government; should winnow the number of electoral parties and candidates that enter parliament and ensure that the leading party gains a workable parliamentary majority.	Should maximize electoral choice among multiple parties, fairly translate vote shares into seat shares, and be socially inclusive in parliamentary representation.
Ideal Function of Opposition Parties	Should provide adversarial scrutiny of government policy proposals and actions.	Should be part of the consultation process and act as an important check on the power of the largest party.
Ideal Function of Citizens	Should be able to evaluate the performance of the governing party and the prospective policies offered by alternative electoral parties in opposition.	Should be able to evaluate the performance and policies of parties that are empowered to negotiate, bargain, and compromise on behalf of their supporters.
Ideal Function of Elected Representatives	Should act as community spokespersons reflecting local concerns and representing all local constituents in parliament.	Should deliberate, negotiate, and bargain as spokespersons on behalf of their party supporters.
Potential Dangers	May lead to "elective dictatorship" characterized by entrenched power for predominant majority populations, disregard for minority rights, and lack of effective checks and balances.	May lead to problems of governance associated with extreme multiparty fragmentation, unstable governments, lack of accountability for the government and for elected representatives, and indecisive election results.

A: Adversarial model

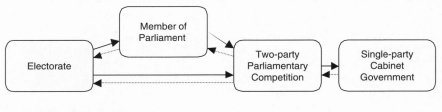

B: Consensual model

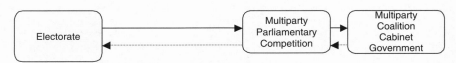

FIGURE 3.1. Models of representative democracy

Tweedledum and Tweedledee, is the essence of popular government."[11] By facilitating a veto on governing incumbents, elections function as instruments of democratic control. At the end of its tenure in office, the single party in government remains collectively accountable for its legislative record and policy performance, and, if the "trains do not run on time" or if there is evidence of corruption, malfeasance, or incompetence, then the electorate can punish the incumbent administration, if they so wish. In comparison, where PR electoral systems generate multiparty parliaments and coalition governments, it is believed that this process makes it more difficult for voters to assign blame or praise for the government's performance and to reward or punish parties accordingly, even if the public becomes deeply dissatisfied with those in power.[12] Proponents argue that under majoritarian and plurality electoral systems, the party with the largest share of parliamentary seats usually forms the government, so that there is a direct link between the votes cast and the outcome for government. Where PR produces multiparty parliaments, the process of coalition building after the result, not the election per se, determines the allocation of cabinet portfolios and government policies. For proponents of adversarial political systems, representative democracy is preserved by the ability of the electorate to reward or punish parties when asked to judge their performance and promises, by rigorous scrutiny of government actions, and by vigorous debate between government and opposition parties.

The closest analogy to adversarial democracy is the legal arguments propounded by public defenders and prosecutors, with the judge (constitutional courts) ensuring fair play, the news media functioning as official recorders, and the electorate serving as the ultimate jury. In the courts, the function of the defender and prosecutor is to argue the pros and cons of each case to the best of their abilities, within the boundaries of legal ethics, irrespective of their personal beliefs about the guilt or innocence of their clients because through the battle of courtroom debate it is believed that justice will be done. In this conception, drawing upon the classical liberal theory of John Stuart Mill, adversarial parliamentary debate reveals flaws in any political argument, weaknesses in policy proposals, and mistakes or errors by government ministers, and, as such, it is to be valued more than a false consensus that could potentially stifle debate, hide certain failings from the public eye, and exclude the full range of alternative proposals from consideration. Parliament ideally functions in this view as the nation's forum for debate, where the government proposes and the opposition's duty, like the public prosecutor, is to oppose in principle.

Strong Voter-Member Accountability

At the local level, advocates argue that the link between citizens and their member of parliament elected in geographically based single-member districts provides local communities with a voice in the nation's affairs as well as makes elected members directly responsive to constituency concerns. Due to single-member districts and candidate-ballots, elected members are believed to remain individually accountable to their local party organization on a day-to-day basis and to all their local constituents at regular intervals. Members are thought to have stronger electoral incentives to provide constituency service, and, thereby, to build a personal vote, in single-member districts using candidate-ballots.[13] In this context it is believed that members will prioritize local constituency service with individual casework, sorting out such problems as housing or welfare benefits, as well as listening to community concerns and raising these matters in parliamentary debates. The independence and autonomy of MPs from the central party leadership is further strengthened where local party members and activists determine the recruitment, nomination, and selection process for parliamentary candidates in their constituency.[14] By contrast, members are thought to be more accountable to party leaders under electoral systems with party-ballots, especially in large multimember constituencies with closed party lists and nomination procedures controlled by the central party.[15] Such a system is believed to promote parliamentary discipline within programmatic and cohesive legislative parties because the leadership has the power to sanction rebels by refusing their renomination.

Governability

Majoritarian and plurality electoral systems used in legislative contests have strong reductive effects designed to generate single-party executives and to limit the degree of party fragmentation in parliaments. What they thereby lose in fairness to minor parties, proponents argue, they gain in governing capacity, as the single party in cabinet government is thereby empowered to implement its programmatic manifesto promises during its term of office, if a majority of parliamentary seats are held and the support of cohesive and disciplined parliamentary backbenchers is maintained. By systematically exaggerating the seat lead for the winning party with the largest share of votes, these electoral systems generate either a "natural" or a "manufactured" majority, producing a decisive outcome in seats. This process, thereby, legitimates the governing authority of the winner, even in relatively close contests in the share of the popular vote. Single-party governments, with an overall parliamentary majority, can enact whatever policies they feel are necessary during their terms of office, making difficult or unpopular decisions they believe are in the country's long-term interests, while knowing that they face the judgment of the electorate when their terms end and the potential sanction of losing power.

Given the concentration of executive power in the hands of a single party, the main check on the cabinet during its term of office is a vote of confidence in parliament. Governments capable of surviving such a vote, which in practice usually means carrying their own backbenchers with them, often face few other effective curbs on power, beyond the courts. For advocates, this system has certain decisive advantages: providing government with the authority to legislate and the capacity to implement its policies, especially radical proposals; to respond decisively and in a timely fashion to contingent events and sudden emergencies; to overcome parliamentary stalemate on controversial and divisive issues; and to make difficult decisions that may generate short-term unpopularity, if they believe that these policies are in the country's long-term interests. Majoritarian systems remove the need for closed-door postelection negotiations and policy compromises with other parties or for frequent coalition changes between elections.[16] There is a single democratic chain of accountability within each nation stretching from citizens to particular members of parliament, from parliamentarians to cabinet ministers, and from ministers to civil servants implementing policies. Proponents believe that, in this regard, the provision of accountable single-party government is more important than the inclusion of all parties in strict proportion to their share of the vote. Indeed, the way that majoritarian and plurality electoral systems usually penalize minor and fringe parties can be regarded as a virtue, if this process prevents extremists on the far right or far left from acquiring representative legitimacy, thereby avoiding a fragmented parliament full of "fads and faddists."

Decisive Elections

Majoritarian and plurality electoral systems function as a substantial hurdle that systematically reduces the multiple number of parties and candidates contending for elected office so that, although electoral competition remains open as almost anyone can usually stand (with some minor legal regulations for matters such as citizenship and age requirements), only the leading contenders win parliamentary seats and governing power. Where electoral systems succeed in fulfilling this function, proponents argue, they thereby have the capacity to generate decisive outcomes where voters' preferences determine directly the selection of members of parliament and the overall distribution of parliamentary seats among parties. In turn, the majority of seats awarded to the largest party leads to the formation of single-party cabinet governments. Majoritarian electoral systems thereby maintain a direct and transparent link between the share of the votes cast and the single party in government.

Responsiveness to the Electorate

Proponents claim that government and opposition parties, and also individual elected members, must remain "responsive" to public concerns. In adversarial democracies, the governing party is entrusted with considerable powers during its term in office, with few checks and balances, but, nevertheless, it is thought that politicians remain sensitive to public opinion because those governing are aware that even a small swing in the popular vote in a competitive and balanced two-party system is sufficient to bring the opposition into office. This system can be envisaged as a pulley-and-weights mechanism where a modest pull on the electoral rope can produce a disproportionate displacement of weight. Proponents believe that these characteristics mean that under majoritarian systems governments are granted considerable power during their tenures in office, yet this power is shackled with ultimate accountability to the electorate. Moreover, individual members are thought to remain responsive to their particular community, representing local interests and articulating diverse constituency concerns in national legislative debates, which may be a particularly important function in large and heterogeneous societies.

Critiques

Critics suggest that adversarial democracy suffers from certain well-known dangers. In particular, adversarial democracy involves a zero-sum game between the Ins and the Outs. If one party is returned to government repeatedly over successive elections, with a majority or even just a plurality of votes, the opposition has limited powers of checks and balances. Where communities are divided into multiple cleavages, especially between enduring majority and minority populations, and where these social divisions and ethnic cleavages are reflected in party politics, then the balanced rotation between government and opposition implied in the adversarial model may be absent. Predominant parties can exercise undue power and trample over the interests of minority groups. Exacerbating adversarial debate may work in stable democracies and homogeneous societies, but in deeply divided plural societies and transitional democracies, critics suggest, where there is minimal agreement about the rules of the game as well as about basic policy issues, this can be a recipe for disaster. The potential dangers, it is argued, are "elective dictatorship," disregard for minority rights, administrative corruption arising from insufficient checks and balances, unfairness to minor parties, and public disillusionment if citizens feel that governments are unresponsive to their needs and if fragmented opposition parties mean that elections are unable to insure a regular rotation of parties in power.

Arguments For and Against Consensual Democracy

To guard against these dangers, critics present many alternative visions of how representative democracy should function and what institutions are necessary as the structural foundations for these normative ideals. These arguments can also be discussed and framed in many ways, including as Madisonian, deliberative, or consociational models of democracy.[17] In this study I focus upon the arguments developed by Lijphart in favor of consensus democracy as the most systematic comparative treatment of the subject. The vision of consensual representative democracy emphasizes that political institutions should promote consensual decision-making, bargaining, and compromise among multiple parliamentary parties, each with a stake in power, and dispersed decision-making processes. Proponents of consensual democracy suggest that proportional electoral systems facilitate deliberative and collaborative governance, reduce the barriers to minority parties, maximize voting turnout, and ensure that parliaments faithfully mirror the social and political diversity in society, all of which can be regarded as essential, but not sufficient, conditions for checking and balancing the power of predominant majorities.

Facilitate Deliberative and Collaborative Governance
For those who favor consensual democracy, the primary function of elections is to allow citizens to choose spokespersons to discuss, negotiate, and bargain on their behalf. Representation is less geographical than social. Far from concentrating collective responsibility in the hands of the single-party government, it is believed that the process of governance should be dispersed as widely as possible among elected representatives who are empowered to deliberate, bargain, and achieve compromise acceptable to all actors, with many institutional checks and balances, including multiple political parties in parliament, to ensure that plural interests are heard in a consensual decision-making process. The vision of democracy underlying this perspective is essentially more deliberative and collaborative than adversarial.

Reduce the Barriers to Minor Parties
Advocates of consensual democracy emphasize the need for electoral systems to give fair and just representation so that the distribution of parliamentary seats reflects the share of the popular vote won by all parties. This process is thought to provide Madisonian checks to single-party government and

majority predominance. For many critics, the traditional moral case against majoritarian electoral systems is based on the way this system systematically penalizes the share of seats awarded to minor parties who achieve a significant share of the vote but with support dispersed thinly across many districts, exemplified by the Canadian Progressive Conservatives in 1993, the Alliance Party in New Zealand in 1993, or the British Liberal Democrats in 1983. All electoral systems winnow out the field of candidates and parties that enter office, by translating votes into seats. In theory, pure PR systems have little reductive impact, as the seat share received by each party reflects its vote share. In practice, no PR system is wholly proportional in outcome, even with minimum vote thresholds, large district magnitudes, and proportional formulas. But PR electoral systems are designed to allocate seats more closely to the share of the vote received by each party than are majoritarian and plurality electoral systems, which prioritize different objectives. By facilitating the election of more minor parties, PR systems also broaden electoral choice, providing voters with a wider range of alternatives. By contrast, by discouraging some minor parties from standing, voters face fewer party choices, although also simpler options, under majoritarian electoral systems.

Maximize Electoral Participation

Under majoritarian and plurality electoral systems, supporters of minor and fringe parties, with geographic support dispersed widely but thinly across the country, may feel that casting their votes will make no difference to who wins in their constituencies, still less to the overall composition of government and the policy agenda. The "wasted votes" argument is strongest in safe seats in single-member districts where the incumbent candidate or party is unlikely to be defeated. In contrast, proportional elections with low vote thresholds and large district magnitudes, such as the Party Lists system used in the Netherlands, increase the opportunities for minor parties to enter parliament even with a relatively modest share of the vote and dispersed support, and, therefore, increase the incentives for their supporters to cast a vote. Because fewer votes are wasted in a PR system, it is believed that proportional representation systems should therefore generate higher electoral turnout than majoritarian or plurality electoral systems.[18]

Ensure Parliamentary Diversity

Proponents of consensus democracy also emphasize the importance of social inclusion, so that all voices and multiple interests are brought to the policymaking process, and, in this regard, they emphasize the need for diversity in the composition of parliaments. It is well established that certain social groups are over-represented in elected office, with parliamentary elites commonly drawn from predominant ethnic groups, men, and those of higher occupational status. Although there are substantial variations world-wide, overall, women constitute only one-sixth (14.4%) of national legislators worldwide, with women usually lagging furthest behind in national parliaments using majoritarian electoral systems.[19] Reformers have considered various strategies designed to widen opportunities for women and minorities, including legally binding candidate quotas, dual-member constituencies designated by minority group or gender, and affirmative action for candidacies and official positions within party organizations. Some of these mechanisms can be used in single-member districts, for example, in the mid-nineties the British Labour party adopted all-women shortlists for nomination in half its target seats. But advocates argue that affirmative action can be implemented most easily when applied to balancing the social composition of party lists, for example, by designating every other position on the candidate list for women.[20] These mechanisms, proponents suggest, can also increase the number of regional, linguistic, ethnic, or religious minorities in parliament, although their effects depend upon the spatial concentration of each group. Socially diverse representation can be regarded as intrinsically valuable for consensus democracy, by improving the range of voices and experience brought to policy discussions, and also because the entry of minority representatives into public office can increase a sense of democratic legitimacy and develop leadership capacity.[21] Proponents argue that it is important to maximize the number of "winners" in elections, particularly in divided or heterogeneous societies, so that separate communities can peacefully coexist within the common borders of a single nation-state.[22]

Critiques

Against these arguments, most critics of PR emphasize certain well-known themes, arguing that these electoral systems are prone to generate indecisive electoral results and weak, ineffective, and unstable governing coalitions where it is difficult for voters to assign clear responsibility; create institutional checks and balances characterized by policy stalemate, administrative paralysis, and legislative gridlock; foster cautious, slow, and incremental decision-making and limit the ability of policymakers to respond in timely and coherent fashion to a sudden crisis; encourage the legitimation of extremist parties on the far right and left; reduce the accountability of elected members to local parties and constituents; and weaken the inability of the electorate to throw out some "king making" parties that are semipermanent members of coalition governments.

The alternative visions of democracy have often fuelled attempts to reform the electoral system to achieve either greater government accountability through majoritarian systems or wider parliamentary diversity through proportional systems. Underlying the normative debate are certain important empirical claims about the consequences of electoral rules for voting behavior and for political representation. We, therefore, need to go on to examine systematic evidence to see how far the normative claims are supported by comparative evidence. Do PR systems generate more opportunities for minor parties but also the dangers of excessive party fragmentation? Do majoritarian systems produce decisive outcomes where the leading party is empowered to govern alone for the duration of their term in office but also exclude minor parties from fair representation? It is to these issues that I now turn.

PART II

THE CONSEQUENCES FOR VOTING BEHAVIOR

4

Party Systems

Effective parties that work well can serve multiple functions in democracies: simplifying and structuring electoral choices; organizing and mobilizing campaigns; articulating and aggregating disparate interests; channeling communication, consultation, and debate; training, recruiting, and selecting candidates; structuring parliamentary divisions; acting as policy think tanks; and organizing government.[1] The direct impact of electoral systems on patterns of party competition has long been regarded as one of their most important effects. Electoral engineering has been advocated in nations suffering either from the dangers of excessively unstable and fragmented party systems, such as in Italy and Israel, or from the opposite dangers of unchanging one-party predominant systems, exemplified by Singapore and Japan. But, potentially, electoral systems can indirectly affect many other features of how parties work, such as the strength of bonds between citizens and parties and how far party identification shapes voters' choices. In this chapter, therefore, I explore how far electoral systems are systematically related to patterns of party competition. In subsequent chapters, then, I examine the relationship between electoral systems, the strength of party identification, and general orientations toward political parties, as well as to what extent partisan alignments influence voter decisions in the countries under comparison.

The Mechanical Effects of Electoral Systems on Party Competition

The classic starting point for any analysis has to be Duverger's famous claims about the relationship between electoral systems and party systems. Duverger's first law is: (1) *"the plurality single-ballot rule tends to party dualism."* The second claim is: (2) *"The double-ballot system and proportional representation tend to multipartyism."*[2] Although originally stated as a universal law-like regularity, without exception, subsequently, Duverger suggested that this was only a weaker probabilistic generalization.[3] The conditions under which this relationship holds, and its status as a law, have attracted considerable debate marked by continued reformulations of the original statement and many efforts to define precisely was is to "count" as a party in order to verify these claims.[4] The effects of electoral systems are partly mechanical, depending upon the working of the rules, exemplified by the vote hurdles that single-member districts create for minor parties with dispersed support. The effects can also be partly psychological, by shaping the incentives facing parties and the public, for example, if minor party candidates are discouraged from running in majoritarian elections where they believe they cannot win, or if citizens cast a "strategic," "tactical," or "insincere" vote for a major party in the belief that voting for minor parties in these systems is a wasted vote.[5] Subsequent studies have recognized that the hurdles facing minor parties under majoritarian electoral systems vary under certain conditions, the most important of which concern: (1) the geographic distribution or concentration of party support; (2) specific aspects of electoral systems beyond the basic formula, notably the use of voting thresholds, the size of the district magnitude in proportional systems, and the use of manipulated partisan bias such as gerrymandering to include or exclude minor parties; and also (3) the type of major social cleavages within a nation, an issue explored in the next chapter. The reasons why geography is so important is that minor parties with spatially concentrated support can still win seats in single-member districts and plurality elections, such as regional, nationalist, or ethnic parties that are strong in particular constituencies, exemplified by the success of the Bloc Québécois and the Reform Party in Canada or the Scottish National Party and Plaid Cymru in the United Kingdom. Majoritarian and plurality systems are most problematic for parties with modest support that is widely dispersed across many single-member districts, such as the Australian Greens or the Canadian Progressive Conservatives. Specific aspects of the electoral system are also important because minor parties still face considerable barriers under proportional electoral formulae that combine small district magnitudes with high vote thresholds, exemplified in the countries under comparison by contests for the Polish Sejm. Partisan manipulation of the electoral rules, such as the use of malapportionment (producing constituencies containing differently sized electorates), gerrymandering (the intentional drawing of electoral boundaries for partisan advantage), as well as restrictive legal rules for nomination to get on the ballot, also can function to benefit or penalize minor parties. Last, the number, distribution, and depth of social cleavages, and their politicization by linking groups to political parties, is also critical to differences between the workings of electoral systems in relatively homogeneous and heterogeneous societies, producing an interaction between the type of electoral rules and social heterogeneity.[6]

Before examining the evidence for the relationship between electoral and party systems in the societies under comparison, we first need to consider what is to count as a party. One problem in the literature concerns how to distinguish between fringe parties and independent candidates, a problem particularly evident in the Ukrainian and Russian parliamentary election, where many candidates stood (and were often elected in single-member districts) as a strategy to gain exception from criminal prosecution. Because there is no single best measure, the wisest strategy is to compare alternative summary measures of the number of parties in different countries, ranging from simple to more complex indices, to see if the specific choice of measures makes a substantial difference to the interpretation of the results. *Electoral parties* are defined most simply as all those parties standing for election, and *parliamentary parties* as all those that win at least one seat in the lower house. Yet these simple measures are too generous to capture many of the most important distinctions commonly made between systems: for example, if all electoral parties count equally for "one," then almost every country except those where opposition parties are banned by law would qualify as a multiparty system. In the United States, for example, normally understood as a classic two-party system, the Democrats and Republicans would count as equal to all other fringe parties holding no seats but contesting presidential elections, including the Greens, the Reform Party, the Communist Party, the Natural Law Party, the Libertarians, and the Workers' Party. One way to narrow this measure to generate a more meaningful comparison is to count *relevant parties*, defined as those gaining more than a certain threshold of national votes or parliamentary seats; in this study relevant electoral parties are defined as those gaining 3% or more of the national vote, whereas relevant parliamentary parties are understood as those getting 3% or more of seats in election to the lower house.

Yet adoption of the conventional 3% threshold is in itself arbitrary, as the cut-off point could equally be set slightly higher or lower. Measures of relevant parties can also prove misleading: for example, if four parties are of roughly equal size, each gaining about one-quarter of the parliamentary seats, then there is no problem about counting them all equally as a four-party system. But if there are considerable disparities in size among parties, for example, if two major parties predominate with over 75% of all parliamentary seats, holding the balance of power between the opposition and government, and yet another eight fringe parties each get only 3% of seats, then given the imbalance of power it does not seem satisfactory to count each party equally to produce a ten-party system. The most popular method used to overcome this problem is the Laakso and Taagepera measure of the *Effective Number of Parliamentary Parties* (ENPP) and also the *Effective Number of Electoral Parties* (ENEP), both of which take into account not only the number of parties but also the relative size of each.[7] Although the measure is abstract, it is also fairly intuitively meaningful to grasp the difference between party systems containing, say, 2.6 and 5.5 effective parliamentary parties. Using this measure, Arend Lijphart reexamined the evidence for the Duverger thesis by comparing election results in twenty-seven advanced industrialized democracies from 1945 to 1990. The study estimated that the effective number of parliamentary parties was 2.0 in plurality systems, 2.8 in majoritarian systems, and 3.6 in proportional systems. Yet even here there are important variations beyond the basic formula because Lijphart found that the minimum threshold of votes within proportional systems also had an important effect on the inclusion of minor parties.[8] An alternative study by Richard Katz compared a broader range of countries, using a database with more than 800 national elections held until 1985, and he found many significant deviations around the mean effective number of parliamentary parties, particularly among subtypes within the basic proportional and majoritarian families.[9] Katz concluded that there was little support, as a universal law, for any simple version of Duverger's claim that plurality elections inevitably generate two-party systems, although, nevertheless, as a probabilistic generalization plurality systems usually proved more reductive than PR elections.

To examine the evidence for a wider range of countries in recent years we can compare party systems in national elections for the lower house of parliament held under the different electoral families and their subtypes. For comparison across alternative measures, to see if the results are robust when replicated, the analysis uses three summary indicators to assess levels of party competition:

Party competition

- The mean number of *all* parliamentary parties (defined as all parties winning at least one seat),
- The mean number of *relevant* parliamentary parties (all parties holding 3% or more of parliamentary seats),
- The mean number of *effective* parliamentary parties (calculated for the CSES elections by the Laakso and Taagepera method [1979]).

The estimates are based on the most recent national election for the lower house of parliament, with 170 contests held worldwide from 1995 to 2000, and the thirty-two parliamentary elections in the CSES countries under comparison, with the results derived from *Elections Around the World.*[10]

Table 4.1 shows that worldwide the mean number of parliamentary parties (based on the simplest definition of parties holding at least one seat) was 5.22 in the countries using majoritarian systems, 8.85 in combined systems, and 9.52 in societies with proportional electoral systems. In other words, in countries using any form of PR there are almost twice as many parliamentary parties as in countries using any form of majoritarian electoral system.[11] Confirming this broad pattern, although with less of a sharp contrast between the major types of electoral system, the comparison of the mean number of relevant parties (holding more than 3% of parliamentary seats) was 3.33 in all majoritarian systems, 4.52 for combined systems, and 4.74 for all

TABLE 4.1. *Electoral Systems and Party Systems*

	Mean Number of Parliamentary Parties (with at least one seat)	Mean Number of Relevant Parliamentary Parties (with more than 3% of seats)	Number of Countries
All Majoritarian	5.22	3.33	83
Alternative Vote	9.00	3.00	1
Bloc Vote	5.60	4.57	10
2nd Ballot	6.00	3.20	23
FPTP	4.78	3.09	49
All Combined	8.85	4.52	26
Independent	8.89	3.94	19
Dependent	8.71	6.17	7
All Proportional	9.52	4.74	61
STV	5.00	2.50	2
Party List	9.68	4.82	59
TOTAL	7.05	4.12	170

Notes and Sources: The data include the results for 1,263 parties contesting the latest elections to the lower house of parliament from 1995 to June 2000. Parliamentary parties are defined as those winning at least one seat in the lower house. The results of the elections were calculated from *Elections Around the World.* Available online at www.agora.stm.it/elections/alllinks.htm. The classification of electoral systems is discussed fully in chapter 2 and is derived from Andrew Reynolds and Ben Reilly. 1997. *The International IDEA Handbook of Electoral System Design.* Stockholm: International IDEA, Annex A. combined-independent systems include two electoral systems used in parallel. Combined-dependent systems include two electoral systems used where the results depend upon the combined share of the vote. FPTP, First-Past-the-Post; STV, Single Transferable Vote.

proportional systems. Yet at the same time there are also some important variations evident among subtypes of electoral systems within each family, for example, among proportional systems, systems using party lists had more parliamentary parties (and relevant parliamentary parties) than in the two nations (Ireland and Malta) using the STV. Duverger claims that there is an important difference between simple plurality (FPTP) and majoritarian Second Ballot systems. The comparison shows that there were, indeed, more parliamentary parties (and more relevant parties) in the twenty-three nations using Second Ballot runoff elections than in the forty-nine states using FPTP. Yet, at the same time, under the Second Ballot system far fewer parliamentary parties, and relevant parliamentary parties, were elected than under party list PR.

Nevertheless, despite establishing these broad patterns by electoral family, the means can disguise considerable deviations, as there are important cross-national differences within each of the major types. Deviations from the mean are produced as the relationship between the type of electoral system and party system in each country is conditioned by the geographical distribution of party support, the level of electoral threshold, the average size of the district magnitude, and any manipulated partisan bias in the system. To illustrate this, the mean number of effective parliamentary parties (ENPP) for the 30 countries in the CSES dataset under detailed comparison is illustrated in Figure 4.1. Again the basic pattern by party family is shown, with majoritarian systems having an average ENPP of 2.42, compared with 3.54 in combined systems, and 4.45 in proportional systems. If we break this down further by country, the pattern shows that among Anglo-American countries all using First-Past-the-Post, the mean number of effective parliamentary parties is 2.0 in the United States, 2.1 in the United Kingdom, but 3.0 in Canada; in the latter case, despite FPTP, regional Canadian parties gain seats in their heartland provinces. There is some overlap between plurality systems and the least proportional party list electoral systems, notably Spain with a mean ENPP of 2.7 due to small district magnitude, and Poland (ENPP 3.0) which has a high (7%) vote threshold to enter the Sejm. Nevertheless, as predicted many of the PR systems under comparison can be classified as moderate multiparty systems, with an ENPP ranging from 3.4 to 5.6, whereas Belgium qualifies as a polarized party system with an ENPP of 9.1.

The combined electoral systems show substantial variations in party competition. As expected, some of the combined-independent systems with many single-member districts, including South Korea, Japan, and Taiwan, are closer to the mean ENPP found in majoritarian systems. In comparison, the combined-dependent systems, with the outcome based on the party list share of the vote, exemplified by New Zealand and Hungary, are closer to the multiparty system common under PR systems. The primary exceptions to the overall pattern are Russia and Ukraine, which both have fragmented multiparty systems despite using combined-independent electoral systems. The pattern in these nations is explained by the instability of their party systems, the fragility of the consolidation process in their democratic transitions, along with the existence of multiple social cleavages, and the election of many independents and small parties via the single-member districts,[12] for reasons explored more fully in the next chapter.

Therefore, overall, the analysis of all elections worldwide and the more detailed comparison of elections held in the thirty nations within the CSES dataset support the reductive effect of the basic electoral formula. This generally confirms Duverger's main proposition that plurality electoral systems tend toward party dualism, whereas PR is associated with multipartyism. Yet the extent of the difference in the effective number of parliamentary parties should not be exaggerated, ranging in the CSES countries under comparison from an average of 2.42 in majoritarian systems to 4.45 in proportional systems. Moreover, the variations evident within each electoral family show that the relationship between electoral systems and party systems is probabilistic, not universal, as illustrated by the marked contrast between Spain and Belgium, although both have proportional party list elections.

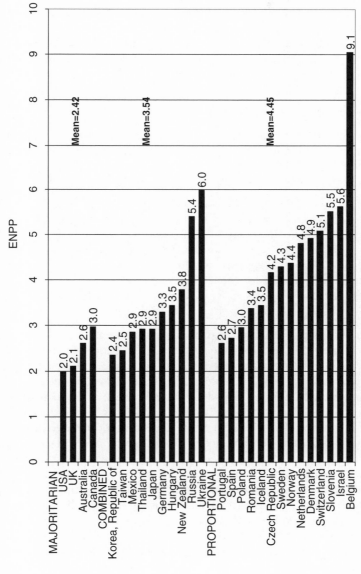

FIGURE 4.1. Effective Number of Parliamentary Parties (ENPP) by electoral family. *Note:* The ENPP is calculated following the method of Laakso and Taagepera (1979). For details of the elections see Table 2.1.

These variations are generated by the factors discussed earlier, namely, (1) the geographic distribution of party support; (2) specific features of electoral design beyond the basic electoral formula, such as formal vote thresholds and district magnitude; and, as we shall see in subsequent chapters, (3) the number and depth of social cleavages within each nation. Smaller parties can do well under FPTP, especially regional or ethnic–national parties with spatially concentrated support. At the same time, minor parties can be heavily penalized in proportional systems with high thresholds and small district magnitudes.

The Proportionality of Votes to Seats

Many studies have commonly found proportionality to be significantly greater under PR than under majoritarian systems, although, again, important variations exist within electoral families and subtypes.[13] Proportionality is gauged in this study by three measures:

- The *percentage share of the vote* won by the party in first place, to provide an indication of the extent to which electoral systems generated a vote majority for the leading party.
- The *percentage share of seats* won by the party in first place, to provide an indication of the extent to which the electoral system generated a parliamentary majority for the leading party.
- The *Rose Index of Proportionality* to show the relationship of votes to seats (a standardized version of the Loosemore-Hanby Index).

All the alternative measures of proportionality summarize the degree to which each party's share of seats corresponds to its share of votes, but alternative measures reflect slightly divergent notions of the underlying concepts. The oldest measure, used by Douglas Rae, simply uses the average of the deviations, summing the absolute differences between the vote percentages and the seat percentages and then dividing by the number of parties. One potential problem with the Rae Index, however, is that it is oversensitive to the number of parties, understating the disproportionality of systems with many small parties.[14] One of the most widely used alternatives is the Loosemore-Hanby Index, which adds the absolute values of all vote-seat share differences and then divides by 2, instead of Rae's division by the number of parties. For ease of interpretation, following Rose, this measure can be standardized, and, in theory, the standardized Loosemore-Hanby Index of Proportionality ranges from 0 to 100. Majoritarian systems provide a winner's bonus for the party in first place, while penalizing others, so the size of the winner's bonus provides another indication of disproportionality. As expected, the variations are predictable; the mean Rose Index of Proportionality was 91.2 for all proportional systems around the world, compared with 85.0 for all combined systems and 81.9 for all majoritarian systems.

To see whether this pattern was generated by the specific measure used or whether it remains robust under alternative indicators, the proportionality of the electoral systems can also be compared by calculating the votes-to-seats ratio for each party in elections held from 1995 to 2000 in 143 nations around the globe, based on the summary unstandardized regression coefficient (beta) for each electoral family. The results in Figure 4.2 further confirm, as expected, that proportional electoral formulae produce the closest reflections of votes-to-seats ratios ($R^2 = .95$). A few parties scatter more widely around the top of the regression line in these systems, but most fall where expected, suggesting a fairly close match between the percentage of votes that a party receives and its percentage of seats won. The combined formula proved marginally less proportional results ($R^2 = .93$). In comparison, the majoritarian formula shows the widest scatter of votes to seats ($R^2 = .81$). This is caused, primarily, by minor and fringe parties failing to gain any or few seats in these elections, shown visually by the parties falling above the regression line. The winner's bonus is illustrated by the parties falling below the regression line, where parties gain a greater percentage of seats than their share of the vote.

The indicators of the capacity of the electoral system to generate a working majority can also be examined by comparing the vote share and the seat share for the leading party in worldwide national elections (see Table 4.2). These comparisons in Table 4.2 confirm, as expected, that the leading party usually won a comfortable majority of votes (54.5%) and seats (56.8%) in majoritarian and plurality electoral systems (with the exception of the Australian Alternative Vote system first preference distribution). Majorities of votes and seats for the leading party were also evident under combined-independent electoral systems. By contrast, the leading party generally failed to gain a majority of votes or seats under combined-dependent and proportional party list systems. Under all proportional systems, the leading party gained on average 45.3% of the vote and 43.8% of the seats. This evidence confirms, as proponents of each type of electoral system claim, that PR systems are more likely to prioritize legislative inclusiveness and multiparty systems whereas, in comparison, majoritarian systems are more likely to provide a decisive outcome and single-party executives. The electoral threshold for government office, if gauged by the average share of the vote for the party in first place, is about 10% higher under majoritarian than under proportional electoral systems worldwide. This is important if, as I argued in the introduction, the higher level of threshold in majoritarian systems provides incentives for parties to develop bridging strategies appealing to multiple sectors of the electorate, and if the lower thresholds in proportional systems provide incentives for bonding strategies designed to mobilize core groups of supporters. These claims are examined further in the next chapter.

To explore the consistency of these patterns further, the distribution of the standardized Loosemore-Hanby Index of Proportionality, a common

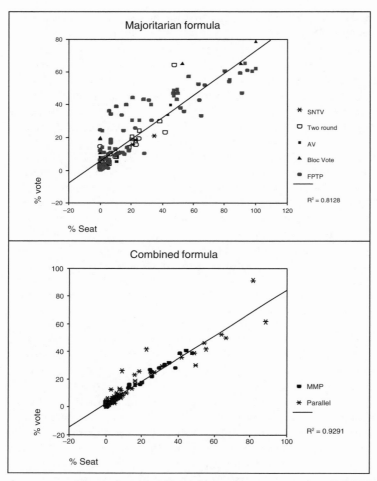

FIGURE 4.2. The proportionality of party votes to seats. SNTV, Single Non-Transferable Vote; AV, Alternative Vote; FPTP, First-Past-the-Post; MMP, Mixed Member Proportion; PR, Proportional Representation. *Source:* See Table 4.2.

measure used in the literature, can be compared in more detail for the nations included in the CSES. Figure 4.3 confirms the pattern observed earlier: the mean proportionality was 85.3 under majoritarian systems, 89.6 under combined systems, and 92.6 under proportional systems. Proportionality was, therefore, usually lower in majoritarian elections, with the exception of the United States, which generated a highly proportional result despite FPTP elections due to the two-party predominance in the House of Representatives and a fairly even share of the vote. Proportionality was usually highest under

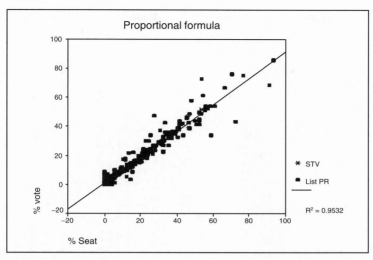

FIGURE 4.2. (*cont.*)

TABLE 4.2. *Electoral Systems and Proportionality*

	Rose's Index of Proportionality	% Vote for the Party in First Place	% Seats for the Party in First Place	Number of Countries
All Majoritarian	81.9	54.5	56.8	83
Alternative Vote	84.0	40.3	45.3	1
Bloc Vote	75.6	52.9	56.2	10
2nd Ballot	92.2	54.8	57.8	23
FPTP	83.0	55.1	57.8	49
All Combined	85.0	46.8	49.5	26
Independent	82.6	51.7	53.9	19
Dependent	90.1	33.9	36.9	7
ALL Proportional	91.2	45.3	43.8	61
STV	93.9	45.3	50.1	2
Party List	91.1	44.5	43.6	59
TOTAL	87.2	48.7	50.0	170

Notes and Sources: The data include the results in elections to the lower house of parliament from 1995 to June 2000 in 170 nations. The results of the elections were calculated from *Elections Around the World*. Available online at www.agora.stm.it/elections/alllinks.htm. The Index of Proportionality was derived from Richard Rose. Ed. 2001. *The International Encyclopedia of Elections*. Washington, D.C.: Congressional Quarterly Press.

The classification of electoral systems is discussed fully in chapter 2 and is derived from Andrew Reynolds and Ben Reilly. 1997. *The International IDEA Handbook of Electoral System Design*. Stockholm: International IDEA, Annex A. Combined-independent systems include two electoral systems used in parallel. Combined-dependent systems include two electoral systems used where the results depend upon the combined share of the vote. FPTP, First-Past-the-Post; STV, Single Transferable Vote.

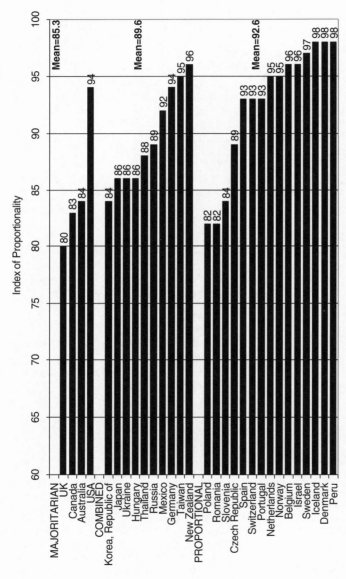

FIGURE 4.3. Proportionality by electoral family. *Note*: The Index of Proportionality, following Rose, is a standardized version of the Loosemore-Hanby Index. This is calculated as the difference between a party's percentage share of the vote and its percentage share of the total seats in parliament, summed, divided by 2 and subtracted from 100. Theoretically, it can range from 0 to 100. For details see Rose, Munro, and Mackie 1998. For details of the elections see Table 2.1.

party list PR, although, again, there are some exceptions, in Poland and Romania, due to high thresholds or low district magnitudes. Combined systems generally fell into the middle of the distribution although dependent-combined systems prove more proportional than independent-combined systems. In the countries under comparison, the average winner's bonus (representing the difference between the vote share and seat share for the leading party, exaggerating their legislative lead over all other parties) is 12.5 percentage points under majoritarian systems, compared with 7.4 under mixed systems and 5.7 under PR. Hence, under majoritarian electoral systems a party that won 37.5% of the vote or more could usually be assured of a parliamentary majority (50%+) in seats, whereas under PR systems a party would normally require 46.3% of the vote or more to achieve an equivalent result. As proponents argue, therefore, one-party governments with a working parliamentary majority are generated more easily in majoritarian than in proportional electoral systems, but at the expense of the legislative representation of minor parties.

Conclusions

Reformers often suggest that constitutional changes, particularly modifications to the electoral system, can contribute toward better governance, either through more majoritarian arrangements that are believed to strengthen governability or through more proportional formulae that are designed to improve power-sharing and social inclusiveness. In this chapter I focused upon the consequences of electoral systems for party systems, and, in particular, whether there is convincing evidence that electoral systems have the capacity to shape patterns of party competition. Throughout the analysis I have assumed that the electoral system is exogenous, so that it is capable of determining patterns of party competition. Where electoral systems have been in existence for many decades, indeed, in some cases for more than a century, it seems safe to assume that the cumulative effect of repeated contests under these rules is capable of shaping the party system, for example, by constantly excluding minor parties from office or by giving them a role as kingmaker in cabinet governments. Nevertheless, where electoral systems have experienced frequent changes from majoritarian to proportional or vice versa, as in France, or where electoral systems in newer democracies have only recently been adopted, it is far more difficult to regard the institutional rules as truly exogenous. In this context, levels of party competition, and the process of bargaining and negotiation over the constitutional rules of the game, are likely to shape the adoption of electoral systems. In newer democracies, then, there is likely to be interaction between the type of electoral system and the type of party system, and estimates that treat electoral systems as exogenous are likely to over-estimate their causal effects.[15] Case studies examining a series of election results within each country and policy studies of the adoption and reform of electoral rules in each nation, as well as more sophisticated models using two-staged least squares analysis, are the most satisfactory approaches to disentangling these relationships, taking us far beyond the scope of this study. Nevertheless, even if unable to establish the direction of the causal relationship within the limitations of the cross-sectional comparison, the results provided in this chapter serve to confirm some of the basic patterns in the relationship between electoral systems and party systems, which is necessary as the basis for subsequent chapters.

Overall, the results of the comparison of elections in all nations world-wide, and the detailed analysis of elections held in the thirty-two countries in the CSES dataset lend further confirmation to support the reductive impact of the basic electoral formula. With the important limitations already noted, the analysis generally supports Duverger's generalization that plurality electoral systems tend towards party dualism, whereas PR is associated with multi-partyism. The comparisons support the classic claims made by proponents on both sides of the normative arguments, namely that majoritarian elections usually generate one-party governments with a secure parliamentary majority, while proportional elections generally lead toward more inclusive multiparty parliaments and more proportional results. Yet two important qualifications should be stressed when interpreting these results.

First, the difference in party competition by electoral family proved relatively modest in size; worldwide, the mean number of relevant parties was 3.33 in majoritarian systems and 4.74 in PR systems. The contrasts were slightly greater in the CSES elections under comparison, where the effective number of parliamentary parties was 2.42 in majoritarian systems and 4.45 in proportional elections. Yet although the relevant or the effective number of parliamentary parties elected under each system may not appear greatly different, the contrast does reflect the classic categorical distinction between a two-party system (or two-and-a-half party), where the organizing principle is a division of the spoils of office between the government and opposition, accompanied by one-party cabinet government resting upon a secure parliamentary majority, and multiparty competition, where parliament contains multiple actors and coalition government among multiple parties is essential to secure a working parliamentary majority.

At the same time, it should be noted that there are important variations in party competition and proportionality within each electoral family. As discussed earlier, the relationship between electoral systems and party systems is conditional upon many factors, including, most important: (1) the geography of electoral support; (2) specific features of electoral design such as the use of formal thresholds and the size of districts; and (3) the number and depth of social cleavages within a nation. Minor parties can do well in gaining seats under First-Past-the-Post, especially regional or ethnic–national parties with spatially concentrated support, while at the same time such parties can also be heavily penalized in proportional systems with high thresholds and small district magnitudes. Having confirmed these basic patterns and tendencies, the next chapters go on to explore the *psychological* capacity of electoral systems to influence the relationship between parties and voters, and, in particular, the strength of social cleavages and partisan identities in the electorate.

5

Social Cleavages

In the previous chapter I documented how electoral systems have important mechanical effects upon party systems. They can also be expected to exercise an indirect psychological impact upon patterns of electoral behavior as well, including to what extent voting choices are determined by social identities. To explore these matters, in the first section of this chapter I outline the framework for understanding these issues by comparing rational-choice institutionalism and cultural modernization theories. In the second section I examine patterns of cleavage politics and the influence of the primary cleavages on voting behavior in the legislative and presidential elections under comparison, including the role of social class and religion. The conclusion considers the extent to which these relationships are contingent upon the incentives provided under different electoral systems and to what degree they are determined by broader secular trends.

Theories of Social Cleavages and Voting Behavior

The seminal sociological studies of voting behavior developed during the 1960s by Seymour Martin Lipset and Stein Rokkan emphasize that social identities formed the basic building blocks of party support in Western Europe.[1] For Lipset and Rokkan, European nation-states were stamped by social divisions established decades earlier, including the regional cleavages of center-periphery, the class inequalities between workers and owners, and the sectarian cleavages over church and state that split Christendom between Catholics and Protestants. These traditional cleavages were powerful for several reasons. First, they reflected major ideological fissures in party politics. Social class mirrored the basic schism between the left, which favored a strong role for the state through egalitarian welfare policies, fiscal redistribution, and interventionist economic management, and the right, which preferred a more limited role for government and laissez-faire market economics. The religious division reflected conservative and liberal moral debates, such as those surrounding the role of women, marriage, and the family. Differences between core and periphery concerned how far the nation-state should be centralized or how far power should be devolved downward to the regions. Lipset and Rokkan theorized that organizational linkages gradually strengthened over the years, as party systems "froze" from around the 1920s until at least the mid-1960s, with stable patterns of party competition revolving around the salient primary cleavages dividing each society, as exemplified by the role of class in Britain, religion in France, and language in Belgium.[2] The electoral systems used in Western Europe at the time that the mass franchise was expanded played a vital role in stabilizing party competition by reinforcing the legitimacy of those parties and social groups that had achieved parliamentary representation, so long as parties remained internally united and maintained their electoral bases. Electoral systems created hurdles for newer parties threatening to disturb the status quo. Party systems, with patterned and predictable interactions in the competition for seats and votes, became settled features of the electoral landscape throughout many established democracies. Of course, this picture exaggerates, as some nations such as Germany and Italy experienced major disruptions, while the Great Depression triggered important realignments in the mass base of parties in the United States. Nevertheless, in the absence of sudden demographic upheavals, the external shock of events such as the Second World War, electoral reforms, or massive new expansions of the electorate, party systems in many European countries seemed to exhibit a rocklike stability, permitting only glacial evolution.[3]

The structural theory provided by Lipset and Rokkan became widely influential as the established orthodoxy in understanding voting behavior and party competition in Western Europe, as well as in many other established democracies such as Australia and Canada, but from the mid-1970s onwards these accounts increasingly came under challenge. New minor parties started to gain electoral momentum and foot-holds of parliamentary representation, including ethno-nationalist parties in Canada, Spain, and the United Kingdom; environmentalists in Germany and France; the anti-immigrant radical right, such as the National Front in Britain; and a range of diverse "protest" parties advocating cross-cutting moral and economic issues in Denmark, Italy, and the Netherlands.[4] This led observers to suggest that the process of societal modernization was eroding the "traditional" social identities of class and religion that predicted the mass basis of party support in late 1950s and 1960s. These identities no longer seemed capable of generating unwavering and habitual party loyalties in many postindustrial societies.[5] If the rocklike ballast of class and religion no longer anchored voters to parties, then this change promised to have significant consequences for patterns of growing volatility in electoral behavior and in party competition, opening the door for more split-ticket voting across different levels, the occasional sudden rise of protest parties, more vote-switching within and across the left–right blocs of party families, and the growing influence of short-term events, party strategy, candidates, and leaders, and media coverage in determining the outcome of election campaigns.

This study lacks time-series data to compare trends in social dealignment since the early 1960s, but it focuses instead upon comparing the cross-national evidence in more than 30 countries for two alternative accounts, seeking to explain where social dealignment should have advanced furthest and fastest. Incentive-based explanations, building upon organizational studies of party politics, emphasize the strategic role of political actors in reinforcing or weakening party–voter bonds, including to what extent social democratic parties make class appeals. I will develop these ideas to consider, in particular, whether electoral rules have the capacity to shape the incentives for parties either to reinforce support among their natural electoral constituencies or, alternatively, to develop catch-all electoral appeals outside their bases.[6] By contrast, cultural theories of societal modernization, providing orthodox "bottom up" accounts grounded in traditional accounts of mass political behavior, focus upon secular trends in the nature of postindustrial societies, both in the cognitive skills of electors and in the value basis of issue conflict, that are believed to have eroded the traditional affective bonds linking citizens to parties. If incentive-based accounts are accurate, then we might expect to find considerable differences in the strength of cleavage politics in elections held under majoritarian and proportional formula. If cultural accounts are closer to the mark, and rising levels of education and cognitive skills have altered the basis of voting decisions, then we would expect that cleavage politics would be weakest in postindustrial societies. Let me first outline these accounts in more detail then turn to consider the available cross-national evidence.

Rational-Choice Institutionalism and Campaign Strategies

Alternative theories based on rational-choice institutionalism emphasize the importance of the electoral rewards facing political parties when either deliberately reinforcing the strength of group-party ties through bonding appeals or weakening these linkages through bridging strategies. These ideas were developed by Adam Przeworski and John Sprague[7] and, subsequently, were expanded by Herbert Kitschelt.[8] The earliest party organizations that evolved from the late eighteenth century onward were essentially elite-driven parliamentary factions, loosely coordinating elected members of parliament and their followers, built around rival leaders.[9] With minimal party discipline in parliament, and a limited franchise, elections were based around informal networks and patron–client relations. When mass suffrage spread throughout different countries in Western Europe during the mid-nineteenth and early twentieth centuries, the electorate became too large to manage through the older associations of local elites. Duverger suggested that the mass-branch party emerged, primarily among trade unionists and Labor and Social Democratic parties, to organize the newly enfranchised working-class populations.[10] European parties had an incentive to foster close links with their natural social bases in the electorate, so that Labor, Socialist, and Communist parties collaborated closely with the organized labor movement, while Christian Democrats created strong links with the Catholic Church and with the business sector. The emphasis on common ideological principles, clear and distinctive programmatic party platforms reflecting these goals, and a sense of one-of-us belonging to a clan with clear boundaries and fee-paying membership demarcating "them" and "us" served multiple functions for parties by helping to mobilize supporters, raise funds, and attract volunteers, and, therefore, contributed ultimately toward their electoral success.

In recent decades, however, due to secular social trends sweeping through postindustrial societies, West European Socialist parties have faced the gradual shrinkage in the size of their working-class base through the contraction of manufacturing industry and the rise in the white-collar service sector. Faced with these developments, Kitschelt suggests that some Social Democratic parties have adapted successfully by altering the basis of their electoral appeals beyond their traditional blue-collar base. The most electorally successful parties of the left have adopted catch-all or bridging strategies designed to attract diverse constituencies by selecting moderate leaders and promoting centrist economic policies, as well as by expanding their programmatic agenda beyond redistributive politics to prioritize diverse issues such as environmental protection, human rights, and women's equality. This strategy is exemplified most dramatically by the popularity of the "middle-England" politics leading to successive electoral victories for Tony Blair's Labour Party in the United Kingdom, where Labour "leapfrogged" over the Liberal Democrats to become the party in the center of the political spectrum. Whereas postwar Labour was pure one-of-us "bonding," concerned with heartland appeals to factory workers, unions, and pensioners, under Blair's leadership, New Labour perfectly illustrates bridging tactics across diverse constituencies.[11] The electoral success of President Bill Clinton's moderate coalition for the Democrats in the United States is another classic example of this approach. Older illustrations include the German Social Democratic Party's abandonment of the "Bad Godesburg" Marxist rhetoric in the late 1950s and its successful shift toward the catch-all middle ground. When Labor, Socialist, and Social Democratic parties and candidates move toward the center ground in the attempt to develop catch-all bridging strategies, they may, thereby, abandon reliance upon their working-class supporters and their trade-union base as well as discard traditional socialist programs advocating egalitarian income redistribution, nationalization, and Keynesian economic management.[12] Similar strategies could influence West European Christian Democrat parties, such as those in Germany and Italy, when faced with shrinking numbers of regular church-goers. Bridging strategies involve dissolving traditional boundaries between "us" and "them," adopting whatever ideas and policy proposals seem more practical and effective regardless of their ideological origins, encouraging fuzzy, inclusive, and consensual party platforms, and fostering easy-entry, easy-exit shifting coalitions of informal support built around particular issues, rather than formal fee-paying membership and life-long loyalties. Bridging strategies trample upon sacerdotal principles and traditional one-of-us boundaries. Reducing dependence upon loyalists carries risks as well as benefits, including the dangers of facing widespread desertion in hard times. It also requires constant attention to the crafting and maintenance of popular support, and, therefore, requires greater attention to the dark arts of political marketing, including polling, publicity, and the press. But successful bridging strategies also allow parties to "cross-over" and, thereby, break out of dependence upon limited sectors of the electorate. Therefore, according to the theory developed by Przeworski and Sprague, the basis of cleavage politics is not an inevitable sociological process; instead, they argue, political actors create, reinforce, and maintain the links between political parties and social groups, within the context of institutional arenas, social structures, and cultural histories that constrain the strategic alternatives facing politicians.

Building upon these ideas, I theorize that one of the institutional contexts shaping the incentives for parties to develop strong and stable bonds with core groups of supporters or to adopt catch-all bridging strategies concerns the basic type of electoral formula. In particular, Donald L. Horowitz has suggested that adoption of majoritarian electoral systems in deeply divided plural societies provides incentives for parties to pool votes by broadening their electoral base beyond their core constituencies.[13] In support of this thesis, Ben Reilly has provided case study evidence that the Alternative Vote system has moderated ethnic appeals made by parties in elections held in Papua New Guinea from 1964 to 1972.[14] If we extend this argument to other core cleavages of class, religion, or language, this suggests that majoritarian electoral systems, exemplified by the Alternative Vote or by Second Ballot systems, should generate strong incentives for political actors to adopt moderate or centrist bridging appeals in heterogeneous constituencies. Indeed, this was the rationale for the adoption of the Second Ballot system by de Gaulle for the Fifth French Republic, as the system was intended to reduce the extreme party fragmentation of the Fourth Republic by encouraging cooperation among rivals within party blocs on the left and on the right. Under majoritarian rules, parties and candidates must appeal to a great variety of diverse interests if they are to secure an absolute majority (50%+) of votes. As such, they face considerable pressures to adopt Broad Church catch-all appeals to multiple social groups distributed throughout the electorate, including working- and middle-class sectors, as well as different religious sects and creeds, and varied ethnic minorities. The Second Ballot system, with a runoff ballot between the two leading contenders, such as that used in single member districts in Hungarian parliamentary elections, and in the Lithuanian and Chilean presidential elections, could be expected to serve this function by encouraging cooperation within party blocs on the left and on the right. Plurality systems exemplified by FPTP could serve a similar function, although with lower voting hurdles and, therefore, more modest incentives for cross-group appeals, as parties and candidates can be elected with less than a majority of votes. STV or party list elections in small multimember heterogeneous constituencies, each electing about three to five members per district, present a similar, if weaker, logic of electoral incentives where parties and candidates need to spread the distribution of their support. By contrast, in proportional electoral systems with low thresholds and large district magnitudes, exemplified by the Netherlands and Israel, parties and candidates can be returned to parliament by appealing to a far narrower segment of the population, which could be expected to exacerbate class, faith-based, or ethnic-bonding strategies in plural societies. Therefore, if electoral systems shape the electoral incentives for political actors to either reinforce their bonds with core homogeneous groups of supporters or to dilute these linkages with bridging appeals to heterogeneous groups, and if parties have the strategic capacity to respond rationally to these electoral rewards, then cleavage voting should be stronger under proportional than majoritarian electoral systems.

Cultural Values and Modernization Theory

Alternative cultural explanation emphasizes that the strength of cleavage politics is primarily the product of bottom-up developments in the nature of mass societies. In this view basic social identities of class, religion, gender, and ethnicity cannot be created or manipulated at the whim of politicians; instead, these reflect deep-rooted cultural phenomena arising from enduring sociological processes. Political actors and institutions, in this view, are the superstructure arising from the broader social base. This perspective has been developed most fully in theories of societal modernization, suggesting that multiple long-term secular trends have transformed political behavior in postindustrial societies in the late twentieth century.[15] Modernization theories originated in the work of Karl Marx, Max Weber, and Emile Durkheim, and these ideas were subsequently revived and popularized in the late 1950s and early 1960s by many developmental theorists, notably Seymour Martin Lipset, Daniel Lerner, Walt W. Rostow, and Karl W. Deutsch.[16] More recently, in the work of Ronald Inglehart and Russell Dalton, these ideas have been developed and applied to understanding changes in the mass basis of political culture.[17] Modernization theories suggest that the shift from agriculture toward industrial production leads toward growing prosperity, higher levels of education, and urbanization, which in turn lay the social foundations for democratic participation in the political system and the rise of mass-based party organizations rooted in the electoral base. Traditional societies are characterized by subsistence livelihoods based largely on farming, fishing, extraction, and unskilled work, with low levels of literacy and education, predominately agrarian populations, minimum standards of living, and restricted social and geographic mobility. Citizens in agrarian societies are strongly rooted to local communities through ties of "blood and belonging," including those of kinship, family, ethnicity, and religion, as well as through long-standing cultural bonds. The shift from traditional agrarian society toward industrialized society concerns the move from agricultural production to manufacturing, from farms to factories, from peasants to workers. Social trends accompanying these developments include migration to metropolitan conurbations, the rise of the working class and the urban bourgeoisie, rising living standards, the separation of church and state, increasing penetration of the mass media, the growth of Weberian bureaucratization and rational-legal authority in the state, the foundations of the early welfare state, and the spread of primary schooling. This phase occurred in the Industrial Revolution in Britain during the mid-to-late eighteenth century and spread throughout the Western world during the nineteenth and early twentieth centuries.

Daniel Bell popularized the view that, after a certain period of industrialization, a further distinct stage of development could be distinguished, as a nonlinear process, with the rise of postindustrial societies.[18] For Bell, the critical tipping point was reached when the majority of the workforce moved from manufacturing into the service sector, working as lawyers, bankers, financial analysts, technologists, scientists, and professionals employed in the knowledge industries. According to Inglehart, the social and economic shifts characterizing postindustrial societies include the rise of a highly educated, skilled, and specialized workforce; the population shifts from urban to suburban neighborhoods and greater geographic mobility including immigration across national borders; rising living standards and growing leisure time; rapid scientific and technological innovation; the expansion and fragmentation of mass media channels, technologies, and markets; the growth of multi-layered governance with power shifting away from the nation-state toward global and local levels; market liberalization and the expansion of nonprofit social protection schemes; and the erosion of the traditional nuclear family and growing equality of sex roles within the home, family, and workforce.[19]

Most important for voting behavior, modernization theories emphasize that in agrarian and industrial societies, religious and class identities orient citizens toward the political system and provide a simple, low-cost guide to voting, enabling information shortcuts that allowed people to decide which politicians and policies to support over successive contests. These cognitive shortcuts are particularly useful for the least-sophisticated citizens with minimal literacy and schooling, and with limited access to political information from the mass media. By contrast, social trends in affluent postindustrial societies have led toward rising levels of education and cognitive skills, providing the human capital that can help to master the complexities of public affairs and the policymaking process. Better-educated and more so-phisticated citizens may have less need to rely upon social cues in electoral choices. Compared with earlier eras, the public in postindustrial societies today has many opportunities to learn about political events and current affairs from regular exposure to multiple nonpartisan information sources in the press, on television news, and on the Internet.[20] These sources allow voters to compare a range of parties, leaders, and public policy issues, po-tentially exposing them to many dissonant values beyond those shared with friends, family, and colleagues in their local communities. Lifestyle changes in postindustrial society include the rise of a more socially and geographically mobile citizenry, less rooted in their local areas. At the same time, patterns of secularization in West European societies have emptied church pews and weakened the traditional organizational linkages between the churches and Christian Democratic parties.[21] The capacity of trade unions to generate support among traditional working-class communities for parties of the left also may have faded in those societies experiencing the decline of manu-facturing industry and falling union membership rolls.[22] Therefore, to sum up, if the modernization thesis correctly identifies the causes of any dealign-ment, then the strength of cleavage politics should vary systematically among different nations in accordance with levels of socioeconomic and human de-velopment. In particular, social class and religion should have the least in-fluence on voting behavior in postindustrial societies, when compared with industrialized nations. The role of class and religion also can be expected to vary between post-Communist and developing societies, in the light of different political legacies, historical traditions, and social structures, such as the role of the Catholic Church in Latin America and Orthodox religion in Eastern Europe.

The Strength of Cleavage Politics

How can we evaluate the evidence for these accounts by comparing the avail-able cross-national survey data? In measuring the strength of cleavage poli-tics, the classification of voting choices along a consistent left–right scale is critical to the reliability of the analysis. The vote in each legislative and presi-dential election was recoded into a consistent 10-point left–right scale, based on the party families identified in the CSES dataset by the international teams of collaborators. Party families were classified as follows: (1) Communist, (2) Ecology, (3) Socialist, (4) Social Democrat, (5) Left-liberal, (6) Liberal, (7) Christian Democrat, (8) Right-liberal, (9) Conservative, and (10) Nationalist/Religious. Parties that could not be categorized reliably by the traditional left–right scale were excluded from the analysis, including regional, ethnic, agrarian, and independent parties.[23] In interpreting the results, a positive coefficient denotes greater voting support for parties of the right. The 10-point scale captures gradations within voting blocs, for example, differences between countries in support for Communist, Socialist, and Social Democratic parties of the left. For ease of interpretation, however, to illustrate the simple distribution of voting without any prior controls, the 10-point scale was collapsed into a left-wing voting bloc (including the parties coded from 1–5) and a right-wing bloc (6–10). The CSES data was weighted to produce national samples of equal size. Figure 5.1 illustrates the distribution of voting support for the left–right voting blocs showing the legislative elections ranging across the spectrum from Japan, Mexico, and Peru, where the right-bloc parties predominated, down to Britain, Denmark, and the Ukraine, where the left-bloc parties were in the clear majority.

For the independent variables, the models monitored the effects of the standard social cleavages that are usually found to influence voting. Models first entered the demographic factors of age (in years) and gender (men = 1, women = 0). The main indicators commonly associated closely with socioeconomic status (SES) were then entered including education (using a 4-point scale from only primary school to university qualifications), household income (using a standardized 5-point quintile scale), occupational class (using a 5-point scale recoding the respondent's employment), and whether the respondent was a union member (0/1). In addition, the main language spoken at home (coded 0/1) was employed to gauge linguistic majorities, and the strength of religiosity was compared using the frequency of attendance at religious services. Last, to compare the strength of social identities against alternative measures of political ideology, the 10-point left–right self-placement scale was included. Comparison with alternative regression models was tested, to see if the inclusion or ordering of certain variables made a significant difference to the interpretation of the analysis, and the results of the core model presented here were found to be reliable and stable irrespective of the exact operationalization.[24] The social characteristics are presented most simply in Figure 5.2, showing the percentage of each group that voted for either the right-wing or left-wing bloc in the pooled sample of legislative elections in twenty-eight nations, without any prior controls. Multivariate regression analysis then used the 10-point left–right voting scale as the dependent variable with the independent variables entered in the order listed.

The results of the baseline regression model for the pooled sample of legislative elections in twenty-eight nations are presented in Table 5.1. In this analysis, Model A included the structural variables, then Model B added the measure of left–right ideology. The results in Model A show two patterns. First, in the pooled sample all the standard structural factors proved significantly related to left–right voting choice in these elections, in the expected direction, confirming many previous studies. Across all countries, younger voters proved slightly more left-wing than their parents and grandparents. Once the model is controlled for age, men proved significantly more right-wing than women, displaying the modern gender gap that first emerged in the

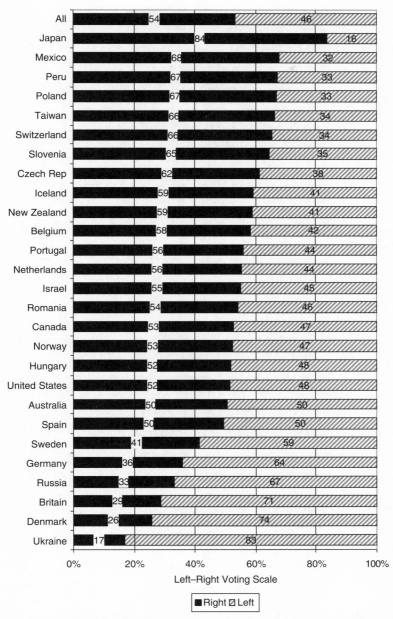

FIGURE 5.1. The distribution of support for the left–right voting blocs in legislative elections. Left–Right Vote: Party vote in legislative elections for the lower house classified on a 10-point scale ranging from Communist (1) to Nationalist (10) then dichotomized into right-wing and left-wing blocs. *Source:* Comparative Study of Electoral Systems, Module I, 1996–2002.

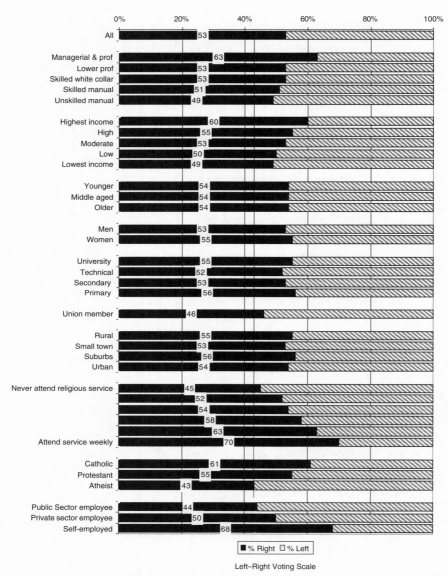

FIGURE 5.2. The social characteristics of right-wing voters. Left–Right Vote: Party vote in legislative elections for the lower house classified on a 10-point scale ranging from Communist (1) to Nationalist (10) dichotomized into right-wing and left-wing blocs. *Source:* Comparative Study of Electoral Systems, Module I, 1996–2002. Pooled sample.

TABLE 5.1. *Baseline Models Predicting Right-Wing Voting Support, Pooled Legislative Elections*

	Model A				Model B				Coding
	B	S.E.	Beta	Sig.	B	S.E.	Beta	Sig.	
SOCIAL STRUCTURE									
Age	−.008	.001	−.05	***	−.006	.001	−.04	***	A2001 Years old
Sex (Male)	.226	.035	.05	***	.112	.032	.02	***	A2002 Male = 1/Female = 0
Education	.040	.018	.02	*	.047	.017	.02	**	A2003 Highest level of education of respondent. Primary 1, secondary 2, post-secondary technical 3, university 4.
Income	.113	.014	.06	***	.081	.012	.05	***	A2012 5-point scale of household income from lowest to highest quintile.
Union member	−.609	.040	−.11	***	−.374	.036	−.07	***	A2005 Respondent is union member 1, else 0
Linguistic majority	.362	.036	.08	***	.224	.033	.05	***	A2018 Language usually spoken at home. Linguistic majority 1, else 0.
Religiosity	.311	.010	.24	***	.189	.009	.15	***	A2015 6-point strength of religiosity scale from never attend religious service (1) to attend at least weekly (6).
IDEOLOGY									
Left-right ideology					.409	.006	.43	***	A3031 Position respondents placed themselves on the 10-point scale from left (0) to right (10).
Constant	4.6								
Adjusted R²	.074				.248				

***p. 001; **p. 01; *p. 05.

Notes: The figures represent the results of ordinary least square (OLS) multiple regression analysis models including unstandardized beta coefficients (B), standardized error (S.E.), standardized beta coefficients (Beta), and their significance (P). Voting Choice: For the dependent measure, votes for each party family are recoded using a 10-point scale ranging from left (low) to right (high) as follows: (1) Communist, (2) Ecology, (3) Socialist, (4) Social Democrat, (5) Left-liberal, (6) Liberal, (7) Christian Democrat, (8) Right-liberal, (9) Conservative, and (10) Nationalist/Religious. A positive coefficient indicates support for parties on the right. The pooled sample of legislative elections includes 28 nations and 17,794 respondents. Data was weighted by A104.1 to ensure that the size of the sample is equal per nation.

Source: Comparative Study of Electoral Systems, Module I, 1996–2002.

United States. Overall, among the indicators of SES, union membership proved the strongest predictor of voting behavior, followed by income and then by education. Language was also important, with linguistic minorities more likely to support parties of the left. Among all the structural factors, the strength of religiosity emerged as by far the best predictor of voting support for parties of the right. Secondly, however, although all the factors proved to be statistically significant, nevertheless, all the structural variables in the pooled sample explained only 7% of the variance in voting behavior, as summarized by the adjusted R^2. Once the additional ideological measure of the respondent's left–right position was added in Model B, however, the proportion of variance explained by the model rose to 25% (measured by the adjusted R^2). In this model, although all the structural variables remain significant and in the predicted direction, nevertheless, none of these proved as strongly related to how people voted as left–right ideology.

But how does this pattern vary across elections in different nations? And, in particular, does the strength of cleavage politics vary, as different theories suggest, according to (a) the basic type of electoral system and (b) the level of socioeconomic development in a country? To examine this further the results were broken down in a series of regression models for each election, with the results presented in Table 5.2. Given some minor differences in the coding and inclusion of certain variables in the different national election studies, the comparison of separate models run in each election proved more reliable than models pooled by the type of electoral system and level of development. Elections are ranked by the adjusted R^2 to summarize the amount of variance in voting behavior explained by each of the models.

Socioeconomic Status

Many observers have documented the decline of traditional cleavage politics based on socioeconomic status and religion in Western Europe, although there has been considerable dispute about the most appropriate measurement and classification of these phenomena.[25] The most comprehensive analysis of the available evidence of postwar trends in class politics in twenty postindustrial nations by Nieuwbeerta and De Graaf (1999) suggests that some degree of dealignment has occurred in many European countries where these linkages used to be strong, and these findings are replicated irrespective of the alternative measures of social class employed for analysis.[26] Even commentators who had argued most strongly in the mid-1980s that class still mattered in Britain, if a revised classification and measurement was used, have accepted more recently that some degree of class dealignment has now occurred.[27] Because the impact of socioeconomic status can be measured, categorized, and analyzed in many ways, reflecting alternative conceptions of the underlying concept, I will use alternative indicators to see if these make any substantial difference to interpreting the results.

Household Income

The cleavage by socioeconomic status (SES) is commonly understood to represent the basic economic and material inequalities in any society. SES can be gauged by household income, the respondent's or head of household's occupational status, educational qualifications, and, as a related proxy, union membership. Employment in the public or private sectors, and shared lifestyle characteristics, function as alternative indicators.[28] The primary classification used in this study is based upon a 5-point standardized household income scale as the most reliable cross-national indicator, given substantial differences in the structure of the labor force in postindustrial and industrial societies, and also given that the classification of occupation was not included in some election studies in the CSES. Income is a basic indicator of socioeconomic status although, of course, there can be affluent households among the skilled manual workers, such as among self-employed plumbers or electricians, as well as less-well-off white-collar workers, such as secretaries, shop assistants, and nurses. Across the pooled sample the analysis shows a steady rise in voting support for parties of the right among more affluent household groups, as expected. The voting gap between the richest and poorest households was 11 percentage points, a significant difference. When the analysis was broken down by country, the multivariate models showed that higher income proved a significant predictor of right-wing voting in about one-third of the elections under comparison, including in all the Anglo-American democracies, as well as in the Netherlands, Sweden, Germany, Russia, and Mexico.

Occupational Class

But are these results due to the use of income to denote socioeconomic status? Because the definition and classification of occupational class produces little consensus in the literature we also need to compare alternative indicators. The respondent's own main occupation (rather than the head of household, to avoid a gender bias) was classified into five categories: senior managerial and professional, technicians and associated professional, other skilled white-collar (including clerical and service sector workers), skilled manual (such as plant and machinery operators), and unskilled manual (including construction, miners, and agricultural laborers). This five-fold classification reflects different levels of pay, skills, and qualifications, as well as job autonomy and authority. In the pooled sample, without any prior controls, the results show the predicted polarized pattern; almost two-thirds (63%) of managers and professionals voted for parties of the right, compared with less than half (49%) of the unskilled manual workers, producing a substantial and significant gap, reflecting that already observed by income.[29] Even if there has been secular dealignment over time, as many studies indicate, nevertheless, occupational class continues to predict a pattern of voting choice in the pooled sample. At the same time we need to be cautious when generalizing

TABLE 5.2. *Predictors of Right-Wing Voting Support in Legislative and Presidential Elections*

Nation	Type of Election	Type of System	Year	Demographic				Socioeconomic Status								Other Social Identities				Ideological		Adjusted R^2
				Age B	Age P	Sex (Male) B	Sex (Male) P	Educ. B	Educ. P	Income B	Income P	Class B	Class P	Union Member B	Union Member P	Linguistic majority B	Linguistic majority P	Religiosity B	Religiosity P	Left–Right Position B	Left–Right Position P	
Sweden	Leg	Prop	1998	.000		.005		.008		.063		.017		-.267	***	.243		.104	***	.461	***	.563
Chile	Pres	Maj	1999	.001		-.153		.113		.058				-.206				-.124		.608	***	.557
Israel	PM	Maj	1996	-.009	*	-.179		-.173	***	-.086	*	-.034				-.087		.172	***	.409	***	.551
Iceland	Leg	Prop	1999	-.007	**	.099		-.175	**	.085	*			-.039						.635	***	.512
Ukraine	Leg	Comb	1998	.025	**	.389		.551	**	-.050		.097		-.110		.100	***	.440	***	.412	***	.478
Switzerland	Leg	Prop	1999	-.004		.262		-.184	**	-.133	*	-.033		-.284		.873	***	.204	***	.539	***	.452
Czech Rep.	Leg	Prop	1996	-.007		.143		-.019		.065		-.099		-.140		.001		.127	*	.666	***	.431
Israel	Leg	Prop	1996	-.011		-.418	*	-.181	*	-.007		-.076		-.055		-.550	*	.383	***	.390	***	.416
Norway	Leg	Prop	1997	.007		.074		.118		-.090	*	.015		-.205	*			.084	**	.591	***	.409
Netherlands	Leg	Prop	1998	.003		.067		.118		.145	***	-.099	*	-.012	***			.326	***	.448	***	.372
Poland	Leg	Prop	1997	-.006		.069		.071		-.082		.017		-.227				.159	***	.311	***	.363
Lithuania	Pres	Maj	1997	.001		.127		.069		-.120										.379	***	.346
Britain	Leg	Maj	1997	.010	***	-.088		-.092		.200	***	-.201	***	-.335	**	.220		.024		.380	***	.304
Spain (i)	Leg	Prop	2000	.009		.021		.178		.096		-.071		-.713	*	-.233		.236	*	.563	***	.279
Russia	Pres	Maj	2000	-.017	*	-.281		.093		.417	***	-.060		.062		.100		.063		.360	***	.272
Belarus	Pres	Maj	2001	-.014		.556	**	.295		.266	***	-.118		-.172				-.132		-.028		.260
Hungary	Leg	Comb	1998	-.016	***	.051		.056		-.046		-.106		-.179				.142	***	.433	***	.255
N. Zealand	Leg	Comb	1996	-.001		.023		-.099		.026		.016		-.463	**	-.241		.145	***	.462	***	.254
Belgium	Leg	Prop	1999	.004		.374	***	-.089		.019		.032		-.009		.799	***	.163	***	.451	***	.243
Germany	Leg	Comb	1998	.006		.112		-.151	**	.109	**	-.023		-.465	***			.139	***	.334	***	.236
USA	Pres	Maj	1996	-.001		.409	***	.027		.338	***	-.083		-.604	***			.154	***	.351	***	.224
Russia	Leg	Comb	1999	-.029		-.628		.297		.659	***	.157		-.752		-.001		.126	***	.611	***	.207
USA	Leg	Maj	1996	-.001		.192		.092		.360	***	-.058		-.808	***			.128	***	.271	***	.184
Australia	Leg	Maj	1996	.003		-.042		-.042		.050		-.051		-.396	***			.071	**	.247	***	.164

Country			Year									(i)	
Denmark	Leg	Prop	1998	−.001	.024	−.030	−.024	−.196 ***	−.312	−.522 **	.087 *	.324 ***	.141
Romania	Pres	Maj	1996	−.023 ***	.186	.077	−.026	.216 ***	.225 *	.484 **	.029	.088 ***	.121
Canada (i)	Leg	Maj	1997	.004	.301 *	.064	−.006	−.132	−.127	−.611 ***	.096 *	.238 ***	.085
Romania	Leg	Prop	1996	−.012 **	.204	.169 *	.084	.071	.143	.010		.053 *	.073
Taiwan	Leg	Comb	1996	.009	−.203	.051	.020		−.281		−.161	.113	.044
Portugal	Leg	Prop	2002	.016 *	−.233	−.003	.149	−.057	.163	.001	−.153 **	.172 ***	.034
Mexico	Leg	Comb	1997	.004	−.060	.022	.166 **		−.313			.128 ***	.033
Mexico	Pres	Maj	2000	−.004	−.139	−.079	.071		−.303	.028		.106 ***	.030
Slovenia	Leg	Prop	1996	.005	−.212	.000	.017		−.023			.079 ***	.023
Taiwan	Pres	Maj	1996	.009	.249	.040	−.087	.127	−.104	−.642 ***	.038	.044	.017
Peru	Pres	Maj	2001	−.082	−.111	.193 ***	−.074					.086 ***	.016
Korea	Leg	Comb	2000	.005	−.072	−.108	.026		.415			.040 *	.013
Peru	Leg	Prop	2001	−.004	.000	.068	−.106 **		−.190			.334 ***	.009

*** p. 001; ** p. 01; * p. 05.

Notes: The figures represent the results of ordinary least square (OLS) multiple regression analysis models including unstandardized beta coefficients (B) and their significance (P). Blank cells represent missing data. Voting Choice: For the dependent measure, votes for each party family are recoded using a 10-point scale ranging from left (low) to right (high) as follows: (1) Communist, (2) Ecology, (3) Socialist, (4) Social Democrat, (5) Left liberal, (6) Liberal, (7) Christian Democrat, (8) Right liberal, (9) Conservative, and (10) Nationalist Religious. A positive coefficient indicates support for parties on the right. For details of the coding used for the independent variables see the baseline model in Table 5.1. (i) Religiosity was measured by frequency of church attendance.

Source: Comparative Study of Electoral Systems, Module I, 1996–2002.

about this pattern, as important variations emerge once the analysis is broken down by nation. In the multivariate regression models, with controls for income and union membership, occupational class is a significant predictor of voting choices in only three nations (Britain, the Netherlands, and Romania). If income and union membership are dropped from the model, class becomes significant in two additional nations (Australia and the Czech Republic).

Trade Union Membership
Trade union membership is another proxy measure commonly related closely to occupational class, although this association may have weakened over the years in countries where unions have sought to diversify their traditional blue-collar industrial base through expanding their membership among clerical, service, and professional employees. Overall levels of union membership vary substantially around the world, with density levels remaining strongest in the mid-1990s in many post-Communist nations of Central and Eastern Europe, as well as in the smaller Nordic welfare states.[30] There are many reasons why union membership should help to predict patterns of party support. Where trade unions are strongly linked to Socialist and Social Democratic parties they can provide organizational resources and mobilizing capacity in election campaigns, including local networks of volunteers, office communication facilities such as computers, telephones, and copiers, and financial assistance. Membership of the organized labor movement can also be understood as an expression of subjective class-consciousness, whereas those who actively attend union meetings become part of social networks that can reinforce left-wing attitudes and partisan affiliations. The results of the analysis in Table 5.1 confirms that even after controlling for other social factors, union membership was significantly linked to voting choices in one-third of the elections where this measure was available, proving to be particularly strongly related in West European states (Sweden, Norway, Germany, the Netherlands, and Spain) and the Anglo-American democracies (Britain, Australia, the United States, and New Zealand), and, by comparison, to be insignificant throughout Central and Eastern Europe.

Education
Education is the last variable under analysis that is closely associated with socioeconomic status, with school and university qualifications determining many subsequent opportunities in the workforce and society. Where education is closely related to social class, we would expect university graduates to be more right-wing in voting choice, even though there could be crosscutting pressures as numerous studies also have found education to be one of the most powerful characteristics that is consistently associated with liberal attitudes toward many social and political issues. Moreover, in countries that have experienced rapid socioeconomic development, education is often strongly associated with other crosscutting cleavages, such as age. The

results of the analysis show that overall, with or without any prior controls, in the pooled sample, education proved a relatively poor predictor of voting choice. When broken down by nations, patterns in the multivariate models in Table 5.2 also proved inconsistent: in countries such as Norway, the Ukraine, and Romania, as expected, greater education was positively associated with support for parties on the right. In contrast, however, in some countries this relationship proved negative, including in Israel, Switzerland, and Germany, where the more educated proved more left-wing in orientation. The impact of education generates patterns that differ across societies. The analysis so far suggests two main conclusions about the impact of socioeconomic status on voting behavior. First, of all the alternative indicators of social status that we have compared, income emerges as the most significant and consistent indicator of voting choices across the range of societies within the CSES dataset, although social class and union membership were important in some nations. Yet even income was only a significant predictor of voting choice in the expected direction – with more affluent households showing greater support for parties on the right – in one-third of the countries under comparison.

Religion

For Lipset and Rokkan, the other classic pillar of partisan alignment in postwar Western Europe was religion. Many accounts suggest that in recent decades the process of secularization has eroded habitual church-going and religious faith in Western Europe. Nevertheless, religious beliefs remain strong in many traditional societies, as well as in the United States, and during the last decade there may even have been a revival of organized religion in post-Communist Europe.[31] Even if some degree of secularization has been experienced in many societies in Western Europe, the results of the analysis demonstrate that religion remains more strongly and more consistently related to voting choice than any of the indicators of socioeconomic status. In the pooled model, almost three-quarters (70%) of the most devout (those who reported attending religious services at least once per week) voted for parties of the right. By contrast, among the least religious, who never attended religious services, less than half (45%) voted for the right. The substantial 25-point mean voting gap by religiosity proved far stronger than that produced by any of the alternative indicators of socioeconomic status. Across all countries, Catholic voters proved more right-wing than Protestants, while atheists were among the most left-wing of any of the social groups under comparison.

The multivariate analysis in Table 5.2 shows that the strength of religiosity (as measured by frequency of attending religious services) consistently predicted support for parties of the right and the association proved significant in two-thirds of the elections where data was available, even with prior social controls. Religiosity was particularly strongly related to voting choice in

Israel, the Netherlands, and Belgium, all countries where religious divisions have long been regarded as some of the most critical components of cleavage politics, as well as in Hungary and the Czech Republic. The explanation for the strength of the linkage is that churches in Western Europe have long been associated strongly with Christian Democrat and Conservative parties and have represented traditional moral values concerning diverse issues such as marriage and divorce, gender equality, and gay rights. In the United States, as well, "born again" fundamentalist churches are closely linked to the Republicans, especially in the South, emphasizing the use of prayer in school and conservative moral values such as those of the Right to Life movement. The role of organized religion elsewhere has developed within varying contexts, for example in Ireland, Poland, and Italy the Catholic Church usually has expressed conservative positions on issues such as divorce and reproductive rights, whereas in Latin American societies the church has supported more liberal causes and defended human rights in opposition to the state.[32]

Demographic Factors: Generation and Gender

Traditional socialization theories suggest that political attitudes and values can be expected to reflect the decisive experiences that shape the formative years of particular generations. These contrasts are exemplified by the experiences of those who grew up with poverty and job insecurity during the interwar Great Depression era of unemployment, inflation, and soup kitchens, in comparison with the experiences of the baby-boom generation that came of age during the postwar era of affluence and the basic safety-net established by the welfare state in postindustrial societies. Substantial generational contrasts also can be expected following the rapid social and political transformations that occurred in post-Communist Europe during the 1990s, following the fall of the Berlin Wall and the end of the Soviet state, and the sharp shocks of economic market adjustments. The "Asian tigers" such as Taiwan and the Republic of Korea have experienced equally profound social and economic transformations in shifting from agrarian to industrialized societies during the late twentieth century. The more fundamental and radical the social change, the stronger the generational differences that can be expected to flow from these developments. By itself, in the pooled sample across countries, all the main age groups display similar patterns of voting behavior. Yet the result of the multivariate analysis of voting choice by age group broken down by countries shows two distinct patterns (see Figure 5.3). In one or two West European nations, including Britain and Portugal, the generation that grew up during the interwar years proves slightly more conservative than the younger postwar cohorts. The generational voting gap in these countries is not large, but it is significant. Similar patterns are evident in Australia, Norway, and Germany, although not approaching conventional levels of statistical significance. The theory of postmaterialism developed by Ronald Inglehart provides, perhaps, the most

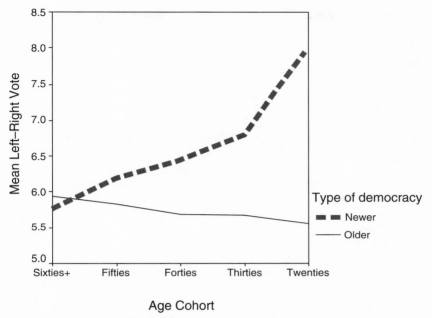

FIGURE 5.3. Age cohorts and voting support. *Notes:* Cases weighted by CSESWGT. Left–Right Vote: Party vote in legislative elections classified on a 10-point scale ranging from Communist (1) to Nationalist (10). *Source:* Comparative Study of Electoral Systems, Module I, 1996–2002.

plausible explanations for this phenomenon, suggesting that growing levels of affluence and the existence of the welfare state safety net experienced by the postwar baby-boom generation in Western Europe fostered more liberal values among the young compared with their parents' or grandparents' generations, leading younger voters to prioritize issues such as environmental protection, sexual equality, and international human rights, advocated by many parties of the left.[33] In sharp contrast, the reverse pattern is evident in some post-Communist societies, where the youngest generation proves far more right-wing than older voters. This pattern is most evident in Russia, Hungary, and Romania. The values of older generations in post-Communist nations were shaped by the existence of the managed economy and the security of the welfare state for health care, education, and pensions. The youngest generation growing up in Central and Eastern Europe have had the greatest experience of the neo-liberal market reforms and "shock" therapies experienced in these countries, as well as of the free and fair elections held during the last decade and the consolidation of representative democracy. The younger generation has adapted most rapidly to social and political change so that they now express greater support to parties on the right in this region, while the older generation remains more wedded to the values expressed by the reformed Communist and the Social Democratic parties of the left.[34]

Generational changes are important not just for themselves but also for the way that these trends have altered in different ways the voting behavior of women and men. During the postwar era the conventional wisdom in political science held that women in Western democracies were politically more conservative than men.[35] Gender differences in party preferences were never as marked as the core cleavages of class and religion; there were no mass "women's parties" in Western Europe, such as those associated with trade unions and churches. Nevertheless "women's conservatism" was seen as a persistent and well-established phenomenon. Part of the reason concerns the patterns of religiosity we have already observed because more women than men tend to be regular churchgoers. During the 1980s this conventional wisdom came under increasing challenge. In many West European countries a process of gender dealignment appeared, with studies reporting minimal sex differences in voting choice and party preferences.[36] And in America the phenomenon of the gender gap manifested itself in the early 1980s, with women shifting their allegiances toward the Democratic Party, while men moved toward the Republican Party on a stable and consistent basis, reversing the previous pattern of voting and partisanship.[37] The initial explanations of the gender gap in United States focused on factors specific to American politics, such as the appeal of President Reagan, programmatic differences between the parties on issues such as reproductive rights and childcare, or particular social conditions affecting American women. But the most recent comparative research has found that far from being specific to the United States, there is a broader generational transformation evident in many established democracies, so that although older women remain slightly more right-wing than older men, among younger generations in affluent nations this situation is commonly reversed.[38] In post-Communist and developing societies, however, reflecting historical experiences, the generational patterns are different.

The gender gap in the pooled sample of all countries is negligible: 53% of women support right-wing parties compared with 55% of men. Yet once voting patterns are analyzed by nation, the gender gap becomes significant in about one-third of the elections under comparison. Nevertheless, there are mixed patterns, with women slightly more left-wing than men in a few countries, including Belgium, Canada, and the United States, whereas women are more conservative than men in Israel. Moreover, interesting patterns emerge once the patterns are broken down by age and by type of society. As Figure 5.4 shows, in established democracies there has been a reversal of the traditional gender gap, so that older women remain slightly more conservative than older men, while among the younger generation, women are now more left-wing than younger men. Because the values of older women and

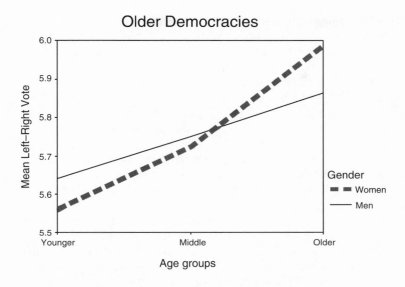

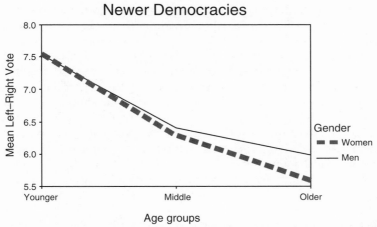

FIGURE 5.4. The gender–generation gap. *Notes:* Cases weighted by CSESWGT. Age groups: Younger (Low through 39 years old), Middle-aged (40 thru 59 years old), Older (60+). Left–Right Vote: Party vote in legislative elections classified on a 10-point scale ranging from Communist (1) to Nationalist (10). *Source:* Comparative Study of Electoral Systems, Module I, 1996–2002.

younger women "cancel out" in the overall figures, there appears to be no significant gender gap in many older democracies. If these patterns persist, however, as cohorts change, then the process of demographic replacement, as older generations die out and younger generations take their place, can be expected to gradually shift women increasingly toward the left in these nations, producing a modern gender gap as in the United States. In contrast, among newer democracies, as one can see, there is a different pattern: among the older generation women remain more left-wing than men, perhaps because women have been affected more than men by the economic shock therapy and the cuts in welfare benefits such as state pensions and child-care. Yet among the youngest generation in these societies the gender gap disappears. The patterns lend further confirmation to the existence of the gender gap–generation that has been observed in a wider range of 75 societies using the World Values Surveys. The relationship between gender and voting choices is, therefore, complicated by the existence of cross-cutting generational cleavages and by societal histories and cultures.

Linguistic Cleavages
I also compared the existence of linguistic cleavages, which are expected to divide party politics most deeply in plural multilingual societies such as Canada, Switzerland, and Belgium. The predominant language was identified in each nation and was coded to define linguistic majorities by the language usually spoken at home. Of course, this is only an imperfect measure, as second-generation immigrants could be equally fluent in more than one language, but this provides a proxy measure for ethno-linguistic divisions. The results of the analysis proved particularly strong in Switzerland (divided by cantons between the German-speaking majority and the French and Italian minorities), Canada, Belgium (split between Francophones and Flemish Walloons), and the Ukraine (almost evenly divided between Ukrainian and Russian speakers), as well as in significant minority communities in Israel, Taiwan, and Romania. These patterns would probably have been even stronger if I examined support for the ethno-linguistic regional parties separately, rather than left–right support, because ethno-linguistic cleavages often cross-cut socioeconomic ones. This pattern will be analyzed further in Chapter 9 when I look in detail at ethnic minority politics.

Left–Right Ideology
Last, as well as with social cleavages, I also expected that the ideological position of voters would play an important role in predicting patterns of party support. The left–right scale has been found to be one of the most familiar ways that citizens use to identify their own positions and that of the parties along the political spectrum.[39] In the CSES survey, three-quarters of the public could identify their locations on this scale. Because I expect these values to be generated by social cleavages, the self-placement of respondents on the 10-point left–right ideological scale was entered sequentially last in the regression models, after the structural variables. The results show that ideological values were significant predictors of voting choice in every country except for two nations (Belarus and Taiwan). The presidential election in Belarus pitted President Lukashenko, an old-style ex-Soviet apparatchik,

against the former reformist prime minister and opposition leader, Mikhail Chigir, but official observers declared that the election was hardly free and fair; whereas in Taiwan the parties were identified mainly by nationalist issues, about relationships with mainland China, rather than by left–right ideology.[40] Elsewhere the ideological position of voters proved to be strongly and consistently related to party support.

The Effects of Electoral Systems on Cleavage Politics

Given the patterns that we have established, the key question that remains concerns how far the strength of cleavage politics can be related systematically to either the type of electoral system (as suggested by incentive-based theories) or, alternatively, to the level of socioeconomic development (as predicted by culture-based sociological accounts). The adjusted R^2 in Table 5.1 summarizes the amount of variance in voting behavior in each election explained by the social cleavages that I have analyzed so far. The results show considerable cross-national differences, from elections such as those in Sweden, Israel, and the Ukraine, with a high R^2, where social structure and ideology contributed strongly to whether people voted on the left or right of the political spectrum, down to other elections such as those in Taiwan, Peru, and the Republic of Korea, which are ranked at the bottom of the table.

If the logic of the incentive-based theory is correct, then I should expect to find that in majoritarian electoral systems parties will focus their electoral strategies on catch-all bridging appeals, to try to maximize their electoral support to secure a plurality or majority of votes that is necessary to win elected office. Alternatively, under PR electoral systems with low thresholds parties can use bonding strategies among a narrower constituency and still get elected. Strategic theories are based on the premise that parties and candidates can either reinforce or weaken the political salience of social identities such as class and religion by their use of either bridging or bonding appeals. Hence, socialist parties seeking to mobilize their core working-class bases can emphasize the issues of economic equality, redistributive fiscal policies, and investment in welfare services for health and education. In the same way, if Conservative and Christian Democratic parties want to appeal to their core constituencies they can focus on traditional moral values concerning marriage and the family as well as heartland issues such as law and order, defense, and immigration. If, however, they seek to broaden their electoral support, parties can focus on centrist issues such as the importance of economic growth or the need for efficient public services.

To examine the evidence for incentive-based theories, Figure 5.5 compares the strength of cleavage politics, measured by the R^2 listed in Table 5.2 in legislative and presidential elections held under majoritarian, combined, and proportional electoral systems. The R^2 coefficient can be understood as the

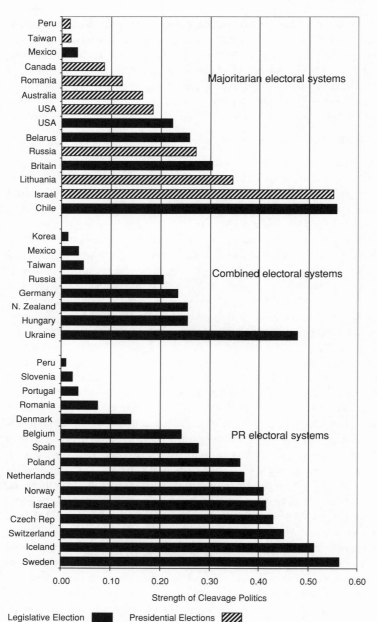

FIGURE 5.5. The strength of cleavage politics by type of electoral system. *Source:* See Table 5.2.

amount of variance in the left–right voting scale explained by the combined effects of social structure and political ideology. The result of the comparison confirms that although there are considerable differences within each category, nevertheless, on balance, cleavage politics was stronger under proportional electoral systems. As summarized by the mean R^2, the strength of cleavage politics was 25% in the fourteen elections conducted under majoritarian systems, 24% in the nine elections conducted using combined systems, but 36% in the 15 elections held under PR systems. That is to say, in predicting how many people voted for parties on the left and on the right of the party scale, more than one-third of the total variance in PR elections was generated by social structure and ideology. As discussed in subsequent chapters, comprehensive explanations of voting behavior would also include many other factors, including patterns of partisanship; the retrospective record of the government's performance on major economic and social issues; the popular appeal of party images, party leaders, and prospective policy platforms; and the impact of campaign events and media coverage. But, nevertheless, social structure and political ideology remain important by explaining between one-quarter and one-third of the variance in left–right electoral behavior in the electoral systems under comparison.

But might the results be due to the type of societies that used different forms of elections? Cultural accounts emphasize that in developing and industrialized societies, traditional social identities of class and religion provide voters with strong cues influencing voting behavior and party loyalties. In postindustrial societies, however, modernization theories suggest that rising levels of education, greater cognitive skills, the erosion of traditional communities, and richer information resources from the mass media have reduced voters' reliance upon traditional social identities and habitual party attachments, increasingly replacing the politics of loyalties with the politics of choice. Figure 5.6 compares the strength of cleavage politics, using the same procedure as before, but dividing societies into industrial and postindustrial levels of human development, classified by the Human Development Index discussed earlier in Chapter 1. Again there are important variations within each category, but, nevertheless, the results show quite clearly that, far from being weaker, in fact, cleavage politics remains stronger in postindustrial societies. The average amount of variance in voting behavior (R^2) explained by cleavage politics was 24% in industrial societies, but it was 33% in postindustrial nations. Many other studies have demonstrated that the cues of class and religion have become less influential in many established democracies, but, nonetheless, social identities continue to have a stronger impact upon voting choices in postindustrial nations. Even if the social bonds anchoring groups to parties have indeed weakened in these nations, as dealignment theories suggest, this does not mean that they have, thereby, become irrelevant to electoral choices. Converse's learning model maintained that the strength of attachment to parties should grow with a

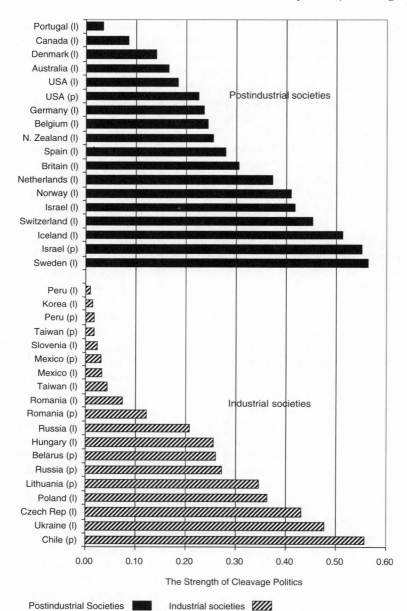

FIGURE 5.6. The strength of cleavage politics by type of society. (p), presidential; (l), legislative. *Source:* See Table 5.2.

history of support for one's preferred party.[41] In many industrial societies and newer democracies, with much shorter experience of a series of free and fair elections, and with less consolidated patterns of party competition along the left–right scale, these bonds between political parties and voters' social identities have yet to develop to anything like the same degree.

Accordingly, we can conclude that, on balance, the evidence leans more toward incentive-based than cultural accounts of social dealignment. Of course, the indicators remain limited in many important ways. In particular, the inclusion of both presidential and legislative elections could produce some important problems of interpretation, if presidential elections tended toward stronger bridging appeals than parliamentary contests. This could be a persuasive criticism because one would expect presidential elections to focus more on personalities and less on ideological and issue-based appeals. For the time being, I will assume that the results presented in this chapter are the product of the electoral system, not any differences between presidential and parliamentary systems, and I will examine this issue further in subsequent chapters that analyze the impact of the personal vote and party reputation for party leaders and parliamentary candidates. The comparative framework is another important limitation. In the best of all possible worlds it would be desirable to have electoral studies drawn from many more countries and regions of the world. In particular, the CSES dataset lacks any newer democracies and industrialized nations using majoritarian systems for parliamentary elections. Against this, it has to be said that, in fact, this dataset represents the broadest range of integrated election studies that is available currently, including electoral democracies from most continents. As cross-national collaboration develops among teams of electoral studies, future comparisons will be able to evaluate to what extent these generalizations hold within a wider range of contexts.

Moreover, without time-series data one is unable to establish trends to demonstrate whether there has been greater social dealignment within majoritarian systems. The incentive-based explanation claims essentially that the type of electoral system will predict the contemporary strength of cleavage politics in different places. If the formal or informal rules of the game change in important regards, for example, if the social composition of constituencies becomes either more homogeneous or more heterogeneous through the process of boundary revisions, demographic shifts, or patterns of population migration, then one would expect that this could have an impact by changing the electoral incentives facing political actors and, thereby, weakening or strengthening voter–party bonds. Yet there is no direct historical evidence to sustain this proposition. What secondary evidence does suggest, however, is that cleavage politics does appear to have eroded further and faster in postindustrial societies with majoritarian electoral systems. The most extensive study of trends in cleavage politics by Franklin et al. examined election surveys from the mid-sixties until the late-eighties in a dozen postindustrial societies. The results strongly indicate that countries with majoritarian electoral systems during this period saw the earliest decline of cleavage politics, including in Canada, the United States, Britain, Australia, France, and New Zealand.[42] Therefore, the type of electoral system may play an important role in helping to explain the timing of the process of dealignment, and the underlying conditions in which this occurs, although as a static theory the incentive-based "top-down" theory cannot by itself explain satisfactorily the process of decline per se, unless the workings of the electoral system alter in important ways. The theory suggests that one should find significant differences among countries today, but it lacks a dynamic element.

Last, perhaps the most important criticism that could be made of the results is that I have not established the direction of causality in any relationship; in particular, the electoral system is treated throughout the discussion as exerting an exogenous impact upon parties, which then shape the political salience of social cleavages. This seems a reasonable assumption in established democracies where the electoral rules are usually a more or less permanent institution that generates "hard" incentives and opportunities for particular patterns of behavior by voters, campaign managers, and party leaders alike. In most older democracies the basic electoral system has existed for more than a century, although major electoral reforms were introduced in the last decade in a few countries, such as Italy, New Zealand, and Britain, and the specific administrative arrangements governing voting procedures have altered more regularly. As a result, it is appropriate to regard electoral systems in these nations as exerting an *independent* effect on political actors. Yet, of course, at the time that electoral systems are initially adopted, it seems plausible that parties would seek to adopt the type of rules serving their rational self-interests. Hence, minor parties in deeply divided plural societies, exemplified by Israel and Ukraine, will seek to adopt PR arrangements, whereas major parties in more homogeneous cultures can be expected to prefer majoritarian rules. In the transition process to democracy, the party system can exert a decisive influence upon the electoral rules, and, therefore, in newer democracies it seems more appropriate to regard electoral systems as both dependent upon parties (when analyzing which systems are adopted) and also as an independent variable (when explaining the effect of the rules on political behavior).

The central claim in incentive-based theories is not that electoral systems *create* the social cleavages or their political relevance, but merely that the initial adoption of certain rules (for whatever reason) creates certain incentives to either maintain or reinforce (and possibly exacerbate) one-of-us bonding, or, alternatively, to modify or downplay (and possibly erode) group consciousness in the political arena by encouraging catch-all bridging strategies. As discussed more fully in Chapter 9, this process can be illustrated most clearly by particularly divisive ethnic cleavages, such as the role of racial conflict over civil rights in 1960s America, the clash between Muslims and Christians in Bosnia-Herzegovina, or discord among Protestants and Catholics in Northern Ireland. In these societies, political actors can either seek to mobilize their base by heightening ethnic tensions through adopting populist rhetoric directed to own-group appeals or, alternatively, they can seek to maximize their support by downplaying such appeals and proposing consensual policies that will appeal to bridging constituencies. Similar logics follow the politicization of any other major social cleavage such as class or region. The evidence in this chapter suggests that the electoral rules of the game can contribute toward this process as majoritarian rules in heterogeneous geographic constituencies provide greater incentives toward moderate bridging strategies. But does one find patterns similar in terms of party loyalties to those evident concerning social identities? It is to this issue that I now turn.

6

Party Loyalties

I demonstrated in Chapter 4 the mechanical effects of the electoral rules upon party systems, but we know far less about their indirect psychological impact upon patterns of party loyalties. The first part of this chapter reviews briefly both cultural modernization and rational choice accounts to establish the theoretical framework. The second part compares the strength of partisan identification, the social and political characteristics of partisans, and, also, to what degree these attachments vary under different electoral systems. The third part of the chapter goes on to consider to what extent these partisan bonds, in conjunction with social identities, help to explain voting behavior in the countries under comparison.

Theories of Partisan Identification

Cultural Modernization and Partisan Identification

Classic Michigan theories of electoral behavior by Campbell et al., which dominated the field of the study of voting behavior in the United States for many decades, focused on individual-level voting choices rather than on their broader institutional context. The model, derived from social psychology, suggested that most voters in the United States were anchored over successive elections, and sometimes for their lifetimes, by persistent loyalties to a particular party.[1] *Partisan identification* was understood in the original theory as an *affective* orientation or habit of the heart, where American voters came to see themselves as habitual Democrats or Republicans, as part of their core self-identity, rather as they came to see themselves as Southerners or New Englanders, Catholics or Protestants, and fans of the Yankees or the Red Sox. Partisan identification has two main components: its *direction* (in support for particular parties across the left–right spectrum) and its *strength* (whether people feel lasting bonds or whether they only lean toward a particular party). These attachments, acquired through the socialization process in early childhood and adolescence, were believed to provide citizens with a long-standing orientation toward electoral choices and their places within the political system. Partisan identification has been regarded as a stable anchor providing a cognitive shortcut that guided voting decisions and reduced the costs of participation, even where people lacked detailed information about the particular candidates standing for office, or if they had little understanding of complex policy issues and party programs.[2] Because people saw themselves as Democrats or Republicans, they were thought to adopt political attitudes congruent with these identities, for example, reflecting core beliefs about the need to reduce taxation in the GOP or the importance of preserving Medicare and Medicaid in the Democrats. Social structure remained an important component in this theory, as partisan identification was believed to be the product of a cohesive socialization process that reinforced the acquisition of early political values within the family, school, work group, and social milieu, so that attachments reflected long-standing structural cleavages of class, religion, gender, and race dividing the American electorate. Cultural accounts stress that habitual loyalties should strengthen with age, as it takes time for people to acquire stable ties with parties.[3] The theory emphasized that the existence of habitual partisan identities in the mass electorate had important consequences, not just for how voters decide, but also for the behavior of political actors and for processes of stable governance. According to this view, in most U.S. elections each party sought to mobilize and get-out-the-vote for its "normal base" of support. This concept requires splitting the actual vote cast for a party into two parts: a normal or baseline vote to be expected from a group, based on its habitual behavior over successive elections in the past, and the current deviation from that norm, due to the immediate circumstances of the specific election, such as particular leaders, events, and issues. The outcome of elections, and therefore, American government, rested upon stable and predictable processes. For the traditional Michigan model, therefore, most American voters were anchored psychologically to a particular party for long periods of time, perhaps for their lifetimes, through unwavering attachments that are, in turn, rooted in social structure.

When the Michigan model was applied to other established democracies in Western Europe, including Britain, France, and Norway, early electoral surveys confirmed that most voters expressed a party identification and that this sense of attachment was strongly associated with voting behavior in these nations as well.[4] In 1964, for example, 96% of British citizens identified with one of the three main parties, and 44% were "strong" identifiers. Nevertheless, even in the 1960s Butler and Stokes observed that vote switching was more often accompanied by a parallel shift of party identification in Britain than in the United States.[5] A voluminous literature in voting behavior developed around the topic and from the mid-1970s onward the Michigan school came under increasing challenge. Panel studies monitoring the behavior of the same voters over successive elections in various countries, including in

Canada, the Netherlands, Sweden, Japan, and Britain, reported commonly that party identification switched over successive elections in tandem with voting, as well as in response to short-term changes in material conditions and other preferences, rather than proving itself to be a stable, enduring anchor for electoral choices and political orientations.[6] If party identification and voting choices essentially co-varied as two sides of the same coin in Western Europe, representing the expression of current political preferences, then models explaining voting decisions that include party identification as an independent variable could prove circular, artificially inflating the impact of party identification on vote choice.[7] Others argued that the concept of party identification needed to be reinterpreted as it represented a running tally of party performance, and therefore a more rational orientation, rather than a simple affective sense of loyalty.[8]

But the most sustained and fundamental critique of the Michigan school came from accounts of societal modernization suggesting that, even if one accepts the traditional concepts and measures, there is substantial evidence that traditional party loyalties – particularly *strong* attachments – have been fraying gradually in many advanced industrialized societies from the 1970s onward, including in the United States. Social psychological theories of partisan dealignment make three major claims: (1) in postindustrial societies, many citizens no longer have strong and stable affective identities anchoring them to political parties; (2) as a result, many voters have become more volatile in their electoral behavior and increasingly willing to desert the major parties, thereby, producing erratic waves of support for minor parties; and, also, (3) short-term factors have become more influential components in voting choice, including the impact of the outgoing government's policy record, party programs on the major issues of the day, the personal qualities and experience of political leaders and candidates, and the role of the mass media and campaigns. Dealignment theories suggest that in established democracies this development could have significant consequences for many aspects of voting behavior, by potentially boosting electoral volatility, the proportion of late-deciders and non-voters, and split-ticket voting, as well as possibly by reducing turnout and weakening beliefs about the legitimacy of the political process and trust in government.[9] At systemic level, with less ballast, a fall in partisanship could generate more unpredictable outcomes, strengthen the prospects for minor parties, further fractionalize party systems, and, therefore, complicate coalition building and the government formation process.

Considerable survey evidence has now been accumulated that suggests that party attachments have eroded in many established democracies during the late twentieth century,[10] although heated debate continues about the causes and the consequences of this phenomenon. Less systematic research is available to make reliable comparisons with the strength of voter-party attachments in elections held in a wide range of newer transitional and consolidating democracies, although most studies suggest that stable party loyalties will take years or even decades to develop.[11] Schmitt and Holmberg developed one of the most comprehensive analyses of trends in the United States and Western Europe, based on national elections studies and the Eurobarometer survey from the mid-1960s until the early 1990s.[12] The authors were fairly cautious about drawing any sweeping conclusions from the data, but they noted that a general decline of partisanship had occurred in many places, although they emphasized that the depth and spread of any partisan dealignment differed across countries and time. More recently, Dalton analyzed trends in national election studies conducted in nineteen advanced industrialized democracies from the mid-sixties to the late nineties, excluding the "newer" (third wave) democracies of Spain, Portugal, and Greece.[13] The study concluded that the proportion of party identifiers dropped across all advanced industrialized democracies under comparison, with a fall that was statistically robust in two-thirds of the nations. The significant erosion in the proportion of strong identifiers occurred in all but three nations (Finland, the Netherlands, and Denmark). The similarity of trends across postindustrial democracies led Dalton to conclude that similar processes of modernization within these countries, particularly the effects of generational change and rising cognitive mobilization, had caused these developments: "In short, the process of cognitive mobilization has *increased* voters' political sophistication and their ability to deal with the complexities of politics – and this may have *decreased* the functional need for partisanship among many better educated and politically involved citizens." This assumes that partisan attachments function as an organizing device or perceptual prism for political evaluations, facilitating judgments about unfamiliar candidates and cueing attitudes toward new issues, a process thought particularly important for voting choice among less informed citizens. Cultural explanations of the strength of partisan identification typically focus at individual-level upon the social characteristics of voters, including levels of education and age, as well as stress the linkages between partisanship and subsequent political attitudes and behavior, such as feelings of political efficacy, satisfaction with democracy, and propensity to vote.

Rational-Choice Institutionalism

The social psychological perspective emphasizes long-term processes of societal modernization affecting decision-making processes in the mass electorate. If there has been a weakening of party bonds, then the primary cause is believed to lie in secular trends such as growing levels of cognitive skills, the rise of the mass media, or generational shifts in postmaterial values and issue concerns. Yet ever since Downs, a substantial literature has provided an alternative understanding of the notion of partisan identification, where the role of political actors is regarded as critical, in particular, how parties place themselves strategically when competing along the left-right ideological spectrum.[14] Schmitt and Holmberg exemplify this claim when they argue that the strength of partisanship lies in the hands of political actors more than in society.[15] If so, then one might expect to find considerable cross-national variations in the vitality of voter–party bonds, both within postindustrial societies and also within the broader universe of electoral democracies, based on systematic features of electoral institutions and party systems. In this perspective, the strength of partisan attachments in different countries vary according to factors such as the extent of party competition and the degree of ideological polarization around divisive issues; the historical legacy of party systems including the continuity of older parties and the mobilization of new contestants; the performance of parties in government when serving the needs of their core supporters; the structure of party organizations and the strength of their linkages with affiliated associations such as unions and churches; systematic organizational and ideological differences among party families such as the Greens, Communists, and Social Democrats; the primary face-to-face and mediated channels of campaign communications; the basic type of electoral rules; and the overarching constitutional arrangements such as differences between presidential and parliamentary systems, as well as federal or unitary states.

Many of these explanations would take us far beyond the scope of this limited study, but, nevertheless, I will examine some of the characteristics of parties and electoral systems that could plausibly be associated with strong partisanship. Rational-choice institutionalism accounts suggest that political actors such as party leaders, campaign managers, and parliamentary candidates respond to the electoral incentives present in their broader context, particularly to the logic of electoral rules and party competition. Strong party-voter linkages and affective loyalties are regarded commonly as an electoral advantage for parties, by helping to mobilize support and to provide a cushion of true believers in good times and bad. Yet under majoritarian rules parties have a strong incentive to develop bridging appeals to meet higher electoral thresholds to office. In this context they may decide to advocate broad and diffuse ideological positions, to adopt consensual issue stances, and to stress their competence at managing government, in the attempt to maximize their support across all groups in the electorate, even if they calculate that this strategy comes at the cost of some erosion of their core party identifiers. By contrast, under proportional rules parties can get elected to office with a lower share of the vote, and, in this context, they have a stronger incentive to adopt bonding appeals based on their core issues and party image, as an economical way of mobilizing their own party identifiers. Where political actors focus upon partisan appeals this process, in turn, is thought to have an *indirect* influence upon the enduring potency of party-voter attachments among the mass public.[16]

The Strength of Partisan Identification

Comparing voting behavior in many countries allows for the testing of these theories, although one immediately encounters debates about the best measurement of partisan identities.[17] The standard question on partisanship, carried since 1952 in the American National Election Study (NES) and in many subsequent election studies elsewhere, has traditionally asked: *"Generally speaking, do you usually think of yourself as a Republican, a Democrat, an Independent, or what?"* The follow-up items then probe for the strength of any partisanship.[18] The word *usually* is thought to prompt respondents to consider long-term orientations beyond voting in the particular election. By contrast, the core concept of partisan identification that we can compare from the CSES survey was measured by the following questions:

1. [Party identification] *"Do you usually think of yourself as close to any particular political party?"* (A3004)
2. [Direction] If 'yes,' *"Which party is that?"* [A3005_1]
3. [Strength] *"Do you feel very close to this [party/party block], somewhat close, or not very close?"* (A3012)

The key difference is that the first question in the CSES battery does not carry any cues that refer to specific parties, unlike the standard items carried in the NES and many other national election studies. The choice of wording could be important, as direct comparison across items in the NES and British Election Studies (BES) suggests that the CSES version generates significantly lower numbers of partisans than the "cued" question. Nevertheless, the essential point for cross-national analysis is the consistency of the item used across different election studies, to generate reliable comparisons. The first part of the battery was carried in all the national election studies contained in the dataset.

The basic distribution of partisans by nation based on this measure is illustrated in Figure 6.1. The results show considerable contrasts between countries, with widespread partisanship in Australia, Israel, and the Ukraine, compared with the weak partisanship in countries ranking at the bottom of the list, including Chile, Thailand, and Belarus. It might be assumed that there should be some straightforward differences in the strength of partisanship between older democracies with long-established party systems and newer democracies with more recently founded parties. Yet the contrasts between nations do not appear to fall into any simple pattern that could be easily explained by a single predominant cause, for example, by differences between presidential and parliamentary executives, between Anglo-American or West European nations, or between multiparty and two-party systems. To explore this pattern further, I will compare explanations for the strength of partisanship based on three factors: the characteristics of the political and electoral system at national or macro-level; the type of party, including the

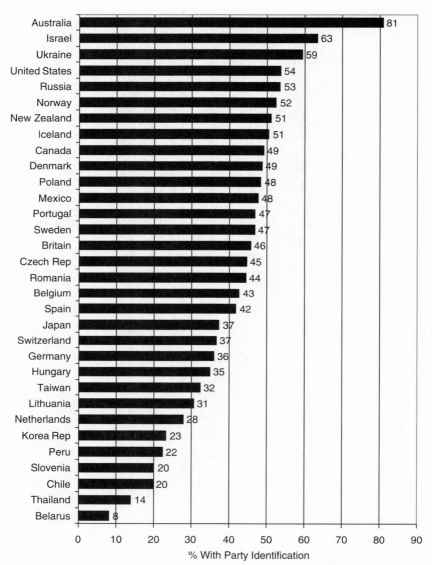

FIGURE 6.1. Proportion of partisans by nation. *Note:* Q: "*Do you usually think of yourself as close to any particular political party?*" (% '*Yes*'). *Source:* Comparative Study of Electoral System, Module I, 1996–2002.

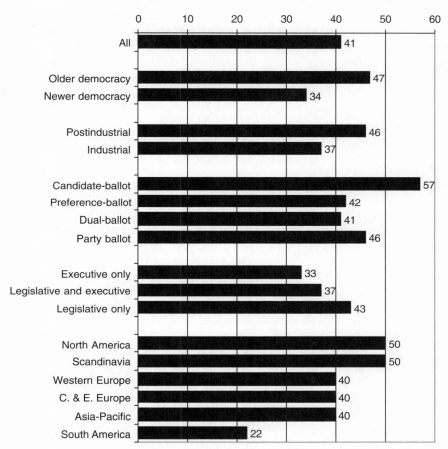

% With Party Identification

FIGURE 6.2. National context of partisanship. *Note:* Q: "*Do you usually think of yourself as close to any particular political party?*" (% 'Yes'). *Source:* Comparative Study of Electoral Systems, Module I, 1996–2002.

party family and longevity, at meso-level; and then the social background and the political attitudes of voters at individual level.

National Context

Figure 6.2 shows some of the main variations in the proportion of partisans by type of society and political system. Many assume that the bonds between voters and political parties should strengthen with the democratic consolidation process, and, indeed, this is what we find, with almost one-half (47%)

of the electorate living in older democracies expressing a party identification, compared with about one-third (34%) of those living in newer democracies. Most major parties in older democracies have established familiar images in the public's mind, and many parties have continuous historical roots and traditional identities on the left or right of the political spectrum that can be traced back for many decades, in some cases for more than a century. If it takes time for people to acquire stable ties with parties, then party loyalties should be strongest among long-established political parties.[19] By contrast, party attachments are weakest in newer democracies where patterns of party competition have not yet stabilized and where party discipline in parliament remains loose, where party images are fluid, where mass-branch party organizations are under-developed, where parties remain personalistic rather than based on programmatic differences in policy manifestos, and where voters have not yet acquired a lifetime habit of party support reinforced over successive elections.[20] Party systems have often failed to institutionalize in many newer electoral democracies in Latin America and Asia. Given the strong link between socioeconomic and political development in the countries under comparison in the CSES data, not surprisingly, similar patterns of partisanship were evident in the gap between postindustrial and industrial societies.

The electoral system may also have an important influence upon patterns of partisanship. As discussed in detail in Chapter 8, in election campaigns, candidates can choose to focus on *personal* appeals, including their records in the delivery of public services to their local districts, as well as their individual leadership qualities such as their backgrounds and experiences, to become well known and to develop personal reputations. Alternatively, they can decide to stress *party* appeals such as the collective party record, policy program, and leadership team. If electoral prospects depend upon winning votes cast for the individual politician instead of, or in addition to, votes cast for the party, then politicians face a tradeoff between the value of personal and party reputation. In extremely candidate-centered systems, the personal appeal of particular local politicians can be expected to influence the calculus of voters' decisions more strongly than general party labels. In legislative elections, I theorize that the electoral incentive for candidates to emphasize party labels or to emphasize personalistic appeals varies according to the ballot structure:[21]

1. The highest incentive to stress personal appeals comes from *candidate-ballots*: used in single-member districts with plurality elections such as those used for the U.S. Congress and the U.K. House of Commons.
2. A moderate incentive to stress personal appeals comes from *preference-ballots*: used in open party list PR systems allowing preferential voting where voters can rank their ballot choices from among candidates within the same party, such as that used in Brazil and Belgium.

Preferential ballots are also used in multimember constituencies with low district magnitude where candidates compete for popular votes with others from within their own party, exemplified by the Single Transferable Vote in Ireland and the Single Non-Transferable Vote used for some districts in Taiwan.

3. Under *dual-ballots*, there are mixed incentives, as used in combined systems where electors can express their preferences through some mix of candidate and preferential or party ballots.

4. Last, politicians have the greatest incentive to emphasize their collective record in the context of *party-ballots*, used in proportional electoral systems with closed party lists, such as in Norway, the Netherlands, and Romania. In these contests, all parliamentary candidates on the ticket win or fail together, as votes are pooled, and voters are unable to determine which particular members are elected from the party list.

This argument assumes that campaigns reflect the type of electoral rewards facing vote-seeking politicians, and also that the public will recognize and respond to the type of electoral appeals made by political actors.

The type of candidate selection process is also believed to be important to the type of strategies that candidate will emphasize since this process determines which applicants succeed in becoming adopted as official parliamentary candidates for each party. Parties can be classified according to the degree of centralization of the selection process, ranging from the most open systems determined mainly by voters, such as the Canadian Conservatives or the U.S. Democrats, to the most closed systems determined mainly by party leaders, exemplified until recently by the Mexican PRI or by Berlosconi's Forza Italia. Between these poles, a range of political actors may play a role: including party members, local delegates, factions, affiliated groups, and regional party leaders, as well as external gatekeepers such as financial donors, local notables, and journalists.[22] Extremely party-centered systems combine closed PR lists, so that voters can only choose from among parties, with nomination processes where party candidates are determined by the party leadership. In such circumstances, parliamentary candidates have no incentive to engage in any real campaigning beyond lending their name to the party list. At the opposite pole, extremely candidate-centered systems combine open voter primaries determining party nominees with open-list PR. Most systems fall somewhere between these polar extremes. In all these regards, electoral systems, nomination processes, and parties can be expected to influence whether elections foster strong or weak party–voter linkages in the mass electorate.

One cannot compare all aspects of this theory since there is no way of classifying the process of candidate selection used by each party in the countries under comparison on any systematic basis. This process can vary substantially among parties even within a country, and, in most cases, it remains a "black box" where we have more information about the formal rules than the informal procedures and norms guiding the outcome.[23] Nevertheless, we can compare the strength of partisanship among the basic types of electoral system and ballot structures that we have already classified.

The results of the comparison in Figure 6.2 show some modest support for this proposition: 46% of those voting in party-ballots had a partisan identification compared with 42% of those voting with preferential-ballots. Nevertheless, it must be stressed that this difference, while statistically significant, remains extremely modest. Moreover, contrary to the theory, those voting with candidate-ballots displayed by far the strongest partisanship, as 57% expressed a party identification. Further analysis with a much wider range of countries would be necessary to explore this relationship further, including classifying the degree of centralization of the party recruitment process. But the initial evidence presented here provides limited or, indeed, contradictory support for the claim that the strength of partisan identification varies systematically according to the ballot structure. In later chapters I will explore how far the ballot structure influences other characteristics of the electorate, such as their knowledge of candidates and their contact with elected members.

Presidential vs. Parliamentary Executives

The basic type of parliamentary or presidential executive is another factor that could influence the strength of party-voter attachments. The results confirm that partisanship is strongest in legislative general elections, where 43% expressed a partisan identity, partisanship is slightly weaker in elections combining legislative and executive contests, and it is weakest of all in presidential elections, where only one-third expressed a party identity. In parliamentary systems, where the legislature determines the executive and maintains the prime minister in office, then we would expect party cohesion to be important, as all members win or lose together. If the prime minister fails to win a vote of confidence in parliament, then the government falls, and either the leader of the opposition attempts to form an administration with a working majority or parliament is dissolved and all representatives have to fight an election campaign. All elected politicians in the governing party or parties have a high incentive to maintain party unity in parliamentary systems or they face the threat of potential electoral defeat. In presidential systems with strong party discipline, where the party leader can play an important role in the selection of parliamentary candidates, the presidential nominee can campaign with a unified platform and coherent set of policies. In presidential systems with weaker party discipline, however, legislative candidates may distance themselves from an unpopular incumbent at the head of the ticket and, indeed, from others within their own party or from incumbent politicians as a class, by focusing strategic campaigns upon local issues and their personal records of constituency service.

More detailed aspects of the ballot structure also may play an important direct role by influencing voters' decision-making processes. In presidential systems, electors have the option of splitting their vote for different levels of office. This complexity of choices is illustrated most clearly in the United States, where voters face multi-level elections with candidates ranging from the local city council, state representatives, judicial office, gubernatorial contestants, and nominees for the House and Senate, all the way up to the president and vice president. Multi-level ballots can be expected to weaken partisanship, by encouraging candidates to make localized personal appeals. Presidential elections held under Second Ballot systems are designed to weaken allegiance to smaller parties by encouraging coalitions between left-wing and right-wing coalitions to achieve an overall majority. By contrast, in parliamentary general elections under PR list and majoritarian systems, voters face the single choice of either a party list or a party candidate for parliament. European general elections can be held in conjunction with those for other levels of office, including for the president in France and the prime minister in Israel, but even so, there are far fewer elected offices in European democracies than in the United States, and elections in Europe are held normally at less frequent intervals.[24] Given these considerations, it is not surprising that partisanship proves stronger in parliamentary than in presidential systems.

The last comparison in Figure 6.2 shows the patterns of partisanship broken down by major world region. The results show that partisanship was strongest in North America and Scandinavia. Interestingly, it was slightly weaker in Western Europe and similar to the levels found in Central and Eastern Europe and the Asia-Pacific region. Although we might expect that parties would have far stronger roots in Western European nations, where there is a long tradition of free and fair elections and parties have historical roots dating back sometimes more than a century, nevertheless, patterns are similar in the post-Communist nations under comparison. Partisan identification proves weakest of all in the South American nations, namely Chile and Peru, although this could be affected by the fact that both elections under analysis in this region were for presidential office. Data for a wider range of nations and elections that is more generally representative of different world regions is needed before we can establish more reliable generalizations about these patterns.

Party Systems

The strength of attachments also could plausibly be influenced by many aspects of political parties, including their mass-branch organization and the

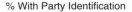

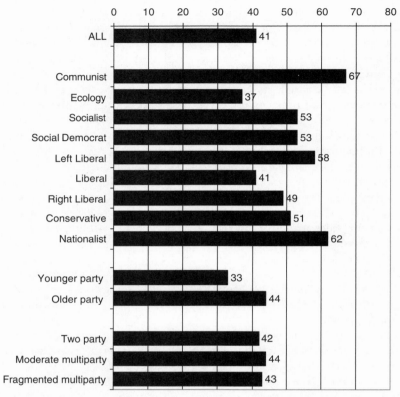

FIGURE 6.3. Party characteristics of partisans. *Note:* Q: *"Do you usually think of yourself as close to any particular political party?"* (% '*Yes*'). The differences between groups are all significant at the .001 level using Cramer's V. *Source:* Comparative Study of Electoral Systems, Module I, 1996–2002.

strength of their links with other groups in the community. Here we can compare the type of party family based on how people voted; as expected, the pattern in Figure 6.3 confirms that party identification was strongest among the most ideologically polarized parties, including among reformed Communist parties on the far left as well as among the nationalist far right. About two-thirds of people who voted for these parties also expressed a party identification. More centrist or moderate parties attracted slightly fewer party identifiers, while Liberal and Ecology parties attracted the weakest partisan attachments. As will be observed later, even clearer patterns are evident if we compare the position of respondents on the left–right ideological scale. We would expect supporters to be less loyal where parties focus their strategies on middle-of-the-road ideological or issue appeals, as it becomes easier for voters to switch among contestants. Where parties compete in the middle or center ground, so that voters cannot perceive much difference between them, this generates fewer hurdles to switching parties, and partisan loyalties prove weaker voting anchors. This pattern may be particularly important today when many of the classic economic and foreign policy issues that formerly divided left and right are no longer so salient, following the end of the Cold War, and where newer issues that cross-cut the old left–right cleavage have risen on the policy agenda, exemplified by public concern about terrorism, environmental protection, and globalization. We find stronger patterns of party attachments where parties are more ideologically polarized because in this context higher barriers exist to switching between or among parties.

The historical traditions and longevity of party organizations should play an important role in the strength of partisan attachments. As expected, older parties (defined as those established for at least twenty years or more) attracted more party identifiers than did younger parties founded more recently. Moreover, this is not just a matter of contrasts between older and newer democracies, as there are considerable variations in the longevity of parties, even within Western Europe and North America. Although there have been major changes in the composition of American parties, their basic identities and labels remain some of the oldest in the world. Elsewhere party systems usually have seen far greater innovations, exemplified by developments in the Netherlands, Belgium, or Canada, with older parties occasionally fading away or splitting into different factions, and newer parties emerging into prominence.

Party competition also could play a role, and, as discussed earlier in Chapter 4, the effective number of parliamentary parties varies substantially in the countries under comparison. Yet the pattern in Figure 6.3 shows that, by itself, the type of party system did not show a substantial difference in the strength of partisan attachments.

Social Structure and Partisanship

Social psychological accounts suggest many reasons why the strength of partisanship should vary according to the social and political characteristics of citizens. In particular, Dalton argues that we would expect partisanship to play the strongest role in voting decisions among the least educated and politically informed groups, who lack cognitive skills and, therefore, have most need to rely upon partisan shortcuts.[25] Because education is related closely to other indicators of SES, partisanship also should be associated with patterns of social class and household income. If habits develop over time, we would also expect that partisanship should be least developed among the younger

% With Party Identification

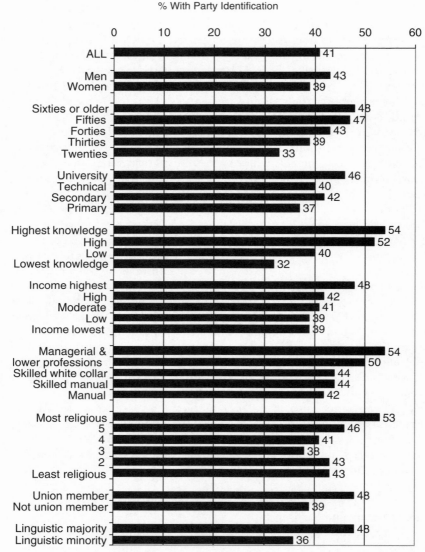

FIGURE 6.4. Social characteristics of partisans. *Note:* Q: "*Do you usually think of yourself as close to any particular political party?*" (% '*Yes*'). The differences between groups are all significant at the .001 level using Cramer's V. *Source:* Comparative Study of Electoral Systems, Module I, 1996–2002.

generation of citizens, and these attachments are expected to strengthen with age, as many previous studies have found.[26] Voter–party bonds also are expected to be stronger among those who belong to voluntary organizations and community associations, such as trade unions and churches, if social networks and membership of these organizations function to reinforce political attitudes among like-minded groups. Identification with a particular party also should be stronger among those who hold positive orientations toward parties in general.

The patterns evident in Figure 6.4 show that partisanship was, indeed, stronger by age group, as expected, with a substantial 15-point gap between the youngest cohort and those over age sixty. Partisanship was also more advanced among those with ties to affiliated organizations such as unions and churches. But contrary to Dalton's suggestions, partisan attachments were stronger among the well-educated, as well as among the highest income and class groups and among those who scored highest on political knowledge tests (although this latter association could be interpreted as the product of partisanship, if party ties generate greater interest in public affairs, as much as its cause). Partisan ties also were slightly stronger among men than women. What this social profile suggests is that general party loyalties tend to reflect the type of characteristics that also predict more active engagement in parties as members or as activists.[27] In this regard, it might be more appropriate to understand partisanship as an orientation similar to political participation, so that a similar range of factors predict whether someone is close to a party and whether she or he will vote.

Political Attitudes and Partisanship

The political characteristics in Figure 6.5 confirm the patterns that many others have noted, with partisanship associated with many indicators of system support, although here the question of the direction of causality is open to interpretation. A sense of closeness to a particular party could lead people to be more likely to participate, to have a sense of efficacy and the belief that they can influence the political process, and to display greater satisfaction both with democracy in general and with the fairness of the electoral process. Alternatively, those who display these characteristics also are more likely to feel close to one of the parties, as this is another form of positive engagement with the political process. Probably, a reciprocal process is at work here that cannot be disentangled without either time-series panel surveys or careful experimental designs.

The political profile also confirms the observation that ideology plays a critical role, with those who place themselves at either the far left or far right displaying the strongest sense of partisanship. By contrast, those who see themselves in the moderate center of the political spectrum have the lowest

% With Party Identification

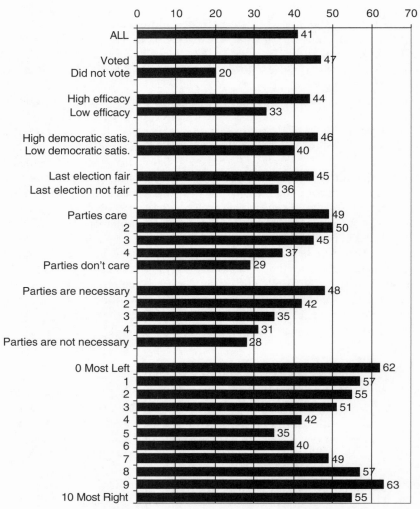

FIGURE 6.5. The political characteristics of partisans. *Note:* Q: "*Do you usually think of yourself as close to any particular political party?*" (% 'Yes'). *Source:* Comparative Study of Electoral Systems, Module I, 1996–2002.

feelings of partisanship. To confirm these overall patterns, Table 6.1 used binary logistic regression models comparing the influence of the social and attitudinal predictors of partisanship, using the pooled sample of legislative elections. All these factors prove to be significant, as predicted, with the coefficients pointing in the expected direction.

TABLE 6.1. *Baseline Models Predicting Partisanship, Pooled Legislative Elections*

	Model A Social Structure			Model C Plus Political Attitudes			Coding
	B	S.E.	Sig.	B	S.E.	Sig.	
SOCIAL STRUCTURE							
Age	.01	.001	***	.01	.001	***	A2001 Years old.
Sex (Male)	.11	.025	***	.11	.026	***	A2002 Male = 1/Female = 0.
Education	.17	.013	***	.17	.013	***	A2003 Highest level of education of respondent. Primary 1, secondary 2, post-secondary technical 3, university 4.
Income	.05	.010	***	.06	.010	***	A2012 5-point scale of household income from lowest to highest quintile.
Union member	.15	.028	***	.14	.026	***	A2005 Respondent is union member 1, else 0.
Linguistic majority	.56	.025	***	.58	.007	***	A2018 Language usually spoken at home. Linguistic majority 1, else 0.
Religiosity	.10	.007	***	.09	.011	***	A2015 6-point strength of religiosity scale from never attend religious service (1) to attend at least weekly (6).
PARTISAN ATTITUDES							
Parties care				.17	.012	***	"Political parties in [country] care what ordinary people think." % Agree
Parties necessary				.13	.009	***	"Political parties are necessary to make our political system work in [country]." % Agree
Ideological extremism				.27	.091	***	A3031 Position respondents placed themselves on the 10-point left–right scale, recoded from moderate center (1) to extreme (5).
Constant	−2.0			−3.7			
% Correctly predicted	59%			63%			Proportion of cases correctly predicted by the model.
Nagelkerke R²	.06			.13			Overall variance explained by the model.

Notes: The figures represent the results of binary logistic regression models including unstandardized beta coefficients (B), standardized error (S.E.), and their significance (Sig): ***p.001 **p.01 *p.05. Partisan identity: The dependent variable is coded from the following item: *"Do you usually think of yourself as close to any particular political party?"* The pooled sample of legislative elections includes 28 nations and 31,124 respondents. Data was weighted by sample (A1041) to ensure that the size of the sample is equal per nation.

Source: Comparative Study of Electoral Systems, Module I, 1996–2002.

Partisan Identities and Voting Choice

But do partisan identities help to explain voting choices in the different countries under comparison? The baseline regression models of voting behavior in Table 6.2 first entered the structural controls of age, gender, education, income, union membership, linguistic majorities, religiosity, and left–right ideology, using the measures that were discussed in the previous chapter. I have established already the importance of these factors in determining voting choice, and they also can be expected to exert a similar influence on partisanship. Model B then entered the party that respondents felt closest toward, after recoding to reflect the left–right scale of voting choice. The results confirm that even with the prior social controls, the direction of partisan identification played a major role in voting decisions, with the amount of variance explained by the models rising from 8% in Model A to 83% for the combined effects of social structure and partisan identities in Model B. Nevertheless, I need to note an important qualification to interpreting these results. If party attachments are understood, as social psychological accounts claim, as an affective general orientation toward parties, then the results suggest that they still remain capable of exerting an important influence on voting choice. If, alternatively, we interpret these partisan identities as essentially co-varying with voter choice, as revisionist accounts caution, then including these measures in models of voting choice provides little additional explanatory power.

But to what extent can variations in the degree to which these models predict voting behavior in different nations be explained? On the one hand, theories of cultural modernization suggest that we should observe important contrasts by the basic type of society, in particular, that patterns of human development and rising education levels and cognitive skills should have gradually reduced reliance upon party loyalties. If so, partisan identification should exert a stronger influence upon voting behavior in industrialized than in postindustrial nations. On the other hand, if incentives matter, then we expect to find important differences among elections using different types of electoral rules. One expects homebase appeals and, therefore, partisan identities to be stronger under PR than under catch-all parties in majoritarian systems. Table 6.3 replicates the baseline voting model in all the elections under comparison, showing just the summary amount of variance explained by social structure (in Model A) and by both partisan attachments and social structure (in Model B). Table 6.3 shows that countries vary substantially in the degree to which voting behavior can be explained by the combination of these two factors. In many elections, exemplified by those in the Czech Republic, Sweden, and Hungary, social structure and partisan identities can account for more than 90% of the variance in voting choice, without the need to bring in other medium- or short-term factors such as the record of the incumbent administration, the type of issues that feature in

TABLE 6.2. *Baseline Models Predicting Right-Wing Voting Support, Pooled Legislative Elections*

	Model A Social Structure				Model B Social Structure Plus Partisan Identification				Coding
	B	S.E.	Beta	Sig.	B	S.E.	Beta	Sig.	
SOCIAL STRUCTURE									
Age	-.010	.001	-.07	***	.000	.001	-.01		A2001 Years old.
Sex (Male)	.310	.045	.06	***	.007	.020	.01		A2002 Male = 1/Female = 0.
Education	.049	.023	.02	*	.035	.010	.02	**	A2003 Highest level of education of respondent. Primary 1, secondary 2, post-secondary technical 3, university 4.
Income	.093	.017	.05	***	.006	.008	.01		A2012 5-point scale of household income from lowest to highest quintile.
Religiosity	.366	.012	.27	***	.024	.006	.02	***	A2015 6-point strength of religiosity scale from never attend religious service (1) to attend at least weekly (6).
PARTISANSHIP									
Partisan identification					.908	.004	.90	***	*"Do you usually think of yourself as close to any particular political party?"* If 'yes,' *"Which party is that?"* Parties were recoded on a 10-point scale from left (0) to right (10).
Constant	4.53				.360				
Adjusted R²	.076				.826				

Notes: The figures represent the results of ordinary least square (OLS) multiple regression analysis models including unstandardized beta coefficients (B), standardized error (S.E.), standardized beta coefficients (Beta) and their significance (Sig.): ***p<.001 **p<.01 *p<.05. Voting Choice: For the dependent measure, votes for each party family are recoded using a 10-point scale ranging from left (low) to right (high) as follows: (1) Communist, (2) Ecology, (3) Socialist, (4) Social Democrat, (5) Left-liberal, (6) Liberal, (7) Christian Democrat, (8) Right-liberal, (9) Conservative, and (10) Nationalist/Religious. A positive coefficient indicates support for parties on the right. The pooled sample of legislative elections includes 28 nations and 17,794 respondents. Data was weighted by sample (A1014_1) to ensure that the size of the sample is equal per nation. Party Identification: *"Do you usually think of yourself as close to any particular political party?"* If 'yes,' *"Which party is that?"* Parties are recoded into a 10-point scale using the same classification as voting choice.

Source: Comparative Study of Electoral Systems, Module 1, 1996–2002.

TABLE 6.3. *Social Structure, Partisan Identification, and Left–Right Voting Support in 37 Legislative and Presidential Elections*

	Model A	Model B	
	Social Structure and L–R Vote (i)	Increase When Party ID is Added (ii)	Total Variance Social Structure + Party ID (iii)
	Adj. R²	Adj. R²	Adj. R²
Czech Rep.	0.64	0.32	0.97
Sweden	0.67	0.27	0.94
Hungary	0.42	0.50	0.92
Ukraine	0.53	0.35	0.88
Iceland	0.62	0.25	0.87
Netherlands	0.54	0.33	0.87
Germany (p)	0.41	0.46	0.87
Israel (p)	0.65	0.22	0.86
Britain	0.39	0.47	0.86
Norway	0.50	0.35	0.86
Denmark	0.14	0.69	0.83
Switzerland	0.50	0.31	0.81
Russia	0.27	0.54	0.80
United States (p)	0.30	0.51	0.80
Israel	0.50	0.30	0.80
Australia	0.21	0.59	0.80
Poland	0.46	0.31	0.77
Portugal	0.07	0.70	0.77
Peru (p)	0.04	0.72	0.76
Belgium	0.19	0.56	0.75
Taiwan	0.08	0.66	0.74
Japan	0.01	0.69	0.70
Slovenia	0.12	0.58	0.70
Mexico	0.06	0.63	0.69
Canada	0.13	0.54	0.68
Lithuania (p)	0.51	0.16	0.67
New Zealand	0.32	0.34	0.66
Taiwan (p)	0.03	0.63	0.65
United States	0.21	0.42	0.63
Spain	0.33	0.25	0.58
Romania	0.08	0.51	0.58
Korea	0.06	0.47	0.53
Peru	0.01	0.49	0.50
Romania (p)	0.10	0.37	0.47
Belarus (p)	0.32	0.11	0.43
Chile (p)	0.42	0.01	0.43
Mexico (p)	0.01	0.09	0.10

Notes: (i) Model A: The amount of variance (Adjusted R²) in ordinary least square (OLS) regression analysis models explained by the effects of social structure including sex, age, education, income, union membership, linguistic majority, and religiosity on the left–right voting scale. For the items and coding see Table 6.1. (ii) Model B: The increase in the amount of variance when partisan identification is added to the models. (iii) Model B: The total amount of variance explained by social structure and party identification. Voting scale: For the dependent measure, votes for each party family in legislative and presidential elections are recoded using a 10-point scale from left (low) to right (high) as follows: (1) Communist, (2) Ecology, (3) Socialist, (4) Social Democrat, (5) Left-liberal, (6) Liberal, (7) Christian Democrat, (8) Right-liberal, (9) Conservative, (10) Nationalist/Religious. Party Identification: *"Do you usually think of yourself as close to any particular political party?"* If 'yes,' *"Which party is that?"* Parties are recoded into a 10-point scale using the same classification as voting choice. (p) Presidential elections. Significance: ***p.001 **p.01 *p.05.

Source: Comparative Study of Electoral Systems, Module I, 1996–2002.

TABLE 6.4. *Mean Variance in Voting Behavior Explained by Social Structure and Party Identities*

	Model A	Model B		
	Social Structure (%)	Party Identification (%)	Total Combined Social Structure and Party (%)	Number of Elections (N)
	(i)	(ii)	(iii)	
Cultural Modernization				
Postindustrial	33	44	77	20
Industrial	24	41	65	17
Electoral System				
Majoritarian	25	37	63	13
Combined	24	52	76	9
PR	36	41	77	15

Notes: Calculated from Tables 5.2 and 6.3, in 37 legislative and presidential elections. (i) Model A: The amount of variance on the left–right voting scale (Adjusted R^2) in ordinary least square (OLS) regression analysis models explained by the effects of social structure including sex, age, education, income, union membership, linguistic majority, and religiosity. (ii) Model B: The increase in the amount of variance in voting behavior when partisan identification is added to the models. (iii) Model B: The total amount of variance in voting behavior explained by the combined effects of social structure and party identification. PR, Proportional Representation.
Source: Comparative Study of Electoral Systems, Module I, 1996–2002.

the campaign, or the personalities of the party leaders. Although there is substantial evidence that dealignment may have weakened social and partisan identities, nevertheless, in these societies citizens continue to behave in ways predicted by the classic theories of voting behavior established more than four decades ago. Nevertheless, there are many other elections under comparison where these factors seem to exert little grip on the outcome, notably those in Belarus, Chile, and Mexico. In these cases, we need to turn to other types of factors such as the personality of political leaders, the government's economic record, or the type of election campaign to account for voting behavior.

Table 6.4 summarizes the key comparisons by type of electoral system and by type of society. If cultural modernization theories are correct then we should find that party and social identities remain stronger anchors of voting behavior in industrialized societies but that these influences should be weaker in postindustrial nations. Instead the results show that the impact of party attachments on electoral choice proved marginally higher (44%) in postindustrial than in industrial societies (41%), a modest difference, but one in the *contrary* direction to that predicted by theories of cultural modernization. Figure 6.6 illustrates the variance by type of society. Alternatively, if incentive-based theories are correct then we would expect the main

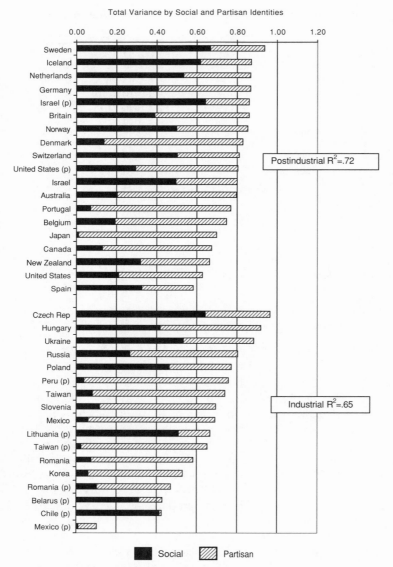

FIGURE 6.6. Total variance produced by social and partisan identities, by type of society. *Note:* (p), presidential.

contrasts to lie between majoritarian electoral systems promoting catch-all vote-maximizing campaign strategies and PR list systems that facilitate more niche-marketing home-base appeals. And, indeed, this is what one finds, as illustrated in Figure 6.7, which compares the combined effects of social and

Total Variance Produced by Social and Partisan Identities

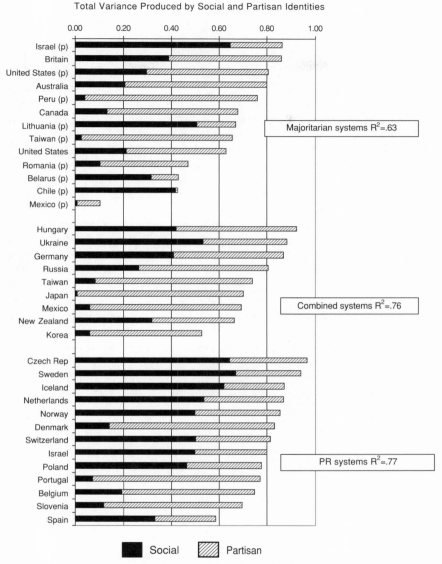

FIGURE 6.7. Total variance produced by social and partisan identities, by electoral system. *Note:* PR, Proportional Representation.

partisan identities. The total variance explained by these factors (derived from the final column of Model B) was 63% on average in elections held under majoritarian rules, significantly less than in combined systems (76%) and in PR list systems (77%). That is to say, social structure and partisan attachments explained two-thirds of the variance in voting behavior under majoritarian rules and more than three-quarters in combined and PR systems.

Yet certain important qualifications need to be made to these results. Given the limited range of nations and elections, these summary figures should be regarded with considerable caution, and it remains to be seen whether these generalizations remain robust when tested with a broader range of contexts. As the figures show, there are also substantial differences among elections within each type of electoral system, rather than a wholly consistent pattern. Other factors exogenous to the model, and well beyond the scope of this study, such as the government's record, leadership popularity, and economic performance, also contribute toward comprehensive explanations of these patterns. The main variance in voting behavior among elections comes from the *combined* effects of social plus partisan identification, rather than from the latter alone. Yet the summary results lend further confirmation to the basic pattern established in the previous chapter, with the combined effects of social structure and party identities exerting a weaker influence upon voting behavior in majoritarian electoral systems than in proportional systems. The rational-choice institutionalism theory suggests that this pattern can best be understood through the way that the electoral system has a direct impact upon the incentives facing parties and, therefore, an indirect impact upon voting behavior.

From the analysis presented so far in this study I have established a fairly predictable pattern of voting behavior in the electorate. But do electoral systems and detailed voting procedures exert an important influence, not on *whom* people vote for but on whether they cast a ballot at all? I turn next to this topic.

7

Turnout

In many established democracies, concern about eroding participation at the ballot box has been expressed widely, with commentators suggesting that we are seeing the "vanishing voter," especially in America.[1] Yet patterns of voting turnout in the United States are far from typical and, indeed, always have been during the postwar era. Levels of electoral participation today vary dramatically among democracies. In the countries under comparison, on average more than 80% of the voting age population (VAP) turned out in legislative elections held during the 1990s in Iceland, Israel, and Sweden, compared with less than half of the equivalent group in the United States and Switzerland (see Figure 7.1). The comparison shows that turnout cannot simply be explained by differences in the historical experiences of older and newer democracies, as the Czech Republic, Chile, and South Korea all rank in the top third of the comparison, whereas the United States, Canada, and Japan lag near the bottom. Worldwide there are even greater disparities, with more than 90% of the voting age population (Vote/VAP) participating in legislative elections during the last decade in Malta, Uruguay, and Indonesia, compared with less than a third in Mali, Colombia, and Senegal. To explain these patterns, the first part of this chapter considers accounts based on rational-choice institutionalism and the cultural modernization theories. The second part examines the evidence and analyzes the extent to which turnout varies by political institutions, by electoral laws, and by voting procedures, as well as by the social characteristics and cultural attitudes of voters, and by levels of societal modernization. The conclusion considers the implications of the findings for electoral engineering, including to what degree attempts to boost voting participation through electoral reform and civic education can hope to succeed.

Mean Vote/VAP, 1990s

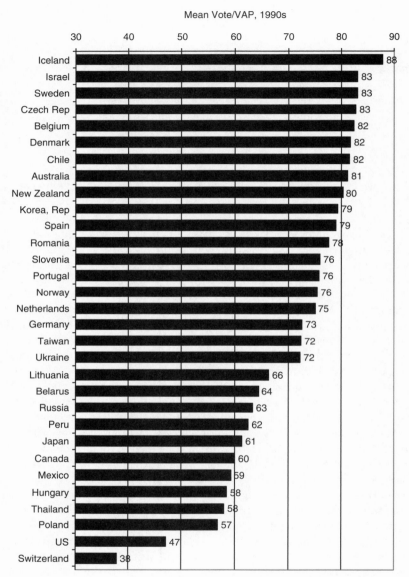

FIGURE 7.1. Votes cast as a proportion of the voting age population, 1990s. *Note:* Mean Vote/VAP is measured as the number of valid votes as a proportion of the Voting Age Population in parliamentary elections during the 1990s held in the 32 nations in the CSES dataset under comparison. VAP, Voting Age Population. *Source:* International IDEA database, *Voter Turnout from 1945 to 2000.* Available online at www.idea.int.

Rational-Choice and Cultural Modernization Theories of Voting Participation

Comparative research has long sought to understand the reasons for voting participation and the explanations for cross-national differences in turnout.[2] As noted in previous chapters, debate surrounds the extent to which this process is affected by the strategic incentives derived from electoral rules and by the cultural habits arising from the socialization process and societal modernization.

The Costs and Benefits of Participation

Attempts at constitutional engineering are based on the premise that the electoral design can shape the behavior of parties, candidates, and citizens. Rational-choice accounts emphasize that taken-for-granted institutions, rules, and regulations are not neutral in outcome; instead they set the context through facilitating participation for some actors while discouraging or restricting others. Three types of factors are believed to be important: (1) political institutions set the broadest context, most distant from the specific act of casting a ballot, including arrangements such as the type of electoral system, whether the executive is presidential or parliamentary, and the type of party system; (2) the legal system determines more specific features of electoral regulations, exemplified by the use of compulsory voting laws and the age qualifications for suffrage; last, (3) electoral administrative procedures are most proximate to the act of voting, such as registration processes, the distribution of polling stations, and the facilities for voting. These factors could shape the behavior of political actors *indirectly*; in majoritarian electoral systems, for example, minor parties could decide to focus their effort and resources in their strongest target seats, rather than campaigning across the country. In countries with compulsory voting laws, parties may invest less effort in get-out-the-vote drives. These factors could also influence citizens *directly*, through shaping the costs and benefits of voting.

Many comparative studies have emphasized the importance of the institutional and legal arrangements for electoral activism, suggesting that rules do matter. Hence, Powell established that turnout in established democracies was boosted by the use of compulsory voting laws, by automatic registration procedures, and by the strength of party-group alignments, whereas it was depressed in one-party predominant systems allowing no rotation of the parties in government.[3] Jackman and Miller confirmed that political institutions and electoral laws provided the most plausible explanation for variations in voter turnout, including levels of electoral proportionality, multipartyism, and the use of compulsory voting.[4] Blais and Dobrzynska analyzed voter turnout as a proportion of the registered electorate in parliamentary elections in 91 democracies from 1972 to 1995 and concluded that turnout was influenced by the use of compulsory voting, the age at which citizens became eligible to vote, the type of electoral system, the closeness of the electoral outcome, and the number of parties, as well as by levels of socioeconomic development and the size of the country.[5] Franklin analyzed postwar elections in 22 established democracies and argued that an important part of the reason for any decline in turnout during the last decade concerned changes in the institutional context, such as the abandonment of compulsory voting laws and the lowering of the age of qualifying for the franchise, yet the impact of any such changes was lagged rather than immediate, as there was a cohort effect upon new generations entering the electorate.[6] In the United States as well, turnout is believed to be depressed by the hurdle of registration requirements, where the onus lies with the applicant, generating attempts at partial reforms such as the "Motor Voter" initiative.[7] Yet even if "institutions matter" it remains unclear *why* they matter, whether because they reinforce and reflect long-term cultural habits and taken-for-granted traditions within each society, or because they alter the rational calculus when voters decide whether to participate. Moreover, the link between the broader cultural context, and how voters perceive and weigh the costs, choices, and decisiveness of elections, is only poorly understood.

Cultural Modernization, Civic Skills, and Motivational Attitudes

Theories of cultural modernization advanced by Ronald Inglehart and Russell Dalton, discussed in the introduction to this book, suggest that common social trends, including rising affluence, the growth of the service sector, and expanded educational opportunities, have swept through postindustrial societies, contributing toward a new style of citizen politics in Western democracies.[8] This process is believed to have increased demands for more active public participation in the policymaking process through direct action, new social movements, and protest groups, as well as weakened deferential loyalties and support for traditional organizations such as churches, parties, and unions, and also eroded conventional participation via the ballot box.[9] Growing levels of human capital are regarded as critical to this process because education, and the cognitive skills that it provides, is one of the factors that most strongly predict political activism.[10] If this process is, indeed, critical, as theorists suggest, then we would expect to find different patterns of electoral participation in industrial and in postindustrial societies.

Rather than calculating consciously the potential rewards and benefits of voting, cultural accounts emphasize that the propensity to participate or abstain is a habit of the heart acquired early in life and reinforced through experience of successive elections, along with other closely related civic attitudes and values such as partisan attachments and political trust. In this view, some people will turn out to vote through rain or shine because they are interested in public affairs, they believe it is their civic duty to vote, they want to express support for a particular party, or they want to express disapproval of the incumbent's performance, irrespective of whether they believe that the vote "matters" by influencing which particular candidate or party gets elected. Indeed, because one vote will not determine the outcome, as Downs argued, if voters are calculating the strategic benefits of casting a ballot for maximizing their interests, the well-known "paradox" of elections is why anyone votes at all.[11] Cultural theories stress that habits of civic engagement take many years to become engrained over successive elections, so that attempts to boost turnout by administrative fixes and legal modifications, such as the simplification of registration procedures through the Motor Voter Act in the United States, the introduction of all-postal ballots in Oregon, or the use of Internet voting in Geneva, are misguided and impractical. Cultural theories suggest that although institutional reforms are unlikely to achieve their goals in the short term, in the longer term they may have a more glacial impact, if younger generations gradually start to participate at higher levels by using the new opportunities, and the process of demographic replacement eventually transforms the composition of the electorate. This process is exemplified clearly by the expansion of the franchise to women because it took many decades after the franchise was granted before women achieved parity with men at the ballot box, before eventually overtaking them.[12] Moreover, if the early socialization process stamps the younger generation with participatory habits, then it follows that civic education is one of the most important mechanisms available for encouraging political engagement, by influencing what children learn about democracy and citizenship in schools while habits remain plastic and fluid.[13]

Ever since Almond and Verba's *Civic Culture* (1963), a long series of studies have stressed that political participation requires motivational attitude, as well as possession of the resources that facilitate civic engagement.[14] This perspective suggests that psychological orientation toward the political system and participatory habits are learned at an early age from parents, teachers, colleagues, and neighbors, when people are open to change. Among these civic attitudes, Almond and Verba emphasized three elements: (1) *cognitive* orientations, which include knowledge and beliefs about the nation-state, political leaders, and major policy issues, as well as an awareness of citizens' rights; (2) *affective* orientations toward the political system, which include the belief that citizens are competent and capable of influencing the democratic process (termed *internal political efficacy* or *subjective competence*), the sense that government is responsive to public needs and demands (*external political efficacy*), and interest in politics and public affairs; and (3) *evaluative* orientations, which concern judgments about the political process, such as the fairness of elections or the performance of government.[15] Lack of trust and confidence in government also has been regarded as depressing activism because the rising tide of political cynicism in the United States occurred during roughly the same period as the fall in turnout, although others have argued that dissatisfaction may have the reverse effect by stimulating involvement.[16] For Almond and Verba, the civic culture works most effectively where the predominant psychological orientations are congruent with the political system.

Resources are also regarded as important because time, money, and civic skills, derived from family, occupation, and associational membership, make it easier for individuals who are predisposed to take part to do so. The fact that resources are distributed unevenly throughout societies helps to explain the disparities in participation related to gender, race/ethnicity, age, and social class. Education, in particular, is one of the best predictors of many types of civic engagement, furnishing cognitive skills and civic awareness that allow citizens to make sense of the political world and increase feelings of subjective competence.[17] People of higher SES – in terms of education, income, and occupation – are commonly far more active in politics. The most thorough study of generational trends in the United States, by Miller and Shanks, emphasized that a long-term secular trend generated turnout decline, with the post-New Deal generation consistently less likely to vote than their fathers or grandfathers. This phenomenon was not a product of life-cycle, or aging, they suggest, but rather represents an enduring shift among the generation who first came to political consciousness during the turbulent politics of the 1960s. The long-term slide in American turnout, they conclude, is due to the process of generational replacement, not to a fall in the propensity of the older generations to turnout: *"It was the gradual replacement of the habitual voters of the pre-New Deal generations with the non-voting post-New Deal cohorts that produced the thirty-year national decline in aggregate voter turnout from the early 1960s to the late 1980s."*[18] More recently, Robert Putnam has presented a formidable battery of evidence illustrating lower levels of civic engagement among the postwar generation, including electoral participation.[19] In a comparative study, Franklin also emphasizes the role of generational cohorts in "dampening" the effects of any institutional reforms.[20] If *culture* were important, then we would expect to see considerable variations in voting participation evident at individual-level, associated with patterns of education, age, and SES, as well as a strong relationship between turnout and motivational attitudes such as political efficacy and partisan identification. If cultural *modernization* is important, then we would also expect that patterns of turnout would vary systematically with levels of human development in different societies, as greater human capital (education and cognitive skills) would contribute toward rising levels of citizen activism.

Analyzing Turnout

Multivariate models help us to evaluate the evidence for these accounts. If voters respond to electoral rules, then levels of turnout should vary systematically under different institutional arrangements. If societal modernization affects the civic culture, then national levels of human development, as well as individual civic resources and attitudes, should predict turnout. To test the evidence for these propositions, binary logistic regression analysis is used where the dependent variable is whether the respondent reported voting or not in the legislative elections in the countries under comparison in the CSES dataset. As with other surveys, levels of reported turnout were nearly always slightly higher in each country than the official estimate of either the votes cast as a proportion of the voting age population (Vote/VAP) or as a proportion of the registered electorate (Vote/Reg). Model A in Table 7.1 first entered levels of human development, then added the main political institutions commonly thought to influence electoral participation, for reasons discussed fully later. These include whether the electoral system is majoritarian, combined, or proportional; the average population size of electoral districts; the frequency of national elections; the use of any compulsory voting regulations; whether the political system has a presidential or parliamentary executive; patterns of party competition (measured by the percentage vote for the party in first place); and the type of party system (measured by ENPP). After including these factors, the model explains 7% of the overall level of variance in turnout (measured by the Nagelkerke R^2). Model B then enters the social and cultural factors at individual level, including the standard factors of age, gender, education, income, union membership, and religiosity (used in earlier chapters), as well as partisan identification and external political efficacy, explaining in total 20% of the variance in turnout. This suggests that Model B improves the goodness-of-fit, although many other factors not included in this limited analysis also influence political participation, including the role of mobilizing agencies such as parties, social networks, and the news media.[21]

Overall, the models suggest that the institutional context and the cultural factors contribute about equally toward explaining voting turnout. In the countries under comparison, all other things being equal, among the *political institutions* that matter, voting participation is likely to be maximized in elections using PR, with small electoral districts, regular but relatively infrequent national contests, and competitive party systems, and in presidential contests. But even controlling for the institutional context, there are significant inequalities in electoral participation related to human development, socioeconomic resources, and cultural attitudes. The formal rules help to determine overall levels of turnout from one country to another, but even so, within each society citizens who are more educated, affluent, and motivated remain more likely to participate than others, and activism is higher in postindustrial nations. Let us examine the meaning and interpretation of these results in more detail.

Cultural Modernization

Theories of cultural modernization advanced by Ronald Inglehart and Russell Dalton, discussed in the introduction to this book, suggest that common social trends, including rising affluence, the growth of the service sector,

TABLE 7.1. *Models Explaining Turnout, Pooled Legislative Elections*

	Model A			Model B			Coding
	b	(s.e.)	Sig.	b	(s.e.)	Sig.	
SOCIETAL MODERNIZATION							
Human development	3.02	.585	***	4.59	.621	***	Human Development Index (reversed). UNDP 2000.
INSTITUTIONAL CONTEXT							
Electoral system	.329	.035	***	.493	.038	***	Majoritarian (1), combined (2), proportional (3).
District size	−.001	.035	***	−.001	.035	***	Mean population per elected representative.
Parliamentary or presidential executive	1.505	.095	***	1.96	.105	***	Parliamentary executive (1), presidential election (0).
Frequency of national elections	−.008	.003	**	−.002	.003		Mean number of national elections (parliamentary and presidential) held during the 1990s.
Use of any compulsory voting	1.82	.106	***	1.50	.109	***	Compulsory Voting: Yes (1), No (0).
Party competition	.089	.004	***	.094	.004		Mean% vote for the party in 1st place in legislative elections during the 1990s.
Party system	.178	.013	***	.124	.014	***	Effective number of parliamentary parties (ENPP).
SOCIAL STRUCTURE							
Age				2.12	.113	***	A2001 Logged Years.
Gender				.003	.037		A2002 Male = 1, female = 0.
Education				.294	.021	***	A2003 Highest level of education of respondent. Primary 1, secondary 2, post-secondary technical 3, university 4.
Income				.102	.014	***	A2012 5-point scale of household income from lowest to highest quintile.
Union membership				.188	.047	***	Union member = 1, not = 0.
Religiosity				.095	.012	***	A2015 6-point strength of religiosity scale from never attend religious service (1) to attend at least weekly (6).

CULTURAL ATTITUDES

	b	s.e.	Sig.	
Left–right ideology	.019	.008	**	10-point self-position scale.
Party identification	.929	.040	***	"Do you usually think of yourself as close to any particular political party?" 'Yes' = 1, no = 0.
External political efficacy	.154	.009	***	10-point scale from two agree–disagree items: "Who is in power can make a difference" and "Who people vote for makes a difference."
Constant	−.467	−5.9		
% Correctly predicted	83.1	84.0		
Nagelkerke R²	*.072*	*.198*		

Notes: The table lists unstandardized logistic regression coefficients (b), standard errors (s.e.), and significance (Sig.), with reported voting turnout in legislative elections as the dependent variable in 32 nations. * = p < .05; ** p < .01; *** p < .001. Human Development: *Human Development Report 2000*, New York: United Nations Development Programme. Electoral system: See Table 2.1. Party System: See Table 4.1.

Source: Comparative Study of Electoral Systems, Module I, 1996–2002, N. 24413.

and expanded educational opportunities, have swept through postindustrial societies, contributing toward a new style of citizen politics in Western
democracies.[22] This process is believed to have increased demand for more
active public participation in the policymaking process through direct action,
demonstrations, and protest politics. Also, it is believed to have weakened deferential loyalties and support for traditional organizations such as
churches, parties and unions, and also to have eroded conventional participation in elections.[23] Growing levels of human capital are regarded as
vital because education, and the cognitive skills that it provides, strongly
predicts political activism.[24] The comparison of turnout (Vote/VAP) in legislative elections worldwide during the 1990s confirms these predictions, as
shown in Figure 7.2; overall 74% of the voting age population cast a ballot in industrial societies, compared with 80% in postindustrial societies.

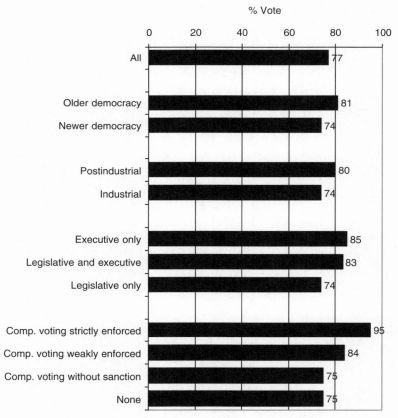

FIGURE 7.2. Systemic characteristics of turnout. Comp., Compulsory. *Source:* Comparative Study of Electoral Systems, Module I, 1996–2002.

The multivariate model in Table 7.1, using the CSES dataset, confirms that human development is significantly related to higher voting participation. As argued elsewhere, societal modernization does, indeed, matter, with the main effects of education occurring in the initial stages of the expansion of schooling and literacy in the shift from agrarian to industrial society, and the effects leveling off and, thereby, proving curvilinear at later stages of societal development.[25] That is to say, it is basic schooling and literacy that make the fundamental difference for patterns of turnout, a relatively undemanding act but one that does require some basic familiarity with the major parties and where these can be placed across the political spectrum, as well as some understanding of the electoral process. Basic education facilitates comprehension of political coverage in the news media, particularly newspapers. Further participation in college- and university-level education makes a difference for more demanding forms of civic engagement, such as protest politics, but the spread of access to higher education in a society does not in itself add incrementally to greater electoral turnout. Given the strong interrelationship between levels of economic and democratic development in the 32 nations in the CSES dataset, not surprisingly, similar patterns are evident in Figure 7.2, when turnout is compared in older and newer democracies.

The Impact of Political Institutions

Electoral Systems

Previous studies have commonly found that the type of electoral formula shapes participation, with PR systems generating higher turnout than majoritarian systems.[26] This pattern seems well supported by the evidence: Table 7.1 shows that, even after controlling for levels of human development, the basic type of electoral system remains a significant indicator of turnout. Legislative elections held during the 1990s in the CSES countries under comparison generated 75% turnout (Vote/VAP) under PR systems, 10% higher than in those elections contested in majoritarian systems, and a similar pattern was confirmed in a broader comparison of all 164 nations holding competitive elections worldwide during the 1990s. Because the type of electoral system is a categorical rather than a continuous variable, Table 7.2 provides further details about the impact of different electoral systems on worldwide levels of voter turnout in the 1990s, measured in the standard way by vote as a proportion of the voting age population (Vote/VAP) and, for comparison with some previous studies, by vote as a proportion of the registered electorate (Vote/Reg). The results without any controls confirm that average turnout (using either measure) was highest among nations using PR, namely, Party Lists and the STV electoral systems. In contrast, voter participation was fairly similar among the different types

TABLE 7.2. *Electoral Systems and Turnout Worldwide, 1990s*

Type of Electoral System	Mean Vote/VAP 1990s	Mean Vote/Reg 1990s	N.
MAJORITARIAN			
Alternative Vote	65.5	92.9	2
2nd Ballot	58.5	65.0	21
First-Past-the-Post	61.2	67.7	43
Single Non-Transferable Vote	52.6	59.8	2
Bloc Vote	56.5	70.9	9
All majoritarian	**60.4**	**68.3**	77
COMBINED			
Combined-Dependent	66.6	71.9	7
Combined-Independent	63.5	69.0	19
All combined	**64.0**	**70.4**	26
PROPORTIONAL			
List PR	70.0	74.7	59
Single Transferable Vote	83.4	81.7	2
All PR Systems	**70.0**	**74.6**	61
ALL	65.0	70.8	164

Notes: Mean Vote/VAP is measured as the number of valid votes as a proportion of the voting age population (VAP) in all nations worldwide that held parliamentary elections during the 1990s. Mean Vote/Reg is measured as the number of valid votes as a proportion of the registered electorate (Reg) in all nations worldwide that held parliamentary elections during the 1990s. N., Number of nations; PR, proportional representation.

Source: Calculated from International IDEA database, *Voter Turnout from 1945 to 2000.* Available online at www.idea.int.

of majoritarian and combined systems, with turnout across all these systems at about 7.5 to 11 points less than under PR. The results indicate that the basic type of electoral system does, indeed, shape the incentive to participate, with the key distinction between PR systems and all others. The exact reasons for this relationship remain unclear,[27] but incentive-based explanations focus on the differential rewards facing citizens under alternative electoral arrangements. Under majoritarian systems, supporters of minor and fringe parties with geographic support dispersed widely but thinly across the country, such as the Greens, may believe that casting their votes will make no difference to who wins in their constituency, still less to the overall composition of government and the policy agenda. The wasted votes argument is strongest in safe seats where the incumbent party is unlikely to be defeated. In contrast, PR elections with low vote thresholds and large district magnitudes, such as the Party Lists system used in the Netherlands, increase the opportunities for minor parties with dispersed support to enter parliament with only a modest share of the vote, and, therefore, this could increase the incentives for their supporters to participate.

Electoral Districts

Many other aspects of the electoral system could shape voter participation, such as the ballot structure, the use of open or closed party lists, and levels of proportionality, but district magnitude, and in particular, the population size of the average electoral district, can be expected to be especially important because this may determine the linkages between voters and their representatives. Observers have long noted a relationship between the size of a country and democracy, although the reasons for this association remain unclear.[28] It is possible that the smaller the number of electors per member of parliament, the greater the potential for constituency service and for elected representatives to maintain communications with local constituents, and, therefore, the higher the incentive to turnout based on any "personal" vote.[29] Voters may not be able to shape the outcome for government, but in smaller single-member or multimember districts, as I shall examine in later chapters, they may have greater information, familiarity, and contact with their elected representative or representatives, and, therefore, they may be more interested in affecting who gets into parliament.[30] The simplest way to measure district size is to divide the number of seats in the lower house of the legislature into the total population in each country. There are considerable cross-national variations in the average number of electors per representative depending upon the size of the population and the number of seats in parliament, ranging from India with 1.7 million electors per member of the Lok Sabha down to about 5,500 per MP in the Bahamas, Malta, and Cape Verde. The results in Table 7.1 confirm that, indeed, the size of electoral districts proved a significant predictor of turnout, in a negative direction, with smaller districts generally associated with higher voter participation.

Presidential versus Parliamentary Executives

Another factor commonly believed to influence the incentives to turnout concerns the power and level of the office and, in particular, whether there is a parliamentary or presidential (or directly elected) executive. *First-order elections* are the most important national contests, including legislative elections in countries with parliamentary systems of government and presidential contests in countries with strong presidencies. In contrast, *second-order* elections are all others, including state, provincial, or local contests, referenda, and initiatives, and direct elections to the European Parliament among the 15-member European Union states.[31] In parliamentary systems, the head of government – such as the prime minister, premier, or chancellor – is selected by the legislature and can be dismissed by a legislative vote of no confidence. In presidential systems (in the case of Israel, direct elections for the prime minister), the head of government is popularly elected for a fixed term and is not dependent upon the legislature.[32] Rational-choice theory suggests that the incentive to vote is likely to be greatest with the most salient elections determining the composition of government. In countries with presidential systems of government where elections for the president and legislature are held on separate occasions, like the mid-term elections in the United States, more people are likely to participate in executive rather than in legislative contests. Where presidential and parliamentary elections are held on the same date then there is likely to be no substantial difference in levels of turnout in both types of contest. The result of the analysis presented in Table 7.1 confirms that overall turnout was significantly higher in legislative contests with parliamentary executives than in countries with presidential executives, where these become second-order contests. In the countries under comparison in the CSES dataset, turnout was 85% in executive-only elections, 83% in elections combining legislative and executive office, and 74% in legislative-only contests.

Frequency of Contests

The frequency of elections has also been thought to be important for participation because this increases the costs facing electors and may produce voting fatigue. Franklin et al. have demonstrated that the closeness of national elections immediately before direct elections to the European Parliament is a strong predictor of turnout in European elections.[33] The cases of Switzerland and the United States are cited commonly as exemplifying nations with frequent elections for office at multiple levels, as well as with widespread use of referenda and initiatives, and both are characterized by exceptionally low voter participation among Western democracies.[34] California, for example, has primary and general elections for local and state government, including for judicial, mayoral, and gubernatorial offices, congressional midterm elections every two years for the House and Senate, presidential elections every four years, as well as multiple referenda issues on the ballot, all producing what Anthony King has termed the "never-ending election campaign."[35] If the frequency of elections generates voter fatigue, the increase in contests associated with the growth of primaries in the United States after 1968, the introduction of direct elections to the European Parliament in 1979, and contests for regional bodies following devolution and decentralization in countries such as Spain, France, and the United Kingdom could help to explain any decline in turnout in recent decades. A simple measure of electoral frequency can be calculated by the number of national-level parliamentary and presidential elections held during the decade of the 1990s, ranging from only one contest in a few semidemocracies to up to seven or more elections in the United States and Taiwan. It should be noted that this measure provides the most consistent and reliable cross-national indicator that is available, although it is likely to represent a conservative estimate since it does not count many other types of contest held during this decade including national or local referenda and initiatives, pre-nomination primaries, or European, regional/state, and local contests. The results in

Table 7.1 confirm that the frequency of national elections was strong and significant, in a negative direction: the more often national elections are held, the greater the voter fatigue. This result is likely to provide important clues to some of the sharpest outliers in turnout in the elections under comparison, such as Switzerland and the United States, both among the richest and most developed countries on earth yet characterized by relatively low levels of voter participation.

Political Parties

As we have seen in Chapter 4, the type of party system and patterns of electoral competition are related closely to the basic type of electoral system, although there is not a perfect one-to-one fit. Ever since Duverger, it is well known that the plurality method of elections favors two-party systems, by systematically over-representing the largest party when translating votes into seats.[36] We have already demonstrated that as disproportionality rises, so the effective number of parliamentary parties falls.[37] The analysis in Chapter 4 showed that the majoritarian elections under comparison were contested by 5.2 parliamentary parties on average, compared with almost twice as many parties (9.5) in proportional systems. In Israel, for example, the May 1999 elections to the 120-member Knesset returned seventeen parties, and no single party won more than 14% of the popular vote. In the Ukraine, thirty parties and party blocs contested the 1998 parliamentary elections and, as a result, eight parties were elected via party lists and seventeen won seats via the single-member districts, along with 116 Independents.[38] By contrast, in the 1996 U.S. midterm elections, while some minor party challengers such as the Greens contested a few districts, only one independent was returned to the House of Representatives. In the 2000 parliamentary elections in South Korea, the two major parties (the Grand National Party and the Millennium Democratic Party) and the minor party (United Liberal Democrats) swept up all seats. Yet there are a number of important exceptions to this rule, with plural societies such as Papua New Guinea and India characterized by multiple parties in majoritarian electoral systems, as well as Malta and Austria characterized by two-party and two-and-a-half party systems despite PR elections. Beyond the electoral formula, the electoral fortunes of smaller parties can all be shaped by the existence of social cleavages in plural societies, the geographic distribution of heterogeneous populations, the use of high voting thresholds, and the geographical drawing of constituency boundaries.[39]

The party system can, therefore, be expected to influence voter turnout, but there is little agreement in the literature about the exact nature of this relationship, and there is a complex interaction between electoral choice and electoral competition. Some suggest that the greater the range of alternative parties listed on the ballot, stretching from the nationalist far right through the moderate center to the post-Communist left, the more people are stimulated to vote.[40] This claim assumes that wider electoral choices across the ideological spectrum mean that all sectors of public opinion and all social groups are more likely to find a party to represent their views, preferences, and interests. Yet the counter argument also is heard from those who suggest that the higher the level of party fragmentation, the greater the probability of coalition government, the less the share of votes cast determines the formation of government, and, therefore, the lower the inducement for electors to turnout.[41] As Jackman has argued, voters in multiparty systems that produce coalitions do not directly choose the government that will govern them, instead they vote for the parties in the legislature that will select the government that will determine the policy agenda. Under multiparty coalitions voters appear to be offered a more decisive choice among policies, whereas, in fact, they are offered a less decisive one.[42] The range of parties contesting an election is related to levels of electoral competition. Where the outcome is anticipated to be close, this seems likely to increase the incentive to participate, while parties have greater inducements to get out the vote. To measure the party system I use the ENPP, a measure discussed in Chapter 4, as a summary indicator of the range of electoral choice: Table 7.1 confirms that in the countries under comparison the ENPP was related significantly to voting turnout, with more parties maximizing the range of choices on the ballot paper. Nevertheless, the 32 CSES nations included only a limited range of party systems, as shown in Figure 4.1, ranging from the two-party system of the U.S. Congress (with an ENPP of 1.99) through to the fragmented multipartyism of Belgium (with an ENPP of 9.05). Elsewhere in the world there are wider variations in party competition, including one-party systems where opposition movements are suppressed (such as Uganda, Zimbabwe, or Singapore) and even more extreme fragmentation. Examination of the full range of 876 parliamentary elections held worldwide from 1945 to 2000, explored elsewhere, reveals that the relationship between turnout and party competition is actually curvilinear: voting participation is depressed both by extreme fragmentation (where the leading party wins less than 30% of the vote) and (even more) by one-party predominance (where the leading party gains more than 60% of the vote).[43] In both cases, the party systems hinder the ability of citizens to generate a decisive result if their vote is an attempt to "throw the rascals out" and achieve turnover of the governing party or parties.

Although it might be thought that voters would be more easily mobilized by the more extreme parties across the ideological spectrum, Figure 7.3 shows that although there were some variations by the type of party family, the differences were fairly modest. Overall, turnout was slightly lower for the moderate liberal parties, but elsewhere across the political spectrum turnout was spread fairly evenly among parties of the left and right. Clearly, many other factors beyond the ideological position of parties may be at work here, including the party's organizational strength and ability to mobilize to

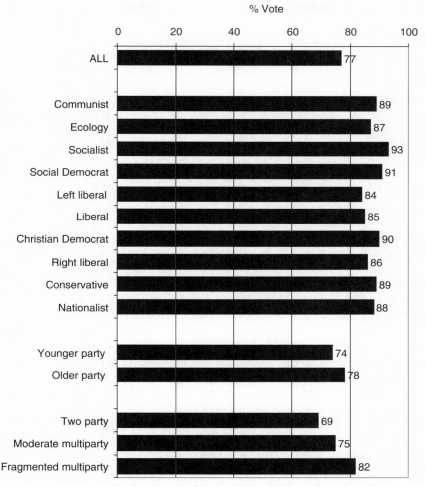

% Vote

FIGURE 7.3. Partisan characteristics of turnout. *Note:* The proportion of party supporters that vote is classified by partisan identification. Younger parties: Under 20 years old. Older parties: Over 20 years old. Party System: Classified based on the effective number of parliamentary parties. *Source:* Comparative Study of Electoral Systems, Module I, 1996–2002.

turn out their supporters, as well as the party's chances of electoral success. Even if partisanship is stronger among supporters of the far-left and far-right parties, as already shown in Figure 6.5, this does not necessarily mean that their supporters will be more active as the wasted vote calculation becomes relevant, where minor parties on the extreme left and right stand less chance of being returned to office. If we compare the age at which parties were founded, there is a modest (4-point) gap between older parties (founded more than 20 years ago) and younger parties, but this is far less than might be expected.

Electoral Laws

Compulsory Voting

The use of compulsory or mandatory voting laws can be expected to have an obvious impact on turnout, although the strength of the effect depends upon how strictly such regulations and any associated sanctions are implemented and enforced.[44] In practice, legal rules for voting may be de jure or de facto. The most common legal basis is statutory law, although the obligation to vote also may be rooted in constitutional provisions.[45] Implementation ranges from minimal de facto enforcement to the imposition of various sanctions. Fines are most common, as in Brazil, Egypt, and Luxembourg, although other punishments include the denial of official documents such as passports, identity cards, drivers licenses, or government benefits (used in Italy and Greece) and even, occasionally, the threat of imprisonment (up to six months in Cyprus) as a criminal offence. The effectiveness of any legal penalties is dependent upon the efficiency of the prior registration process and, where the initiative falls upon the elector, whether there are fines or other penalties associated with failure to register. Where implementation is enforced loosely, then the impact of any mandatory regulations has to operate largely through the impact of the law on social norms, similar to the effect of no-parking restrictions on city streets. Mandatory voting regulations may be genuine attempts to increase widespread public involvement in the political process, or they may be employed by less democratic regimes to compel the public to vote, in the attempt to legitimize one-party contests. Even in democratic states the use of legal regulations may have unintended consequences for participation because it may reduce the incentive for parties to organize and mobilize their heartland supporters, to get them to the polls.[46] Worldwide, twenty-three countries currently use compulsory voting in national parliamentary elections, including seven older democracies such as Australia, Belgium, Greece, Luxembourg, and Italy. In addition, this practice also is used for national elections in a few provinces in Austria and in Switzerland, and until 1970 the Netherlands also used such regulations. Voting also is mandatory in many Latin American countries at different levels of democratization, as well as in nondemocratic regimes in Singapore and Egypt.[47]

Most previous studies have found that compulsory voting is associated with higher turnout, but these have been limited mainly to established democracies, most of which are in Western Europe. Table 7.1 demonstrates that in national elections held worldwide, the use of compulsory voting was related to turnout. To explore this further, Table 7.3 shows the levels of turnout in

TABLE 7.3. *Compulsory Voting and Electoral Turnout Worldwide, 1990s*

		Mean Vote/VAP	Mean Vote/Reg	N. of Nations
Older democracies	Compulsory	79.4	86.9	7
	Noncompulsory	71.7	72.7	32
	Difference	+7.7	+14.2	39
Newer democracies	Compulsory	67.7	75.8	9
	Noncompulsory	69.3	73.9	31
	Difference	−1.6	+1.9	40
Semi-democracies	Compulsory	53.9	60.6	5
	Noncompulsory	56.6	67.0	40
	Difference	−2.7	−6.4	45
Nondemocracies	Compulsory	40.9	70.6	2
	Noncompulsory	61.8	67.8	38
	Difference	−20.9	+2.8	40
ALL	Compulsory	65.9	75.4	23
	Noncompulsory	64.2	70.0	141
	Difference	+1.9	+5.4	164

Notes: Mean Vote/VAP is measured as the number of valid votes as a proportion of the Voting Age Population (VAP) in all nations worldwide that held parliamentary elections during the 1990s. Mean Vote/Reg is measured as the number of valid votes as a proportion of the registered electorate (Reg) in all nations worldwide that held parliamentary elections during the 1990s. Compulsory Voting: The following 23 nations were classified as currently using compulsory voting: Older democracies: Australia, Belgium, Costa Rica, Cyprus, Greece, Italy, Luxembourg; Newer Democracies: Argentina, Bolivia, Chile, Dominican Republic, Ecuador, Liechtenstein, Panama Canal Zone, Thailand, and Uruguay; Semi-democracies: Brazil, Guatemala, Honduras, Peru, and Venezuela; Non-democracies: Singapore and Egypt.
Source: Calculated from International IDEA database, *Voter Turnout from 1945 to 2000.* Available online at www.idea.int.

the 1990s found in all twenty-three countries worldwide with compulsory voting regulations, broken down by type of democracy. The results show that in older democracies there is, indeed, a positive relationship; levels of vote as a proportion of the voting age population are 7.7% higher in nations using mandatory voting laws, and are a remarkable 14.2% higher in terms of vote as a proportion of the registered electorate. Where these laws exist in established democracies in Western Europe, the Asia-Pacific, and South America, then the registered electorate, the group that is most obviously subject to any sanctions, is far more likely to cast a ballot. Yet in all other types of political systems the result is very different, with vote/VAP actually slightly lower among newer democracies and semi-democracies with mandatory laws, and far lower in Egypt and Singapore, the only two nondemocratic states with mandatory regulations and at least semicompetitive elections.

There may be a number of explanations for this intriguing finding. First, the law may be enforced more strictly, and the registration processes may be more efficient, in the older democracies, so that voters face stronger negative incentives to participate. In addition, it may be that the impact of mandatory laws depends primarily upon broader social norms about the desirability of obeying the law and those in authority, which may prove stronger in established democratic states in Western Europe than in many Latin American cultures. Last, newer democracies characterized by low electoral turnout may be more likely to introduce laws in the attempt to mobilize the public, but without strict implementation these laws may prove ineffective correctives. Some evidence to evaluate these propositions is available in the CSES dataset, where it is apparent that in countries where compulsory voting is strictly enforced then 95% of the public voted (see Figure 7.2). In countries where the laws on compulsory voting were without any sanction, however, turnout was no greater than in nations without any such laws. This pattern helps to account for some of the striking differences in the impact of compulsory voting laws in different types of political systems and suggests the need for caution in generalizing about how these laws work across nations.

Eligibility for the Franchise

The restrictions to the minimum age at which people qualify to vote is important because in most West European countries for which we have survey data, the young are consistently less likely to vote than are older groups, and similar patterns are well established in the United States.[48] *Ceteris paribus*, we would expect to find that the lower the age at which citizens are eligible to vote, the lower the turnout. Blais and Dobrzynska confirmed that, all other things being equal, turnout is reduced by almost two points when the voting age is lowered by one year.[49] Latin American states were the first to lower the age of the franchise from twenty-one to eighteen, beginning in the nineteenth century, and it was only in the 1970s that the United States and Western European countries followed suit.[50] Today the age of the franchise is usually in the region of eighteen to twenty years old. Studies demonstrate that the age of voting eligibility is now unrelated to cross-national variations in turnout, probably because most democracies now have standardized to within a relatively similar age range.[51]

Restrictions on the franchise vary from one country to another, such as the disenfranchisement of felons, bankrupts, resident aliens, and groups such as the mentally incapacitated.[52] Waves of immigration or increases in the prison population can have an important dampening effect on vote/VAP. In the United States the claim of steadily declining turnout since 1972 has been challenged as an artificial product of the rise in the number of ineligible voters (due to increased numbers of resident aliens and felons in prison or on probation), which swelled the size of the voting age population.[53] The enfranchisement of women has had a dramatic impact on electoral participation. Only four countries enfranchised women before the start of World War I: New Zealand in 1893, Australia in 1902, Finland in 1907, and Norway in 1913. Women had attained suffrage by the end of World War II in 83 nations, and in 171 nations in total by 1970. In another 20 nations this occurred even later, for example in 1971 in Switzerland, 1976 in Portugal, 1980 in Iraq, 1984 in Liechtenstein, and 1994 in Kazakhstan, and today women continue to be barred from voting in Qatar, Saudi Arabia, Oman, and the United Arab Emirates.[54] The first election following the enfranchisement of women usually has seen a sudden drop in overall levels of vote/VAP, as older generations of women who had never participated before suddenly become eligible to vote, followed by a slow recovery in rates of turnout. In the United States and Britain, for example, women were first enfranchised in the early 1920s, and the first election afterward saw an immediate sharp drop in overall turnout. Subsequent decades saw a slow and steady increase in levels of female turnout until the early 1980s, when women came to participate at similar, or even slightly higher, levels than men. Similar patterns have been found elsewhere.[55] The residual effect of this pattern is found more widely; countries that enfranchised women prior to 1945 had average turnout (vote/VAP) of 69% in the 1990s, compared with 61% for countries that granted women the vote in the postwar era. Nor is this simply due to a close association between women's rights and overall levels of democracy. Studies have found this difference to be strong and significant; even after controlling for general levels of political rights and civil liberties, countries that enfranchised women earlier tend to have higher turnout today than those that reformed in more recent decades.[56]

Electoral Administration

Turnout may also be affected by the administration of registration procedures and facilities for voting that alter the costs for certain groups, such as the use of absentee, advance, overseas, and postal ballots; proxy votes; the distribution of mobile polling facilities for special populations such as the elderly, infirm, or disabled in nursing homes and hospitals; and polling scheduled for weekends or holidays rather than workdays.[57] The Bush-Gore debacle in Florida illustrated vividly the importance of seemingly minor and routine practices such as the design and layout of the ballot paper, the security checks used for verifying registration lists, and the type of counting mechanism.[58] Reformers often focus on administrative procedures, on the grounds that lowering the barriers and simplifying the procedures for registration and voting, while maintaining the integrity of the electoral process, will boost participation. This process is exemplified through special electoral arrangements for mobile populations, such as facilitating the casting of postal, proxy, absentee, or overseas votes, as well as providing polling facilities for the elderly and disabled in nursing homes and hospitals, locating polling stations in areas like shopping centers and supermarkets, and holding elections with lengthy hours on a nonworkday. Registration procedures are often thought to be another important hurdle, if citizens have to apply to register, often well ahead of the election, and if complicated, time-consuming, or restrictive practices depress participation.[59] Registration is by application in the United States, France, and Brazil, whereas in many other countries eligible citizens are enrolled automatically to vote, and registration is the responsibility of the government, conducted via a door-to-door canvas, an annual household census, or a rolling register. Under other regimes, voters can be deterred by far more serious barriers, such as in Belarus, where citizens faced the threat of intimidation at polling places. Incentive-based theories commonly assume that reducing the hurdles to registration and casting a ballot will boost participation. Yet if broader features of the political system remain unchanged, such as the range of parties contesting elected office, then tinkering with administrative procedures may produce minimal change.

Registration Processes

The facilities for registration and casting a ballot commonly are expected to affect turnout. The evidence that the registration process matters is most persuasive in comparisons of regulations that vary from state to state within the United States. Rosenstone and Wolfinger examined the difference in turnout between those states with the easiest registration requirements, for example, those such as North Dakota that allow registration at polling places on election day, and those with the strictest requirements. Their estimates suggest that if all American states had same-day registration, this would provide a one-time boost of turnout of about 5 to 9%.[60] Since their study during the 1970s, many states have experimented with easing the requirements, through initiatives such as the Motor Voter registration (where citizens can register to vote at the same time as they complete the form used for motor vehicle registration), with limited effects on voter participation.[61] Some states such as Oregon have also experimented with postal voting. The 1993 National Voter Registration Act requires all states to make voter registration available in motor vehicle bureaus, as well as by mail and at various social service agencies, and it also forbids removing citizens from the rolls simply for not voting. Nevertheless, as the Florida case in the 2000 presidential contest vividly illustrated, the efficiency of the registration and voting procedure at state level can leave much to be desired. Studies suggest that easing voter registration processes has improved slightly American voter turnout, with a one-time bump when new processes are introduced, but that the impact is not uniform across the whole electorate, as it has had the most impact increasing participation among middle-class citizens.[62]

Yet the comparative evidence is less well established. Studies have long assumed that voluntary registration procedures, where citizens need to apply to be eligible to vote, are an important reason why American turnout lags well behind many comparable democracies.[63] In countries with application processes, including the United States, prospective voters usually must identify themselves before an election, sometimes many weeks in advance, by registering with a government agency. In other countries the state takes the initiative in registering eligible citizens, through an annual census or similar mechanism. But what is the impact of this process? Katz compared the electoral regulations in thirty-one nations and found that nineteen states used an automatic registration process, whereas, in contrast, twelve registered citizens by application.[64] The analysis of electoral participation based on this classification of registration procedures found that these hurdles might be less important than is often assumed because average vote/VAP proved to be identical in the democracies using either automatic or voluntary registration procedures.[65]

Polling Facilities

In terms of other voting facilities, most countries hold their elections on a single day, usually at the weekend, which makes it easier for employed people to visit a polling station. In a few countries, however, elections are spread over more than one day; in India, for example, where there are more than 600 million voters and some 800 thousand polling stations, balloting takes place on a staggered basis during a month across the whole country. In addition, there are important variations in the use of absentee, overseas, postal, advance, and proxy ballots, and how far polling stations are distributed widely throughout the community for groups who might otherwise have difficulty in getting to the polls, such as the population in residential homes for the elderly, in hospitals, and military personnel posted overseas.[66] Franklin compared average turnout for 1960–95 in parliamentary elections in twenty-nine countries and found that compulsory voting, Sunday voting, and postal voting facilities all proved important predictors, along with the proportionality of the electoral system, although not the number of days that polls were open.[67] Studies found that after controlling for levels of development, only polling on a rest day proved to provide a significant boost to turnout in established democracies; in contrast the use of proxy voting and the number of days that the polling stations were open proved to be associated negatively, perhaps because countries concerned about low turnout try to increase the opportunities to get to the polls.[68] Other special voting facilities also all proved unrelated to turnout.

Cultural Attitudes and Individual Resources

Yet it is well established that even within particular political systems, some groups and individuals remain far more likely to participate than others. Cultural accounts stress that some people choose to vote for largely affective reasons, such as a general sense of civic duty or to express support for a party or cause without any hope of electoral gain, even if other instrumental citizens are motivated by the rational tradeoff between electoral costs and benefits. We, therefore, need to turn to analyze the motivation and resources that help predict why some individuals have higher civic engagement than others. Moreover, theories of societal modernization suggest that the process of human development may produce fundamental changes to patterns of political participation. Rising levels of human capital (literacy, education, and the cognitive skills that schooling produces), along with access to the mass media, the rising middle classes, and urbanization, can be expected to facilitate political activism, although previous studies have established that modernization operates in a curvilinear pattern, as human development increases turnout most in the transition from agrarian to industrial societies, rather than in the stages from industrial to postindustrial.[69]

The results of the multivariate analysis presented in Table 7.1, and the proportion of people who voted illustrated in Figure 7.4, confirms the familiar pattern: turnout was higher among the middle classes, with a 10-point gap between the unskilled manual working class and managers and professionals. Not surprisingly, a similar pattern was reflected in household income, generating an 8-point voting gap between the top and bottom quintiles. The education gap was even larger; 68% of those with only primary school education voted compared with 82% of those with either technical or university qualifications. The age profile was familiar; three-quarters of the younger thirties voted, compared with 81% of the over-sixties. The gender gap was modest and, as noted with the patterns of partisanship, varied by type of society, with the gap proving insignificant in the pooled sample of all legislative elections. Moreover, both union membership and church attendance contributed toward higher turnout, suggesting that the social networks and mobilizing resources of these organizations contributed toward civic engagement. In terms of cultural attitudes, as expected, partisan identification produced a dramatic voting gap: 91% of those who expressed a strong party identification cast a ballot compared with 76% of those who had only a weak party attachment. External political efficacy also mattered: as cultural theories have long emphasized, people who felt that the system was responsive were more likely to participate. In the multivariate models, political ideology also counted, with those on the right slightly more likely to participate, even controlling for their SES. Last, as expected, turnout was slightly higher in more developed societies, as gauged by the United Nations Development Programme (UNDP) Human Development Index. The societal changes associated with the modernization process do strengthen electoral participation, as anticipated. A wider range of nations, covering many poorer agrarian economies, could be expected to strengthen this association further.

Conclusions: Culture, Incentives, and Voting Participation

Rational-choice theories suggest that the primary incentives facing citizens in national elections may be understood as a product of the electoral *costs* of

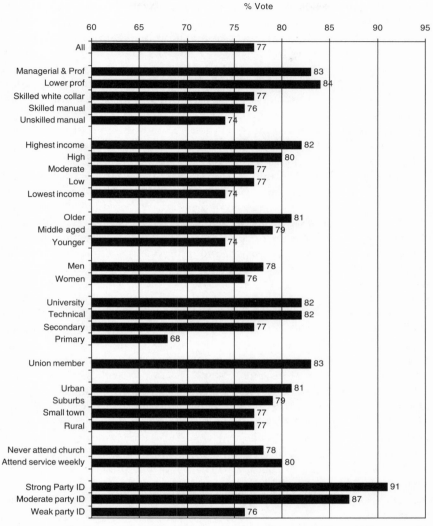

FIGURE 7.4. Social and attitudinal characteristics of turnout. *Source:* Comparative Study of Electoral Systems, Module I, 1996–2002.

registering and voting, the party *choices* available to electors, and the degree to which casting a ballot determines the composition of parliament and government. There are multiple costs, including the time and effort required to register and to vote, any legal sanctions imposed for failure to turnout, and the frequency with which electors are called to the polls. All other things being equal, among postindustrial societies one would expect turnout to be higher in political systems that reduce the costs of voting, such as those with automatic processes for maintaining the electoral register and electoral arrangements that maximize party competition but which also maintain a strong link between voters' preferences and the outcome for parliament, for government, and for the policy agenda. In this view, as well, effective electoral engineering designed to change the institutional context, such as easier registration processes or the use of all-postal voting facilities, should generate improvements in turnout.[70] In contrast, cultural accounts suggest that electors are influenced more by their SES and their political attitudes, beliefs, and values, generating habitual and deeply rooted patterns of participation, so that mass political behavior will respond only sluggishly, if at all, to changes in political institutions, electoral law, or electoral administration.

In the countries under comparison in the CSES dataset, all other things being equal, the results of the analysis confirm further that political institutions matter, in particular, that voting participation is maximized in elections using PR, with small electoral districts, regular but relatively infrequent national contests, competitive party systems, and in presidential contests. These factors lend further confirmation to the pattern established in an earlier study comparing a wider range of nations around the globe. Nevertheless, the policy implications of these results are far from straightforward because these institutions represent fundamental parts of political systems that are extremely difficult, if not impossible, to alter in practice. More *specific voting facilities*, such as the role of registration processes and the use of transfer voting or advance voting, are more practical to reform, but comparison of established democracies presented elsewhere shows that these arrangements often produce little significant effect on voting turnout. In established democracies, the use of compulsory voting regulations was an important indicator of higher turnout, whereas this was not found among the broader comparison of elections worldwide. The pooled model showed that levels of human development, the institutional context, the social characteristics of electors, and cultural attitudes were all important predictors of turnout. Therefore, rather than a false dichotomy, between rational-choice strategic incentives and cultural modernization, we should conclude that both these factors contribute toward understanding patterns of political participation, in a "nested" model. In Chapters 1 through 7, therefore, I have established that the type of electoral rules *does* affect mass voting behavior in terms of patterns of cleavage politics and the strength of partisan identities, as well as in terms of contributing toward electoral turnout. But do these rules have a more direct impact upon patterns of PR, such as the diversity of legislative bodies and the role of elected members? The third part of this book turns to these important issues.

PART III

THE CONSEQUENCES FOR POLITICAL REPRESENTATION

8

Women's Representation

The first part of this book examined how electoral rules influenced the strategies adopted by parties and the behavior of the mass electorate. But so far I have not considered the potential impact of rational-choice institutionalism and cultural modernization upon political representation. Debates about electoral reform have revolved around the practical impact of changes to the status quo, including how to achieve social diversity in legislatures so that parliaments look more like the people they serve. Recent decades have witnessed growing demands for the inclusion and empowerment of women in elected office, as well as a stronger voice for ethnic minorities (as discussed fully in the next chapter). Feminist theorists suggest that the presence of women leaders facilitates the articulation of different perspectives on political issues, where elected representatives are not just "standing as" women but also "acting for" women as a group.[1] An accumulating body of evidence in North America, Scandinavia, and Western Europe suggests that women legislators do, indeed, raise distinctive concerns and issue priorities.[2] If so, then their under-representation in parliament may have important consequences for the public policy agenda and for the articulation of women's interests, as well as for the legitimacy of democratic bodies.

As is well known, today women continue to be strongly under-represented in elected office. This pattern persists despite trends in the home, family, school, and workforce that have been transforming women's and men's lives during the postwar era, as well as despite the growth of the second wave feminist movement strengthening demands for gender equality in politics. NGOs, parties, and international agencies have often expressed the need for equal opportunities for women. Governments have signed official National Action Plans and have held international conventions designed to establish conditions of gender equality in the public sphere, exemplified by the 1979 Convention on the Elimination of All Forms of Discrimination against Women (CEDAW) favoring the principle of equal opportunities in public life, ratified by 163 nations.[3] The *1995 UN Beijing Platform for Action* expressed commitment to the empowerment of women based on the conviction that: "*Women's empowerment and their full participation on the basis of equality in all spheres of society, including participation in the decision-making process and access to power, are fundamental for the achievement of equality, development and peace.*"[4] The *Platform for Action* aims explicitly for a 50–50 gender balance in all areas of society, and its analysis places full participation in decision-making in the foremost role.

In practice, however, multiple barriers continue to restrict women's advancement in elected office. Out of 193 nations worldwide, only nine women are at the pinnacle of power as elected heads of state or government. Despite some redoubtable and well-known world leaders, such as Margaret Thatcher, Gro Harlem Bruntland, Mary Robinson, and Golda Meir, only 39 states have *ever* elected a woman president or prime minister. According to estimates by the United Nations, women represent less than one-tenth of the world's cabinet ministers and one-fifth of all sub-ministerial positions.[5] The Inter-Parliamentary Union estimates that about 5,600 women sit in parliament worldwide in mid-2002, representing 14.7% of all members.[6] This is a rise from 9% in 1987, yet if growth at this level is maintained (0.36% per annum), a simple linear projection predicts that women parliamentarians will achieve parity with men at the turn of the twenty-second century.

Regional variations show sharp contrasts to these global patterns (see Figure 8.1). Women parliamentarians do best in the Nordic nations, constituting 39% of MPs in the lower house. Sweden leads the world; women are half of all cabinet ministers, and 149 female members sit in the Riksdag (43%), quadrupling from 10% in 1950. Women political leaders also have moved ahead in the other Nordic countries.[7] Elsewhere, the proportion of women members of parliament is lower, including in the Americas (16%), Asia (15%), Europe, excluding the Nordic states (15%), Sub-Saharan Africa (14%), and the Pacific (14%). The worst record remains in Arab states, where women are 5% of elected representatives. Women continue to be barred by law from standing for parliament in Kuwait, Qatar, Saudi Arabia, Oman, and the United Arab Emirates. There have been some moves toward reforms in the region, for example, Moroccan law introduced thirty reserved seats for women, and, after the September 2002 elections, 11% of the legislature were female. In Bahrain legal revisions allowed women to stand in elections for the first time, but none were elected, although women constituted 10% of the candidates in the May 2002 local elections and 5% of the candidates for the national parliament five months later. A glance at the rank order of the proportion of women in office in the countries under comparison in Figure 8.1 suggests that the level of socioeconomic development and length of democracy may be important, but these are neither necessary nor sufficient for gender equality in parliaments; in Mexico, Lithuania, and the Czech Republic, for example, women politicians are more successful than in the United States and Japan, two of the most affluent democracies in the world.

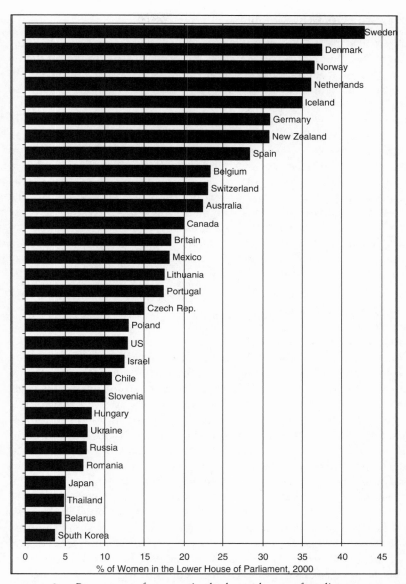

FIGURE 8.1. Percentage of women in the lower house of parliament, 2000. *Source:* Inter-Parliamentary Union. 2002. *Women in National Parliaments.* Available online at www.ipu.org.

Analyzing Women's Representation

The literature suggests that multiple reasons lie behind this phenomenon.[8] The funnel model in Figure 8.2 identifies the primary steps in the candidate selection process, from the earliest and most diffuse factors operating within each country through more specific stages in each party until the final step of election to parliament. This limited study cannot examine the evidence for all these phases, especially the way the selection process operates within different parties, which is explored in depth elsewhere.[9] But here we can focus upon to what extent women's representation is influenced by cultural modernization and by electoral laws, the most diffuse factors in any political system, illustrated on the left in the model. *Electoral laws*, including the basic type of electoral system, the statutory adoption of gender quotas, and the use of reserved seats for women, shape the strategic incentives facing party selectors and candidates. *Cultural modernization* relates to either egalitarian or traditional attitudes toward gender equality in the home, workplace, and public sphere, particularly attitudes toward the role of women as political leaders.

Rational-Choice Institutionalism

Rational-choice institutionalism assumes that selectors are vote-maximizers seeking to pick party standard-bearers who will appeal to electors and, therefore, be returned to parliament.[10] Gatekeepers controlling the nomination and selection of legislative candidates are the party "selectorate," whether centralized in national office or operating at regional or local level, and they include party voters, members, activists, leaders, and officers.[11] Multiple factors may determine the decision of party selectors, beyond the pursuit of votes, for example, ideologues may favor one-of-us nominees within organizational or leadership factions. Selectors may be swayed by personal loyalties to particular colleagues or by the rhetorical skills of certain outstanding speakers. But if selectors fail to act, at least in part, in a rational vote-maximizing manner, then the theory predicts that any candidates they nominate will probably be less successful among the electorate and, therefore, less likely to enter parliament. Yet when taking their decisions, selectors possess limited information about public preferences. To minimize electoral risks, it is rational for them to re-select incumbents. Members of parliament enjoy the advantages of any personal vote built up from an established legislative track record and parliamentary experience on key committees, as well as the cachet of name-recognition and the organizational resources that accompany office. In the absence of an existing incumbent, to reduce uncertainty, for selectors the default option is to nominate new candidates that share similar social and political characteristics to previous MPs. Because many parliamentary elites are usually disproportionately male, middle-aged professionals, such as lawyers, teachers, and journalists, as well as part of

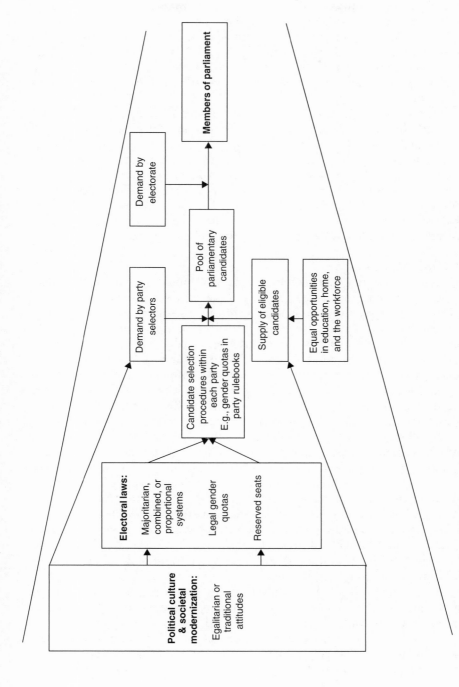

FIGURE 8.2. Funnel model of the candidate selection process

the predominant ethnic group in any society, it minimizes electoral risks for selectors to prefer candidates with similar characteristics for future contests. Moreover, the profile of the typical member of parliament will shape broader role models about who is regarded as most likely to succeed in political careers, encouraging aspirants with the standard characteristics to seek nomination, while discouraging members of nontraditional groups from coming forward.

Due to these tendencies, without external intervention, the selection process can be expected to reproduce the status quo, picking incumbents or new candidates who reflect the typical social background and experience displayed by most MPs. In this context, opportunities for women may be influenced by electoral law, including the basic type of electoral system, the statutory adoption of gender quotas, and the use of reserved seats for women. Rational-choice institutionalism suggests that electoral laws determine the balance of incentives operating in the selection process, for example, the use of statutory gender quotas creates sanctions regulating the outcome.

Cultural Modernization

By contrast, cultural modernization accounts emphasize that societal values reflect levels of human development. The theory developed by Inglehart and Norris also suggests that the cultural values in any society are not accidental, instead they are related systematically to levels of human development.[12] In many societies, rigid gender roles determine the rights, resources, and powers of women and men, notably the division of labor in the home and workplace. In others, men's and women's roles are more interchangeable, and innate biological differences lead to fewer social expectations. Where a culture of gender equality predominates, it provides a climate where de jure legal rights are more likely to be translated into de facto rights in practice; where institutional reforms are implemented in the workplace and public sphere; where women embrace expanded opportunities in literacy, education, and employment; and where the traditional roles of women and men are transformed within the household and family. Moreover, the critical importance of culture is that women as well as men share the predominant attitudes, values, and beliefs about the appropriate division of sex roles within any society. Sex discrimination reflects deep-rooted attitudes toward gender equality, so that where traditional cultural values prevail, then selectors will prefer to select men for political leadership. Moreover, in traditional cultures, parties will fail to introduce equal opportunity or positive action policies voluntarily, and they will fail to comply with any statutory positive action laws and disregard any legal penalties against sex discrimination. Where traditional values prevail, women are not limited just by society in terms of the opportunities they seek, but they also choose to limit themselves. Inglehart and Norris argue that cultural change is not an ad hoc and erratic process, rather patterns of human development and societal modernization underpin attitudinal shifts. The broad direction of value change is predictable although the pace is conditioned by the cultural legacy and institutional structure in any given society, exemplified by the role of an Islamic heritage in the Middle East, the legacy of Communism in Central Europe, and the egalitarian traditions in Scandinavia.

Evidence

Multivariate models allow us to analyze the evidence using the same logic adopted throughout the book. The models assume that if electoral laws are critical, then levels of female representation should vary systematically under different rules. On the other hand, if cultural values are important, then religious traditions, as a proxy for gender equality attitudes, should prove significant. The summary models presented in Table 8.1 allow us to compare the proportion of women elected to the lower house in the most recent general election prior to 2000. The analysis draws upon worldwide data in 171 nations from the Inter-Parliamentary Union. Model A first enters levels of development (measured by the UNDP's Human Development Index). Electoral systems are classified into the basic types of proportional, combined, and majoritarian categories used throughout the book, as categorized in Chapter 2.[13] The model then entered the use of positive action policies implemented by law, including the level of either statutory gender quotas or reserved seats, and also the length of women's suffrage in a country as a broader indicator of women's political rights and civil liberties. One important limitation is that the multivariate analysis does not include the use of voluntary gender quotas adopted through internal party rules and regulations because these vary among different parties within the same country. Their effects are best understood and studied through case studies and comparisons of trends over time conducted at national-level, as will be discussed later.[14]

In Model A, the type of electoral system, the use of reserved seats, and the year of women's suffrage are all found to be associated significantly with women's representation, and the measures of human development only prove significant at the .10 level. In Model B, to compare the role of structure and culture, the predominant religion in different countries of the world is then entered, as an indirect proxy for cultural differences toward the role of women and men. The amount of variance explained by the analysis increases from 25% based on electoral law in Model A to 37% with the addition of cultural factors in Model B. Nevertheless, although fewer women are elected in Muslim and Orthodox societies, after controlling for development and the electoral system, none of the cultural indicators of religiosity emerge as statistically significant. After discussing the results in detail, and the reasons for the patterns that are uncovered, the final section of this chapter then considers their implications.

TABLE 8.1. *Explaining the Proportion of Women in Parliament, 171 Nations Worldwide, 2000*

	Model A Electoral Laws				Model B Electoral Laws+Culture			
	B	SE	Beta	Sig.	B	SE	Beta	Sig.
DEVELOPMENT:								
Level of human development	6.642	3.882	.131	.089	6.642	3.882	.131	.089
ELECTORAL LAWS:								
Electoral system	2.265	.623	.248	.000	2.077	.600	.227	.001
Legal gender quotas (%)	.081	.071	.076	.257	.029	.072	.027	.689
Legal reserved seats (%)	.458	.209	.149	.030	.489	.196	.159	.013
Length of women's suffrage (years)	.186	.028	.437	.000	.152	.030	.356	.000
RELIGIOUS CULTURE:								
Protestant					2.594	7.378	.124	.726
Catholic					.063	7.389	.003	.993
Orthodox					-4.283	7.292	-.211	.558
Muslim					-8.072	7.640	-.222	.292
Other					-.647	7.363	-.025	.930
Constant	-2.968	2.006			-4.119	7.362		
Adjusted R²	.253				.370			

Notes: The coefficients represent beta (B), standard errors (SE), standardized beta (Beta), and significance (Sig.) derived from ordinary least square (OLS) regression analysis models, with the proportion of women in the lower house of parliament in 171 nations worldwide as the dependent variable. The variables were entered in the listed order. The coefficients significant at the p.01 level are displayed in **bold**.

Level of human development: *Human Development Index, 1998.* UNDP. 2000. *United Nations Development Report, 2000.* New York: UNDP/Oxford. Available online at http://www.undp.org.

Electoral system: See Chapter 2. Majoritarian (1), Combined (2), and Proportional (3). Proportion of women in parliament: Inter-Parliamentary Union, 2000. *Women in National Parliaments.* Available online at www.ipu.org. Legal reserved seats: see Table 8.4. % of reserved seats set in Tanzania, Uganda, Pakistan, Zimbabwe, Bangladesh, Sudan, Morocco, Botswana, and Lesotho. Legal gender quotas: see Table 8.5. % of gender quota set in Argentina, Belgium, Bolivia, Brazil, Costa Rica, Dominican Republic, Ecuador, France, Mexico, Panama, Paraguay, Peru, and Venezuela. Religious culture: The predominant religion in each nation classified as dummy variables using the *CIA World Factbook.* Available online at www.cia.gov.

TABLE 8.2. *Women's Representation by Type of Electoral System, 2000*

	% of Women in the Lower House of Parliament, 2000	Number of Nations
All Majoritarian	8.5	89
Alternative Vote	11.2	2
Bloc Vote	7.1	9
2nd Ballot	9.6	24
First-Past-the-Post	8.5	54
All Combined	11.3	29
Combined-independent	8.7	21
Combined-dependent	18.0	8
ALL Proportional	15.4	64
Single Transferable Vote	10.6	2
Party Lists	15.6	62
TOTAL	11.7	182

Note: The percentage of women in the lower house of national parliaments 2000, 182 nations worldwide. For the classification of electoral systems see Chapter 2.
Source: Calculated from Inter-Parliamentary Union. 2000. *Women in Parliament Database.* Available online at www.ipu.org.

Electoral Laws

The thesis that more women have usually been elected to parliament under party-list PR than under majoritarian electoral systems has been confirmed in a series of studies since the mid-eighties, based on research comparing both established democracies and also a broader range of developing societies worldwide.[15] Within proportional electoral systems, district magnitude has commonly been regarded as a particularly important factor, with more women usually elected from large multimember constituencies. The results of the multivariate analysis in Table 8.1 confirm that proportional electoral systems are significant predictors of the proportion of women in parliament, even after controlling for levels of human development. The comparison in Table 8.2, without any controls, shows how women are far more successful under PR list systems. As a simple rule, *women proved almost twice as likely to be elected under proportional than under majoritarian electoral systems.* Women were on average 8.5% of MPs in majoritarian systems, 11.3% in combined systems, and 15.4% of members in PR systems. Contrasts were also evident in the proportion of women MPs in combined-independent systems (8.7%) and in the more proportional combined-dependent systems (18.0%).

Considerable variations also were clear within each major electoral family, however, which could be attributed to many intervening conditions, including levels of district magnitude (the mean number of candidates per district) and proportionality, the use of legal and voluntary gender quotas, party ideologies (with the left generally more sympathetic toward gender equality),

TABLE 8.3. *Women's Representation by Electoral Family and Type of Society*

Type of Society	Electoral Family	% of Women in the Lower House, 2000	Number of Nations
Postindustrial	Proportional	29.5	12
	Combined	19.4	4
	Majoritarian	16.9	5
	Difference	**12.6**	
Industrial	Proportional	12.6	24
	Combined	12.9	12
	Majoritarian	10.8	19
	Difference	**1.8**	
Agrarian	Proportional	11.7	24
	Combined	8.6	11
	Majoritarian	7.4	57
	Difference	**4.3**	

Note: The mean percentage of women in the lower house of the national parliament, 168 nations worldwide (2000). Type of society: classified according to the level of human development, based on data from *Human Development Index, 1998*. UNDP. 2000. *United Nations Development Report, 2000*. New York: UNDP/Oxford. Available online at http://www.undp.org. For the classification of electoral systems see Chapter 2.

Source: Calculated from Inter-Parliamentary Union. 2000. *Women in Parliament Database*. Available online at www.ipu.org.

and the type of party organization.[16] More women were elected in certain majoritarian electoral systems, such as in Australia and Canada, than in other highly proportional Party Lists systems, as exemplified by Israel. Although there is a strong and consistent association, by itself the basic type of electoral system is neither a necessary nor a sufficient condition to guarantee women's representation. Table 8.3 breaks down the analysis by the type of society, showing that the link between the basic type of electoral system and women's representation was strongest among postindustrial societies, where there was a 12-point gap between PR and majoritarian systems. There was a far more modest 4-point gap among poorer agrarian nations, although even in developing societies, proportional electoral systems do function as a facilitating mechanism, which expedites women's entry into legislative office.

Strategic incentive theory suggests three main reasons why women usually benefit from PR. First, under proportional systems, each party presents the public with their collective list of candidates for each multimember district. As such, parties have an electoral incentive to maximize their collective appeal in such lists by including candidates representing all the major social cleavages in the electorate, for example, by including both middle-class professionals and blue-collar workers, farmers and urban shopkeepers, Catholics and Protestants, as well as women and men. Multimember districts encourage collective party accountability for the complete list of candidates. Where parties have to nominate a slate of candidates for a multimember district, the exclusion of any major social sector, including women, could signal discrimination, and could, therefore, risk an electoral penalty at the ballot box. By contrast in First-Past-the-Post systems, parliamentary candidates are selected to run within each single-member district. Where the selection process is in the hands of the local constituency party, this creates minimal incentive for each particular constituency to pick a ticket that is "balanced" at the district or national level. Local party members often want a representative who will maximize their chances of winning in that constituency, irrespective of the broader consequences for the party or parliament.[17] The selection of the default option (i.e., a candidate reflecting the traditional characteristics and qualifications of previous parliamentarians) may be expected to predominate in many cases, as the rational vote-maximizing strategy designed to minimize electoral risks.

Moreover, the type of electoral system also is related to patterns of incumbency turnover. One major barrier to women candidates lies through the strength of incumbency, with elected officials returned over successive contests, due to the personal vote advantages of familiarity, name recognition, and media attention, as well as to greater financial and organizational resources that accompany legislative office.[18] In many contests the key challenge facing women is not just becoming nominated per se, but contesting a winnable seat in single-member districts, or being ranked near the top of the party list of candidates in PR systems. In the United States, for example, 85% of incumbent congressional representatives have been returned in successive election from the late 1970s to the mid-1990s. A broader comparison of elections to the lower house of the national parliament in twenty-five established democracies from 1979 to 1994 found that on average about two-thirds of all incumbents were returned from one general election to the next, including 66% in PR electoral systems and 70% in majoritarian elections.[19] This difference is modest but it could generate slightly more opportunities for challengers, including women, in the pipeline for elected office.[20] For example, in Britain it was the massive turnover in MPs following Labour's landslide victory in 1997, coupled with the use of positive action placing women in target seats, that doubled the number of women in the U.K. House of Commons. As incumbents, Labour women MPs were reelected in the 2001 British general election, despite the fact that the original positive action strategy was discontinued. In the United States, studies have established that from 1998 to 2000 women increased their numbers in states with term limitations more than elsewhere, although this effect is reversed in states such as California where women representatives have already made much progress.[21]

Finally, as discussed next, party list PR also facilitates the use of positive action designed to boost women's representation, exemplified by legal or

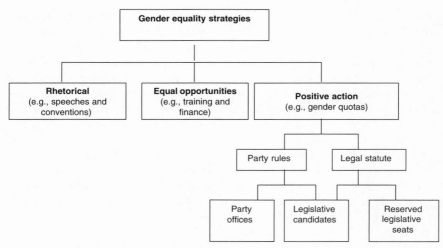

FIGURE 8.3. Gender equality strategies

voluntary gender quotas in candidate selection procedures. Positive action strategies can also be used under majoritarian electoral systems as well, as shown by the British case, but it can be harder to implement within single-member districts than within party lists. For all these reasons, PR systems are likely to be more "women-friendly" than majoritarian electoral systems. These qualities are also present in combined electoral systems, so that in Germany, Hungary, and New Zealand more women are usually successful via party lists rather than through single-member districts.

Electoral Laws and Positive Action

During the last decade many policy initiatives have attempted to increase the number of women in elected and appointed office. As shown in Figure 8.3, the most common strategies fall into three main categories.

Rhetorical strategies are exemplified by signature of international conventions on women's rights, and official speeches and statements applauding the principles of equal opportunities for women and men. Where leaders are committed to these statements, and where they have the power of patronage, then this can lead to the promotion of women in elected and appointed office. Yet gains that are not institutionalized may be easily lost again under different leadership, and women who benefit from patronage may appear as token representatives without their own electoral or party base. Rhetorical strategies are the weakest and most ineffective instruments, although capable of producing some modest gains.

Equal opportunity policies are designed to provide a level playing field so that women can pursue political careers on the same basis as men. Common examples include programs of financial aid to assist with electoral expenses, candidate training in the skills of communication, public speaking, network-ing, campaigning, and news-management, and the provision of crèches and childcare facilities within legislative assemblies. Equal opportunity strategies can be gender-neutral in design, for example, opportunities for training can be offered to both women *and* men parliamentary candidates, and child-care can be used by both parents, although their effects may be beneficial primarily to women.

Last, *positive action policies*, by contrast, are designed explicitly to benefit women as a temporary stage until such a time as gender parity is achieved in legislative and elected bodies. Positive action includes three main strategies:

- The use of *reserved seats* for women established in electoral law;
- *Statutory gender quotas* controlling the composition of candidate lists for all parties in each country; and also
- V*oluntary gender quotas* used in the regulations and rules governing the candidate selection procedures within particular parties.

Positive action has become increasingly popular in recent decades, as one of the most effective policy options for achieving short-term change, although the use of these policies remains a matter of controversy within and outside of the women's movement.

Reserved Seats

By electoral law, some countries have stipulated a certain number of reserved seats that are only open to women or ethnic minority candidates. This pol-icy has been adopted to boost women's representation under majoritarian electoral systems in developing nations in Africa and South Asia, particularly those with a Muslim culture (see Table 8.4). Reserved seats have been used for the lower house in Morocco (elected from a national list of 30 women mem-bers out of 325 representatives), Bangladesh (30/300), Pakistan (60/357), Botswana (2 women appointed by the president out of 44 members), Taiwan (elected), Lesotho (3 women appointed out of 80 seats), and Tanzania (48 women out of 295 members are distributed according to parties according to the party share of seats in the House of Representatives).[22] This mechanism guarantees a minimum number of women in elected office, although some have argued that it may be a way to appease, and ultimately sideline, women. Being elected does not necessarily mean that women are given substantive decision-making power, especially given the weakness of many of these leg-islative bodies. Where appointed by the president, if lacking an independent electoral or organizational base, women may be marginalized from any real decision-making responsibility, and their appointment can reinforce control of parliament by the majority party. Many of the countries using this policy have limited democratic rights and civil liberties, with power concentrated in

TABLE 8.4. *Reserved Seats for Women Used in the Lower House of Parliament Worldwide, 2000*

	Election	Total Number of MPs in the Lower House	Number of Seats Reserved for Women	% of Seats Reserved for Women	Appointed or Elected
Uganda	2001	292	56	19.1	Indirectly elected
Pakistan	2002	357	60	16.8	Elected
Tanzania	2000	295	48	16.2	Appointed
Zimbabwe	2000	274	37	13.5	Appointed
Djibouti	2003	65	7	10.7	Elected
Bangladesh	1996	300	30	10.0	Appointed
Sudan	2000	360	35	9.7	Elected
Morocco	2002	325	30	9.2	Elected
Botswana	1999	44	2	4.5	Appointed
Lesotho	1998	80	3	3.8	Appointed
Taiwan	1996	334	Varies	Varies	Elected
Jordan	2003	120	5	4.2	Appointed

Note: Reserved seats in the lower house of the national parliament are defined as those that by law can only be filled by women, either by appointment or election. It should also be noted that in Nepal three seats are reserved for women in the upper house, according to the 1990 constitution.
Sources: The Electoral Institute of Southern Africa (EISA). Available online at www.eisa. org.za; *Elections Around the World.* Available online at www.electionworld.org; International IDEA. Available online at www.idea.int.

the executive. In Uganda, for example, 56 parliamentary seats out of 292 are reserved for women (19%), which are indirectly elected, along with seats set aside for representatives drawn from the groups such as the army, youth, the disabled, and trade unions, despite a ban on opposition parties standing for election.[23] Nevertheless, against these arguments, reserved seats also have been used at local level in India, with considerable success. In India 33% of seats on local municipal elections are reserved for women, although when it was proposed to extend this practice for elections to the national parliament (Lok Sahba) in 1996 the issue aroused heated debate and was defeated.[24] As discussed further in the next chapter, reserved seats based on regional, linguistic, ethnic, or religious ethno-political cleavages also have been used, although their effects depend upon the size and spatial concentration of such groups.

Legal Gender Quotas

Positive action strategies also include statutory gender quotas applied by law to all political parties, specifying that women must constitute a minimal proportion of parliamentary candidates or elected representatives within each party. Quotas represent an instrument that introduces specific formal selection criteria, in the form of minimal or maximal thresholds for a given group, into selections procedures, whether for elected or appointed office in the public sphere or for personnel recruitment in the private sector, such as for trade union office. There is an important distinction drawn between *statutory* gender quotas introduced by law, and, thereby, applying to all parties within a country, and *voluntary* gender quotas implemented by internal regulations and rule books within each party. Quotas can be specified for women and men, or for other relevant selection criteria, such as ethnicity, language, social sector, or religion. Statutory gender quota laws have been applied to elections in Belgium, France, and Italy, to many nations in Latin America (see Table 8.5), as well as for appointments to public bodies and consultative committees in many countries such as Finland and Norway.[25]

As shown by the last column in Table 8.5, monitoring short-term change in the election immediately before and after passage of the law, in some countries and in some elections, legal gender quotas appear to have worked far more effectively than in other cases, hence, the substantial rise in women in parliament found in Argentina, the modest growth in Peru and Belgium but minimal progress evident in France, Mexico, or Brazil. Moreover, the general comparison of the use of legal gender quotas in the nations where these have been introduced proves insignificant in the multivariate model in Table 8.1. Why is this? The effective implementation of legal gender quotas depends upon multiple factors, including, most important, how the statutory mechanisms are put into practice, the level of the gender quota specified by law, whether the rules for party lists regulate the rank order of women and men candidates, whether party lists are open or closed, and also the penalties associated with any failure to comply with the law. Positive action policies alter the balance of incentives for the party selectorate. Where these laws are implemented, then selectors need to weigh the potential penalties and benefits if they do or do not comply. Selectors still may prefer the default option of nominating a male candidate under certain circumstances, for example, if the laws are designed as symbolic window-dressing more than as de facto regulations; if the regulations specify that a certain proportion of women have to be selected for party lists but they fail to specify their rank order so that female candidates cluster in unwinnable positions at the bottom of the list; or if any sanctions for noncompliance are weak or nonexistent. As in many attempts to alter the incentive structure, the devil lies in the details, so apparently similar legislative policies turn out to have different consequences in different nations.

In Belgium, the Electoral Act of May 24, 1994 specified that no more than two-thirds of the candidates on any party electoral list may be of the same sex. The minimum representation requirement is, thus, exactly the same for men and women. It applies to the Chamber of Representatives and the

TABLE 8.5. *Statutory Gender Quotas in Use Worldwide*

Country	Date of Law	Gender Quota%	Legislative Body	Electoral System	List Open or Closed	% Women MPs Before Law (i)	% Women MPs After Law (ii)	Change (i)–(ii)
France	1999	50	Lower House	Majoritarian	–	11	12	+1
Costa Rica	1997	40	Unicameral	Proportional	Closed	14	19	+5
Belgium	1994	33	Lower House	Proportional	Open	18	23	+5
Bosnia & Herzegovina	2001	33	Lower House	Proportional	Open		14.3	
Argentina	1991	30	Lower House	Proportional	Closed	6	27	+21
Peru	1997	30	Unicameral	Proportional	Open	11	18	+7
Venezuela	1998	30	Lower House	Combined	Closed	6	13	+7
Panama	1997	30	Unicameral	Combined	Closed	8	10	+2
Venezuela	1998	30	Senate	Combined	Closed	8	9	+2
Bolivia	1997	30	Lower House	Combined	Closed	11	12	+1
Mexico	1997	30	Senate	Combined	Closed	15	16	+1
Bolivia	1997	30	Senate	Combined	Closed	4	4	0
Brazil	1997	30	Lower House	Proportional	Open	7	6	–1
Mexico	1996	30	Lower House	Combined	Closed	17	16	–1
Indonesia	2003	30	Lower House	Proportional	Closed	9	N/a	N/a
Macedonia	2001	30	Lower House	Combined	Closed		17.5	N/a
Serbia	2002	30	Lower House	Proportional	Open	7.5	N/a	N/a

Dominican Rep.	1997	25	Lower House	Proportional	Closed	12	16	+4
Ecuador	1997	20	Unicameral	Combined	Open	4	15	+11
Paraguay	1996	20	Senate	Proportional	Closed	11	18	+7
Paraguay	1996	20	Lower House	Proportional	Closed	3	3	0
Korea, North	–	20	Lower House	Majoritarian	–		20.1	
Philippines	1995	20	Lower House	Combined	Closed		17.8	
Armenia	1999	5	Lower House	Combined	Closed		3.1	
Nepal	1990	5	Lower House	Majoritarian	–		5.9	
Average		*30*				*10*	*14*	*+4*

Note: Legal gender quotas for the lower house of national parliaments are defined as laws which specify that each party must include a minimum proportion of women on party lists of candidates. Change is estimated based on the percentage of women MPs in the parliamentary election held immediately before and after implementation of the gender quota law.

Sources: Mala Htun. 2001. "Electoral rules, parties, and the election of women in Latin America." Paper for the annual meeting of the American Political Science Association, San Francisco, August 30, 2001; Mala Htun and Mark Jones. 2002. "Engendering the Right to Participate in Decision-making: Electoral Quotas and Women's Leadership in Latin America." In *Gender and the Politics of Rights and Democracy in Latin America*, Eds. Nikki Craske and Maxine Molyneux. London: Palgrave; International IDEA. *Global Database of Quotas for Women.* Available online at www.idea.int.

Senate, and also to regional, community, provincial, and municipal councils, as well as to elections to the European Parliament. If this requirement is not respected, the list candidacies that would otherwise have been held by women have to be left blank or the whole list is declared invalid.[26] The Act was first fully enforced in the 1999 European elections that saw the proportion of Belgian women MEPs rise from 18.5 to 23.3%. This was an increase, albeit a modest one, but the power of incumbency means that it will take many successive elections under the new rules before women become a third or more of Belgian parliamentarians.

In 1999 France passed the parity law, a constitutional amendment requiring parties to include 50% representation of women in their party lists for election, with financial penalties attached for failure to do so. The gender parity law passed in June 2000 specified that for elections to the National Assembly between 48 and 52% of all candidates presented nationwide by any given political party must be women. If this percentage is higher or lower, the state will cut its financial contribution. The results of the first elections held in March 2001 under the new rules indicate a substantial impact at municipal level, almost doubling the number of women in local office from 25 to 47%. Nevertheless, in the first elections to the French National Assembly held under the parity rules, in June 2002, the proportion of elected women rose by only 1.4%, from 10.9 to 12.3%. Only eight more women entered the Assembly, dashing the hopes of the reformers. The main reasons were that the parity law failed to specify the selection of women for particular types of single-member seats, so that women nominees could be concentrated in unwinnable constituencies. Moreover, the major parties decided to favor incumbents, largely ignoring the financial penalty of reduced party funding associated with imbalanced party lists.[27] The sanction is a reduction in the public funding received for each party's campaign on a sliding scale of 5% for a gender difference of 10% on party lists of candidates, 30% for a difference of 60%, and a maximum 50% for a difference of 100%. Hence an all-male list would still get half the public funding. Despite the parity law, the proportion of women in the Chamber of Deputies means that France is ranked 61st worldwide after reform, compared with 59th before parity was introduced.

Another parallel European case concerns Italy, where a quota system was introduced in 1993 into the legislation governing municipal, provincial, and national elections.[28] These laws asserted that a minimum of 30% of both sexes had to be present in electoral lists. In 1995, however, the Italian Constitutional Tribunal repealed these regulations, considering that they were contrary to the principle of equality. Some parties have introduced voluntary gender quotas into their party rules, set at 50% for Verdi, 40% for DS, 40% for the PRC, and 20% for the PPI. Yet in the 2001 election women remained only 9.8% of the Italian Chamber of Deputies, ranking Italy 77th worldwide. In Armenia, the 1999 Electoral Code states that the voting lists of the parties involved in the proportional parliamentary electoral system should contain not less than 5% female candidates, but the low level and poor implementation meant that women in the June 1999 elections were only 3.1% of the national parliament.

During the early 1990s, with the expansion of democracy, the popularity of statutory gender quotas spread rapidly in Latin America. The first and most effective law (Ley de Cupos) was passed in Argentina in 1991, introducing an obligatory quota system for all parties contesting national elections to the Chamber of Deputies: "*lists must have, as a minimum, 30% of women candidates and in proportions with possibilities of being elected. Any list not complying with these requisites shall not be approved.*" Most important, the law stipulates that women must be ranked throughout party lists, not consigned to the end where they face no realistic chance of election. Party lists failing to comply with the law are rejected. If a rejected list is not corrected so as to bring it into compliance with the law, the party in question cannot compete in that district's congressional election. The provincial branches of the political parties create the closed party lists from which the Argentine deputies are elected, although at times the national party intervenes to impose a list. Following the implementation of the law, in the 1993 Chamber election, 21.3% (27 of 127) of the deputies elected were women, compared with only 4.6% (6 of 130) in the election of 1991. A decade after passage, the proportion of women in the Chamber of Deputies had risen to 30.7% (79 out of 257), ranking Argentina 9th from the top worldwide in the representation of women. In total, eleven Latin American countries now have adopted national laws establishing a minimum percentage for women's participation as candidates in national elections, and a twelfth – Colombia – had approved a quota of 30% for women in senior positions in the executive branch.[29] Although in these countries the impact has been varied, a comparison in Table 8.4 of the elections held immediately before and after passage of these laws suggests that legislative quotas generated on average an eight-percentage-point gain in women's election to congress. Variation in the effectiveness of the quotas can be explained by whether the PR list is open or closed (with the latter most effective), the existence of placement mandates (requiring parties to rank women candidates in high positions on closed party lists), district magnitude (the higher the number of candidates in a district, the more likely quotas are to work), and good faith party compliance.

Statutory gender quotas have also been applied to local, municipal, and regional contests. In South Africa the Municipal Structures Act states that political parties must seek to ensure that women comprise 50% of lists submitted for election at the local level. Following the municipal elections in 2000, women were 28.2% of local councilors. In the Namibian local authority elections in 1992 and 1998, the law required political parties to include at least 30% women on their party candidate lists.

The comparison of legal gender quotas suggests grounds for caution for those who hope that these strategies will automatically produce an immediate short-term rise in women legislators. The French case, in particular, illustrates the way the detailed aspects of how such quotas are implemented, and the sanctions for noncompliance, can generate very different results even for municipal and national elections within the same country. The variations in the results across Latin America confirm these observations.

Voluntary Gender Quotas in Party Rules

Most commonly, however, voluntary gender quotas have been introduced within specific parties, particularly those of the left, rather than being implemented by electoral law.[30] Rules, constitutions, and internal regulations determined within each party are distinct from electoral statutes enforceable by the courts. Parties in Scandinavia, Western Europe, and Latin America often have used voluntary gender quotas, and Communist parties in Central and Eastern Europe employed them in the past. It is difficult to provide systematic and comprehensive analysis of party rules worldwide, but in spring 2003 International IDEA's *Global Database of Quotas for Women* estimates that 181 parties in 58 countries use gender quotas for electoral candidates for national parliaments.[31] The effects of these measures can be analyzed by focusing on their use within the European Union because this allows us to compare a range of representative democracies at similar levels of socio-economic development. Table 8.6 compares the use of gender quotas for the candidate selection process in national elections in the fifteen EU-member states. By 2000, among 76 relevant European parties (with at least ten members in the lower house), almost half (35 parties) use gender quotas, and two dozen of these have achieved levels of female representation in the lower house of parliament over 24%.[32] Among the European parties using gender quotas, on average one-third (33%) of their elected representatives were women. By contrast, in the European parties without gender quotas, only 18% of their members of parliament were women. Of course, it might be misleading to assume any simple cause and effect at work here because parties more sympathetic toward women in public office also are more likely to introduce gender quotas. European parties of the left commonly introduced voluntary gender quotas during the 1980s, including the Social Democratic, Labour, Communist, Socialist, and Greens parties, before the practice eventually spread to other parties. Nevertheless the "before" and "after" test, exemplified by cases such as their deployment by parties in Scandinavia, in Germany, and in the British Labour Party, suggests that the effect of voluntary gender quotas within parties also varies substantially.

Many of the parties ranking at or near the top of the proportion of women MPs in Table 8.6 are in Scandinavia. The Norwegian Labour Party was the first in this region to implement a 40% gender quota for all elections

TABLE 8.6. *Voluntary Gender Quotas in Party Rules Used in 15 EU Member States, 1996–2000*

	Party	Country	Election Year	Total Number of Party MPs	% Women	Gender Quota
1.	VIHR	Finland	1999	11	81.8	✓
2.	PDS	Germany	1998	36	58.3	✓
3.	B90/Grüne	Germany	1998	47	57.4	✓
4.	Centerpartiet	Sweden	1998	18	55.6	✗
5.	GroenLinks	Netherlands	1998	11	54.5	✓
6.	Miljöpartiet de Grona	Sweden	1998	16	50.0	✓
7.	Social Democrats	Sweden	1998	131	49.6	✓
8.	PvdA	Netherlands	1998	45	48.9	✓
9.	Ecolo	Belgium	1999	11	45.5	✓
10.	SDP	Finland	1999	51	43.1	✓
11.	D'66	Netherlands	1998	14	42.9	✗
12.	Vänsterpartiet	Sweden	1998	43	41.9	✓
13.	Christian Democrats	Sweden	1998	42	40.5	✓
14.	SKL	Finland	1999	10	40.0	✓
15.	Socialstick Folkeparti	Denmark	1998	13	38.5	✗
16.	Venstre Liberale Parti	Denmark	1998	42	38.1	✗
17.	KOK	Finland	1999	46	37.0	✓
18.	Social Democrats	Denmark	1998	63	36.5	✗
19.	SPÖ	Austria	1999	65	35.5	✓
20.	Folkpartiet Liberelna	Sweden	1998	17	35.3	✓
21.	Social Democrats	Germany	1998	298	35.2	✓
22.	IU	Spain	1996	21	33.3	✓
23.	KF	Denmark	1998	16	31.3	✗
24.	Christian Democrats	Netherlands	1998	29	31.0	✓
25.	Dansk Folkeparti	Denmark	1998	13	30.8	✗
26.	Moderata Samlings	Sweden	1998	82	30.5	✗
27.	VAS	Finland	1999	20	30.0	✓
28.	PCP	Portugal	1999	17	29.4	✗
29.	ÖVP	Austria	1999	52	28.4	✓
30.	PSOE	Spain	1996	141	27.7	✓
31.	KESK	Finland	1999	48	27.1	✗
32.	VVD	Netherlands	1998	39	25.6	✓
33.	SFP/RKP	Finland	1999	12	25.0	✓
34.	Rifond. Communista	Italy	1996	32	25.0	✓
35.	CIU	Spain	1996	16	25.0	?

(continued)

TABLE 8.6 *(continued)*

	Party	Country	Election Year	Total Number of Party MPs	% Women	*Gender Quota*
36.	**Labour**	**U.K.**	**1997**	**418**	**24.2**	✓
37.	POSL/LSAP	Luxembourg	1999	13	23.1	✓
38.	PRL – FDF	Belgium	1999	18	22.2	✗
39.	FDP	Germany	1998	43	20.9	✗
40.	Party Socialist	Portugal	1999	115	20.0	✓
41.	PD	Luxembourg	1999	15	20.0	✗
42.	CDU	Germany	1998	200	19.5	✓
43.	PDS	Italy	1996	156	19.2	✗
44.	CVP	Belgium	1999	22	18.2	✓
45.	KKE	Greece	2000	11	18.2	?
46.	VLD	Belgium	1999	23	17.4	✗
47.	FPÖ	Austria	1999	52	17.3	✗
48.	**Partie Socialiste**	**France**	**1997**	**251**	**16.7**	✓
49.	PCS/CSV	Luxembourg	1999	19	15.8	✓
50.	Popular Party	Spain	1996	156	14.1	?
51.	PSD	Portugal	1999	81	13.6	✗
52.	CSU	Germany	1998	45	13.3	✗
53.	Labour	Ireland	1997	17	11.8	✓
54.	**PCF**	**France**	**1997**	**36**	**11.1**	✓
55.	Fianna Gael	Ireland	1997	54	11.1	?
56.	PASOK	Greece	2000	158	10.8	✓
57.	Party Socialist	Belgium	1999	19	10.5	✗
58.	Fianna Fáil	Ireland	1997	77	10.4	?
59.	Lega Nord	Italy	1996	59	10.2	✗
60.	PSC	Belgium	1999	10	10.0	✗
61.	Verdi (Greens)	Italy	1996	21	9.5	✗
62.	Forza Italia	Italy	1996	123	8.1	✗
63.	New Democrats	Greece	2000	125	8.0	✓
64.	**Conservative**	**U.K.**	**1997**	**165**	**7.9**	✗
65.	P-S-P-U-P	Italy	1996	67	7.5	✗
66.	CDS-PP	Portugal	1999	15	6.7	?
67.	Vlaams Blok	Belgium	1999	15	6.7	✗
68.	**Liberal Democrat**	**U.K.**	**1997**	**45**	**6.5**	✗
69.	**RCV**	**France**	**1997**	**33**	**6.1**	?
70.	**UDF**	**France**	**1997**	**113**	**5.3**	✗
71.	Alleanza Nazionale	Italy	1996	93	4.3	✗
72.	Lista Dini	Italy	1996	25	4.0	✗

	Party	Country	Election Year	Total Number of Party MPs	% Women	Gender Quota
73.	**RPR**	France	1997	140	3.6	✗
74.	CCD-CDU	Italy	1996	30	3.3	✗
75.	**UUP**	U.K.	1997	10	0.0	✗
76.	SP	Belgium	1999	14	0.0	✗

Notes: Voluntary gender quotas are defined as internal party rules, regulations, or constitutions specifying that the party should include a minimum proportion of women as candidates for elected office. The table only includes relevant parties (i.e., those with at least ten seats in lower house of the national parliament). The data, derived originally from the Council of Europe database, has some important limitations. It should be noted that the definition and meaning of "quota" can differ among parties, and some may use this only for internal organizational posts rather than for candidate nomination. Parties without a formal quota may instead apply a "gender target," adhered to more or less rigidly in candidate selection. Parties **in bold** are in countries using majoritarian electoral systems.

√ Gender quota is currently used by this party for parliamentary nominations.

✗ Gender quota is not currently used by this party for parliamentary nominations.

? Information on gender quotas is not available from this source.

Source: Meg Russell. 2000. *Women's Representation in U.K. Politics: What can be done within the Law?* London: The Constitution Unit Report. University College. The original data in the report was compiled from the Council of Europe. "Women and Politics Database." Available online at http://www.db-decision.de/index.html.

in 1983, although this did not specify the location of women candidates within their lists. Other Norwegian parties followed suit, including the Social Left, the Center Party, and the Christian Democrats.[33] This was followed by Denmark where the Social Democratic Party introduced a 50% quota for elections in 1988.[34] Because the rank position of candidates on the party list is critical to their success in being elected, in 1994 the Swedish Social Democratic Party introduced the principle of including a woman as every second name on the list – the "zipper" or "zebra" principle. This means that every second name on the party's nomination list must alternate between women and men. In Sweden, since the general election in 1994, the largest political party, the Social Democrats, and later the Greens and the Christian Democrats, systematically have alternated women's and men's names in their lists of the constituency candidates for parliamentary, local, regional, and the EU Parliament elections. If we compare the Swedish parties ranked high in Table 8.6, it is apparent that gender quotas are used by some such as the Social Democrats and the Vänsterpartiet, although not all the credit should go to the use of positive action, by any means, as other Swedish parties including the Centerpartiet also have a substantial number of women MPs despite not using any gender quotas.

Elsewhere in Western Europe, as shown in Table 8.6, formal practices vary among countries and parties. In Germany, for example, three of the five major political parties have a 40 to 50% quota system in their party rules. In 1980, when the Greens turned from a social movement into a political party, they instilled gender balance by including a strict 50% quota combined with a zipper system in their statutes. Except for the very top positions in government, the Greens have been more or less able to meet their requirements. In 1988 the Social Democrats followed suit by stipulating in party rules that in all internal party elections at least one-third of candidates must be female. From 1994 onward, 40% of all party positions have to be held by women. For election lists, parliamentarian mandates, and public office a transition period with lower percentages was agreed. It started with one-quarter in 1988, required one-third in 1994, and reached 40% in 1998. The SPD met the targets within the party but fell slightly short for seats in parliaments and in governments. In 1996 the Christian Democratic Party (CDP) introduced the so-called quorum requiring 30% of female representation in both party functions and election lists, but so far these targets have not been met. After German unification the Partei des Demokratischen Sozialismus (PDS, former East German Communist Party) introduced a strict 50% quota in combination with a zipper system. In many elections the PDS has outperformed its own targets. Currently, only the Christlich-Soziale Union (CSU, the Bavarian sister party of the CDP) and the Liberals (Freie Demokratische Partei, FDP) refuse to introduce voluntary gender quotas.

It is often easier to implement positive action in proportional elections using party lists but these strategies can also be used under majoritarian rules. In Britain, the Labour Party first agreed to the principle of quotas to promote women's representation in internal party positions in the late 1980s.[35] In 1988 a minimalist measure was agreed for candidate selection for Westminster, so that if a local branch nominated a woman, at least one woman should be included on the constituency shortlist. In 1993, following an electoral defeat where the party failed to attract sufficient support amongst women voters, it was decided that more radical measures were necessary. Consequently, the Labour Party's annual conference agreed that in half the seats where Labour MPs were retiring, and in half the party's key target marginal seats, local party members would be required to select their parliamentary candidate from an all-women shortlist. Other seats would be open to both women and men. Although this policy was subsequently dropped under legal challenge, it still proved highly effective, contributing toward doubling the number of women in the U.K. House of Commons from 1992 to 1997.[36] Despite abandoning the original policy, low levels of incumbency turnover maintained most of these gains in the subsequent general election in 2001. For the first elections to the new Scottish Parliament, Welsh Assembly, and Great London Assembly, Labour adopted a "twinning" policy. The system "twinned" neighboring seats, taking into account their "winnability," so that each pair would select one man and one woman. This opportunity was uniquely available, given that there were no incumbent members. Under this system, local party selectors in the two constituencies would come together to pick candidates, and each would have two votes – one for a woman and one for a man.

Gender quotas are by no means limited to established democracies. In South Africa, for example, in 1994 the African National Congress implemented a 33.3% gender quota into party rules, while in Mozambique in 1999 the Frelimo Party introduced a 30% quota on electoral lists. This policy has been particularly common among parties of the left, and the Socialist International Women lists fifty-seven socialist parties using gender quotas in April 2002, ranging from 20 to 50%, including the Israeli Meretz (40%), the Mali Adema-Pasj (30%), the Nicaraguan FSLN (30%), and the Turkish CHP (25%).[37] Gathering systematic and reliable data on the use of such strategies worldwide is difficult, but a global review of practices by the Inter-Parliamentary Union in 1993 found that twenty-two parties employed gender quotas for legislative elections, whereas fifty-one parties used them for elections to internal party posts.[38] By contrast, in the first democratic elections following the fall of the Berlin wall, parties within Central and Eastern Europe often moved in the opposite direction, abandoning gender quotas for parliament and local government that were regarded as part of the old Communist state,[39] although, occasionally, subsequently reinstating this practice such as in the Czech Social Democratic Party (SDP) (25%), the Bosnian SDP (30%), and the Lithuanian SDP (30%).

Cultural Modernization

Yet there is no automatic relationship between women's representation and the type of electoral system or, indeed, the use of legal or voluntary gender quotas. For example, in the PR countries under comparison, women are 4 out of 10 members of parliament in Sweden, but they are only about 1 in 10 in Romania and Israel. Even within established democracies, during the 1950s and 1960s there was little difference between the proportion of women elected under PR and under majoritarian systems. It was only from the 1970s onward that the proportion of women elected under PR expanded substantially in Western Europe. This pattern suggests that although the electoral system may function as a facilitating condition, it may well interact with broader cultural factors, for example, the way that women's opportunities in education and the workforce expanded in postindustrial societies and the second wave women's movement generated greater demands for women's inclusion in public life, from the late-1960s onward. Evidence presented elsewhere demonstrates that in recent decades a major shift in cultural attitudes toward the traditional division of sex roles, including the spread of more egalitarian attitudes toward the role of women as political leaders, was far stronger in postindustrial societies than in industrial nations.[40] Therefore, parties may respond to electoral rewards by selecting a more balanced ticket for public office under PR, but the strength of the incentive for parties to respond varies according to cultural attitudes in the general public and, therefore, to levels of societal modernization.

The interaction of political culture and the institutional rules may help to provide insights into persistent puzzles about why apparently similar institutional reforms may turn out to have unanticipated consequences, even among relatively similar political and social systems. Why should party-list PR be associated with many more women being elected to power in, say, the Netherlands than in Israel? Why should the use of gender quotas for candidacies seem to work better in Argentina than in Ecuador? Rather like the failure of Westminster-style parliaments in many African states in the 1960s, uprooted institutions do not necessarily flourish in alien cultural environments. Evidence presented elsewhere suggests that contemporary attitudes toward women's leadership are more egalitarian in postindustrial than in post-Communist or developing societies, and that traditional attitudes toward gender equality remain a major obstacle to the election of women to parliament.[41] Ever since the seminal study on women and politics in the mid-1950s by Duverger,[42] it has often been assumed that traditional attitudes toward gender equality influence women's advancement in elected office, although, despite the conventional wisdom, little systematic cross-national evidence has been available to verify this proposition. Theories of socialization have long emphasized the importance of the division of sex roles within a country – especially egalitarian or traditional attitudes toward women in the private and public spheres. Studies of the process of political recruitment in established democracies like Britain, Finland, and the Netherlands have found that these attitudes influence both whether women are prepared to come forward as candidates for office (the *supply*-side of the equation) as well as the criteria used by gatekeepers such as party members and leaders, the news media, financial supporters, or the electorate when evaluating suitable candidates (the *demand*-side).[43] In cultures with traditional values concerning the role of women in the home and family, many women may be reluctant to run and, if they seek the office, they may fail to attract sufficient support to win. A study by the Inter-Parliamentary Union found that female politicians in many countries nominated hostile attitudes toward women's political participation as one of the most important barriers to running for parliament.[44] Cultural explanations provide a plausible reason why women have made such striking advances in parliaments within the Nordic region compared with other comparable European societies like Switzerland, Italy, or Belgium, since all these are affluent post-industrial welfare states and established parliamentary democracies with proportional representation electoral systems. Karvonen and Selle suggest that in Scandinavia a long tradition of government intervention to promote social equality may have made the public more receptive to the idea of positive action, such as quotas, designed to achieve equality for women in public life.[45] Abu-Zayd suggests that culture is an important reason why many nations with a strict Islamic background often have ranked at the bottom of the list in terms of women in parliament, despite notable exceptions in Islamic societies in top leadership positions.[46]

Commonly, therefore, traditional attitudes toward gender equality have been suspected to be an important determinant of women's entry into elected office, yet, so far, little systematic cross-national evidence has been available to prove this thesis. Most comparative studies have adopted proxy indicators of culture, such as the historical prevalence of Catholicism within West European societies, understood as representing more traditional attitudes toward women and the family than Protestant religions.[47] An early comparison by Margaret Inglehart found that women's political activism was lower in the Catholic than Protestant countries of Western Europe, and it was suggested that this was because the Catholic Church was associated with a culture that was more hierarchical and authoritarian in nature.[48] A more recent worldwide comparison of women in politics in 180 nation states by Reynolds indicated that the greatest contrasts were between dominant Christian countries (whether Protestant or Catholic) and all other religions including Islamic, Buddhist, Judaic, Confucian, and Hindu, all of which had lower proportions of women in legislative and Cabinet office.[49] The key question is whether the well-established relationship between electoral systems and female representation continues to hold in different religious cultures, particularly in a wide range of societies.

To assess the role of religious culture we can classify countries worldwide according to the predominant religion in each society, with data drawn from the CIA *World Factbook* 2002. Evidence presented elsewhere suggests that the type of religion is a suitable proxy indicator of culture because religious values are closely related to attitudes toward women in politics. Direct evidence of attitudes toward sex roles in the home and family, labor force, and public sphere is available in the last two waves of the World Values Survey conducted in seventy-five societies during the mid-to-late 1990s. The basic indicator measuring support for gender equality in political leadership used in this survey is the 4-point scale asking respondents to what extent they agreed or disagreed with the following statement:

People talk about the changing roles of men and women today. For each of the following statements I read out, can you tell me how much you agree with each? Do you strongly agree, agree, disagree, or disagree strongly? ... On the whole, men make better political leaders than women do.

The predominant religion in each society proved one of the strongest indicators of egalitarian or traditional attitudes. Using this measure, countries

TABLE 8.7. *Women's Representation by Predominant
Religious Culture*

	% Women	Number of Nations
Roman Catholic	14.3	57
Protestant	13.6	47
Buddhist	8.6	12
Hindu	7.6	3
Orthodox	7.1	12
Muslim	6.2	49
TOTAL	11.1	180

Note: The mean percentage of women in the lower house of the national parliament, 181 nations worldwide (2000). Religious culture: The predominant religion in each nation is classified using the CIA *World Factbook.* Available online at www.cia.gov.
Source: Calculated from Inter-Parliamentary Union. 2000. *Women in Parliament Database.* Available online at www.ipu.org.

that were most positive toward women's leadership included the Protestant Nordic nations (Norway, Sweden, and Finland), as well as many Protestant Anglo-American societies such as New Zealand, Australia, and the United States. Those that proved most traditional in orientation included the poorer Muslim societies of Egypt, Jordan, Iran, and Nigeria.[50]

Unfortunately, survey evidence of attitudes toward women in politics was only available from the World Values Study in about one-third of the countries under comparison in the CSES dataset, and the latter survey did not collect any direct information on this issue. Accordingly, the predominant religion in a country was selected to function as a proxy measure predicting cultural orientations toward women's leadership roles because Inglehart and Norris had identified the predominant religion as strongly related to support for gender equality. Table 8.7 shows that the proportion of women in parliament was, indeed, lowest in predominately Muslim states (6.3%), as expected, as well as in those countries in Central and Eastern Europe sharing an Orthodox tradition (7.1%). By contrast, women were about twice as successful in being elected to parliament in Catholic and Protestant societies, as Reynolds noted in an earlier study.[51] Nevertheless, despite this pattern, Table 8.8 demonstrates that once controls are introduced for levels of human development and for electoral law, this relationship is not statistically significant. Cultural–religious values do predict women's presence in politics, helping to explain important variations in parliamentary elites within similar electoral systems. Inglehart and Norris compared a wide range of electoral democracies and found that the direct survey indicators of attitudes toward gender equality were very powerful predictors of women in office.[52] But, nevertheless, in the 171 countries under comparison worldwide, structural

TABLE 8.8. *Women's Representation by Electoral Family and Type of Religious Culture*

Type of Society	Electoral Family	% of Women in the Lower House, 2000	Number of Nations
Protestant	Proportional	25.1	13
	Combined	17.7	4
	Majoritarian	8.0	30
	Difference	**−17.1**	
Roman Catholic	Proportional	14.6	30
	Combined	15.4	11
	Majoritarian	13.1	16
	Difference	**−1.5**	
Muslim	Proportional	10.8	7
	Combined	7.3	7
	Majoritarian	5.9	29
	Difference	**−4.9**	
Orthodox	Proportional	7.8	5
	Combined	6.5	4
	Majoritarian	6.7	3
	Difference	**−1.1**	

Note: The mean percentage of women in the lower house of the national parliament, 159 nations worldwide (2000). Religious culture: The predominant religion in each nation is classified using the CIA *World Factbook*. Available online at www.cia.gov.

Source: Calculated from Inter-Parliamentary Union. 2000. *Women in Parliament Database.* Available online at www.ipu.org.

factors appear more influential factors affecting women's role in public life than the proxy indicators of cultural attitudes.

Conclusions

International agencies, governments, parties, and groups concerned with increasing women's representation have advocated a range of initiatives designed to break through the barriers for women in elected office, including using rhetorical strategies, equal opportunity, and positive action policies. Some of the principal options that are available include basic reform of majoritarian electoral systems by moving toward combined or proportional arrangements, the most difficult political strategy, as well as the use of reserved seats for women, the implementation of statutory gender quotas by law, and the adoption of voluntary gender quotas within particular parties. These policies all aim to alter the incentives when parties are selecting candidates for legislative bodies.

The evidence presented in this chapter provides further confirmation that the basic type of electoral system does, indeed, influence opportunities for women in elected office. Women generally are more successful in being nominated and elected under proportional electoral systems. It seems likely that in cultures where the public is broadly sympathetic toward the principles of gender equality, parties have greater incentives to create a balanced ticket, to avoid any electoral penalties from the appearance of sex discrimination against women. This electoral incentive is absent among local selectors with single-member districts in majoritarian elections, where each local party can choose the default option of a male candidate without any collective responsibility for balancing the social profile of candidates at national level. In theory, positive action policies can be adopted under any electoral system, but they are implemented most easily when applied to balancing the gendered composition of PR party lists, just as parties seek to balance collective party lists of candidates by the major electoral cleavages of region, occupational class, or religion. More women are elected to office under PR than majoritarian elections in countries from every religious culture worldwide, although by far the biggest gap by type of electoral system is found among Protestant nations as well as among affluent postindustrial societies. Furthermore, the multivariate analysis shows that the type of electoral system, the use of reserved seats, and the length of women's suffrage were associated with more women in parliament worldwide. Once these factors were introduced, the predominant religious culture (as a proxy for attitudes toward gender equality in different societies) proved to be insignificant. Although insufficient by themselves, the results suggest that PR electoral systems, in combination with positive action strategies, can serve to increase the diversity of legislative bodies, producing parliaments that look more like the people they serve.

9

Ethnic Minorities

Some of the most intractable problems facing democracies concern the management of ethnic conflict. The familiar litany of problems ranges from the inclusion of diverse racial groups in South Africa and Namibia to long-standing tensions between Catholic and Protestant communities in Northern Ireland, violence in the Basque region, the Israeli–Palestinian conflict, the Balkans, and the dramatic civil wars that occurred in Rwanda, Kashmir, and East Timor. Ethnic identities can be best understood as social constructs with deep cultural and psychological roots based on national, cultural–linguistic, racial, or religious backgrounds.[1] They provide an affective sense of belonging and are defined socially in terms of their meaning for the actors, representing ties of blood, soil, faith, and community. Agencies concerned with the peaceful amelioration of such antagonisms have turned increasingly toward "constitutional engineering" or "institutional design" to achieve these ends. The aim has been to develop electoral rules of the game structuring political competition so that actors have in-built incentives to accommodate the interests of different cultural groups, leading to conflict management, ethnic cooperation, and long-term political stability.

One of the most influential accounts in the literature is provided by the theory of consociational or consensus democracy developed by Arend Lijphart, which suggests that the institutional arrangements, particularly the type of electoral system, can maintain stable governments despite countries being deeply divided into distinct ethnic, linguistic, religious, or cultural communities.[2] Consociational systems are characterized by institutions facilitating cooperation and compromise among political leaders, maximizing the number of "winners" in the system, so that separate communities can coexist peacefully within the common borders of a single nation-state. Electoral systems represent, perhaps, the most powerful instrument available for institutional engineering, with far-reaching consequences for party systems, the composition of legislatures, and the durability of democratic arrangements.[3]

As we have seen, majoritarian electoral systems systematically exaggerate the parliamentary lead for the party in first place, to secure a decisive outcome and government accountability, thereby, excluding smaller parties from the division of spoils. By contrast, proportional electoral systems lower the hurdles for smaller parties, maximizing their inclusion into the legislature, and ultimately, into coalition governments. Consociational theories suggest that proportional electoral systems are most likely to facilitate accommodation between diverse ethnic groups, making them more suitable for transitional and consolidating democracies struggling to achieve legitimacy and stability in plural societies.

These are important claims that, if true, have significant consequences. To explore the evidence for these arguments, the first part of this chapter summarizes the key assumptions in consociational theories of democracy and outlines the central propositions examined. The second part describes the research design and methods. Evidence from the CSES facilitates comparison of political attitudes and behavior among a diverse range of ethnic minorities including the Russian-speaking population living in the Ukraine, residents in the Catalan, Galician, and Basque regions in Spain, African-Americans in the United States, the Arab/Muslim populations in Israel, the Scots and Welsh in Britain, the Hungarian minority in Romania, the mainland Chinese in Taiwan, and the Maoris in New Zealand. The third part defines and analyzes the primary ethnic cleavages in each of these societies and tests the central propositions about the effects of electoral systems on differences in minority–majority support. The results suggest a complex relationship between the basic type of electoral system and majority–minority differences in system support. In particular, the study throws doubt on the claim that PR Party Lists systems automatically generate higher levels of system support among ethnic minorities. The conclusion considers the lessons of these findings for issues of effective electoral designs and conflict mediation through constitutional engineering.

The Theoretical Framework

The central issue examined in this chapter derives from Arend Lijphart's theory of consociational democracy, in particular the claim that PR systems are more effective at engendering support for the political system among ethnic minorities. The core argument is that, in contrast to majoritarian electoral systems, PR (1) produces a more proportional outcome; (2) this outcome facilitates the entry of smaller parties into parliament; (3) this entry includes the election of ethnic minority parties; and, in turn, (4) these elections produce greater diffuse support for the political system among ethnic minority populations (see Figure 9.1). Although widely influential, the existing evidence for some of these claims is limited and remains controversial.

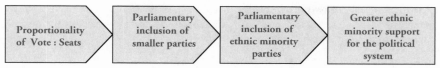

FIGURE 9.1. Proportional representation and outcome

Proportionality

The first claim is that majoritarian electoral systems are less proportional in translating votes into seats. As demonstrated in Chapter 4, considerable evidence supports this proposition. This study confirms the general patterns established in the literature.[4] Using the Gallagher Index, Lijphart compared parliamentary elections from 1945 to 1996 in thirty-six democracies and found that the average electoral disproportionality under PR systems ranged from 1.30 (in the Netherlands) to 8.15 (in Spain), and in majoritarian–plurality systems it ranged from 9.26 (Australia) to 21.08 (France).[5] Lijphart concluded that disproportionality was the product of district magnitude (the number of members elected per district) combined with the effective threshold (that is, the minimum level of votes that a party needs to gain seats).[6]

The Inclusion of Smaller Parties

The second claim is that more proportional electoral systems *lower the barriers for the parliamentary representation of any political minority*, whatever the background or ideological persuasion of its members, if the group seeks to mobilize and contest elections. Although the association between electoral systems and multipartyism is weaker than that between electoral systems and disproportionality, Chapter 4 established that usually more parties are elected under PR than under majoritarian elections. Lijphart's comparison of thirty-six established democracies from 1945 to 1996 found that the level of disproportionality in the electoral system was related negatively to the effective number of parties elected to the lower houses of parliament ($r = -.50$ p.01).[7] Katz concluded that PR is associated with greater party competition, including the election of a wider range of parties across the ideological spectrum.[8]

The Inclusion of Ethnic Minority Parties

By lowering the electoral barrier to smaller parties, it is claimed that PR, thereby, increases the opportunities for any ethno-political minority to enter parliament if its members want to organize as a party and run for office. In plural societies with strong cleavages, consociational arrangements, in general, and PR systems, in particular, are believed to facilitate minority representation. As Lijphart argues:

In the most deeply divided societies, like Northern Ireland, majority rule spells majority dictatorship and civil strife rather than democracy. What such societies need is a democratic regime that emphasizes consensus instead of opposition, that includes rather than excludes, and that tries to maximize the size of the ruling majority instead of being satisfied with a bare majority.[9]

Yet the evidence for the relationship between the electoral system and ethnic representation remains limited and controversial. Systematic comparative data on ethnic minorities is plagued by problems of operationalization and measurement, due to the diversity of ethno-national, ethno-religious, and ethno-linguistic cleavages in different societies. Rather than examining direct indicators, both Lijphart and Taagepera argue that we can generalize, using the proportion of women in elected office as a proxy indicator of minority representation in general.[10] The previous chapter confirmed greater female representation under PR Party Lists systems than under majoritarian electoral systems.[11] But is it legitimate to generalize from the representation of women to the representation of ethnic minorities? In fact, there are reasons why this strategy may prove misleading. Ethnic minorities are often clustered geographically within certain areas, such as the British Asian community in Leicester or African-Americans in Detroit, allowing local gains in particular constituencies in majoritarian electoral systems even within heterogeneous plural societies. By contrast, the male-to-female ratio is usually fairly uniform in distribution across different constituencies, except in a few retirement areas. Moreover, the use of positive action strategies including candidate quotas or reserved seats often differs considerably in the opportunities they provide for women and ethnic minorities. And we also know that, at least in Britain, women and ethnic-racial minorities face different types of discriminatory attitudes among selectors and electors.[12]

Considerable debate also surrounds to what extent generalizations about the workings of electoral systems in plural societies within established democracies can be extended to the management of ethnic tensions in transitional and consolidating democracies. Much existing research on consociational democracies is based on the experience of West European political systems that, by virtue of their very persistence, have come to a shared consensus about many of the basic constitutional rules of the game and a democratic culture. The classic exemplars of plural democracies are the Netherlands, Switzerland, and Belgium. But it may prove difficult to generalize from the context of stable and affluent postindustrial societies, with institutional arrangements and a liberal democratic culture of tolerance that has evolved throughout the twentieth century, to the process of conflict-management in transitional democracies struggling with the triple burden of socioeconomic development, the consolidation of the political system, and the global pressures of the world market. Only limited cross-national survey research has analyzed these issues in countries where ethnic politics often is regarded as particularly critical, such as in Africa.[13] Some older examples of consociational democracies in developing societies, such as Lebanon and Malaysia, have had a mixed record of success.[14]

The growing literature on newer democracies remains divided on this issue. Sisk and Reynolds argue that PR systems generally have been most effective in mitigating ethnic conflict in culturally plural African societies, by facilitating the inclusion of minorities in parliament and encouraging "balanced" lists. But this process is contingent upon multiple factors, notably the degree to which ethnicity is politicized, the depth and intensity of ethnic conflict, the stage of democratization reached by a country, the territorial distribution and concentration of ethnic groups, and the use of positive action strategies in the selection and election process.[15] Saideman et al. used pooled time-series data from the Minorities at Risk dataset and found that PR tends to reduce ethnic conflict.[16] By contrast, Tsebelis suggests that, although PR is useful in gaining agreement to a new constitution during the initial transition from authoritarian rule, in the longer term, proportional arrangements may serve to reinforce and perpetuate rigid segregation along narrow ethnic-cultural, religious, and linguistic cleavages, rather than to promote a few major catch-all parties that gradually facilitate group cooperation within parties.[17] Barkan argues that the cases of Namibia and South Africa show that parties representing ethnic minorities are not necessarily penalized by majoritarian systems.[18] Taagepera warns of the dangers of PR producing extreme multipartyism and fragmentation, which may promote instability in new democracies.[19] Because much of this work is based on country-specific case studies, it remains hard to say to what degree we can generalize more widely, for example, whether power-sharing arrangements in the new South Africa would work if transplanted to Angolan or Nigerian soil, let alone exported further afield to the Ukraine or the Balkans. The unintended consequences of electoral reforms – evident even in the cases of Italy, Japan, Israel, and New Zealand – illustrate how constitutional engineering remains more art than science.[20] Given all these important considerations, and continuing debate in the literature, more evidence is needed to understand the electoral fortunes of ethnic minority parties under majoritarian and proportional electoral systems.

The Impact on Specific and Diffuse Support for the Political System

The last, and perhaps the most controversial and important claim of consociational theory, is that by facilitating the inclusion of ethnic minority parties into parliament, PR systems increase mass-level ethnic minority support for the political system. Lijphart argues that political minorities are persistent electoral losers in majoritarian systems, excluded from representative institutions in successive contests, thereby, reducing their faith in the fairness of the electoral outcome and eroding their diffuse support for the democratic system in general:

Especially in plural societies – societies that are sharply divided along religious, ideological, linguistic, cultural, ethnic, or racial lines into virtually separate sub-societies with their own political parties, interest groups, and media or communication – the flexibility necessary for majoritarian democracy is absent. Under these conditions, majority rule is not only undemocratic but also dangerous, because minorities that are continually denied access to power will feel excluded and discriminated against and will lose their allegiance to the regime.[21]

In contrast under PR, because representatives from ethnic minority parties are incorporated within parliaments and coalition governments, consociational theory assumes that their supporters will gradually come to feel that they have more of a say in the policymaking process, so that minorities will become more satisfied with the fairness of the outcome of specific contests and more supportive at a diffuse level of the electoral system and the democratic rules of the game. Under PR, minorities should display more positive attitudes toward the political system because no group that can mobilize electoral support is excluded systematically from elected office on a persistent basis. Political leaders will learn to collaborate together within parliaments through deliberation, negotiation, and compromise, it is hoped, encouraging conciliation among their grassroots supporters.

Yet there is little direct evidence about the impact of electoral systems on cultural attitudes, such as satisfaction with democracy and support for the political system. Census data about the electorate can be aggregated at district or regional level to analyze ethnic minority voting patterns, for example, Horowitz used this approach to examine election results in Guyana, Trinidad, Congo, Ghana, and India.[22] Blais and Carty compared more than 500 elections across twenty nations to demonstrate greater voter participation in PR than in majoritarian electoral systems.[23] The main limitation with aggregate data is that we cannot establish how minority groups felt about the available electoral choices or the fairness of the electoral system.[24] If the rules of the game mean that some groups are systematically organized into politics and others are systematically organized out, ideally, we need to understand not just how groups voted, but also how they regard democracy and the political system.

Some light on this issue comes from a study by Anderson and Guillory that compared satisfaction with democracy among consensual and majoritarian political systems in eleven EU member states.[25] They hypothesized that: (1) system support would be consistently influenced by whether people were among the winners and losers in electoral contests, defined by whether the party they supported was returned to government; and (2) that this process would be mediated by the type of democracy. The researchers found that in majoritarian democracies, winners expressed far higher satisfaction with democracy than did losers, whereas consociational systems produced a narrower gap between winners and losers. This approach is valuable, but it is confined to Western Europe, it does not allow us to distinguish many national-level factors that may co-vary with the political systems in these nations, such as their historical cultures and traditions, nor does it allow us to distinguish the impact of electoral systems per se from other institutional variables.

Expanding upon Anderson and Guillory, in an earlier study I examined the impact of electoral systems upon confidence in representative institutions by comparing a wider range of twenty-five established and new democracies, using the 1990–93 World Values Survey. Using regression models controlling for social background, levels of democratization, and socioeconomic development, the study found that, contrary to expectation, institutional confidence generally was higher among respondents living in countries using majoritarian rather than PR electoral systems.[26] In an alternative approach, using a single-nation 1993–96 panel study, Banducci, Donovan, and Karp tested whether the move from a majoritarian to a proportional electoral system in New Zealand produced more positive attitudes toward the political system among supporters of minor parties and the Maori population. The study found that after participating in the first Mixed Member Proportional election, supporters of the minor parties displayed greater increases in political efficacy (they were significantly more likely to see their votes as counting and to see voting as important) than did the rest of the electorate, although there was no parallel increase in political trust: "*The lack of change on the main measure of trust in government is particularly striking, suggesting that the roots of distrust in government lie in something other than the rules used to translates votes into seats.*"[27]

We can conclude that consociational theory makes strong claims for the virtues of PR in plural societies. Lijphart argues that consociational power-sharing arrangements, and particularly highly proportional PR electoral systems with low thresholds, are most likely to include ethno-political minorities within legislatures and coalition governments, thereby, promoting support for democracy and cooperation between groups in states deeply divided by ethnic conflict. Yet this brief review of the literature suggests that the direct support for these claims remains mixed. The most convincing and systematic evidence, demonstrated in earlier chapters, concerns the impact of electoral systems upon the proportionality of the outcome and upon the inclusion of smaller parties within parliaments. In turn, under certain conditions, the inclusion of smaller parties in PR systems may influence the electoral fortunes of ethnic minority parties. But it remains an open question whether the inclusion of ethnic minority representatives leads to greater diffuse or specific support for the political system among ethnic minority groups in the electorate, such as stronger feelings of political efficacy, satisfaction with democracy, or trust in government. To go further we need to examine survey evidence measuring support for the political system among members of different minority communities. In Israel, for example, does the Arab community feel that they can influence the Knesset? In the Ukraine, does the Russian-speaking population regard the conduct of elections as free and fair? Does the Hungarian community and Roma (gypsy) groups living in Romania approve of the democratic performance of their political system? Are Basques and Catalans satisfied that their interests are represented through Spanish elections? It is to evidence about these matters that I now turn.

Testing Consociational Theory

Measuring Political Support and Core Hypotheses

What is the best way to measure the concept of "support for the political system"? Elsewhere, building on the Eastonian framework, I have argued that this is essentially multidimensional and so cannot be tapped reliably using single measures, for example, of political trust. This approach distinguishes between five levels of support ranging from the most abstract and diffuse level, measured by support for the political community such as the nation-state, down through support for democratic values, for the political regime, for political institutions, and for political actors. In this view, citizens can logically distinguish between levels, for example, trusting their local representative and yet having little confidence in parliament as an institution or approving of democratic ideals but still criticizing the performance of their government, and so on.[28]

Following this logic, four alternative indicators of political support were used for the analysis. Specific support was measured by perceptions of the *fairness of the electoral system*, the most direct evaluation of how well the election was seen to work. Responses to this could be colored by the outcome of the specific campaign under analysis, for example, by the party that won office. Diffuse support, understood to indicate more general approval of the political system as a whole, was measured by general *satisfaction with the democratic process*. It would remain consistent to approve of how the last election worked and still to remain dissatisfied with how democracy performed in general, or vice versa. The diffuse sense that citizens could influence the political process was tapped by measures of *political efficacy*. Last, *voting turnout* was compared as a critical indicator of involvement in the specific election. Factor analysis (not reported here) revealed that these items fell into two principal dimensions: the "approval" dimension meant that perceptions of the fairness of the electoral system were related closely to general satisfaction with democracy, whereas the "participation" dimension meant that political efficacy was related closely to electoral turnout. Details of the items used in the analysis are listed under Table 9.2.

Survey evidence provides direct insights into political attitudes such as satisfaction with democracy or feelings of political efficacy, but, at the same time, it remains difficult to compare ethnic minorities directly across a diverse range of societies. Multiple factors can influence specific and diffuse levels of support for the political system, including perceptions of government performance, cultural values, and general levels of interpersonal trust and social capital, as well as the standard predictors of political attitudes at individual-level, such as age, education, class, and gender.[29] Even with suitable controls, given a limited range of countries it becomes impossible to isolate and disentangle the impact of the electoral system from all these other factors.

Yet what we can compare is the *relative* gap in majority–minority political support within each nation. Given the existence of social and political disparities within every democracy, in general, we would expect to find that ethnic minorities would prove more negative than majority populations, for example, that African-Americans would be more cynical about the fairness of elections than whites, that Catalans and Basques would be more critical of the performance of Spanish democracy than other compatriots, that Arabs would feel more powerless to influence Israeli politics than the Jewish population, and so on. Therefore, the first core hypothesis is that within each country, ethnic majorities will express greater support than minorities for the political system. Support can be measured by attitudes toward the fairness of particular election outcomes, as well as more diffuse indicators such as satisfaction with democracy, political efficacy, and voting turnout. Focusing on relative differences between groups within a country holds cross-national variations constant.

Based on this process, as a second step we can then examine relative differences in political support among majority and minority populations under different electoral systems. If consociational theories are correct in their assumptions, if ethnic minorities feel that the political system is fairer and more inclusive of their interests under PR, then the second core hypothesis is that we would expect to find that these relative majority–minority differences would be smaller in countries with PR rather than majoritarian electoral rules. In contrast, if we find that the majority–minority gap in political support is as great under PR as under majoritarian systems, this would favor the null hypothesis.

Measuring the Primary Ethnic Cleavage

"Ethnicity" is one of the most complex and elusive terms to define and measure clearly. As mentioned earlier, ethnic identities are understood in this study as social constructs with deep cultural and psychological roots based on linguistic, ethnic, racial, regional, or religious backgrounds. They provide an affective sense of belonging and are defined socially in terms of their meaning for the actors. In Bulmer's words:

An "ethnic group" is a collectivity within a larger society, having real or putative common ancestry, memories of a shared past, and a cultural focus on one or more symbolic elements which define the group's identity, such as kinship, religion, language, shared territory, nationality or physical appearance. Members of an ethnic group are conscious of belonging to the group.[30]

Table 9.1 shows the distribution of the ethnic minority populations in the countries under comparison. The ethno-national category classified

TABLE 9.1. *Major Types of Ethnic Cleavages*

Ethno-National

	% Majority		% Minority Ethno-National Groups					
Czech Rep (ii)	Czech	94.9	Moravian	1.8	Roma	1.2	Other	2.1
Romania (ii)	Romanian	92.0	Hungarian	5.6	Roma (Gypsy)	1.4	Other	1.0
Britain (i)	English	85.7	Scottish	9.1	Welsh	5.2		
Lithuania (ii)	Lithuanian	85.2	Russian	6.9	Pole	5.8	Other	2.1
New Zealand (ii)	NZ European	81.6	Maori	14.4	Asian	1.4	Other	2.6
Spain (i)	Others	78.9	Catalans	15.8	Pais Vasco (Basque)	5.3		
Australia (ii)	Australian	77.8	European	16.6	Asian	3.0	Other	2.6
Taiwan (ii)	Min Nan	75.2	Hakka	11.5	Mainlanders	12.5	Other	0.8
Ukraine (ii)	Ukrainian	72.4	Russian	24.6	Other	3.0		
Czech Rep (i)	Bohemians	62.4	Moravians	37.6				
Israel (ii)	Jewish-Israeli	54.5	Jewish-European	20.1	Arab	14.2	Jewish-Asia	6.0	Jewish-Africa	4.5

Ethno-Racial

	% Majority		% Minority Ethno-Racial Groups					
Britain	White	97.1	Indian/Asian	1.6	Other	1.3		
United States	White	86.2	African-American	11.2	Asian	1.4	Other	1.2

Ethno-Linguistic (iii)

	% Majority		% Minority Ethno-Linguistic Groups					
Britain	English	97.8	Other	2.2				
Romania	Romanian	93.6	Hungarian	5.0	Other	1.4		
New Zealand	English	84.9	Maori	9.1	Other	6.0		
Spain	Spanish	82.6	Catalan	10.6	Galician	5.4	Basque	1.4
Israel	Hebrew	73.6	Arabic	15.0	Russian	10.9		
Taiwan	Min Nan	67.3	Mandarin	28.1	Hakka	4.3		
Ukraine	Russian	50.4	Ukrainian	49.6				

Ethno-Religious (iv)	% Majority		% Minority Ethno-Religious Groups							
Poland	Catholic	97.1	Other	2.9						
Romania	Orthodox	89.1	Protestant	6.3	Other	1.7				
Israel	Jewish	87.0	Muslim	9.6	Christian	2.2				
Taiwan	Confucianism	71.4	Buddhism	8.4	Taoism	8.6	I-Kuan-Tao	6.8		1.8
Ukraine	Orthodox	67.4	None	25.8						
United States	Protestant	55.5	Catholic	25.2	None	12.4	Jewish	1.9		
Britain	Protestant	54.9	None	32.0	Catholic	10.9				
New Zealand	Protestant	47.6	Catholic	13.3	None	26.3	Other	12.8		
Czech Rep	Catholic	45.3	None	46.7	Protestant	3.8				
Australia	Protestant	43.5	Catholic	28.6	None	15.8				

Center-Periphery (v)	% Majority		% Minority Rural Groups
Australia	Urban	76	Rural 24
Poland	Urban	64	Rural 36

Note: The figures represent the proportion of each group in the adult population (of voting age). Only groups over 1% are reported. Note that this survey was of the British electorate, not the United Kingdom, and, therefore, does not include respondents from Northern Ireland. (i) Based on standard regional classifications. (ii) Based on place of birth. (iii) Ethnic-linguistic cleavages are based on the main language spoken at home. (iv) Under religion, "None" includes atheists and agnostics. (v) Urban includes small town, suburbs, or large town/city.

Source: Comparative Study of Electoral Systems, 1996–2002.

respondents by their place of birth in all countries except for Britain, Spain, and the Czech Republic, where this was measured by residency in regions with strong national identities such as Scotland and Catalonia. The ethno-racial category in the United States and Britain was based on racial self-identification. In the third category, the distribution of ethnic-linguistic minorities was measured according to the language usually spoken at home.[31] The linguistic cleavage produced the strongest divisions in the Ukraine, which was equally divided between Ukrainian-speaking and Russian-speaking households; Taiwan, where there were sizable minorities speaking Chinese Mandarin and Chinese Hakka; and Israel, with its Arab population and Russian émigré groups; with Britain emerging as the most homogeneous population in its dominant language. Ethnic-religious minorities were measured by the respondent's religious identity, with Australia, the Czech Republic, New Zealand, Britain, and the United States the most heterogeneous, and Romania and Poland the most homogeneous, societies. It should be noted that this classification does not attempt to measure the strength of religiosity in the society, nor the "distance" between religious faiths, for example between Jewish and Muslim, both of which would increase the intensity of religious differences. The last category taps the center-periphery cleavage, classifying countries by the proportion in rural areas.

One consequence of their social construction is that the distinctions used to differentiate ethnic identities, and the political salience of ethnic cleavages, vary from one society to another. This complicates greatly the comparative analysis because we need to be sensitive to the particular conditions in each society, for example, the role of race in the United States, regional–national divisions in Britain and Spain, or the critical importance of religion in Israel. The relevant cleavages based on divisions of ethnic identity, race, language, region, or religion varied in the different countries under comparison. After examining the distribution of different social cleavages in the societies under comparison, as a first step to simplify the patterns under comparison, it was decided to focus the analysis in this study upon groups selected as the most politically salient majority–minority ethnic cleavage within each country (see Table 9.2). For consistent comparison, the aim was to identify the functionally equivalent groups across nations. Groups were selected based on the broader literature on ethnic cleavages in the electorate in each country and also based on scrutiny of the strongest cleavages predicting political support in each nation included within the CSES data.

In three cases the primary ethnic cleavage was defined by language, namely Mandarin Chinese- and Hakka-speaking minorities in Taiwan, the Russian-speaking versus Ukrainian-speaking populations in Ukraine, and the Hungarian-speaking population in Romania. In two cases this was defined by country of origin, namely the Maoris versus European populations in New Zealand and the Lithuanian versus Russian-Polish communities in

Lithuania. In three cases the major cleavages were based on region, including the Basque, Galician, and Catalan minorities in Spain; the Bohemian versus Moravian communities in the Czech Republic; and the Scots/Welsh versus English in Britain. Racial identities were used in the United States to distinguish the White versus African-American/Asian populations. In two nations, Poland and Australia, the main center-periphery cleavage was based on rural versus nonrural populations. Last, religion proved the primary cleavage distinguishing the Arab versus Jewish populations in Israel. In some nations the cleavages were reinforcing, for example, the Hungarian population in Romania and the Arabs in Israel proved distinctive in terms of their country of origin, language, and religion. In some other nations there were two distinct and independent types of ethnic cleavages, for example, in Britain the main racial cleavage concerns the Asian and Afro-Caribbean minorities, estimated to be about 2.9% of the electorate, and the center-periphery cleavage divides Scotland/Wales and England (see Table 9.2). The study excluded the separate scrutiny of single groups below 5% of the population where there were too few cases for reliable analysis.

System Support

What is the relative difference between the majority and minority populations using the four alternative indicators of system support? Table 9.2 shows the distribution of system support, the percentage difference between majority and minority groups ranked by size, and the significance of this difference, estimated using simple correlations without any controls. Where the difference is in a positive direction, this indicates that the minority proved more supportive than the majority. Where the difference is in a negative direction, this indicates the reverse.

In most cases, the results confirm the first hypotheseis, namely that where there were significant differences, the majority groups tended to prove consistently more positive toward the political system than did the minorities. In many cases the gap was substantively large, for example, there was far greater dissatisfaction with democracy among the Catalans, Galicians, and Basques in Spain; among the Hungarians in Romania; and among the Moravians in the Czech Republic. In five countries there was no significant difference in turnout, but in six countries levels of voting turnout were consistently lower for ethnic minorities such as among Arabs in Israel and the rural population in Poland. In only a few cases were there significant indicators of greater political support among minority than among majority populations, notably assessments of electoral fairness in Israel and Spain, and also higher levels of political efficacy among minority populations in Taiwan and the Ukraine. If we compare all types of political support, it is apparent that compared with majority populations, minorities proved more positive on only 4 out of

TABLE 9.2. *Indicators of Majority–Minority Political Support*

State	Major Cleavage	Minority	Majority	Diff. Sig.	Primary Minority Group	Elec. Sys.
Election Fair		*% Fair*	*% Fair*			
Israel	Religion	52	15	38**	Arabs/Muslims	PR
Spain	Region	92	79	12*	Catalans, Galicians, Basques	PR
Czech Rep	Region	83	80	3	Moravians	PR
United States	Racial	74	76	−1	Non-Whites	Maj.
Britain	Region	79	81	−3*	Scots/Welsh	Maj.
Poland	Center-Periphery	70	73	−4*	Rural	PR
Taiwan	Linguistic	58	64	−6*	Mandarin/Hakka	Mixed
Ukraine	Linguistic	33	41	−8*	Russians	Mixed
New Zealand	Ethnicity	71	80	−9**	Maoris	PR
Romania	Linguistic	72	82	−10*	Hungarians	PR
Lithuania	Ethnicity	39	58	−20**	Russians/Poles	Mixed
Satisfaction with Democracy		*% Satisfied*	*% Satisfied*			
Israel	Religion	58	53	5	Arabs/Muslims	PR
Lithuania	Ethnicity	34	35	−1	Russians/Poles	Mixed
Ukraine	Linguistic	9	10	−1	Russians	Mixed
Australia	Center-Periphery	72	80	−8*	Rural	Maj.
Britain	Region	69	78	−9**	Scots/Welsh	Maj.
Poland	Center-Periphery	57	66	−10**	Rural	PR
New Zealand	Ethnicity	62	72	−10**	Maoris	PR
United States	Racial	72	82	−10*	Non-Whites	Maj.
Taiwan	Linguistic	40	51	−10**	Mandarin/Hakka	Mixed
Spain	Region	48	64	−15**	Catalans, Galicians, Basques	PR
Romania	Linguistic	28	45	−17**	Hungarians	PR
Czech Rep	Region	42	62	−20**	Moravians	PR
Political Efficacy		*% High*	*% High*			
Taiwan	Linguistic	60	49	11**	Mandarin/Hakka	Mixed
Ukraine	Linguistic	80	75	6*	Russians	Mixed
Britain	Region	76	76	0	Scots/Welsh	Maj.
Israel	Religion	15	17	−2	Arabs/Muslims	PR
Australia	Center-Periphery	67	70	−3	Rural	Maj.
Czech Rep	Region	81	86	−5	Moravians	PR
United States	Racial	64	72	−8	Non-Whites	Maj.
Poland	Center-Periphery	69	76	−8	Rural	PR

(continued)

TABLE 9.2 *(continued)*

State	Major Cleavage	Minority	Majority	Diff. Sig.	Primary Minority Group	Elec. Sys.
New Zealand	Ethnicity	70	79	−9**	Maoris	PR
Romania	Linguistic	61	71	−10*	Hungarians	PR
Lithuania	Ethnicity	57	68	−11*	Russians/Poles	Mixed
Spain	Region	59	71	−11*	Catalans, Galicians, Basques	PR
Voting Turnout		*% Voted*	*% Voted*			
Romania	Linguistic	91	88	3	Hungarians	PR
Australia	Center-Periphery	95	95	0	Rural	Maj.
Britain	Region	82	83	−1	Scots/Welsh	Maj.
Taiwan	Linguistic	91	92	−2	Mandarin/Hakka	Mixed
Czech Rep	Region	86	90	−4	Moravians	PR
New Zealand	Ethnicity	92	96	−4**	Maoris	PR
Ukraine	Linguistic	74	80	−7**	Russians	Mixed
United States	Racial	68	78	−10**	Non-Whites	Maj.
Spain	Center-Periphery	80	90	−11**	Catalans, Galacians, Basques	PR
Poland	Rural	51	61	−10**	Rural	PR
Israel	Religion	67	86	−18**	Arabs/Muslims	PR

Note: The difference represents the majority minus the minority. The significance of the difference between groups was tested with correlation coefficients. ** = p.01; * = p.05.

Fairness of Election: Q2. "(PLEASE SEE CARD 1) *In some countries, people believe their elections are conducted fairly. In other countries, people believe that their elections are conducted unfairly. Thinking of the last election in [country], where would you place it on this scale of one to five where ONE means that the last election was conducted fairly and FIVE means that the last election was conducted unfairly?*" Percentage who believed election was fair (defined as categories 1 and 2).

Satisfaction with Democracy: Q1. "*On the whole, are you very satisfied, fairly satisfied, not very satisfied, or not at all satisfied with the way democracy works in [country]?*" The figures represent the percentage "very" or "fairly" satisfied.

Political Efficacy: The 15-point political efficacy scale was constructed from the following items that were highly inter-correlated. "High" efficacy was categorized as a total score of 8 or above.

Q11. *(PLEASE SEE CARD 5)* "*Some people say that members of [Congress/Parliament] know what ordinary people think. Others say that members of [Congress/Parliament] don't know much about what ordinary people think. Using the scale on this card, (where ONE means that the members of [Congress/Parliament] know what ordinary people think, and FIVE means that the members of [Congress/Parliament] don't know much about what ordinary people think), where would you place yourself?*"

Q13. *(PLEASE SEE CARD 6)* "*Some people say it makes a difference who is in power. Others say that it doesn't make a difference who is in power. Using the scale on this card, (where ONE means that it makes a difference who is in power and FIVE means that it doesn't make a difference who is in power), where would you place yourself?*"

Q14. *(PLEASE SEE CARD 7)* "*Some people say that no matter who people vote for, it won't make any difference to what happens. Others say that who people vote for can make a difference to what happens. Using the scale on this card, (where ONE means that voting won't make a difference to what happens and FIVE means that voting can make a difference), where would you place yourself?*"

Turnout: The question measured whether the respondent cast a ballot in the election. Functionally equivalent but not identical items were used in each national election survey.

Source: Comparative Study of Electoral Systems, 1996–2002

47 indicators. In all the other cases the gap was either statistically insignificant, or minorities proved more critical of the political system.

The second proposition was that the majority–minority gap would be related to the type of electoral system that operated in each country. Consociational theory suggests that ethnic minorities would prove most critical of the political system where they are systematically excluded from power, due to a majoritarian electoral system. Yet the pattern established in Table 9.1 proves too complex to confirm this proposition. Evaluations of the fairness of elections can be regarded as the most direct support for the electoral system per se. On this indicator, it is apparent that the ethnic minority–majority gap is indeed reversed in Israel and Spain, both using PR. Nevertheless, minorities under PR systems in Romania, New Zealand, and Poland proved far more negative than majorities by this measure. In addition, there was no consistent pattern across indicators. For example, when evaluating the performance of democracy in their country, understood as a more diffuse indicator of political support, minorities proved most critical in the PR nations of Spain, Romania, and the Czech Republic. Similarly mixed patterns, unrelated to the type of electoral system, were evident in terms of the majority–minority gaps on political efficacy and voting turnout. The analysis demonstrates *no simple and clear-cut picture relating the type of electoral system directly to differences in majority–minority political support*. This evidence, favoring the null hypothesis, does not support the claims of consociation theory.

To examine this pattern further, a series of regression models were run in each country predicting levels of political support for majority–minority population, adding social controls for age, education, and income. A positive coefficient indicates that the majority populations were more supportive than minority populations. Insignificant coefficients indicate no difference between majority and minorities. A negative coefficient indicates that the minorities were more supportive than the majority. The results in Table 9.3 show few significant differences in minority political support in Australia, Britain, and the United States, all with majoritarian electoral systems. The only exceptions were the Scots and Welsh who proved slightly more critical of the fairness of the election and of British democracy, a pattern that could be explained at least in part by the heightened salience of the issue of devolution in the 1997 general election. In the countries using mixed electoral systems, the ethnic minority groups tended to be less satisfied with democracy and less convinced about the fairness of the election outcomes. Out of eleven regression models, majorities were more positive than minorities in six models, and the reverse pattern was only evident in two. In the countries using PR, in the 24 separate regression models, where there was a significant majority–minority difference, minorities were more critical of the political system in 14 cases, and the pattern was only reversed in two cases (perceptions of electoral fairness in Israel and Spain, noted earlier). Across all indicators, the Maori population proved consistently more critical of their

TABLE 9.3. *Impact of Majority–Minority Cleavage on Political Support, with Social Controls*

	Main Cleavage		Electoral Fairness		Democratic Satisfaction		Political Efficacy		Voting Turnout	
			Beta	Sig.	Beta	Sig.	Beta	Sig.	Beta	Sig.
Australia	Center-Periphery	Rural	N/a		.035		.005		−.038	
Britain	Regional	Scots/Welsh	.041	**	.077	***	−.012		.000	
United States	Racial	Non-White	−.027		.033		.013		.013	
Lithuania	Ethnic	Russian/Pole	.133	***	.027		.060	*	N/a	
Taiwan	Linguistic	Mandarin/Hakka	−.016		.061	*	−.061	*	.005	
Ukraine	Linguistic	Russian	.061	*	.060	*	−.057	*	.088	**
Czech Rep	Regional	Moravia	−.003		.110	***	.012		.007	
New Zealand	Racial	Maori	.079	***	.094	**	.075	***	.067	***
Israel	Religious	Muslim	−.295	***	.041		.053		.169	***
Poland	Center-Periphery	Rural	.027		.048	*	.013		.013	
Romania	Linguistic	Hungarian	.077	***	.095	***	.040	*	.092	**
Spain	Regional	Catalan/Basque	−.068	**	.071	***	.091	***	.123	***

Note: These figures represent standardized regression coefficients for the effects of majority–minority membership of the main ethnic group within each country on the four indicators of support for the political system after controlling for age (years), gender (0 = female, 1 = male), standardized household income (5-point scale), and education (8-point scale). All models use ordinary least square (OLS) regression except for turnout, which uses logistic regression. For the scaling of the dependent variables see the footnotes to Table 9.2. Significant positive coefficients indicate that majority populations are more supportive of the political system than minorities. Insignificant coefficients indicate that there is no difference between majority and minority populations. Negative coefficients indicate that the minority population is more supportive of the political system than majorities. * = p.05; ** = p.01; *** = p.001.

Source: Comparative Study of Electoral Systems, 1996–2002.

political system, as did the Hungarian population in Romania, and a similar pattern was evident on three indicators for the Catalan/Basque population in Spain. Therefore overall the evidence examined here fails to support the consociational claims, which have to be regarded as unproven by this analysis.

Conclusions and Discussion

The issue of the most effective institutional design for managing ethnic tensions has risen in salience in the last decade, along with attempts at democratic aid and state-building. The strategy in this chapter has been to compare relative levels of satisfaction with the political system among majority–minority populations to see whether the gap was reduced, or even reversed, under PR Party Lists systems, as consociational theory suggests. The findings indicate that there is a complex pattern at work here, and the claim that PR Party Lists systems are associated directly with higher levels of political support among ethnic minorities is not confirmed by this study.

Yet it could be argued that perhaps the model within this study is too simple, and there are a number of reasons why any relationship may be conditional and indirect. First, the territorial distribution of different ethnic minority groups varies considerably, and, as Ordeshook and Shvetsova suggest, geography has a considerable impact on the working of electoral systems.[32] Some populations are clustered tightly in dense *networks* within particular geographic localities with distinct territorial boundaries, such as the British Sikh and Bangladeshi communities in the center of Bradford, African-Americans living in inner-city Detroit, or the French-speaking population in Montreal. Some are living in *mosaics* where two or more groups are so intermingled within a territory that it is impossible to identify boundaries, such as in Northern Ireland, the South Tyrol, and the Balkans. Other *diasporas* are spread thinly over a wide area across the boundaries of many nation-states, notably the large Russian populations in the "Near Abroad" such as in Ukraine and Lithuania, the Roma (gypsy) community in Central Europe, and the Kurdish population in the Middle East.[33] The geographic dispersion or concentration of support is important particularly for the way votes get translated into seats in elections that require winning a plurality of votes within a particular single-member district, not across the region or whole nation. In British general elections, for example, Plaid Cymru can win seats roughly proportional to their share of the vote because of the heavy concentration of Welsh speakers in a few North Coastal Wales constituencies, but in contrast, the more dispersed Liberal Democratic supporters are heavily penalized by FPTP.[34] African-Americans concentrated in inner-city districts can get many more House seats than minorities dispersed widely across legislative districts.[35] Territorial clustering allows homogeneous electoral districts representing different groups within heterogeneous societies.

Furthermore, the way that the electoral system shapes ethnic representation can be expected to vary according to the degree of politicization and mobilization of ethnic populations into the political system, as well as in the type of cleavages, whether based on ethno-national, cultural-linguistic, ethnic-religious, or racial identities. Some groups represent little more than a formal census categorization, which may have little resonance for the common identity of particular groups, such as "Asians" in the United States (Asian-Americans) bringing together émigrés from diverse cultures in India, Korea, Vietnam, Indonesia, and China; others share a single predominant cleavage, such as Hispanic groups in the United States sharing a common language but drawn from diverse national and political backgrounds; whereas still others such as African-Americans are bound together by communities based on their common experience of racial and social inequalities, and a shared historical heritage. As Lijphart points out, it is misleading to treat demographic classifications as equivalent to political divisions, for example, to regard the Protestant–Catholic division in Northern Ireland as equivalent to that in Switzerland.[36] Some societies are sharply segmented organizationally into separate subcultures, where groups have distinct political organizations, educational facilities, and cultural associations, whereas others integrate groups into the mainstream culture. Within the countries in this study, certain minorities find organizational expression within parties, such as the Hungarian Democratic Party in Romania, the (Arab) National Democratic Alliance in Israel, the Catalan Nationalist Party in Spain, the Scottish Nationalist Party in Britain, Sinn Fein in Northern Ireland, or the pro-mainland unification New Party in Taiwan.[37] Yet other distinct ethnic groups forward their issue agenda as broader coalitions within mainstream parties, such as African-Americans and Hispanics within the Democratic Party. Ethnicity is a particularly difficult concept to operationalize and measure, and single-dimension indicators based on the number and size of ethnic groups in different countries are unsatisfactory unless we can also gauge the geographic distribution and degree of politicization of these groups.[38] As with conceptions of class differentials, there is an important distinction between objective indicators of group membership (such as formal religious affiliations) and subjective consciousness of the political saliency of these group identities (such as religious debates over reproductive rights). Consociational theory assumes that ethno-political identities are given and proportional electoral systems, therefore, serve to mobilize ethnic parties into the political system. Yet as argued in Chapter 5, in the long-term there is probably a more complex process of interaction at work, whereby potential ethno-political identities are accommodated, but also mobilized and strengthened, by PR systems facilitating their organization and political expression through bonding parties.

Furthermore, majoritarian systems, even if they discriminate systematically against smaller parties, can still make special arrangements for minority representation. As discussed in the previous chapter, reserved seats for ethno-political minorities have been adopted in countries as diverse as Jordan (for Christians and Circassians), Pakistan (10 seats for non-Muslim minorities), New Zealand (for Maoris), Kurdistan (for Assyrians and Turkmens), Lebanon (for Maronites, Sunnis, Shiites, Greek Orthodox, Druses, Green Catholics, and other groups), and Slovenia (for Hungarians and Italians).[39] Another option is the over-representation in the seats allocated to certain districts or regions, to increase the election of minority groups. This practice is exemplified by the smaller size of the electoral quota used in Scottish constituencies, and affirmative gerrymandering (or redistricting) for African-Americans, Latinos, and Asian Americans in the United States.[40] As with positive action strategies for women, discussed earlier, legal statutes and party rules can regulate the selection of parliamentary candidates to ensure that minority candidates are chosen for single-member districts or for party lists.[41] Lijphart acknowledges that majoritarian electoral systems can make special provision for the inclusion of certain specified ethnic or religious groups in parliament, but he argues that highly proportional electoral systems with low thresholds automatically minimize the barriers to office, which has the virtue of being seen as fairer than special provisions for special groups:

PR has the great additional advantage of enabling any minority, not just those specifically favored by the electoral law, to be represented (as long as they attain a stipulated minimum level of electoral support). Compared with majoritarian systems, PR can be said to have the advantage of permitting representation by minorities that define themselves as groups wishing to have representation as minority parties. PR thus avoids any invidious choices in favor of certain minority groups and, as a consequence, against other minorities.[42]

But the existence of alternative strategies implies that constitutional engineers could achieve minority parliamentary representation either through the choice of low-threshold PR systems or through majoritarian systems with deliberate recognition of predetermined minority groups.

Last, the electoral system, while important, remains only one component in consociational systems of democracy. Other institutional arrangements can be expected to prove equally influential in shaping minority views of the political system, such as federal or decentralized designs for regional power-sharing, executive-legislative arrangements including single-party or multiparty coalitional governments, the adoption of parliamentary or presidential systems, the division of powers between legislative houses, rigid constitutions protecting minority rights and subject to judicial review, and pluralist or corporatist interest group systems. Nevertheless, consociational theory suggests that PR electoral systems combined with parliamentary government are the fundamental institutions upon from which many other arrangements flow.

Of course, the evidence presented here remains limited, both in terms of the range of democracies included within the dataset and the way that ethnic minorities have been measured. If there is a relationship, it may well be one that is more complex and indirect, depending upon intermediary conditions such as the geographical clustering of ethnic minority populations, their levels of politicization as a group, and the relationships between ethnic identities, party systems, and parliamentary representation. Special arrangements, such as reserved seats for the aboriginal community in Taiwan or affirmative gerrymandering in the United States, can overcome some of the barriers facing minority groups within majoritarian electoral systems. We need to take account of how far ethnic minorities believe that they share a common identity with distinct political interests, and how far they believe parties within the existing power structure represent these interests. All these factors serve as intervening variables mediating the links between the electoral rules and how minorities perceive the political system. Understanding these issues is a major challenge before we can make any sweeping claims about electoral engineering. Nevertheless, given these important qualifications, the idea that more proportional electoral systems *directly* generate greater support for the political system among ethnic minority groups, as consociational theory claims, is not supported by these results.

Constituency Service

The lesson from earlier chapters is that we can identify some of the probable "mechanical" results of electoral systems with a fair degree of confidence – such as their impact on the structure of party competition or the proportionality of votes to seats. But what are the *psychological* effects of electoral systems on the attitudes and behavior of politicians, and, thus, on broader issues of political representation and accountability in democratic societies? The incentives for legislators to develop a personal vote or incumbency advantage may be determined by many formal rules, including most important, (1) the ballot structure; (2) the centralization of the candidate selection processes within parties; (3) the size of multimember districts; and (4) the use of any term limitations on legislators.[1] In this chapter I scrutinize some of the available evidence for these claims, focusing particularly upon the idea that candidate-ballots promote the individual accountability of elected members, by fostering stronger links between citizens and their parliamentary representatives than party-ballots. If true, we would expect that citizens voting via candidate-ballots should be more knowledgeable about parliamentary candidates, and should also have more contact with elected representatives, than those expressing their electoral choices through party-ballots.

What is the reasoning behind these claims? The ballot structure, determining how voters can express their choices, is assumed to be paramount in the chain of accountability linking representatives to the central party leadership and to local communities of citizens.[2] As discussed earlier, ballot structures can be classified into the following categories based on the choices facing electors when they enter the voting booth:

Candidate-Ballots

- In *single-member districts, citizens in each constituency cast a single ballot for an individual candidate.* The candidate winning either a plurality or majority of votes in each district is elected. Through casting a ballot, electors indirectly express support for parties, but they have to vote directly for a particular candidate. In this context, politicians have a strong incentive to offer particularistic benefits, exemplified by casework helping individual constituents and by the delivery of local services (pork), designed to strengthen their personal support within local communities. This inducement is particularly powerful in marginal seats where a handful of additional votes may make all the difference between victory and defeat.

Preference-Ballots

• In *open-list multimember districts electors cast a ballot for a party, but they can express their preference for a particular candidate or candidates within a party list.* Where citizens exercise a preference vote (otherwise known as an open or nonblocked vote), this strengthens the chances that particular candidates from the list will be elected and, therefore, changes their rank. Under these rules, politicians have a moderately strong incentive to offer particularistic benefits, to stand out from rivals within their own party. In most nations, the choice of exercising one or more preferential votes is optional, and the practical effect of preference-ballots is contingent upon how many citizens choose to just vote the party ticket without expressing a preferential vote. If most people decide to vote for the party list, then the effects are similar to party-ballots, whereas if most choose to exercise a preferential vote for an individual on the list, then the effects are similar to candidate-ballots.

Preference-ballots are employed in party list PR used in 27 electoral systems worldwide, including in Belgium and the Czech Republic, as well as in STV elections in Ireland. But this ballot is also used in plurality and majoritarian electoral systems, such as in the SNTV that has been used in the Republic of Korea, Japan, and Taiwan.[3] The majoritarian Bloc Vote also allows citizens to vote for individual candidates in multimember districts with party lists of candidates, and it is used in Bermuda, the Philippines, and Mauritius. There are some variants to these rules. In Finland, people must vote for individual candidates, and the number of votes won by candidates determines their party's share of seats. The *panachage* systems used in Luxembourg and Switzerland give each elector as many votes as there are seats to be filled, and electors can distribute them either within or across different party lists.

Dual-Ballots

• In *combined (or mixed) electoral systems voters can cast separate ballots in both single-member and multimember districts,* as exemplified by elections in Italy, Germany, and New Zealand. This category can be divided into either combined-independent (where the votes in both types of seats determine the results independently of each other) or combined-proportional (where the share of the vote cast for the party list PR determines the final allocation of seats). Where combined systems operate, most use closed-list multimember districts, so that citizens can cast a ballot for a candidate in their single-member districts as well as for a party in their multimember districts. The effects of dual-ballot elections depend upon what proportion of seats are allocated through single or multimember districts: where most seats are single-member then the effects will be closer to candidate-ballots, and where most are multimember then the effects will be closer to party-ballots.

Party-Ballots

• Lastly, in *closed-list multimember districts, citizens cast a single ballot for a party.* Each party ranks the order of the candidates to be elected within their list, based on the decisions of the party selectorate, and the public cannot express a preference for any particular candidate within each list. Closed-list multimember districts, where voters can only vote the ticket rather than supporting a particular candidate, are expected to encourage politicians to offer programmatic benefits, focused on the collective record and program of their party, and to strengthen cohesive and disciplined parliamentary parties.

This system is used in party list PR in 35 electoral systems worldwide, such as in Norway and Romania. It also operates in the Party Bloc Vote system, where electors can cast a ballot for the party list, and the party with a simple plurality of votes in each district is duly elected, as used in Singapore, Ecuador, and Senegal.

Although there are many reasons to believe that the ballot structure is important for the chain of accountability from legislators to voters and parties, nevertheless, it is only one factor at work here. A related arrangement is the mean district magnitude (referring to the number of seats per district). Extremely large multimember districts are likely to weaken the incentive to cultivate a personal vote in preference-ballot elections, as it will be difficult for any individual candidate to stand out from the throng. Moderate or small multimember districts, on the other hand, are expected to have the opposite tendency, for example, where four or five candidates are rivals in STV seats in Ireland.

Although beyond the scope of this chapter, the candidate selection and nomination process operating within parties is also expected to influence channels of accountability, in particular whether decisions are within the hands of the central party leadership or devolved downward to regional or local party activists, members, or voters (see Figure 10.1). The greater the degree of decentralization, then the stronger the incentive for politicians to

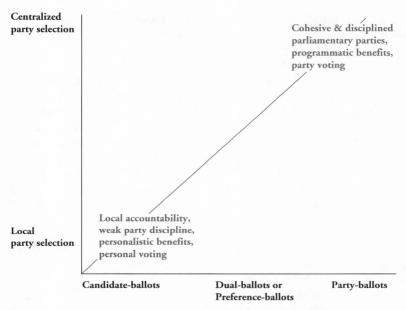

Centralized
party selection

Cohesive & disciplined
parliamentary parties,
programmatic benefits,
party voting

Local accountability,
weak party discipline,
personalistic benefits,
personal voting

Local
party selection

Candidate-ballots   Dual-ballots or   Party-ballots
                           Preference-ballots

FIGURE 10.1. The interaction of selection rules and ballot structures

emphasize local concerns. Although many expect that party rules will reflect
the structure of the electoral system, in fact, the degree of centralization of the
candidate nomination process is quite complex and diverse among parties,
depending upon their structure and organization. In mass-branch parties
with a tradition of internal democracy, such as in many Scandinavian parties, candidate selection decisions can be localized even within party-ballot
elections. At the same time, the party leadership can play an important role
in internal party decisions about nominations, even in candidate-ballot
elections.[4] In noncongruent cases, it remains to be seen whether members
see themselves as more accountable to the party selectorate or the electorate.
The rules governing the candidate nomination process are usually a matter
determined by each party, rather than by law, and there can be considerable variations even within the same country (such as the United Kingdom),
so that these rules cannot be compared through cross-national levels of
comparison.

Given accurate information about the ballot structure, rational vote-
seeking politicians are expected to adopt whichever particularistic or
programmatic strategy is necessary for gaining and maintaining office.
Candidate-ballots are expected to generate members who are highly responsive and accountable to local communities. Politicians have limited time
and energies, and in considering multiple demands vying for their attention, they have to decide among alternative priorities. Some politicians focus

their resources upon the delivery of particularistic benefits, and campaign upon their personal record of individual casework with government departments, tackling constituency concerns and delivering public services to their home district, working with groups on community problems, and being responsive to personal contact with local voters and grassroots party activists through attention to their mail, community meetings, party meetings, and doorstep canvassing.[5] By contrast, party-ballots, where voters can only vote the ticket, are expected to generate strong, disciplined, and cohesive parliamentary parties that are capable of passing their collective platform in the legislature. In this context, politicians are expected to emphasize the delivery of programmatic benefits, campaigning upon their party's collective record, policy platform, ideological image, and leadership team, with the aim of cultivating votes from party loyalists and identifiers. Preferential-ballots and dual-ballots are expected to fall somewhere along the continuum between candidate-ballots and party-ballots.

Of course, some politicians may fail to conform to these expectations. Yet the Darwinian logic suggests that, if citizens reward constituency service in single-member districts, under these rules politicians who fail to behave strategically will be less likely to be returned to parliament. Natural selection through the ballot box means that, over time, the legislature will gradually become composed of politicians pursuing more successful electoral strategies.

This model predicts that ballot structures (the independent variable) directly impact the behavior of rational politicians (the activities that they prioritize, as the intermediate variable) and that, by shaping voting choices, rules also exert an *indirect* impact upon citizens (the dependent variable). If we can establish certain systematic patterns of electoral behavior that are associated consistently with the type of ballot structure, then we can infer the linkages between electoral rules, political actors, and voting behavior.

It follows that reforms that alter the design of the ballot structure, a relatively simple legal procedure although one that can be politically fraught, should have the capacity to engineer important consequences for legislatures. For example, in parliaments with party-ballot elections, individual legislators are only weakly accountable to citizens, and the only way to get rid of lazy, ineffective, scandal-ridden, or corrupt politicians is to "throw the baby out with the party bathwater." Altering the ballot design could strengthen the accountability of elected members to local communities. In countries with party-ballots, where legislators neglect constituency service or casework, the priorities of representatives could be altered by the adoption of preference-ballots. Legislatures using candidate-ballots may suffer from an excessive focus on individualistic pork-barrel local politics to the detriment of collective public goods, party discipline, and government instability. In this context, the theory predicts that the cohesion of parliamentary parties could be strengthened by the adoption of party-ballots.

Review of the Literature

Despite the plausibility of these arguments, the evidence about these claims from previous studies remains mixed and inconclusive. The focus of so much of the literature on the U.S. Congress means that systematic cross-national research remains underdeveloped.[6] Some of the most plausible work is provided by Bernhard Wessels, who compared the role orientations of national MPs in Europe and Members of the European Parliament in the 15 EU-member states.[7] He found that district magnitude was related significantly to role orientations: the smaller the district magnitude – and, therefore, the more personalized the electoral competition – the more members said they prioritized work to represent their constituency. Another important indicator in favor of this proposition is a study where Curtice and Shively examined the evidence that voters were contacted more often and had better knowledge of candidates under single-member district systems rather than under PR multimember districts and concluded that in both cases there was a positive and significant effect.[8]

Evidence within particular countries confirms that parliamentarians in Britain and Australia, like members of the U.S. Congress, dedicate a considerable proportion of their time to constituency service.[9] British MPs face multiple conflicting demands, but in recent years they have devoted a growing amount of time to "service responsiveness": dealing with government departments on behalf of individual citizens and local groups, working with the community in their local areas, holding regular surgeries, and attending constituency functions.[10] MPs can help shortcut the bureaucratic maze of housing regulations, police complaint procedures, or social security claims for individuals or local groups, mediating on behalf of constituents to ensure government officials uphold their rights. The growth of such activities in the postwar period has been well documented in Britain. In the 1950s, Norton and Wood suggested, constituency service by members of the House of Commons was limited, or even non-existent.[11] The amount of constituency correspondence was minimal, perhaps two or three letters a day, while one-third of members did not hold regular surgeries, and two-thirds lived outside the seat. By contrast, from the mid-1960s onward the constituency role expanded: today local surgeries, correspondence, and spending time in the constituency occupy a significant proportion of the workload of most MPs. Estimates of timekeeping are never wholly reliable, but a 1971 survey found most MPs spent about eleven hours per week working "on behalf of constituents." A decade later this had increased to sixteen hours. By 2001 MPs estimated that they devoted thirty-three hours per week to constituency work, representing more than one-third of their workload. Another indicator is the growth in MPs' correspondence: in 1970 the average member received 25 to 74 letters per week. By 2001 the weekly mail had expanded to about 260 letters, just under half from constituents. Most hold weekly surgeries. These indicators suggest that constituency work for British MPs may have more than doubled in the last two decades.[12] Nevertheless, the strength of any rewards from voters for such activity should not be exaggerated. In Britain it has commonly been found that the personal vote for MPs is normally limited in scope.[13] Nor is there good evidence that the increase in constituency services offered by British MPs during the postwar era has strengthened any personal vote because the incumbency advantage remains small and sporadic.[14]

What remains less clear is whether members elected via other types of ballot structures also provide similar local services, especially under preference-ballots. Studies in Ireland under the STV elections, for example, have shown that representatives work hard for their constituents, and they may actually undertake more constituency business than their British equivalents.[15] Carey and Shugart argue that small-to-moderate multimember districts with preferential ballots may promote *greater* incentives for constituency service than single-member districts because candidates in multimember seats need to distinguish themselves from other contestants within their own parties.[16] In Colombia and Brazil, where party-ballots are used, studies suggest that the national legislatures devote much of their time to pork barrel politics with members focused upon district concerns, at the loss of party discipline and legislative cohesion in congress.[17] One reason for this behavior among members in the Brazilian Congress may be an indirect relationship, if pork generates campaign funds that, in turn, lead to personal votes.[18]

Moreover, it is not well established whether legislators in dual-ballot electoral systems differ in their priorities and activities if elected through party-ballots or candidate-ballots, such as in Germany, Mexico, and the Ukraine. Studies suggest a complex relationship between the type of electoral system, the degree of constituency casework, and knowledge of candidates, mediated by political culture, the traditional role of legislators, and the structure of government services. For example, Wessels suggests that few members of the German Bundestag engage in constituency service, irrespective of whether members are elected via the party lists or single-member districts because local services like housing, education, and welfare are the responsibility of the Lander level.[19] Yet others suggest that members of the Bundestag do vary, with those elected via single-member districts being more likely to be on committee assignments that could help them to serve their districts and, thus, gain reelection.[20] In dual-ballot systems, such as in the Ukraine, members of the Duma entering via party lists display greater party cohesion than those elected via single-member districts, although this relationship is contingent also upon the marginality of districts.[21] The strength of any voter-legislator linkages may be determined by the size of the constituency along with the provision of legislative staff, more than by the type of districts. Consider, for example, the amount of mail that can be generated in a populous U.S. Senate seat such as California compared with a small U.K. constituency such as the Western Isles. Based on a comparison of a dozen West European democracies,

Vernon Bogdanor was skeptical about assuming any simple and direct re-lationship between the basic type of electoral system and voters' aware-ness of candidates or levels of constituency service. The study concluded that cultural and historical traditions play a far more important role in de-termining parliamentarian–constituent relationships than the electoral rules per se.[22] Moreover, skeptics argue that attempts at electoral engineering – changing the electoral rules to alter legislative behavior – commonly fail. For example, although constituency service is entrenched strongly within Anglo-American democracies, the adoption of mixed-ballots in the Italian Chamber of Deputies, the Russian Duma, or the Israeli Knesset may not generate similar behavior in these parliaments if the predominant values, social norms, and institutional customs operating in these institutions are deeply rooted in historical traditions and socially determined.

Indicators of Personal Voting

These considerations suggest that we need to re-examine whether voter-member linkages are actually higher under candidate-ballot elections than under party-ballots, as claimed. This issue can be investigated in many ways. One approach is through comparing the workings of different ballot struc-tures within a particular country, with appropriate controls, which allow ideal "natural experiments" for testing these propositions. Hence, voters' awareness of candidates can be compared under different contests within the United Kingdom, including dual-ballots used for elections to the Scottish Parliament, party-ballots used for the European Parliament, and candidate-ballots used for the House of Commons.[23] To compare like with like, how-ever, this strategy can only attribute any differences to the type of ballot per se after a series of contests have been held. Even then, any differences in the public's awareness of candidates, or in the provision of constituency ser-vice, could be due to the functions and visibility of members of these bodies, rather than to the ballot structures per se. The comparison of before and after natural experiments, such as New Zealand or Italy, also provide valu-able insights,[24] although again much else can change in successive elections beyond the basic ballot structures, such as the role of particular issues, party leaders, and campaign events.

Direct information about constituency service was not included in the CSES survey, but we can use two common proxy indicators to gauge the strength of personal voting, namely (1) the name-recognition of candidates and (2) the reported contact that voters experience with elected members. Both of these measures have been used widely in the literature, and both should be higher where politicians focus upon personal campaign appeals. In comparing the strength of personal voting in different nations, we also need to control for many intervening factors that could influence this process. This includes aggregate levels of socioeconomic and human development in each country, as well as the standard social background factors operating at individual level, including age, education, gender, and income, which previous studies have found to be associated commonly with levels of political knowledge and with voter-initiated contact activity.[25]

The Impact of Electoral Systems

Citizens' Knowledge of Politicians

To examine the claims that the ballot structure affects citizens' awareness about parliamentary candidates, we need to establish what citizens knew about those seeking their vote. The CSES asked people whether they recalled any candidates in their district in the last parliamentary election and, if so, they were asked to identify their names. Up to three candidate names were recorded and these were verified as correct against official lists. It can be argued that citizens may still know much about the elected member or members from their district, and they may be familiar with opposing candidates standing for election, even if they remain unable to recall their names. Citizens may use heuristic shortcuts if they support "the Labour man" or "the Christian Democrat woman." Nevertheless, name-recognition is a significant indirect indicator of broader awareness of electoral choices, it has long been used in surveys to test political knowledge, and it is important as a minimal criteria before citizens can evaluate the record of elected members and, thereby, hold individual politicians to account.

Table 10.1 illustrates how far people could correctly identify candidates, without any controls. The results show that, overall, almost half of all citizens (47%) could not identify a single candidate. Most important, the data confirm that party-ballots generated the lowest level of candidate awareness: two-thirds of those casting a vote in party-ballots failed to recognize a single candidate. On the other hand, levels of awareness were moderate in preference-ballot elections, and highest in candidate-ballot and dual-ballot elections. Moreover, the pattern shows considerable variation among individual countries. The Japanese, Thai, and Korean electorates display the highest awareness of those standing for office: only 6 to 8% failed correctly to identify any candidate in these elections. In contrast at the other extreme, awareness was particularly low in Belarus, Mexico, Portugal, and Spain, where three-quarters or more of the electorate could not identify a single candidate. The other important pattern shown in the comparison is that the countries using candidate-ballots – Britain, Australia, and the United States – emerged as about average, and below the dual-ballot systems in Hungary, Germany, and New Zealand. In the United States, for example, 52% failed to recognize a single politician, while only one-quarter could correctly identify at least two. Citizens have similar levels of candidate awareness in candidate-ballot and dual-ballot elections, although both these types of contests show stronger knowledge than under party-ballot elections.

TABLE 10.1. *Knowledge of Candidates*

	% None Correct	% One Correct	% More than One Correct	Electoral System	Type of Ballot
Portugal	81	10	9	Party List PR	Party-ballot
Spain	74	15	11	Party List PR	Party-ballot
Romania	71	19	10	Party List PR	Party-ballot
Norway	31	18	51	Party List PR	Party-ballot
Iceland	17	14	70	Party List PR	Party ballot
All party-ballots	**66**	**15**	**18**		
Sweden	67	23	10	Party List PR	Preference-ballot
Poland	62	22	16	Party List PR	Preference-ballot
Switzerland	50	16	35	Party List PR	Preference-ballot
Czech Republic	42	21	37	Party List PR	Preference-ballot
Peru	35	34	32	Party List PR	Preference-ballot
Denmark	23	20	58	Party List PR	Preference-ballot
All preference-ballots	**45**	**24**	**31**		
Mexico	82	11	7	Combined	Dual-ballot
Taiwan	63	13	24	Combined	Dual-ballot
Ukraine	61	18	21	Combined	Dual-ballot
Hungary	37	24	40	Combined	Dual-ballot
Russia	29	17	55	Combined	Dual-ballot
Germany	24	43	33	Combined	Dual-ballot
New Zealand	21	20	60	Combined	Dual-ballot
Korean Rep.	8	51	41	Combined	Dual-ballot
Thailand	7	17	75	Combined	Dual-ballot
Japan	6	14	80	Combined	Dual-ballot
All dual-ballots	**41**	**20**	**39**		
Belarus	84	10	7	FPTP	Candidate-ballot
United States	52	24	24	FPTP	Candidate-ballot
Australia (i)	43	58		AV	Candidate-ballot
Britain	40	32	29	FPTP	Candidate-ballot
Canada	32	22	46	FPTP	Candidate-ballot
All candidate-ballots	**41**	**26**	**33**		
ALL	47	20	32		

Note: Q: *"Do you happen to remember the name of any candidates who ran/stood in your [lower house primary electoral district] in the last [parliamentary/congressional] election? [If YES] What were their names?"* (i) Only two categories were coded in Australia. AV, Alternative Vote; FPTP, First Past the Post.

Source: Comparative Study of Electoral Systems, 1996–2002.

Voter Contact with MPs

An alternative indicator of the strength of personal voting was measured by asking people whether they had any contact with an MP during the previous twelve months. This need not necessarily have involved constituency work or local service per se because contact could have been generated by forms of election campaign such as telephone or household canvassing, or by party rallies, as well as by constituency surgeries. Nor does this specify the direction of who originated the contact activity, whether bottom up from voters or top down from politicians. Nevertheless, in general, citizen contact with politicians should be strongest where legislators have the greatest incentive to cultivate a personal vote, under candidate-ballot elections.

Table 10.2 shows that on average about 12% of the public reported contact with an elected representative during the previous year, with the highest levels in Iceland, New Zealand, and Canada, and minimal contact activity in the Netherlands, Russia, and Spain. Without any controls, the initial pattern shows that voter-legislator linkages were greatest in candidate-ballot elections, as expected, where one-sixth of the electorate (16%) reported some contact. Moreover, candidate-ballot elections generated twice as much contact as party-ballot elections (8%). This supports the claim that candidate-ballots strengthen member–voter linkages, yet at the same time there were minimal differences among all the other types of ballot structures. The national distribution shows that the United States is about average in contact activity. A closer look at the rankings, however, indicates that some party-ballot elections, such as those held in Iceland, Israel, and Norway, are also above average in contact activity, as are some mixed-ballot contests such as those held in New Zealand and Lithuania. As discussed further in the chapter conclusion, multiple factors also may be contributing toward variations in the overall pattern – including the processes of candidate selection and nomination – as much as the ballot structure.

Multivariate analysis is required to examine these relationships in more depth. Logistic regression models can be used to examine the impact of the ballot structure upon the core measures of contact activity and knowledge of candidates. The models first entered controls for the level of development in each country (measured by the UNDP Human Development Index 1998) that might be expected to shape societal modernization, and the standard individual-level social factors that are found commonly to influence both contact activity and political knowledge, namely age, sex, education, and household income (the latter as a proxy for socioeconomic status). The second step then entered the electoral system variables, using dummies for whether elections had candidate-ballots, dual-ballots, or preference-ballots, with party-ballots used as the default category. The mean district magnitude was also entered. Details of the coding used for all items are listed in the notes to Table 10.3.

TABLE 10.2. *Contact with Elected Representatives*

	% With Contact	Electoral System	Type of Ballot
Iceland	31	Party List PR	Party-ballot
Israel	16	Party List PR	Party-ballot
Norway	15	Party List PR	Party-ballot
Romania	7	Party List PR	Party-ballot
Portugal	6	Party List PR	Party-ballot
Netherlands	5	Party List PR	Party-ballot
Spain	3	Party List PR	Party-ballot
All party-ballots	**8**		
Denmark	20	Party List PR	Preference-ballot
Switzerland	20	Party List PR	Preference-ballot
Chile	12	Party List PR	Preference-ballot
Sweden	11	Party List PR	Preference-ballot
Peru	9	Party List PR	Preference-ballot
Czech Republic	8	Party List PR	Preference-ballot
Poland	6	Party List PR	Preference-ballot
All preference-ballots	**9**		
New Zealand	24	Combined	Dual-ballot
Thailand	17	Combined	Dual-ballot
Korean Republic	16	Combined	Dual-ballot
Lithuania	15	Combined	Dual-ballot
Germany	11	Combined	Dual-ballot
Mexico	10	Combined	Dual-ballot
Japan	8	Combined	Dual-ballot
Taiwan	8	Combined	Dual-ballot
Ukraine	8	Combined	Dual-ballot
Hungary	7	Combined	Dual-ballot
Russia	3	Combined	Dual-ballot
All dual-ballots	**10**		
Canada	22	First-Past-the-Post	Candidate-ballot
Australia	16	Alternative Vote	Candidate-ballot
Britain	13	First-Past-the-Post	Candidate-ballot
USA	12	First-Past-the-Post	Candidate-ballot
Belarus	9	First-Past-the-Post	Candidate-ballot
All candidate-ballots	**16**		
ALL	12		

Note: Q: *"During the last twelve months, have you had any contact with a [Member of Parliament/ a Member of Congress] in any way?"*

Source: Comparative Study of Electoral Systems, 1996–2002.

TABLE 10.3. *Models Predicting Contact with Elected Members*

	Model I			Model II		
	B	SE	Sig.	B	SE	Sig.
SOCIAL CONTROLS						
Level of development	3.18	.220	.000	2.82	.253	.000
Age	.002	.001	.012	.001	.001	.130
Gender (male)	.365	.029	.000	.375	.029	.000
Education	.249	.015	.000	.225	.015	.000
Income	.098	.011	.000	.101	.011	.000
BALLOT STRUCTURE						
Candidate-ballot				.297	.054	.000
Dual-ballot				.329	.045	.000
Preference-ballot				−.196	.041	.000
Mean district magnitude				−.004	.000	.000
Constant	−6.25			−5.36		
% Correctly predicted	89.0			89.0		
Nagelkerke R^2	.040			.053		

Notes: The models using logistic regression analysis provide the unstandardized beta (B), the standard error (SE), and the significance (Sig.) with knowledge of candidates as the dependent variable. Model I: Models without the electoral variables. Model II: Complete model including electoral rules. Ballot structure: Preference-ballots, dual-ballots, and candidate-ballots are all coded as dummy variables, where party-ballot is the default category. Mean district magnitude: see Table 2.1. Level of development is measured by the UNDP Human Development Index 1998 (including longevity, education, and per capita GDP). *UNDP Human Development Report, 2000.* New York: UNDP/Oxford University Press.
Age: In years. Education: 8-point scale from none (1) to university graduate (8).
Income: Household income on a standardized 5-point scale.
Source: Comparative Study of Electoral Systems 1996–2002.

Table 10.3 shows that the Human Development Index and the demographic variables behaved in the expected way: there was greater contact between voters and elected members in more developed countries. Education, income, and gender also proved significant predictors of the amount of contact activity (although, interestingly, age proved a weak or insignificant predictor). That is to say, greater than average contact activity was reported among the most educated, affluent and men, reflecting patterns found commonly in many other forms of political activism. After controlling for these factors, the ballot structures and the mean district magnitude all proved significant. The candidate-ballot and dual-ballot elections showed significantly more contact activity than did party-ballot elections. At the same time, preference-ballots proved negatively related to contact activity, as did the mean size of the district magnitude. Table 10.4 repeats this exercise for analyzing knowledge of candidates, and a similar pattern is found for the level of development and the role of education and gender. After introducing

TABLE 10.4. *Models Predicting Knowledge of Candidates*

	Model I			Model II		
	B	SE	Sig.	B	SE	Sig.
SOCIAL CONTROLS						
Level of development	1.09	.195	.000	7.72	.246	.000
Age	−.012	.001	.000	−.038	.001	.000
Gender (male)	.140	.026	.000	.264	.030	.000
Education	.092	.013	.000	.103	.016	.000
Income	.067	.010	.000	−.019	.012	.129
BALLOT STRUCTURE						
Candidate-ballot				6.82	1.37	.000
Dual-ballot				1.11	.049	.000
Preference-ballot				1.00	.035	.000
Mean district magnitude				−.009	.000	.000
Constant	.413			−5.81		
% Correctly predicted	69.1			80.8		
Nagelkerke R^2	.017			.395		

Notes: The models using logistic regression analysis provide the unstandardized beta (B), the standard error (SE), and the significance (Sig.) with knowledge of candidates as the dependent variable. Model I: Models without the electoral variables. Model II: Complete model including electoral rules. Ballot structure: Note that party-ballot is the default category.
Source: Comparative Study of Electoral Systems, 1996–2002.

these controls, the use of candidate-ballots, dual-ballots, and preference-ballots all displayed significantly greater knowledge of candidates than did party-ballot elections. The coefficients were strongest for the candidate-ballots, as expected, followed by dual-ballots and preference-ballots. The mean district magnitude was also significant and in the expected negative direction, suggesting that the larger the candidate list, the lower the ability to recognize any particular candidate names. Extrapolating from these results, they confirm as expected that the two indicators of personal voting – candidate awareness and voter–member contact activity – are stronger in candidate-ballot elections and weaker in party-ballot elections. The effects of the intermediate types of ballot structure varied among particular countries, and, probably, they are contingent upon other related rules discussed earlier, including the centralization of the nomination procedures used within each party, an issue well beyond the limited scope of this study.

Conclusions and Implications

Proponents argue that one of the primary virtues of candidate-ballots, used for the majoritarian electoral systems with single-member districts, is the chain of collective and individual accountability. The core argument is that parliamentary representatives are accountable via elections so that citizens can sanction those in office, retaining those that perform well and ousting those who do not.[26] Four channels of accountability exist within majoritarian systems. (1) The first principle of parliamentary government is that the executive emerges from, and is responsible to, the legislature, so that the cabinet is accountable collectively on a day-to-day basis to MPs. The ultimate penalty is a legislative vote of no confidence that removes the party leader and the cabinet from office. (2) Moreover, at general elections, the party in government can be held accountable collectively for their actions, and punished or rewarded accordingly by the electorate. (3) Given single-member districts, strong party discipline, and mass-branch party organizations, MPs are accountable for their actions on a regular basis to party members in their local constituency, as well as to party leaders and whips in the House. Members who do not support party policies, or who are seen to fail in their personal conduct, may not be re-nominated for their local seats.

All these forms of democratic accountability may or may not operate. (4) But even if all these mechanisms fail simultaneously, in the final stage, proponents claim that candidate-ballots allow citizens in each community to hold their individual local representatives to account. Under FPTP elections in parliamentary democracies, voters cannot directly pick the prime minister, the cabinet, or even (directly) the overall balance of parties in the House of Commons, but they can select their local member of parliament. The territorial basis of single-member districts is believed to provide a strong incentive for constituency service, ensuring that members remain concerned about the needs and concerns of all their constituents, not just their party faithful.[27] By contrast, under party-ballots, used in multimember districts with closed party lists, electors are powerless to reward or punish individual candidates. Citizens can only signify their dissatisfaction with the performance of particular representatives by casting a ballot against the whole party ticket, which may throw the baby out with the bathwater. Preference-ballots, used in PR systems with open party lists, allow electors to prioritize candidates within each party, but it requires more information for voters to evaluate many candidates than to scrutinize the legislative record and performance of a particular local representative standing in a single seat. Dual-ballots used in combined-electoral systems are expected to fall somewhere along the continuum between candidate-ballots and party-ballots, depending upon certain specific features, such as the number of seats falling into each category.

But are these normative claims substantiated by the available evidence? To summarize, the results of this study suggest that the use of *candidate-ballots does strengthen the extent to which individual politicians emphasize personalistic over party appeals.* This process potentially holds many important consequences for representative democracy, including for the strength of party discipline and cohesion in the legislature, the accountability and independence of members from the party leadership, and the primary activities and role priorities of elected members. With preference-ballots, voters can either opt for the party ticket or they can prioritize particular candidates within the list, and their effects depend upon how many citizens choose to exercise their preferential vote. Dual-ballots, with elections combining both single-member and multimember districts, are an intermediate category falling somewhere between polar types, and their effects depend upon the balance between single-member and multimember districts. By contrast party-ballots, where citizens can only vote the party ticket rather than prioritizing any particular candidate on each list, generate stronger incentives for politicians to emphasize collective party and programmatic appeals in election campaigns. Attempts to strengthen legislatures in newer democracies through institutional capacity-building remain limited. Nevertheless, the picture that emerges from this evidence suggests that in the long term, the design of the ballot structure does have the capacity to shape legislative behavior in important ways. Reformers aiming to strengthen the local responsiveness and accountability of legislators should consider the use of candidate-ballots. Alternatively, reformers seeking to strengthen party discipline and cohesion should consider the adoption of party-ballots.

Attempts at electoral reform assume that the formal electoral rules have far-reaching consequences for the rest of the political system. The choice of ballot structure has been important in this debate. In the British discussion about electoral reform, for example, *The Report of the Independent Commission on the Voting System*, popularly known as the Jenkins report, was given a wide-ranging brief by the Labour government, but the terms specified that any reform had to maintain accountability to local communities: "*a link* between MPs and geographic constituencies" should be maintained (my italics).[28] Although electoral systems with a small district magnitude, such as the STV, and mixed systems, such as the Additional Member System, could be and were considered for the U.K. House of Commons, this effectively ruled out any consideration for regional party list PR with large multimember districts.

The results of the chapter suggest that the type of ballot structure plays an important role in constitutional design in newer democracies or electoral reform in older democracies. Decisions about the basic rules of the game are likely to prove important in the long term for making legislatures "work." If countries did want to encourage their elected politicians to be more accountable and responsive to grassroots communities, then the evidence suggests that the adoption of candidate-ballots would encourage this process. There are many reasons to believe that changing the ballot structure cannot automatically alter legislative behavior overnight; it would be naïve to assume that the adoption of candidate-ballot elections could, by itself, suddenly transform the accountability of legislators in the Ukrainian, Italian, or Russian parliaments, so that politicians in these countries suddenly become similar to members of the U.S. Congress or Westminster MPs, who inherit a long tradition of local community representation and parliamentary norms of constituency service. Nevertheless, in the longer term over a series of elections, through the Darwinian natural selection process, we would expect that legislative behavior would gradually adapt to the electoral incentives created by the formal rules.

PART IV

CONCLUSIONS

The Impact of Electoral Engineering

The starting point for this book was the observation that during the last decade issues of electoral engineering have arisen on the policy agenda in many countries. Major reforms in established democracies have challenged the notion that electoral systems are necessarily stable institutions. In most Western democracies, once the great debate about the universal franchise was resolved and the mass party system consolidated, electoral systems seemed, for the most part, settled and enduring features of the constitutional landscape. Lijphart's study of the electoral systems used in twenty-seven established democracies from 1945 to 1990 found that only one (France) had experienced a fundamental change from plurality to PR, or vice versa.[1] Furthermore, Bartolini and Mair noted only 14 unbroken transitions in Europe between 1885 and 1985, meaning a major shift in electoral rules between two democratic elections, excluding disruptions caused by wars, dictatorships, the establishment of a new state, or the reappearance of an old one.[2] In Western countries the electoral rules of the game, within which political scientists could get on with analyzing individual-level voting behavior, appeared settled and predictable. No longer. In the 1990s some established democracies experienced the most radical reforms to electoral systems in over a century.[3] Major changes from majoritarian to PR, or vice versa, have occurred in 5 of the 21 countries originally identified by Lijphart in the mid-1970s as established postwar democracies (Israel, Japan, New Zealand, Britain, and Italy), and more modest amendments also have been adopted in Austria, Portugal, and Switzerland.[4] Moreover, the international community has become deeply invested in attempts to generate free and fair competition in dozens of nations around the globe, exemplified by the transitions following the collapse of the Milosevic regime in Bosnia and Herzegovina, independence from Indonesia in East Timor, and the end of the bloody civil war in Cambodia. The constitutional settlements in post-Communist Europe, dissatisfaction with political systems in Latin America, and the rise of electoral democracies in Asia, as well as attempts at state-building and regime change in the Middle East and Africa, have all revived interest in what might once have appeared the rather technical, dull, and rather abstruse issue of electoral engineering.

Beyond the basic electoral formula, in many countries debates have arisen about the best way to overhaul electoral procedures. The legal statutes and party rules governing party eligibility and candidate nomination have been reformed to widen the inclusiveness of elected bodies and bring more diverse voices to the political arena. As we have seen, positive action policies have implemented voluntary gender quotas in parties throughout Latin America, Scandinavia, and Western Europe. Even stronger statutory gender quotas have been employed in Argentina, Belgium, France, and Mexico and re-served seats have been used in Uganda, Pakistan, Bangladesh, and Morocco. Renewed attention has focused on the administrative process of electoral registration and voting facilities, including the creation of independent elec-toral commissions responsible to parliament and the professionalization of electoral management through formal guidelines, training, and awareness of best practices. The regulation of campaign finance and political broad-casting has generated a series of initiatives, designed to make the process of party fundraising and expenditure fairer and more transparent, although with mixed or limited success given the numerous loopholes in this process.[5] Democracies have introduced a series of minor reforms to electoral rules, including switching between d'Hondt and LR-Hare formulae, adjusting the effective voting threshold for minor parties to qualify for parliamentary rep-resentation, expanding the conditions of electoral suffrage, and amending the size of legislative assemblies.[6]

During the postwar era, issues of basic electoral reform, although politi-cized in many countries by the exclusion of minor parties in majoritarian sys-tems and by serious problems of government stability in PR elections, were marginalized on the mainstream policy agenda in the United States, with the notable exception of civil rights. By 1961, coast-to-coast, only Cambridge, Massachusetts, retained the STV. In the early 1990s, Lani Guinier's fairly modest proposals for electoral reform were regarded as incendiary.[7] Yet re-cent years have seen renewed debate about electoral procedures in the United States, spurring new legislation, generated by diverse movements concerned about soft money in campaign finance, low levels of voter registration and turnout, the continued lack of women and ethnic minorities in Congress, and serious flaws of electoral administration highlighted by Florida during the 2000 Bush–Gore race.[8] In October 2002 the *Help America Vote Act* was signed into law, giving states almost $4 billion in federal funds to replace outdated voting machines, improve voter education, and train poll workers. States are required to have computerized voter registration systems in place by the 2004 elections, as well as to provide provisional ballots, which will be counted once valid registration is verified, for citizens whose names do not appear on voter rolls. The McCain-Feingold *Bipartisan Campaign Reform Act* came into force in November 2002, limiting the amount of "soft" money that an individual could donate to a party, as well as restricting issue ads that mention a candidate by interest groups. The full consequences of these initiatives for voter turnout and campaign funding can only be evaluated in subsequent elections.

Moreover, many countries have experimented with newer technological innovations in electoral administration. This includes pilot e-voting schemes, whether casting an electronic vote via the Internet from a home or workplace location, or more simply using new communication and information technologies in existing polling stations and as part of the vote tabulation process. For example e-voting has been used in municipal elections in Geneva,[9] and the May 2002 British local elections allowed citizens in selected wards and boroughs to vote electronically using mobile phone text message services, touch telephone, local digital television, as well as on-line voting methods using home computers, local libraries, and council-run information kiosks.[10] Proponents argue that the most innovative uses of technology hold potential for facilitating voter participation, mainly by reducing the time and effort required for casting a ballot.[11] Yet there are major practical, legal, and technical challenges in e-voting, so that task forces reviewing the evidence have generally proved skeptical about the claims that new technology could automatically either entice more citizens to vote, prevent electoral fraud, improve the accuracy and efficiency of vote-counting, or make elections more representative.[12] Electoral procedures have to meet stringent standards, including high levels of security, secrecy, reliability, accuracy, efficiency, integrity, transparency, and equality. Despite the rise of the Internet, the administrative challenges of e-voting are far more difficult than the implementation of many common forms of electronic commerce or government. Even if the major technical, practical, and legal issues could eventually be overcome, the digital divide in Internet access evident even in affluent nations means that, at present, it would be premature to consider adopting e-voting at home or at work on a wide-scale basis.[13] Nevertheless, technological solutions to electoral management will continue to attract continued attention in the future as one potential avenue for voting reform.

Do Rules Matter?

In evaluating the impact of any of these attempts at electoral engineering – whether major reforms proposed to the basic electoral system or more minor modifications to voting procedures and electoral management – we need clear evidence to guide the choice of policy options. Debate about constitutional choices are divided over the ultimate goals that electoral systems should fulfill, as well as disagreements about the extent to which formal rules can best achieve these goals. Proponents of adversarial democracy argue that links between citizens and their elected representatives are strongest in contests using candidate-ballots, promoting accountability and constituency service via territorial representation. The decisive outcome produced by the "exaggerative winner's bonus" in majoritarian electoral systems, and the electoral penalties for minor parties, are regarded by proponents as assets. Under these rules, strong but accountable governments are believed capable of taking difficult decisions and implementing their programs during their terms of office, yet they can ultimately be reined in by citizens and thrown out of power if they overstep the bounds of public preferences. Proponents of consensus democracy respond commonly that proportional systems are fairer for minority parties and groups, promoting an inclusive legislative assembly containing multiple voices across the political and social spectrum, capable of checking and balancing executive power. Party-ballots can be regarded as more effective in promoting party discipline, coherence, and programmatic campaigning rather than personalistic politics.

Constitutional engineering has risen on the policy agenda in recent years. Institutional inertia has often blocked effective reforms, as incumbents protect the rules from which they have benefited and the policy options are often highly technocratic, even where there is widespread dissatisfaction with existing arrangements. Unless there are dramatic scandals or cases of misadministration, dry issues of electoral reform are rarely going to excite public concern in the same way as bread-and-butter matters of jobs, prices, and pay. Even with Florida, the media hullabaloo and public interest faded fast outside the beltway following President Bush's inauguration. Where major reforms have been implemented, the new rules can sometimes rigidify quickly, preventing further changes. In this context, it has become even more important to piece together the available evidence for and against arguments about the consequences of electoral reform.

Attempts at electoral engineering are based, implicitly or explicitly, upon the simple claim that formal rules matter, with both mechanical and psychological effects. Rational-choice institutionalism emphasizes that formal rules generate incentives shaping the rational goal-seeking behavior of politicians, parties, and citizens. This theory makes certain simple assumptions about the self-interested aims of rational actors and then seeks to outline and test the predictions that flow logically from these premises. Through altering strategic incentives, this account suggests that reformers have the capacity to shape the electoral appeals of political actors, and that, in turn, the voting behavior of the electorate will respond to these choices. Rules are, therefore, believed to generate important and far-reaching consequences. In particular the theory of rational-choice institutionalism explored throughout this book is based on the assumptions that electoral rules can influence the incentives for rational vote-seeking politicians to offer either particularistic or programmatic benefits; for parties to campaign using either bridging or bonding strategies; or for party selectors to pick either socially homogeneous or diverse parliamentary representatives. In turn, it is believed that citizens will respond to these voting choices, so that rules influence political behavior both indirectly (via the strategies adopted by political elites) and directly (for example, where rules are designed to reduce the costs of casting a ballot). If these premises are, indeed, correct then it follows that reforming the formal electoral rules should have the capacity to alter the behavior of politicians, parties, and citizens.

Yet skeptics argue that despite the seductive elegance of rational-choice institutionalism, in practice legal rules reflect rather than transform society, so that our capacity to design formal rules for social engineering is strictly limited. Cultural modernization theories, conventional in social-psychological accounts of voting behavior, emphasize how secular social trends common in postindustrial nations have transformed citizens, notably rising educational levels and cognitive skills, broader access to a variety of information sources through the mass media, and the erosion of participation through traditional political organizations including mass-branch parties, trade unions, and churches. Because these processes have been progressing glacially throughout all postindustrial societies, they are thought to have undermined the traditional anchors of voting behavior common in democracies during the postwar decade, including party loyalties based on identities of class, faith, and community. These processes are thought to have operated on affluent mass societies irrespective of the particular electoral rules within each state. In this view, like a flood tide at full rip, political actors, particularly parties of the left, have had to adapt to these inevitable forces of mass society, or go under. Cultural accounts doubt the more far-reaching claims of rational-choice institutionalism as well as the capacity of mechanistic fixes for social engineering.

By deducing the rational logic of how rules may influence the behavior of political actors and, therefore, the mass electorate, and by piecing together evidence derived from a classification of the electoral rules combined with cross-national surveys of voting behavior, we can unravel at least part of the puzzle surrounding these issues. Inevitably the available evidence presented in this study remains limited, in many important ways. It would have been desirable to compare more countries, including parliamentary elections held under majoritarian rules in developing societies. Subsequent analysis should also break down the unit of comparison, to examine the patterns underlying attitudes and behavior at regional, district, and precinct-level, rather than comparing across nations. The richness of detailed case studies focused on particular campaigns also could illuminate important issues about the electoral strategies used by parties. We need to know far more about patterns of campaign spending, the use of political advertising, campaign coverage by the news media, and grassroots local party activism, as well as the dynamics of voter choice and issue priorities during the elections held in each country. The choice of electoral systems also involves many other considerations, beyond the scope of this study, such as their effects on government stability and coalition politics, the public policy process, and feelings of democratic satisfaction and legitimacy. The second module of questions used in the CSES (2001–2005) expands the range of research questions to explore the issues of government accountability and representation.[14] Nevertheless, the preliminary analysis presented in this limited study helps us to understand the behavior of parties, politicians, and citizens located within the context of the formal electoral rules in each country, comparing both industrial and postindustrial societies.

The Consequences for Voting Behavior

After considering the most appropriate classification of electoral systems, and the normative debate between adversarial and consensus arguments in democratic theory, Chapter 4 considered the impact of electoral rules for party systems. Effective parties that work well can serve multiple functions in democracies: simplifying electoral choices, organizing campaigns, aggregating interests, channeling debate, selecting candidates, structuring parliamentary divisions, acting as policy think tanks, and organizing governments.[15] The direct impact of electoral systems on patterns of party competition has long been regarded as one of their most important effects. The comparison of elections in all nations worldwide, and the detailed analysis of the contests held in the thirty-two countries in the CSES dataset, lends further confirmation about the reductive effect of the basic electoral formula. The evidence presented in this comparison supports Duverger's generalization that plurality electoral systems tend toward party dualism, whereas PR is associated with multipartyism. The contrast between party systems under majoritarian and proportional electoral systems is not large, depending upon the precise measure employed, but all indicators pointed consistently in the same direction. According to the most restrictive measure, of ENPP, in the thirty-two countries under detailed comparison there were almost twice as many parliamentary parties under PR than under majoritarian systems. Yet at the same time there are important variations within each electoral family due to many factors, including, most important, (1) the geography of electoral support; (2) specific features of electoral design, such as the use of voting thresholds and the size of districts; and (3) the number and depth of social cleavages within a nation. Minor parties can still gain a disproportionate share of seats under FPTP, common especially for smaller regional or ethnic-national parties, if their share of votes is concentrated spatially in particular districts. At the same time, minor parties can also be heavily penalized in proportional electoral systems, if these have high voting thresholds and/or small average district magnitudes.

These conclusions suggest that, if reforms to the electoral law could be passed and implemented, moves toward more majoritarian arrangements should mitigate some of the problems experienced in countries suffering

currently from the dangers of excessively unstable, undisciplined, and fragmented party competition, exemplified by Italy, Brazil, the Ukraine, and
Israel. At the same time, again if measures could be effectively passed and
implemented, electoral reforms should help to overcome the dangers of unchanging one-party-predominant party systems, where voters cannot hold
governments to account, exemplified by the cases of Singapore, Mexico (until
2000), and Japan. In this regard, at least, electoral engineering can contribute
toward effective party competition as well as levels of proportionality. Policy analysis can also contribute toward understanding the more technical
aspects of the formal rules with a fair degree of accuracy, including assessing
the consequences of the basic type of electoral system, the vote threshold,
the votes-to-seats formulae, the average district magnitude, and the legal
regulations governing the registration of candidates and parties.

Social Cleavages

But do formal rules generate important consequences for the campaign
strategies that parties adopt, with an impact upon mass electoral behavior?
This issue remains far more contentious. Chapter 5 considered the impact
of electoral rules on the strength of cleavage politics. The basic social divisions of class, faith, and community traditionally have been the building
blocks of stable social and partisan identities, anchoring voters to parties
over successive elections. The central claim of rational-choice institutionalism is not that electoral rules *create* social cleavages, or even manufacture
their political relevance, but rather that the initial adoption of certain rules
(for whatever reason) will create certain incentives for parties to adopt either
bonding strategies that will maintain and reinforce (and possibly exacerbate)
cleavage politics or, alternatively, to adopt catch-all bridging strategies that
will modify and downplay (and possibly erode) group consciousness in the
political arena.

The evidence in this study suggests that the electoral rules of the game
can, indeed, contribute toward this process. Compared with proportional
rules, the analysis confirms that majoritarian elections are significantly associated with weaker cleavage politics. In predicting how many people voted
for the left and right on the party scale, about one-quarter of the variance
in majoritarian elections was generated by the combined effects of social
structure and ideology, compared with about one-third in the PR elections.
The reason is that under majoritarian rules, parties and candidates must
appeal to multiple diverse interests and social groups in order to generate the plurality or majority of votes necessary to win office. In this context, rational vote-seeking parties have strong incentives to adopt Broad
Church catch-all bridging strategies that appeal to working- and middle-
class sectors, as well as to different religious sects and creeds, and diverse
ethnic groups. Focusing exclusively upon any single sector, whether farmers or pensioners, environmentalists or blue-collar workers, carries serious

electoral risks. This consideration is important particularly for socialist, social democrat, and Communist parties facing a shrinking traditional base, given the contraction in the number of manual workers employed in the manufacturing industry and the rising proportion of service-sector professionals.[16] In these circumstances, left-wing parties will probably shift more and more toward the center ground in the attempt to develop bringing strategies and cross-class appeals. These patterns are exemplified by the move toward straddling the center-ground experienced under the leadership of Tony Blair in the British Labour Party and under Bill Clinton for the U.S. Democrats, both countries using majoritarian systems for legislative elections. By contrast, in countries with PR systems, especially those with low voting thresholds and large district magnitudes, parties can be returned to power based on a far narrower segment of the population, one based on class, faith-based, or ethnic electoral appeals. Under these rules, parties have less incentive to broaden and moderate their electoral base.

Furthermore, far from cleavage politics being weaker in postindustrial societies, as modernization theory suggests, these linkages actually proved to be stronger. The amount of the total variance in voting behavior explained by the models used for analysis was about one-quarter in industrial nations, but it was one-third in postindustrial societies. Of course, other factors could be offered to account for these patterns, notably the way that strong party–voter linkages take generations to develop over successive elections, so that patterns of cleavage politics have not yet had time to become established and consolidated in newer democracies. It also is true that many studies provide a wealth of evidence that the strength of cleavage politics, especially the link between parties and class or religious identities, has eroded in many established democracies, and many accounts have commonly linked these developments to processes of societal modernization and the rise of a new citizen politics. Nevertheless, rational-choice institutionalism provides an alternative interpretation of the underlying reasons for this decline, by emphasizing top-down patterns of party strategies and electoral incentives to predict the countries where cleavage politics has eroded most clearly.

Partisan Identification
Subsequent analysis of party identification served to further confirm this general pattern. Theories of cultural modernization suggest that important contrasts in the strength of partisan identification should be evident by the basic type of society, in particular that patterns of human development, especially rising education levels and cognitive skills associated with societal development, gradually should have reduced reliance upon party loyalties. If so, partisan identification should exert a stronger influence upon voting behavior in industrialized than in postindustrial nations. Yet if institutional incentives play a stronger role, then important differences should be evident among countries using different types of electoral rules, in particular partisan

identities should exert a stronger impact on voting choices under PR than under majoritarian systems.

The results of the analysis showed that in combination, the joint effects of social structure and partisan attachments explained about two-thirds of the variance in left–right voting behavior under majoritarian rules, but over three-quarters in combined and PR systems. This is far from a complete explanation, as there are also substantial differences among contests within each type of electoral system, rather than a wholly consistent pattern. A comprehensive explanation of voting choices would include many other standard factors exogenous to the model, such as the role of prospective issues and policy platforms, the popularity of party leaders, and the retrospective record of the parties in office, and it is well beyond the scope of this limited study. Furthermore, the main variance in voting behavior comes from the *combined* effects of social plus partisan identification, rather than from the latter alone. Nevertheless, the final model does explain a substantial amount of variance in voting behavior for parties on the left and right, suggesting that if we can identify the basic social characteristics and party loyalties of electors, we can predict their voting choices with considerable confidence. Rational-choice institutionalism proved more persuasive than accounts based on societal modernization because party attachments were similar, or even slightly higher, in postindustrial nations than in industrial societies.

Turnout
Do the rules also affect political mobilization and voter participation? Many attempts at mechanical fixes have been based on the assumption that voting turnout could be boosted either by "sticks" (such as the introduction of compulsory voting laws) or by "carrots" (for example, simpler facilities for electoral registration and postal voting for casting a ballot). Rational-choice institutionalism suggests that the incentives for citizen participation in elections can best be understood as a product of the electoral *costs* of registering and voting, the party *choices* available to electors, and the degree to which casting a ballot determines the composition of parliament and government. All other things being equal, turnout is expected to be higher in electoral arrangements that reduce voting costs, maximize party competition, and also maintain a strong link between voters' preferences and the outcome for government. In contrast, cultural modernization theories emphasize that habitual and deeply rooted patterns of civic participation arise from overall societal levels of human development, social characteristics such as education, age, and class, and attitudes such as a sense of political efficacy and interest. In this latter perspective, habits of mass political participation will respond only sluggishly, if at all, to changes in electoral law or administration.

The results of this study analyzing the nations in the CSES dataset suggest that institutional rules do indeed matter: voting participation is maximized in elections using PR, with small electoral districts, regular but relatively infrequent national contests, and competitive party systems, and in presidential contests. These factors confirm the general pattern established in an earlier comparison of nations around the globe.[17] In established democracies, the use of compulsory voting laws is associated with higher turnout, whereas this is not evident among the broader comparison of elections worldwide. Yet the pooled regression models indicated that, even after controlling for the institutional context, human development, social background, and cultural attitudes also remained important predictors of turnout. Therefore, rather than a false dichotomy, between rule-based incentives and cultural habits, both these factors contribute toward understanding patterns of political participation, in a nested model.

The Consequences for Political Representation

The first part of the book considered how electoral rules influenced the strategies adopted by parties and the behavior of the mass electorate. It then went on to analyze the potential impact of rational-choice institutionalism and cultural modernization upon political representation.

Gender Equality in Legislative Office

Agencies have advocated a range of positive action strategies designed to encourage more socially diverse legislative bodies. Opportunities for women may be influenced by electoral law, including the basic type of electoral system, the statutory and voluntary adoption of gender quotas, and the use of reserved seats for women, as well as by the predominant cultural values within any society. Rational-choice institutionalism suggests that electoral laws determine the balance of incentives operating in the selection process, for example the use of statutory gender quotas creates legal or financial sanctions regulating the outcome, whereas multimember constituencies generate a potential electoral penalty if parties fail to present socially balanced collective lists of candidates, including all major sectors of society. By contrast, cultural modernization accounts emphasize that sex discrimination reflects deep-rooted attitudes toward gender equality; so that where traditional cultural attitudes prevail in less developed societies then selectors will choose men for public office. Moreover, in traditional societies, parties may fail to introduce equal opportunity or positive action policies voluntarily, and they may refuse to comply with any statutory positive action laws and disregard any legal penalties against sex discrimination.

The evidence presented in this chapter provides further confirmation that the basic type of electoral system does, indeed, influence opportunities for women in elected office. Women generally are more successful in being nominated and elected under proportional electoral systems using party-ballots. In cultures where the public is broadly sympathetic toward the principles of gender equality, under PR, parties have considerable incentives to develop a balanced ticket of legislative candidates, to avoid any electoral penalties from the appearance of sex discrimination against women. This electoral incentive is absent in candidate-ballots used in single-member districts in majoritarian elections, where each local party can choose the default option of a male candidate without any collective responsibility for balancing the social profile of candidates at national level. The multivariate analysis comparing countries worldwide showed that the type of electoral system, the use of reserved seats, and the length of women's suffrage were all associated with more women in parliament, although once these factors were introduced, the predominant religious culture (as a proxy for traditional or egalitarian attitudes toward gender equality in different societies) proved insignificant. The employment of voluntary gender quotas was extremely important in particular cases, using pre-post comparisons, although their effects vary from party to party within each country according to detailed matters such as their level and implementation procedures. Party-ballots, in combination with positive action strategies, generate more opportunities for women in legislative bodies, producing parliaments that look more like the people they serve and overcoming cultural barriers through traditional attitudes.

Ethnic Minorities

Can we deduce that similar consequences follow for the representation of ethnic minorities? Although a common strategy, considerable caution is needed before making such a leap. Consociational theories suggest that proportional electoral systems are most likely to facilitate accommodation between diverse ethnic groups, making them more suitable for transitional and consolidating democracies struggling to achieve legitimacy and stability in plural societies. Yet little direct evidence has compared the impact of electoral rules on the inclusion of ethnic minority parties in different countries, still less indications of general satisfaction with democracy and support for the political system among ethnic minority voters. The strategy used in this study compared relative levels of satisfaction with the political system among majority–minority populations, to see whether the majority–minority gap was reduced, or even reversed, under proportional PR party list systems, as consociational theory suggests. The findings indicate that a complex pattern is at work here, and the claim that PR party list systems are associated directly with higher levels of political support among ethnic minorities is not confirmed by this study. One reason could be that other contingent factors could determine this relationship, particularly the geographical dispersion of minority groups; the use of positive action strategies under majoritarian rules, such as reserved seats; other features of the broader political system including the degree of regional autonomy and decentralization; and also the role of political leaders in either mitigating or heightening ethnic tensions. Further research around these complex issues is necessary to further disentangle these relationships and the broader meaning of ethnicity for party politics and voting behavior.[18]

Constituency Service

Moreover, the legitimacy of legislative bodies is founded upon the democratic principles of political representation and accountability. Proponents of candidate-ballots used in majoritarian single-member districts argue that these have the important advantage of allowing citizens to use elections to hold elected members individually responsible for their actions. Preference-ballots used with open-list PR and systems such as the STV also share some of these characteristics. By contrast, party-ballots used in closed-list PR elections remove the ability of citizens to sanction or reward individual politicians. Rational politicians standing in party-ballots will logically focus upon collective campaigns, emphasizing the achievement of their party's record or programmatic platform since they all sink or swim together. Party-ballots should, therefore, strengthen party discipline and cohesion yet weaken the incentive for constituency service. By contrast, candidate-ballots should provide greater incentives for incumbents to appeal on their personal record of constituency service and local representation. If true, citizens voting in candidate-ballots should be more knowledgeable about parliamentary candidates, and they should have more contact with elected representatives, than those voting via party-ballots.

Theoretically, incentive-based models offer many plausible reasons why single-member districts should have strong linkages between citizens and representatives, promoting contact, constituency service, and voter awareness about candidates. The results of this study suggest that the use of candidate-ballots does strengthen how far individual politicians emphasize personalistic over party appeals. This process potentially holds many important consequences for representative democracy, including for the strength of party discipline and cohesion in the legislature, the accountability and independence of members from the party leadership, and the primary activities and role priorities of elected members. With preference-ballots, voters can either opt for the party ticket or they can prioritize particular candidates within the list, and their effects depend upon how many citizens choose to exercise their preferential votes. Dual-ballots, with elections combining both single-member and multimember districts, are an intermediate category falling somewhere polar types, and their effects depend upon the balance between single-member and multimember districts. By contrast party-ballots, where citizens can only vote the party ticket rather than prioritizing any particular candidate on each list, generate stronger incentives for politicians to emphasize collective party and programmatic appeals in election campaigns. Reformers seeking to strengthen the responsiveness and accountability of legislators to local communities should consider adopting candidate-ballots. Alternatively, those seeking to strengthen party discipline and cohesion in parliaments that are fragmented and factionalized should consider the adoption of party-ballots. Yet dual-ballot systems, where *some* members of parliament are elected from single-member districts, as in Germany, Mexico, Japan, or New Zealand, combine some of the advantages of both systems. More cross-national research needs to be conducted on other rules that plausibly could affect this process, including the use of term limitations and the centralization of the candidate selection process.

The Lessons for Electoral Engineering

We have demonstrated, as many others have long believed, that electoral systems represent some of the most powerful instruments available for institutional engineering, with far-reaching consequences for party systems, the composition of legislatures, and democratic representation.[19] I have outlined in this book the logic for three core expectations in rational-choice institutionalism: namely, that the electoral threshold would influence whether parties adopted bridging or bonding strategies; that the ballot structure would shape how far parties adopt socially diverse or homogeneous lists of candidates; and that the ballot structure would affect the emphasis on programmatic or particularistic campaigning. I also considered the evidence for certain propositions arising from cultural modernization theory, namely that patterns of political behavior and cultural attitudes surrounding these same phenomena would be influenced by levels of societal development. This account has been examined and tested by classifying the rules, deducing the way that rational vote-seeking political actors respond, and then examining the patterns of behavior in the electorate.

It should be recognized that in considering the evidence surrounding these issues the research design used in this book, and the comparative framework, remain limited in many important ways. In the best of all possible worlds, one would be able to examine time-series case studies to understand how the process of electoral engineering works in more depth, especially more before and after natural experiments with rule reform. Moreover, the cross-sectional research design is most limited when considering how far the electoral system can, indeed, be regarded as exogenous to party competition, although this is arguably less problematic when considering the logic of how the rules interact with voting behavior. In countries where the electoral system has existed for many decades the impact of the rules upon patterns of party competition is a reasonable assumption. Where the electoral system is newer, it becomes more contentious to assume that there is a simple one-directional causal arrow from the rules to party competition, and instead an interactive process seems more plausible, where party competition shapes the adoption of certain rules and then the rules serve to constrain patterns of party competition. Analytical models can try to examine this process, but only time-series case study analysis provides a truly satisfactory way of disentangling these complex pathways. Cross-national surveys of voting behavior would be extended to a wider range of countries and electoral systems, including contests in developing societies, to broaden the reliable generalizations that can be drawn from their study. Rather than deductive theories about the logic of campaign strategies, direct evidence would be examined and integrated with surveys of the electorate, such as patterns of campaign expenditure or content analysis of party political manifestos. A more comprehensive range of factors would be brought into models of electoral choice, including analyzing the importance of leadership popularity, evaluations of economic performance, and prospective policy platforms. This study has not sought to even consider many of the other important consequences believed to flow from the electoral rules and cultural modernization, whether questions concerning "strategic" or "tactical" voting, direct evidence for the wasted vote syndrome, the role of campaign communications, and broader issues of political participation beyond the act of voting. All these strategies remain open to further work where the comparative study of voting behavior is analyzed using multi-level and multimethod research designs, using the burgeoning range of cross-national social and political surveys. Further modules of the CSES, as well as the development and availability of cross-national surveys such as the Afrobarometer and Asiabarometer, are bringing these issues into sharper focus for the research community. This book has sought to explore only part of the agenda concerning how the comparative study of electoral systems can be reintegrated with the mainstream study of voting behavior.

The results of the analysis serving to confirm the assumptions arising from rational-choice institutionalism have important implications, not just for our theoretical understanding of these issues, but also for all those concerned with the public policy process and practical issues of constitutional reform. In many nations the rules of the electoral system, for many decades accepted as stable and immutable, indeed, often bureaucratic and technical, have become increasingly politicized and contentious. The wave of constitution building following the surge of newer democracies in the early 1990s generated a series of negotiations about electoral laws that needed to be resolved before other constitutional issues could be agreed. After the first elections, far from being settled, the consolidation process in these nations frequently has seen continued adjustments in electoral regulations, such as in threshold levels, the use of electoral formulae, and the size of legislative bodies.[20] More practical matters of electoral management also have risen in salience on the policy agenda of many national and international agencies, notably the issues of the prevention of electoral fraud, intimidation and corruption, voter registration, polling day administration, ballot counting, campaign finance regulation, and free and fair access to political broadcasting in transitional democracies.[21] Disentangling the effects of formal rules and cultural modernization is important, not only for the understanding this provides into the behavior of politicians, parties, and citizens, but also because this gives insights into the possibilities and limits of electoral engineering.

How we interpret the findings in this analysis, and how they feed into the reform process in particular countries, is heavily contextual. Cultural modernization remains important for political behavior, but the effect of social development upon the predominant political attitudes and values in any society is gradual and incremental, and, therefore, this strategy is of limited use as an instrument of short-term reform in the policy process. By contrast, formal rules are changeable, by definition, whether by legislative initiative, bureaucratic decree, or procedural reform. Parliaments, executives, and courts can alter the basic electoral rules, with far-reaching consequences. There is no single best bespoke electoral system that suits all. Instead, as many have commonly observed, there are tradeoff public goods. Majoritarian electoral systems systematically exaggerate the parliamentary lead for the party in first place, to secure a decisive outcome and government accountability, thereby, excluding smaller parties from the division of spoils. By contrast, proportional electoral systems lower the hurdles for smaller parties, maximizing their inclusion into the legislature and ultimately into coalition governments. Any recommendations for electoral reform, therefore, relate to perceptions of the type of problems experienced by any political system.

In plural societies characterized by deeply divided social cleavages, for example, rational-choice institutionalism suggests that adopting majoritarian rules should encourage parties to widen their campaign appeals, thereby encouraging cross-cutting cleavages. Alternatively, in polities characterized by weak linkages between parties and voters, where party competition is centrist and based around personalities, then this account predicts that the adoption of more proportional arrangements should counteract these tendencies, thereby, widening party competition and voter choice.

In countries where legislators currently focus their time and energies on parliamentary debates or committee work while neglecting constituency service, the theory predicts that electing at least some members via candidate-ballots would be one strategy that could change the priorities of parliamentarians. By contrast, in countries where there is an excessive focus on personalistic pork-barrel politics and clientelism, to the detriment of collective public good, party discipline, and government effectiveness, then the theory suggests that the adoption of party-ballots could potentially alter parliamentary behavior.

And in most countries around the world women's voices continue to be under-represented in parliamentary elites. In this context, the use of positive action policies and the adoption of more proportional electoral arrangements could expand opportunities for women in public life, and, thereby, increase the diversity of representative bodies.

The logic of the arguments about why these effects occur is hardly novel, admittedly we lack direct proof of the strategic behavior of political actors, and, often, this study has probably merely confirmed what many have long suspected. Nevertheless, the reasoning developed in the introductory framework and the cross-national survey evidence presented in successive chapters serves to increase our confidence that, in general, formal rules do have significant consequences for electoral behavior, as many have often believed and argued. The study of electoral systems may appear unduly technical and dry, far removed from the central passions of politics, but by determining the structure of the body politic in representative democracies, much else follows. The consequences of formal electoral rules are, therefore, important for basic issues of political representation and accountability, for patterns of participation and party competition, and for the effective health of democratic institutions around the world.

Bibliography

Aarts, Kees, S.E. MacDonald, and G. Rabinowitz. 1999. "Issues and party competition in the Netherlands." *Comparative Political Studies* 32(1): 63–99.

Achen, Christopher. 1992. "Social psychology, demographic variables and linear regression: Breaking the iron triangles in voting research." *Political Behavior* 14(3): 195–211.

Ahmed, Amel. 1999. "Sources and Dynamics of Electoral Reform." Paper presented at the American Political Science Association annual meeting, Atlanta, GA, September 2–6.

Aldrich, John H. 1993. "Rational choice and turnout." *American Journal of Political Science* 37: 246–278.

_____. 1995. *Why Parties? The Origin and Transformation of Party Politics in America.* Chicago: University of Chicago Press.

Alford, Robert R. 1967. "Class Voting in the Anglo-American Political Systems." In *Party Systems and Voter Alignments: Cross National Perspectives.* Eds. Seymour M. Lipset and Stein Rokkan. New York: The Free Press.

Almond, Gabriel A., and Sidney Verba. 1963. *The Civic Culture: Political Attitudes and Democracy in Five Nations.* Princeton, NJ: Princeton University Press.

Ames, Barry. 1995. "Electoral strategy under open-list proportional representation." *American Journal of Political Science* 39(2): 406–433.

_____. 2001. *The deadlock of democracy in Brazil.* Ann Arbor, MI: University of Michigan Press.

Amy, Douglas J. 1996. *Real Choices/New Voices: The Case for Proportional Representation Elections in the United States.* New York: Columbia University Press.

_____. 2000. *Behind the Ballot Box: A Citizen's Guide to Electoral Systems.* Westport, CT: Praeger.

Anderson, Benedict. 1996. *Imagined Communities: Reflections on the Origin and Spread of Nationalism.* London: Verso.

Anderson, Christopher J. 1995. *Blaming the Government: Citizens and the Economy in Five European Democracies.* New York: M.E. Sharpe.

Anderson, Christopher J., and Christine A. Guillory. 1997. "Political Institutions and Satisfaction with Democracy." *American Political Science Review* 91(1): 66–81.

Araujo, C. 2001. "Gender quotas for candidacy to the legislature: The Brazilian case as compared to international experience." *Dados-Revista De Ciencias Sociais* 44(1): 155–194.

Archer, J.C. 2002. "The geography of an interminable election: Bush v. Gore, 2000." *Political Geography* 21(1): 71–77.

Arian, Asher, and Michal Shamir. 2001. "Candidates, parties and blocs: Israel in the 1990s." *Party Politics* 7(6): 689–710.

Ashford, Sheena, and Noel Timms. 1992. *What Europe Thinks: A Study of Western European Values*. Aldershot, U.K.: Dartmouth.

Auer, Andreas, and Alexander H. Trechsel. 2001. *Voter par Internet? Le projet e-voting dans le canton de Geneve dans une perspective socio-politique et juridique*. Available online at www.helbing.ch.

Austen-Smith, David, and Jeffrey S. Banks. 1988. "Elections, coalitions, and legislative outcomes." *American Political Science Review* 82(2): 405–422.

———. 1990. "Stable governments and the allocation of policy portfolios." *American Political Science Review* 84(3): 891–906.

Aylott, N. 1995. "Back To The Future – The 1994 Swedish Election." *Party Politics* 1(3): 419–429.

Bagehot, Walter. (1867) 1964. *The English Constitution*. London: C.A. Watts & Co., p.59.

Banducci, S.A., T. Donovan, and J.A. Karp. 1999. "Proportional representation and attitudes about politics: Results from New Zealand." *Electoral Studies* 18(4): 533–555.

Banfield, Edward C., and James Q. Wilson. 1963. *City Politics*. Cambridge, MA: Harvard University Press.

Barber, James D. 1992. *The Presidential Character*. Eaglewood Cliffs, NJ: Prentice Hall.

Barkan, Joel. 1998. "Rethinking the Applicability of Proportional Representation for Africa." In *Electoral Systems and Conflict Management in Africa*. Eds. Timothy D. Sisk and Andrew Reynolds. Washington, D.C.: U.S. Institute of Peace Press.

Barnes, Samuel, and Janos Simon. Eds. 1998. *The Post-Communist Citizen*. Budapest, Hungary: Erasmus Foundation.

Barnes, Samuel, and Max Kaase. 1979. *Political Action: Mass Participation in Five Western Democracies*. Beverley Hills, CA: Sage.

Bartels, Larry. 1993. "Message received: The political impact of media exposure." *American Political Science Review* 87: 267–285.

Bartle, John. 1998. "Left-right position matters, but does social class? Causal models of the 1992 British general election." *British Journal of Political Science* 28: 501–529.

———. 2001. "The measurement of party identification in Britain: Where do we stand now?" In *British Elections and Parties Review* 11. Eds. Jonathan Tonge, Lynn Bennie, David Denver, and Lisa Harrison. London: Frank Cass.

Bartolini, Stefano. 2000. "Franchise Expansion." In *International Encyclopedia of Elections*. Ed. Richard Rose. Washington, D.C.: Congressional Quarterly Press.

Bartolini, Stefano, and Peter Mair. 1990. *Identity, Competition, and Electoral Availability: The Stabilization of European Electorates, 1885–1985*. Cambridge, U.K.: Cambridge University Press.

Bass, L.E., and L.M. Casper. 2001. "Impacting the political landscape: Who registers and votes among naturalized Americans?" *Political Behavior* 23(2): 103–130.

Bawn, K. 1999. "Voter responses to electoral complexity: Ticket splitting, rational voters and representation in the Federal Republic of Germany." *British Journal of Political Science* 29(3): 487–505.

Bean, Clive. 1986. "Electoral law, electoral behavior, and electoral outcomes: Australia and New Zealand compared." *The Journal of Commonwealth and Comparative Politics* 24(1): 57–73.

———. 1994. "Issues in the 1993 election." *Australian Journal of Political Science* 29: 134–157.

———. 1996. "The 1996 Australian federal election." *Electoral Studies* 15(3): 422–424.

———. 1997. "Australia's experience with the alternative vote." *Representation* 34(2): 103–110.

Bean, Clive, and Jonathan Kelley. 1995. "The Electoral Impact of New Politics Issues – The Environment in the 1990 Australian Federal-Election." *Comparative Politics* 27(3): 339–356.

Bean, Clive, Scott Bennett, Marian Simms, and John Warhurst. Eds. 1997. *The Politics of Retribution: The 1996 Australian Federal Election.* Sydney: Allen & Unwin.

Beetham, David. Ed. 1994. *Defining and Measuring Democracy.* London: Sage.

———. 2001. *International IDEA Handbook of Democracy Assessment.* New York: Kluwer.

Beilin, Yossi. 1996. "An Accident Named The Direct Election to Prime Minister." In *The Electoral Revolution.* Ed. Gideon Doron. Tel Aviv: Hakibutz Hameuchad Publishing House.

Bell, Daniel. 1999. *The Coming of Post-Industrial Society: A Venture in Social Forecasting.* New York: Basic Books.

Beltran, U., and M. Valdivia. 1999. "Accuracy and error in electoral forecasts: The case of Mexico." *International Journal of Public Opinion Research* 11(2): 115–134.

Bendix, Reinhard. 1963. "Concepts and Generalizations in Comparative Sociological Studies." *American Sociological Review* 28(4): 523–539.

Benoit, Ken. 2001. "District magnitude, electoral formula, and the number of parties." *European Journal of Political Research* 39(2): 203–224.

———. 2002. "The endogeneity problem in electoral studies: A critical re-examination of Duverger's mechanical effect." *Electoral Studies* 21(1): 35–46.

Berelson, Bernard. R., Paul F. Lazarsfeld, and W.N. McPhee, 1954. *Voting.* Chicago: University of Chicago Press.

Berglund, Sten, and Jan A. Dellenbrant. 1994. *The New Democracies in Eastern Europe: Party Systems and Political Cleavages.* Aldershot, U.K.: Edward Elgar.

Bergqvist, Christina, A. Borchorst, A. Christensen, V. Ramstedt-Silén, N.C. Raaum, and A. Styrkársdóttir. Eds. 1999. *Equal Democracies? Gender and Politics in the Nordic Countries.* Olso: Scandinavian University Press.

Berinsky, A.J., Nancy Burns, and Michael W. Traugott. 2001. "Who votes by mail? A dynamic model of the individual-level consequences of voting-by-mail systems." *Public Opinion Quarterly* 65(2): 178–197.

Bielasiak, Jack. 2002. "The institutionalization of electoral and party systems in post-communist states." *Comparative Politics* 34(2): 189.

Billig, Michael. 1995. *Banal Nationalism.* London: Sage.

Birch, Sarah. 1997. "Ukraine: The Perils of Majoritarianism in a New Democracy." In *The International IDEA Handbook of Electoral System Design.* Eds. Andrew

Reynolds and Ben Reilly. Stockholm: International Institute for Democracy and Electoral Assistance.

——. 1998. "Electoral reform in Ukraine: The 1988 parliamentary elections." *Representation* 35(2/3): 146–154.

Birch, Sarah, and Andrew Wilson. 1999. "The Ukrainian parliamentary elections of 1998." *Electoral Studies* 18(2): 276–282.

Bird, Karen. 2002. "Who Are the Women? Where Are the Women? And What Difference Can They Make? The Effects of Gender Parity in French Municipal Elections." Paper presented at the *Annual Meeting of the American Political Science Association*, Boston, August 28–September 1, 2002.

Biondel, Jean. 1970. *Votes, Parties and Leaders*. London: Penguin.

Black, Jerome H. 1978. "The Multi-candidate Calculus of Voting: Application to Canadian Federal Elections." *American Journal of Political Science* 22(3): 609–638.

——. 1991. "Reforming the context of the voting process in Canada: Lessons from other democracies." In *Voter Turnout in Canada*. Ed. H. Bakvis. Toronto: Dundurn Press.

Blackburn, Robin. 1995. *The Electoral System in Britain*. New York: St. Martin's Press.

Blackburn, Robin, and Raymond Plant. Eds. 1999. *Constitutional Reform: The Labour Government's Constitutional Reform Agenda*. London: Longmans.

Blais, André. 1988. "The classification of electoral systems." *European Journal of Political Research* 16(1): 99–110.

——. 2000. *To Vote or Not to Vote? The Merits and Limits of Rational Choice Theory*. Pittsburgh: University of Pittsburgh Press.

Blais, André, and Agnieszka Dobrzynska. 1998. "Turnout in electoral democracies." *European Journal of Political Research* 33(2): 239–261.

Blais, André, Elizabeth Gidengil, Richard Nadeau, and Neil Nevitte. 2001. "Measuring party identification: Britain, Canada, and the United States." *Political Behavior* 23(1): 5–22.

Blais, André, and Louis Massicotte. 1997. "Electoral formulas: A macroscopic perspective." *European Journal of Political Research* 32(1): 107–129.

——. 1999. "Mixed electoral systems: A conceptual and empirical survey." *Electoral Studies* 18(3): 341–366.

——. 2002. "Electoral Systems." In *Comparing Democracies 2: Elections and Voting in Global Perspective*. Eds. Lawrence LeDuc, Richard G. Niemi, and Pippa Norris. London: Sage.

Blais, André, Louis Massicotte, and Agnieszka Dobrzynska. 1997. "Direct presidential elections: A world summary." *Electoral Studies* 16(4): 441–455.

Blais, André, Louis Massicotte, and A. Yoshinaka. 2001. "Deciding who has the right to vote: A comparative analysis of election laws." *Electoral Studies* 20 (1): 41–62.

Blais, André, and R. Kenneth Carty. 1990. "Does proportional representation foster voter turnout?" *European Journal of Political Research* 18(2): 167–181.

——. 1991. "The psychological impact of electoral laws – measuring Duverger's elusive factor." *British Journal of Political Science* 21(1): 79–93.

Blashke, Sabine. 2000. "Union density and European integration: Diverging convergence." *European Journal of Industrial Relations* 6(2): 217–236.

Blount, S. 1999. "The microeconomic voter." *Electoral Studies* 18(4): 505–517.

Bogdanor, Vernon. 1984. *What is Proportional Representation?* Oxford: Martin Robertson.

————. Ed. 1985. *Representatives of the People? Parliamentarians and Constituents in Western Democracies.* Aldershot, Hants, U.K.: Gower.

————. Ed. 2003. *The British Constitution in the Twentieth Century.* Oxford: Oxford University Press.

Bogdanor, Vernon, and David Butler. Eds. 1983. *Democracy and Elections.* Cambridge, U.K.: Cambridge University Press.

Boggards, Matthis. 2000. "The uneasy relationship between empirical and normative types in consociational theory." *Journal of Theoretical Politics* 12(4): 305–493.

Bohrer, R.E, A.C. Pacek, and B. Radcliff. 2000. "Electoral participation, ideology, and party politics in post-communist Europe." *Journal of Politics* 62(4): 1161–1172.

Boix, C. 1999. "Setting the rules of the game: The choice of electoral systems in advanced democracies." *American Political Science Review* 93(3): 609–624.

Borre, Ole. 1984. "Critical Electoral Change in Scandinavia." In *Electoral Change in Advanced Industrial Democracies: Realignment or Dealignment?* Eds. Russell J. Dalton, Scott C. Flanigan, and Paul Allen Beck. Princeton, NJ: Princeton University Press.

Boston, Jonathan, Stephen Levine, Elizabeth McLeay, and Nigel S. Roberts. 1996. *New Zealand Under MMP: A New Politics?* Auckland: Auckland University Press.

Bowler, Shaun, and Bernard Grofman. 1996. "STV's place in the family of electoral systems: Theoretical comparisons and contrasts." *Representation* 34: 43–47.

————. Eds. 2000. *Elections in Australia, Ireland and Malta under the Single Transferable Vote: Reflections on an Embedded Institution.* Ann Arbor, MI: University of Michigan Press.

Bratton, Michael, and Nicolas van de Walle. 1997. *Democratic Experiments in Africa.* Cambridge, U.K.: Cambridge University Press.

Brians, Craig Leonard. 1997. "Residential mobility, voter registration, and electoral participation in Canada." *Political Research Quarterly* 50(1): 215–227.

Brians, Craig Leonard, and Bernard Grofman. 1999. "When registration barriers fall, who votes? An empirical test of a rational choice model." *Public Choice* 99(1–2): 161–176.

————. 2001. "Election day registration's effect on US voter turnout." *Social Science Quarterly* 82(1): 170–183.

Brody, Richard A., and Lawrence S. Rothenberg. 1988. "The instability of party identification: An analysis of the 1980 presidential election." *British Journal of Political Science* 18: 445–465.

Brown, Michael, Owen Cote, Sean M. Lynn-Jones, and Steven E. Miller. 1997. *Nationalism and Ethnic Conflict.* Cambridge, MA: The MIT Press.

Bruce, Steve. 1996. *Religion in the Modern World: From Cathedrals to Cults.* Oxford: Oxford University Press.

————. Ed. 1992. *Religion and Modernization.* Oxford: Oxford University Press.

Brynin, M., and David Sanders. 1997. "Party identification, political preferences, and material conditions – Evidence from the British Household Panel Survey, 1991–2." *Party Politics* 3(1): 53–77.

Budge, Ian, David Robertson, and Derek Hearl. Eds. 1987. *Ideology, Strategy and Party Change: Spatial Analysis of Postwar Election Programmes in 19 Democracies.* Cambridge, U.K.: Cambridge University Press.

Budge, Ian, Ivor Crewe, and Dennis Farlie. Eds. 1976. *Party Identification and Beyond.* New York: John Wiley.

Budge, Ian et al. 1997. *The Politics of the New Europe*. London: Longmans.

Bulmer, Martin. 1986. "Race and Ethnicity." In *Key Variables in Social Investigation*. Ed. Robert G. Burgess. London: Routledge and Kegan Paul.

Burns, Nancy, Kay Lehman Schlozman, and Sidney Verba. 2001. *The Private Roots of Public Action*. Cambridge, MA: Harvard University Press.

Butler, David E. 1963. *The Electoral System in Britain Since 1918*. Oxford: Clarendon Press.

Butler, David E., and Donald Stokes. 1974. *Political Change in Britain*. Revised ed. London: Macmillan.

Butler, David, Howard Penniman, and Austin Ranney. 1981. *Democracy at the Polls: A Comparative Study of Competitive National Elections*. Washington, D.C.: American Enterprise Institute.

Butler, David E., and Austin Ranney. Eds. 1994. *Referendums around the World: The Growing Use of Democracy?* Washington, D.C.: American Enterprise Institute.

Cain, Bruce E. 1978. "Strategic voting in Britain." *American Journal of Political Science* 22(3): 639–655.

Cain, Bruce E., John A. Ferejohn, and Morris P. Fiorina. 1987. *The Personal Vote: Constituency Service and Electoral Independence*. Cambridge, MA: Harvard University Press.

Cameron, L., and M. Crosby. 2000. "It's the economy stupid: Macroeconomics and federal elections in Australia." *Economic Record* 76(235): 354–364.

Campbell, Angus, and Henry Valen. 1961. "Party identification in Norway and the United States." *Public Opinion Quarterly* 22(4): 505–525.

Campbell, Angus, Philip Converse, Warren Miller, and Donald Stokes. 1960. *The American Voter*. New York: Wiley.

————. 1966. *Elections and the Political Order*. New York: Wiley.

Caress, S.M. 1999. "The influence of term limits on the electoral success of women." *Women & Politics* 20(3): 45–63.

Carey, John M. 2000. "Parchment, equilibria, and institutions." *Comparative Political Studies* 33(6–7): 735–761.

Carey, John M., and Matthew S. Shugart. 1995. "Incentives to cultivate a personal vote: A rank ordering of electoral formulas." *Electoral Studies* 14(4): 417–440.

Carothers, Thomas. 1999. *Aiding Democracy Abroad: The Learning Curve*. Washington, D.C.: Carnegie Endowment.

————. 2002. "The end of the transition paradigm." *Journal of Democracy* 13(1): 5–21.

Carroll, Susan. Ed. 2001. *The Impact of Women in Public Office*. Bloomington, Indiana: University of Indiana Press.

Carroll, Susan J., and K. Jenkins. 2001. "Unrealized opportunity? Term limits and the representation of women in state legislatures." *Women & Politics* 23(4): 1–30.

Carstairs, Andrew McLaren. 1980. *A Short History of Electoral Systems in Western Europe*. London: George Allen & Unwin.

Carton, A. 2001. "The general elections in Belgium in June 1999: A real breakthrough for women politicians?" *European Journal of Women's Studies* 8(1): 127–135.

Cassel, C.A. 1999. "Voluntary associations, churches and social participation theories of turnout." *Social Science Quarterly* 80(3): 504–517.

Catt, Helena, Paul Harris, and Nigel S. Roberts. 1992. *Voter's Choice: Electoral Change in New Zealand?* Palmerston North, New Zealand: Dunmore Press.

Caul, Miki. 1999. "Women's representation in parliament: The role of political parties." *Party Politics* 5(1): 79–98.

――――. 2001. "Political parties and the adoption of candidate gender quotas: A cross-national analysis." *Journal of Politics* 63(4): 1214–1229.

Chan, K.K.L. 2001. "Idealism versus realism in institutional choice: Explaining electoral reform in Poland." *West European Politics* 24(3): 65–88.

Cheles, Luciano, Ronnie Ferguson, and Michalina Vaughan. 1995. *The Far Right in Western and Eastern Europe.* New York: Longman.

Chen, D.Y. 1999. "A popularly-elected presidency as a focus of constitutional choice: Explaining the Taiwanese case, 1986–1996." *Issues & Studies* 35(5): 1–42.

Chibber, Pradeep, and Ken Kollman. 1998. "Party aggregation and the number of parties in India and the United States." *American Political Science Review* 92(2): 329–342.

Chibber, Pradeep, and M. Torcal. 1997. "Elite strategy, social cleavages, and party systems in a new democracy – Spain." *Comparative Political Studies* 30(1): 27–54.

Choe, Yonhyok, and Staffan Darnoff. 1999. "Evaluating the Structure and Functional Role of Electoral Administration in Contemporary Democracies." Paper presented at the *Annual Meeting of the American Political Science Association*, Atlanta, GA, September 2–5.

Christy, Carol. 1987. *Sex Differences in Political Participation: Processes of Change in Fourteen Nations.* New York: Praeger.

Citrin, Jack. 1974. "Comment: The political relevance of trust in government." *American Political Science Review* 68(3): 973–988.

Clark, Terry Nichols, and Seymour Martin Lipset. Eds. 2001. *The Breakdown of Class Politics.* Baltimore, MD: The Johns Hopkins University Press.

Clarke, Harold, and Marianne Stewart. 1998. "The decline of parties in the minds of citizens." *Annual Review of Political Science* 1: 357–378.

Clarke, Harold, and Paul Whitely. 1990. "Perceptions of macroeconomic performance, government support and conservative party strength in Britain." *European Journal of Political Research* 18: 97–120.

Collier, David. 1991. "The Comparative Method: Two Decades of Change." In *Comparative Political Dynamics: Global Research Perspectives.* Eds. Dankwart A. Rustow and Kenneth Paul Erickson. New York: HarperCollins.

Colomer, J. M. 1991. "Benefits and costs of voting." *Electoral Studies* 10(4): 313–325.

Converse, Philip E. 1964. "The Nature of Belief Systems in Mass Publics." In: David Apter. Ed. *Ideology and Discontent.* New York: The Free Press.

――――. 1969. "Of time and partisan stability." *Comparative Political Studies* 2(2): 139–171.

――――. 1970. "Attitudes vs. Non-attitudes: The Continuation of a Dialogue." In E.R. Tufte. Ed. *The Quantitative Analysis of Social Problems.* Reading. MA: Addison-Wesley.

Converse, Phillip E., and Roy Pierce. 1985. "Measuring partisanship." *Political Methodology* 11(4): 143–166.

Cook, Rhodes. 1989. "Key to survival for democrats lies in split-ticket voting." *Congressional Quarterly Weekly Report 1989* 47(3): 1710–1716.

Coppedge, M. 1997. "District magnitude, economic performance, and party-system fragmentation in five Latin American countries." *Comparative Political Studies* 30(2): 156–185.

Council of Europe. 2000. *Positive Action in the Field of Equality between Women and Men: Final Report of the Group of Specialists on Positive Action in the Field of Equality between Women and Men.* Strasbourg, France. Available online at: www.humanrights.coe.int.

Cox, Gary W. 1987. *The Efficient Secret: The Cabinet and the Development of Political Parties in Victorian England.* Cambridge, U.K.: Cambridge University Press.

———. 1990. "Centripetal and centrifugal incentives in electoral systems." *American Journal of Political Science* 34(34): 903–935.

———. 1997. *Making Votes Count: Strategic Coordination in the World's Electoral Systems.* Cambridge, U.K.: Cambridge University Press.

Cox, Gary W., and M.F. Thies. 1998. "The cost of intra-party competition: The single, non-transferable vote and money politics in Japan." *Comparative Political Studies* 31(3): 267–291.

Cox, Gary W., F.M. Rosenbluth, and M.F. Thies. 1998. "Mobilization, social networks, and turnout – Evidence from Japan." *World Politics* 50(3): 447–474.

———. 1999. "Electoral reform and the fate of factions: The case of Japan's Liberal Democratic Party." *British Journal of Political Science* 29: 33–56.

Crewe, Ivor. 1981. "Electoral Participation." In *Democracy at the Polls.* Eds. David Butler, Howard Penniman, and Austin Ranney. Washington, D.C.: American Enterprise Institute.

Crewe, Ivor, and Anthony Fox. 1995. *The British Electorate 1963–92.* Cambridge, U.K.: Cambridge University Press.

Crewe, Ivor, and David Denver. Eds. 1985. *Electoral Change in Western Democracies: Patterns and Sources of Electoral Volatility.* New York: St. Martin's Press.

Crewe, Ivor, Jim Alt, and Bo Sarlvik. 1977. "Partisan dealignment in Britain 1964–1974." *British Journal of Political Science* 7(2): 129–190.

Criddle, Byron. 1992. "Electoral systems in France." *Parliamentary Affairs* 45(1): 108–116.

Crisp, Brian, and R.E. Ingall. 2002. "Institutional engineering and the nature of representation: Mapping the effects of electoral reform in Colombia." *American Journal of Political Science* 46(4): 733–748.

Curtice, John. 2001. "The Electoral System: Biased to Blair." In *Britain Votes, 2001.* Ed. Pippa Norris. Oxford: Oxford University Press.

———. 2002. "The state of election studies: Mid-life crisis or new youth?" *Electoral Studies* 21(2): 161–168.

Curtice, John, and Michael Steed. 1982. "Electoral choice and the production of government: The changing operation of the electoral system in the United Kingdom since 1955." *British Journal of Political Science* 12(July): 249–298.

———. 1986. "Proportionality and exaggeration in the British electoral system." *Electoral Studies* 5(3): 209–228.

———. 2001. "Appendix 2: The Results Analyzed." Table A2.8. In *The British General Election of 2001.* Eds. David Butler and Dennis Kavanagh. London: Palgrave.

Curtice, John, and Phil Shively. 2000. "Who Represents Us Best? One Member or Many?" Paper presented at the *International Political Science Association World Congress,* Quebec, August 1–6.

Curtice, John, and Roger Jowell. 1997. "Trust in the Political System." In *British Social Attitudes: The 14th report*. Eds. Roger Jowell et al. Aldershot, U.K.: Ashgate.

———. 1998. "Is there really a demand for constitutional change?" *Scottish Affairs special issue: Understanding Constitutional Change*. Edinburgh: University of Edinburgh.

Czudnowski, Moshe M. 1975. "Political Recruitment." In *Handbook of Political Science, Volume 2: Micro-Political Theory*. Reading, MA: Addison-Wesley.

———. 1976. *Comparing Political Behavior*. Beverly Hills, CA: Sage Publications.

Dahl, Robert A. 1966. *Political Oppositions in Western Democracies*. New Haven, CT: Yale University Press.

———. 1971. *Polyarchy: Participation and Opposition*. New Haven, CT: Yale University Press.

———. 1982. *Dilemmas of Pluralist Democracy*. New Haven, CT: Yale University Press.

———. 1989. *Democracy and its Critics*. New Haven, CT: Yale University Press.

Dahlerup, Drude. 1998. "Using Quotas to Increase Women's Political Representation." In *Women in Parliament: Beyond Numbers*. Ed. Azza Karam. Stockholm: International IDEA.

Dalton, Russell J. 1993. "Citizens, Protest and Democracy." Special issue of *The Annals of Political and Social Sciences* (July): 8–12.

———. 1999. "Political Support in Advanced Industrial Democracies." In *Critical Citizens: Global Support For Democratic Governance*. Ed. Pippa Norris. Oxford: Oxford University Press.

———. 2000. "Citizen attitudes and political behavior." *Comparative Political Studies* 33(6–7): 912–940.

———. 2002. *Citizen Politics*. 3rd edition. Chatham, NJ: Chatham House.

Dalton, Russell J., and Martin Wattenberg. Ed. 2001. *Parties without Partisans*. New York: Oxford University Press.

Dalton, Russell J., Scott Flanagan, and Paul Allen Beck. Eds. 1984. *Electoral Change in Advanced Industrial Democracies: Realignment or Dealignment?* Princeton, NJ: Princeton University Press.

de Mesquita E.B. 2000. "Strategic and nonpolicy voting – A coalitional analysis of Israeli electoral reform." *Comparative Politics* 33(1): 63–80.

De Winter, Leuvan, and J. Ackaert. 1998. "Compulsory voting in Belgium: a reply to Hooghe and Pelleriaux." *Electoral Studies* 17(4): 425–428.

Deletant, Dennis, and Peter Saini-Davies. 1998. "The Romanian elections of November 1996." *Representation* 35(2/3): 155–167.

Denemark, D. 2000. "Partisan pork barrel in parliamentary systems: Australian constituency-level grants." *Journal of Politics* 62(3): 896–915.

Denemark, D., and Shaun Bowler. 2002. "Minor parties and protest votes in Australia and New Zealand: Locating populist politics." *Electoral Studies* 21(1): 47–67.

Deutsch, Karl W. 1964. "Social mobilization and political development." *American Political Science Review* 55(3): 493–514.

DeVaus, David, and Ian McAllister. 1989. "The changing politics of women: Gender and political alignments in 11 nations." *European Journal of Political Research* 17(3): 241–262.

Diskin, Abraham, and Hanna Diskin. 1995. "The Politics of electoral reform in Israel." *International Political Science Review* 16(1): 31–46.

Dix, Robert H. 1984. "Incumbency and electoral turnover in latin America." *Journal of InterAmerican Studies and World Affairs* 26(4): 435–448.

———. 1989. "Cleavage structures and party systems in Latin America." *Comparative Politics* 22(1): 23–38.

———. 1992. "Democratization and the institutionalization of Latin American political parties." *Comparative Political Studies* 24(4): 488–511.

Dolan, J. 1997. "Support for women's interests in the 103rd Congress: The distinct impact of congressional women." *Women & Politics* 18(4): 81–94.

Donovan, Mark. 1995. "The politics of electoral reform in Italy." *International Political Science Review* 16(1): 47–64.

Dorling, Danny, Colin Rallings, and Michael Thrasher. 1998. "The epidemiology of the Liberal Democrat vote." *Political Geography* 17(1): 45–70.

Dorussen, H., and M. Taylor. 2001. "The political context of issue-priority voting: Coalitions and economic voting in the Netherlands, 1970–1999." *Electoral Studies* 20(3): 399–426.

Dow, J.K. 2001. "A comparative spatial analysis of majoritarian and proportional elections." *Electoral Studies* 20(1): 109–125.

Downs, Anthony. 1957. *An Economic Theory of Democracy*. New York: Harper and Row.

———. 1972. "Up and down with ecology – The issue-attention cycle." *Public Interest* 28: 38–50.

Duerst-Lahti, Georgina, and Rita May Kelly. Eds. 1995. *Gender, Power, Leadership and Governance*. Ann Arbor, MI: University of Michigan Press.

Dummett, M. 1997. *Principles of Electoral Reform*. Oxford: Oxford University Press.

Dunleavy, Patrick, and Helen Margetts. 1995. "Understanding the dynamics of electoral reform." *International Political Science Review* 16(1): 9–30.

———. 1997. "The electoral system." *Parliamentary Affairs* 50: 602–16.

———. 2001. "From majoritarian to pluralist democracy? Electoral reform in Britain since 1997." *Journal of Theoretical Politics* 13(3): 295–319.

Dunleavy, Patrick, Helen Margetts, Trevor Smith, and Stuart Weir. 2001. "Constitutional reform, new labour in power and public trust in government." *Parliamentary Affairs* 54(3): 405–424.

Duverger, Maurice. 1954. *Political Parties, Their Organization and Activity in the Modern State*. New York: Wiley.

———. 1955. *The Political Role of Women*. Paris: UNESCO.

———. 1986. "Duverger's Law: Forty Years Later." In *Electoral Laws and their Political Consequences*. Eds. Bernard Grofman and Arend Lijphart. New York: Agathon Press.

Eagle, Maria, and Joni Lovenduski. 1998. *High Time or High Tide for Labour Women?* London: Fabian Society.

Ebbinghaus, Bernhard, and Jelle Visser. 1999. "When institutions matter: Union growth and decline in Western Europe, 1950–1995." *European Sociological Review* 15(2): 135–158.

Eldersveld, Samuel James. 1982. *Political Parties in American Society*. New York: Basic Books.

Electoral Reform Society. January 2002. The Independent Commission on Alternative Voting Methods. *Elections in the 21st Century: From Paper-Ballot to e-voting.* Available online at: http://www.electoral-reform.org.uk/.

Elklit, Jørgen, and Nigel Roberts. 1996. "A category of its own? Four PR two-tier compensatory member electoral systems in 1994." *European Journal of Political Research* 30(2): 217–240.

Epstein, Leon. 1980. *Political Parties in Western Democracies.* New Brunswick, NJ: Transaction Books.

Eulau, Heinz, and Michael S. Lewis-Beck. Eds. 1985. *Economic Conditions and Electoral Outcomes: The United States and Western Europe.* New York: Agathon Press.

European Consortium for Political Research Manifestos Group. 1992. *Political Manifestos of the Post-War Era, 1945–81.* Kent, U.K.: Bowker-Saur.

Evans, Geoffrey. 1999. *The Decline of Class Politics?* Oxford: Oxford University Press.

———. 2000. "The continued significance of class voting." *Annual Review of Political Science* 3: 401–417.

Evans, Geoffrey, Anthony Heath, and Clive Payne. 1999. "Class: Labour as a Catch-All Party?" In *Critical Elections: British Parties and Voters in Long-term Perspective.* Eds. Geoffrey Evans and Pippa Norris. London: Sage.

Evans, Geoffrey, and Pippa Norris. Eds. 1999. *Critical Elections: British Parties and Voters in Long-term Perspective.* London: Sage.

Fair Vote Canada. Available online at: http://www.fairvotecanada.org.

Farrell, David M. 1997. *Comparing Electoral Systems.* London: Prentice Hall/ Harvester Wheatsheaf.

Fenster, Mark J. 1994. "The impact of allowing day of registration voting on turnout in U.S. elections from 1960 to 1992." *American Politics Quarterly* 22(1): 74–87.

Fidrmuc J. 2000. "Economics of voting in post-communist countries." *Electoral Studies* 19(2–3): 199–217.

Fieldhouse, E., and Andrew Russell. 2001. "Latent liberalism? Sympathy and support for the liberal democrats at the 1997 British General Election." *Party Politics* 7(6): 711–738.

Finer, Samuel E. 1985. "The Contemporary Context of Representation." In *Representations of the People? Parliamentarians and Constituents in Western Democracies.* Ed. Vernon Bogdanor. Aldershot, Hants, U.K.: Gower.

———. 1995. *Comparing Constitutions.* Revised edition. Oxford: Oxford University Press.

———. Ed. 1975. *Adversary Politics and Electoral Reform.* London: Anthony Wigram.

Fiorina, Morris P. 1981. *Retrospective Voting in American National Elections.* New Haven, CT: Yale University Press.

———. 1990. "An Era of Divided Government." In *Developments in American Politics.* Eds. Bruce Cain and Gillian Peel. London: Macmillan.

Flanagan, Scott C., and Russell J. Dalton. 1984. "Parties under Stress: Realignment and Dealignment in Advanced Industrial Societies." *West European Politics* 7(1): 7–23.

Flickinger, Richard, and Donley Studlar. 1992. "The disappearing voters? Exploring declining turnout in Western European elections." *West European Politics* 15(2): 1–16.

Foley, Michael, and Bob Edwards. 1998. "Beyond Tocqueville: Civil society and social capital in comparative perspective." *American Behavioral Scientist* 42(1): 5–20.

Ford, Gerald. 2002. *To Assure Pride and Confidence in the Electoral Process: Report of the National Commission on Federal Election Reform*. Washington, D.C.: Brookings Institute.

Fox, J. 2002. "Ethnic minorities and the clash of civilizations: A quantitative analysis of Huntington's thesis." *British Journal of Political Science* 32(3): 415–434.

Fox Piven, Frances. 1992. *Labour Parties in Postindustrial Societies*. Oxford: Oxford University Press.

Fox Piven, Frances, and Richard Cloward. 1988. *Why Americans Don't Vote*. New York: Pantheon.

———. 2000. *Why Americans Still Don't Vote and Why Politicians Want It That Way*. Boston: Beacon Press.

Frankland, E. Gene, and Donald Schoonmaker. 1992. *Between Protest and Power: The Green Party in Germany*. Boulder, CO: Westview Press.

Franklin, Mark. 1985. *The Decline of Class Voting in Britain: Changes in the Basis of Electoral Choice, 1964–1983*. Oxford: Clarendon Press.

———. 1999. "Electoral engineering and cross-national turnout differences: What role for compulsory voting?" *British Journal of Political Science* 29(1): 205–216.

———. 2000. "Understanding cross-national turnout differences: What role for compulsory voting?" *British Journal of Political Science* 29: 205–216.

———. 2001. "Electoral Participation." In *Comparing Democracies 2: Elections and Voting in Global Perspective*. Eds. Lawrence LeDuc, Richard G. Niemi, and Pippa Norris. London: Sage.

———. 2003. *The Dynamics of Voter Turnout in Established Democracies Since 1945*. New York: Cambridge University Press.

Franklin, Mark, Tom Mackie, Henry Valen, et al. Eds. 1992. *Electoral Change: Responses to Evolving Social and Attitudinal Structures in Western Countries*. Cambridge, U.K.: Cambridge University Press.

Freedom House. 2001. *Freedom in the World: The Annual Survey of Political Rights and Civil Liberties, 2000–2001*. New York: Freedom House. Available online at www.freedomhouse.org.

Fuchs, Dieter, and Hans-Dieter Klingemann. 1989. "The Left-Right Schema." In *Continuities in Political Action*. Eds. M. Kent Jennings and Jan van Deth. Berlin: de Gruyter.

Gallagher, Michael. 1992. "Comparing proportional representation electoral systems: Quotas, thresholds, paradoxes, and majorities." *British Journal of Political Science* 22: 469–496.

———. 1997. "Ireland: The Archetypal Single Transferable Vote System." In *The International IDEA Handbook of Electoral System Design*. Eds. Andrew Reynolds and Ben Reilly. Stockholm: International IDEA.

———. 1998. "The political impact of electoral system change in Japan and New Zealand, 1996." *Party Politics* 4(2): 203–228.

Gallagher, Michael, and Michael Marsh. Eds. 1988. *Candidate Selection in Comparative Perspective*. London: Sage.

Gallager, Michael, Michael Laver, and Peter Mair. 1995. *Representative Government in Modern Europe*. New York: McGraw Hill.

Gay, C. 2001. "The effect of black congressional representation on political participation." *American Political Science Review* 95(3): 589–602.

Gellner, Earnest. 1983. *Nations and Nationalism*. Oxford: Blackwell.

George, Alexander L. 1998. *Presidential Personality and Performance*. Boulder, CO: Westview Press.

Gidengil, Elizabeth, André Blais, Neil Nevitte, and Richard Nadeau. 2001. "The correlates and consequences of anti-partyism in the 1997 Canadian election." *Party Politics* 7(4): 491–513.

Gidengil, Elizabeth, André Blais, Richard Nadeau, and Neil Nevitte. 1999. "Making sense of regional voting in the 1997 Canadian federal election: Liberal and reform support outside Quebec." *Canadian Journal of Political Science-Revue Canadienne de Science Politique* 32(2): 247–272.

Goldthorpe, John. 1987. *Social Mobility and the Class Structure in Modern Britain*. Oxford: Clarendon Press.

Gomez, B.T., and J.M Wilson. 2001. "Political sophistication and economic voting in the American electorate: A theory of heterogeneous attribution." *American Journal of Political Science* 45(4): 899–914.

Gosnell, Harold F. 1930. *Why Europe Votes*. Chicago: University of Chicago Press.

———. 1968. *Machine Politics: Chicago Model*. 2nd edition. Chicago: University of Chicago Press.

Gramm, Gerald, and John Huber. 2002. "Legislatures as political institutions: Beyond contemporary congress." In *Political Science: State of the Discipline*. Eds. Ira Katznelson and Helen V. Milner. New York: W.W. Norton.

Gray, Mark, and Miki Caul. 2000. "Declining voter turnout in advanced industrialized democracies, 1950 to 1997." *Comparative Political Studies* 33(9): 1091–1122.

Grofman, Bernard. 1997. "SNTV, STV, and Single-Member District Systems: Theoretical Comparisons and Contrasts." In *Elections in Japan, Korea and Taiwan under the Single Non-Transferable Vote: The Comparative Study of an Embedded Institution*. Eds. Bernard Grofman, Sung-Chull Lee, Edwin A. Winckler, and Brian Woodall. Ann Arbor, MI: University of Michigan Press.

Grofman, Bernard, and Arend Lijphart. Eds. 1986. *Electoral Laws and Their Political Consequences*. New York: Agathon Press.

Grofman, Bernard, and Chandler Davidson. Eds. 1992. *Controversies in Minority Voting*. Washington, D.C.: Brookings Institute.

Grofman, Bernard, Sung-Chull Lee, Edwin A. Winckler, and Brian Woodall. Eds. 1997. *Elections in Japan, Korea and Taiwan under the Single Non-Transferable Vote: The Comparative Study of an Embedded Institution*. Ann Arbor, MI: University of Michigan Press.

Grotz, Florian. 2000. "Age of Voting." In the *International Encyclopedia of Elections*. Ed. Richard Rose. Washington, D.C.: Congressional Quarterly Press. Pp. 239–261.

Guber, D.L. 2001. "Voting preferences and the environment in the American electorate." *Society & Natural Resources* 14(6): 455–469.

Gudgin, Graham, and Peter Taylor. 1979. *Seats, Votes and the Spatial Organisation of Elections*. London: Pion.

Guerin, D., and Richard Nadeau. 1998. "The linguistic divide and economic voting in Canada." *Canadian Journal of Political Science-Revue Canadienne de Science Politique* 31(3): 557–572.

Guinier, Lani. 1994. *The Tyranny of the Majority: Fundamental Fairness in Representative Democracy*. New York: The Free Press.

Hamann, K. 1999. "Federalist institutions, voting behavior, and party systems in Spain." *Publius-The Journal of Federalism* 29(1): 111–137.

_____. 2000. "Linking policies and economic voting – Explaining reelection in the case of the Spanish Socialist Party." *Comparative Political Studies* 33(8): 1018–1048.

Hassall, Graham, and Cheryl Saunders. Eds. 1997. *The People's Representatives: Electoral Systems in the Asia-Pacific Region*. London: Allen & Unwin.

Hawang, S.D. 1997. "The candidate factor and Taiwan's 1996 presidential election." *Issues & Studies* 33(4): 45–76.

Hazan, Reuven Y. 1996. "Presidential parliamentarism: Direct popular election of the Prime Minister, Israel's new electoral and political system." *Electoral Studies* 15(1): 21–37.

_____. 1997. "Three levels of election in Israel: The 1996 party, parliamentary and prime ministerial elections." *Representation* 34(3/4): 240–249.

_____. 2002. "Candidate Selection." In *Comparing Democracies*. 2nd edition. Eds. Lawrence LeDuc, Richard G. Neimi, and Pippa Norris. London: Sage.

Hazan, Reuven Y., and Abraham Diskin. 2000. "The 1999 Knesset and prime ministerial elections in Israel." *Electoral Studies* 19(4): 628–637.

Hazan, Reuven Y., and G. Rahat. 2000. "Representation, electoral reform, and democracy – Theoretical and empirical lessons from the 1996 elections in Israel." *Comparative Political Studies* 33(10): 1310–1336.

Hazell, Robert. Ed. 1999. *Constitutional Futures: A History of the Next Ten Years*. Oxford: Oxford University Press.

Hearl, Derek J., Ian Budge, and Bernard Pearson. 1996. "Distinctiveness of regional voting: A comparative analysis across the European Community (1979–1993)." *Electoral Studies* 15(2): 167–182.

Heath, Anthony, and Bridget Taylor. 1999. "New sources of abstention?" In *Critical Elections: British Parties and Voters in Long-term Perspective*. Eds. Geoffrey Evans, and Pippa Norris. London: Sage.

Heath, Anthony, and Roy Pierce. 1992. "It was party identification all along – Question order effects on reports of party identification in Britain." *Electoral Studies* 11(2): 93–105.

Heath, Anthony, Geoffrey Evans, and Clive Payne. 1995. "Modelling the class/party relationship in Britain, 1964–92." *Journal of the Royal Statistical Society Series A*, 158: 563–574.

Heath, Anthony, Roger Jowell, and John Curtice. 1985. *How Britain Votes*. Oxford: Pergamon Press.

_____. 2001. *The Rise of New Labour*. Oxford: Oxford University Press.

Heath, Anthony, Roger Jowell, John Curtice, Geoffrey Evans, Julia Field, and Sharon Witherspoon. 1991. *Understanding Political Change: The British Voter 1964–1987*. Oxford: Pergamon.

Heath, Anthony, Roger Jowell, and John Curtice, with Bridget Taylor. Eds. 1994. *Labour's Last Chance? The 1992 Election and Beyond*. Aldershot, U.K.: Dartmouth.

Hedges, A., and C. White. 1999. *New Electoral Systems: What Voters Need to Know: A Qualitative Study*. London: Social and Community Planning Research Paper No. P5819.

Held, David, Andrew McGrew, D. Goldblatt, and J. Perraton. 1999. *Global Transformations: Politics, Economics and Culture*. Stanford, CA: Stanford University Press.

Herron, E.S. 2002. "Electoral influences on legislative behavior in mixed-member systems: Evidence from Ukraine's Verkhovna Rada." *Legislative Studies Quarterly* 27(3): 361–382.

Hibbs, Douglas A., Jr. 1987. *The Political Economy of Industrial Democracies*. Cambridge, MA: Harvard University Press.

———. 2000. "Bread and peace voting in U.S. presidential elections." *Public Choice* 104(1–2): 149–180.

Hirczy, Wolfgang. 2000. "Compulsory Voting." In the *International Encyclopedia of Elections*. Ed. Richard Rose. Washington, D.C.: Congressional Quarterly Press.

Hideo, Otake. Ed. 1998. *How Electoral Reform Boomeranged: Continuity in Japanese Campaigning Style*. Tokyo: Japan Center for International Exchange.

Hill, K.Q., and Jan E. Leighley. 1996. "Political parties and class mobilization in contemporary United States elections." *American Journal of Political Science* 40(3): 787–804.

Hinich, M.J., M.C. Munger, and S. De Marchi. 1998. "Ideology and the construction of nationality: The Canadian elections of 1993." *Public Choice* 97(3): 401–428.

Hinich, M.J., V. Khmelko, and P.C. Ordeshook. 1999. "Ukraine's 1998 parliamentary elections: A spatial analysis." *Post-Soviet Affairs* 15(2): 149–185.

Hirczy, Wolfgang. 1994. "The impact of mandatory voting laws on turnout: A quasi experimental approach." *Electoral Studies* 13(1): 64–76.

———. 1995. "Explaining near-universal turnout: the case of Malta." *European Journal of Political Research* 27: 467–492.

Hirschman, Albert O. 1970. *Exit, Voice, and Loyalty*. Cambridge, MA: Harvard University Press.

Holmberg, Sören. 1994. "Party Identification Compared Across the Atlantic." In *Elections at Home and Abroad*. Eds. M. Kent Jennings and Thomas Mann. Ann Arbor, MI: University of Michigan Press.

Holzhacker, R.L. 1999. "Campaign communication and strategic responses to change in the electoral environment – Germany after reunification." *Party Politics* 5(4): 439–469.

Horowitz, Donald L. 1991. *A Democratic South Africa? Constitutional Engineering in a Divided Society*. Berkeley: University of California Press.

———. 1993. "Democracy in divided societies." *Journal of Democracy* 4(4): 18–38.

Hoskins, Cathryn, and Shirin Rai. 1998. "Gender, class and representation: India and the European Union." *European Journal of Women's Studies* 5(3–4): 345–355.

Hsieh, John Fuh-Sheng. 1997. "Electoral politics in new democracies in the Asia-Pacific region." *Representation* 34(3/4): 157–165.

———. 2001. "The 2000 presidential election and its implications for Taiwan's domestic politics." *Issues & Studies* 37(1): 1–19.

Hsieh, John Fuh-Sheng, and Emerson M.S. Niou. 1996. "Salient issues in Taiwan's electoral politics." *Electoral Studies* 15(2): 219–235.

———. 1996. "Taiwan's March 1996 elections." *Electoral Studies* 15(4): 545–550.

Hsieh, John Fuh-Sheng, D. Lacy, and Emerson M.S. Niou. 1998. "Retrospective and prospective voting in a one-party-dominant democracy: Taiwan's 1996 presidential election." *Public Choice* 97(3): 383–399.

Hsieh, John Fuh-Sheng, and David Newman. Eds. 2002. *How Asia Votes*. New York: Chatham House.

Htun, Mala. Forthcoming. "Women and Political Power in Latin America." In *Women in Parliament. Beyond Numbers*. Eds. Julie Ballington and Myriam Mendez-Montalvo. Latin America edition. Stockholm: International IDEA.

Htun, Mala, and Mark Jones. 2002. "Engendering the Right to Participate in Decisionmaking: Electoral Quotas and Women's Leadership in Latin America." In *Gender and the Politics of Rights and Democracy in Latin America*. Eds. Nikki Craske and Maxine Molyneux. London: Palgrave.

Huang, C., and T.G. Shields. 2000. "Interpretation of interaction effects in logit and probit analyses – Reconsidering the relationship between registration laws, education, and voter turnout." *American Politics Quarterly* 28(1): 80–95.

Huber, John D. 1993. "Restrictive legislative procedures in France and the United States." *American Political Science Review* 86(3): 675–687.

———. 1996. "The Vote of Confidence in Parliamentary Systems." *American Political Science Review* 90(2): 269–283.

Huber, John D., and G. Bingham Powell, Jr. 1994. "Congruence between citizens and policy-makers in two visions of liberal democracy." *World Politics* 46(3): 291–326.

Huckfeldt, Robert, and John Sprague. 1992. "Political parties and electoral mobilization: Political structure, social structure and the party canvass." *American Political Science Review* 86(1): 70–86.

Huntington, Samuel P. 1968. *Political Order in Changing Societies*. New Haven, CT: Yale University Press.

———. 1993. *The Third Wave: Democratization in the Late Twentieth Century*. Norman, OK: University of Oklahoma Press.

Ingall, R.E., and Brian Crisp. 2001. "Determinants of home style: The many incentives for going home in Colombia." *Legislative Studies Quarterly* 26(3): 487–512.

Inglehart, Ronald. 1977. *The Silent Revolution: Changing Values and Political Styles Among Western Publics*. Princeton, NJ: Princeton University Press.

———. 1990. *Culture Shift in Advanced Industrial Society*. Princeton, NJ: Princeton University Press.

———. 1997. *Modernization and Postmodernization: Cultural, Economic and Political Change in 43 Societies*. Princeton, NJ: Princeton University Press.

Inglehart, Ronald, and Pippa Norris. 2003. *Rising Tide: Gender Equality and Cultural Change Around the World*. Cambridge, U.K.: Cambridge University Press.

International IDEA. *Voter Turnout from 1945 to 2000*. Stockholm: International IDEA. Available online at www.IDEA.int.

Inter-Parliamentary Union. 1992. *Women and Political Power*. Geneva: IPU.

——— 1993. *Electoral Systems: A Worldwide Comparative Study*. Geneva: IPU.

——— 2000. *Politics: Women's Insight*. IPU Reports and Documents No. 36. Geneva: IPU.

——— 2002. *Women in National Parliaments*. Geneva: IPU. Available online at www.IPU.org.

Internet Policy Institute for the National Science Foundation. *Report of the National Workshop on Internet Voting. March 2001.* Available online at http://www. internetpolicy.org/research/e_voting_report.pdf.

Isaacharoff, Samuel, Pamela S. Karlan, and Richard H. Pildes. 1998. *The Law of Democracy: Legal Structures of the Political Process.* Westbury, NY: The Foundation Press.

Ishiyama, John. 1997. "Transitional electoral systems in post-communist Eastern Europe." *Political Science Quarterly* 112(1): 95–115.

Jackman, Robert W. 1985. "Cross-national statistical research and the study of comparative politics." *American Journal of Political Science* 29(1): 161–182.

———. 1987. "Political institutions and voter turnout in industrialized democracies." *American Political Science Review.* 81(2): 405–423.

Jackman, Robert W., and Ross A. Miller. 1995. "Voter turnout in industrial democracies during the 1980s." *Comparative Political Studies* 27(4): 467–492.

Jackson, Keith, and Alan McRobie. 1998. *New Zealand Adopts Proportional Representation.* Aldershot, U.K.: Ashgate.

Jacobson, Gary C. 2001. *The Politics of Congressional Elections.* New York: Longman.

Jagodzinski, Wolfgang, and Karel Dobbelaere. 1995. "Secularization and Church Religiosity." In *The Impact of Values.* Eds. Jan W. van Deth and Elinor Scargrough. Oxford: Oxford University Press.

Janda, Kenneth. 1993. "Comparative Political Parties: Research and Theories." In *Political Science: The State of the Discipline II.* Ed. Ada W. Finifter. Washington, D.C.: American Political Science Association.

Jelen, Ted Gerard, and Clyde Wilcox. Eds. 2002. *Religion and Politics in Comparative Perspective.* New York: Cambridge University Press.

Jenkins, Lord. 1998. *The Report of the Independent Commission on the Voting System.* London: Stationery Office. Cm 4090–1. Available online at http://www. officialdocuments.co.uk/document/cm40/4090/4090.htm.

Jenssen, A.T. 1999. "All that is solid melts into air: Party identification in Norway." *Scandinavian Political Studies* 22(1): 1–27.

Johnston, Richard, et al. 1992. *Letting the People Decide: Dynamics of a Canadian Election.* Montreal: McGill-Queens University Press.

Johnston, Ron J., and Charles J. Pattie. 1996. "The strength of party identification among the British electorate: An exploration." *Electoral Studies* 15(3): 295–309.

———. 1999. "Constituency campaign intensity and split-ticket voting: New Zealand's first election under MMP, 1996." *Political Science* 51(2): 164–181.

———. 2001. "Dimensions of retrospective voting – Economic performance, public service standards and conservative party support at the 1997 British general election." *Party Politics* 7(4): 469–490.

———. 2001. "'It's the economy, stupid' – But which economy? Geographical scales, retrospective economic evaluations and voting at the 1997 British General Election." *Regional Studies* 35(4): 309–319.

———. 2002. "Campaigning and split-ticket voting in new electoral systems: The first MMP elections in New Zealand, Scotland and Wales." *Electoral Studies* 21(4): 583–600.

Johnston, Ron J., Charles J. Pattie, Danny F.L. Dorling, and David Rossiter. 2001. *From Votes to Seats: The Operation of the U.K. Electoral System Since 1945.* Manchester, U.K.: Manchester University Press.

Johnston, Ron J., Charles J. Pattie, Danny F.L. Dorling, Ian MacAllister, H. Tunstall, and David J. Rossiter. 2000. "Geographical scale, the 'feel-good factor' and voting at the 1997 general election in England and Wales." *Transactions of the Institute of British Geographers* 25(1): 51–64.

———. 2001. "Social locations, spatial locations and voting at the 1997 British general election: Evaluating the sources of Conservative support." *Political Geography* 20(1): 85–11.

Jones, Mark P. 1994. "Presidential election laws and multipartyism in Latin America." *Political Research Quarterly* 47(1): 41–57.

———. 1995. *Electoral Laws and the Survival of Presidential Democracies.* Notre Dame, IN: University of Notre Dame Press.

———. 1996. "Increasing women's representation via gender quotas: The Argentine Ley de Cupos." *Women & Politics* 16(4): 75–98.

———. 1997. "A guide to the electoral systems of the Americas." *Electoral Studies* 16(1): 13–16.

———. 1997. "A guide to the electoral systems of the Americas: An update." *Electoral Studies* 14(1): 5–22.

———. 1998. "Gender quotas, electoral laws, and the election of women – Lessons from the Argentine provinces." *Comparative Political Studies* 31(1): 3–21.

———. 1999. "Assessing the effectiveness of gender quotas in open-list proportional representation electoral systems." *Social Science Quarterly* 80(2): 341–355.

Jones, M.P., S. Saiegh, P.T. Spiller, and M. Tommasi. 2002. "Amateur legislators, professional politicians: The consequences of party-centered electoral rules in a federal system." *American Journal of Political Science* 46(3): 656–669.

Jung, Courtney, and Ian Shapiro. 1995. "South Africa's negotiated transition: Democracy, opposition, and the new constitutional order." *Politics and Society* 23(3):269–308.

Kaase, Max. 1987. "On the meaning of electoral change." *Political Studies* 35(3): 482–90.

Kabashima, I., and Y. Ishio. 1998. "The instability of party identification among eligible Japanese voters – A seven-wave panel study, 1993–6." *Party Politics* 4(2): 151–176.

Kaminski, M.M. 2001. "Coalitional stability of multi-party systems: Evidence from Poland." *American Journal of Political Science* 45(2): 294–312.

Kaminski, M.M., G. Lissowski, and P. Swistak. 1998. "The 'revival of communism' or the effect of institutions? The 1993 Polish parliamentary elections." *Public Choice* 97(3): 429–449.

Kang, W.T. 1998. "The rise of a third party in South Korea: the Unification National Party in the 1992 National Assembly election." *Electoral Studies* 17(1): 95–110.

Karam, Azza. Ed. 1998. *Women in Politics Beyond Numbers.* Stockholm: International IDEA. Available online at http://www.int-idea.se/women/.

Karp, Jeff A., and Susan A. Banducci. 1999. "The impact of proportional representation on turnout: Evidence from New Zealand." *Australian Journal of Political Science* 34(3): 363–377.

———. 2002. "Issues and party competition under alternative electoral systems." *Party Politics* 8(1): 123–141.

Karp, Jeff A., Jack Vowles, Susan A. Banducci, and T. Donovan. 2002. "Strategic voting, party activity, and candidate effects: Testing explanations for split voting in New Zealand's new mixed system." *Electoral Studies* 21(1): 1–22.

Karvonen, Lauri, and Per Selle. 1995. *Women in Nordic Politics*. Aldershot, U.K.: Dartmouth.

Katz, Richard S. 1980. *A Theory of Parties and Electoral Systems*. Baltimore, MD: The Johns Hopkins University Press.

———. 1986. "Intra-Party Preference Voting." In *Electoral Laws and Their Political Consequences*. Eds. Bernard Grofman and Arend Lijphart. New York: Agathon.

———. 1996. "Electoral reform and the transformation of party politics in Italy." *Party Politics* 2(1): 31–53.

———. 1997. *Democracy and Elections*. Oxford: Oxford University Press.

———. 1999. "Reforming the Italian Electoral Law 1993." Paper presented at the American Political Science Association annual meeting, Atlanta, GA, September 1–4.

———. 1999. "Role Orientations." In *The European Parliament, the National Parliaments, and European Integration*. Eds. Richard S. Katz and Bernhard Wessels. Oxford: Oxford University Press.

Katz, Richard S., and Peter Mair. 1992. "The membership of political parties in European democracies, 1960–1990." *European Journal of Political Research* 22(3): 329–45.

———. 1995. "Changing models of party organization and party democracy: The emergence of the cartel party." *Party Politics* 1(1): 5–28.

———. 1996. "Cadre, catch-all or cartel? A rejoinder." *Party Politics* 2(4): 525–534.

———. Eds. 1992. *Party Organizations: A Data Handbook on Party Organizations in Western Democracies, 1960–1990*. London Sage.

———. Eds. 1994. *How Parties Organize: Change and Adaptation in Party Organizations in Western Democracies*. London: Sage.

Kenworthy, Lane, and Melissa Malami. 1999. "Gender inequality in political representation: A worldwide comparative analysis." *Social Forces* 78(1): 235–269.

Key, V.O., Jr. 1949. *Southern Politics in State and Nation*. New York: Vintage.

———. 1964. *Politics, Parties, and Pressure Groups*. 5th edition. New York: Crowell.

Kim, H., and R.C. Fording. 2001. "Does tactical voting matter? The political impact of tactical voting in recent British elections." *Comparative Political Studies* 34(3): 294–311.

Kinder, Donald R., and D. Roderick Kiewiet. 1981. "Sociotropic politics: The American case." *British Journal of Political Science* 11(April): 129–161.

King, Anthony. 1999. *Running Scared: Why America's Politicians Campaign Too Much and Govern Too Little*. New York: The Free Press.

——— Ed. 2002. *Leaders' Personalities and the Outcomes of Democratic Elections*. Oxford: Oxford University Press.

King, J.D. 1994. "Political culture, registration laws and voter turnout in the American states." *Publius: The Journal of Federalism* 24(4): 115–127.

Kirchheimer, Otto. 1966. "The Transformation of Western European Party Systems." In *Political Parties and Political Development*, Eds. J. La Palombara and M. Weiner. Princeton, NJ: Princeton University Press.

Kish, Leslie. 1993. "Multinational Survey Designs." Ann Arbor, MI: Survey Research Center, Institute for Social Research.

Kitschelt, Herbert. 1988. "Organization and strategy of Belgian and West European parties: A new dynamic of party politics in Western Europe?" *Comparative Politics* 20(2):127–154.

———. 1989. *The Logics of Party Formation: Ecological Politics in Belgium and West Germany.* Ithaca, NY: Cornell University Press.

———. 1992. "The formation of party systems in East-Central-Europe." *Politics & Society* 20(1): 7–50.

———. 1993. "Class-structure and Social-Democratic Party strategy." *British Journal of Political Science* 23(3): 299–337.

———. 1994. *The Transformation of European Social Democracy.* Cambridge, U.K.: Cambridge University Press.

———. 1995. *The Radical Right in Western Europe.* Ann Arbor, MI: The University of Michigan Press.

———. 1995. "Formation of party cleavages in post-communist democracies – theoretical propositions." *Party Politics* 1(4): 447–472.

———. 2000. "Linkages between citizens and politicians in democratic polities." *Comparative Political Studies* 33(6–7): 845–879.

Kitschelt, Herbert, Zdenka Mansfeldova, Radoslaw Markowski, and Gabor Toka. 1999. *Post-Communist Party Systems.* Cambridge, U.K.: Cambridge University Press.

Kleppner, Paul. 1982. *Who Voted? The Dynamics of Electoral Turnout, 1870–1980.* New York: Praeger Publishers.

Klingemann, Hans-Dieter. 1979. "Measuring ideological conceptualizations." In *Political Action.* Eds. Samuel Barnes, Max Kaase, et al. Beverley Hills, CA: Sage Publications.

Klingemann, Hans-Dieter, and Dieter Fuchs. 1995. *Citizens and the State.* Oxford: Oxford University Press.

Klingemann, Hans-Dieter, and Martin Wattenberg. 1992. "Decaying versus developing party systems: A comparison of party images in the United States and West Germany." *British Journal of Political Science* 22(Part 2, April): 131–49.

Klingemann, Hans-Dieter, Richard Hofferbert, and Ian Budge. 1994. *Parties, Policies and Democracy.* Boulder, CO: Westview.

Knack, Stephen. 1995. "Does 'motor voter' work? Evidence from state-level data." *Journal of Politics* 57(3): 796–811.

———. 2001. "Election-day registration: The second wave." *American Politics Research* 29(1): 65–78.

Knack, Stephen, and James White. 2000. "Election-day registration and turnout inequality." *Political Behavior* 22(1): 29–44.

Knapp, Andrew. 1987. "Proportional but bipolar: France's electoral system in 1986." *West European Politics* 10(1): 89–114.

Knight, Kathleen, and Michael Marsh. 2002. "Varieties of election studies." *Electoral Studies* 21(2): 161–168.

Koelble, Thomas. 1992. "Recasting social democracy in Europe: A nested games explanation for strategic adjustment in political parties." *Politics and Society* 20(1): 51–70.

Kollner, P. 2000. "How electoral reform boomeranged: Continuity in Japanese campaigning style." *Politische Vierteljahresschrift* 41(2): 354–366.

Kostadinova, T. 2002. "Do mixed electoral systems matter? A cross-national analysis of their effects in Eastern Europe." *Electoral Studies* 21(1): 23–34.

Kotler-Berkowitz, L.A. 2001. "Religion and voting behaviour in Great Britain: A reassessment." *British Journal of Political Science* 31(Part 3, July): 523–554.

Krasner, S.D. 1993. "Approaches to the state: Alternative conceptions and historical dynamics." *Comparative Politics* 16(2): 223–46.

Krieger, Joel. 1999. *British Politics in the Global Age*. Oxford: Oxford University Press.

Krupavicius, Algis. 1997. "The Lithuanian parliamentary elections of 1996." *Electoral Studies* 16(4): 541–575.

Krupavicius, Algis, and Dagne Eitutyte. 1999. "The 1997–98 presidential elections in Lithuania." *Electoral Studies* 18(1): 127–136.

Kuenzi, Michelle, and Gina Lambright. 2001. "Party system institutionalization in 30 African countries." *Party Politics* 7(4): 437–468.

Laakso, M., and Rein Taagepera. 1979. "Effective number of parties: A measure with application to Western Europe." *Comparative Political Studies* 12(1): 3–27.

Ladner, A., and Henry Milner. 1999. "Do voters turn out more under proportional than majoritarian systems? The evidence from Swiss communal elections." *Electoral Studies* 18(2): 235–250.

Lakeman, Enid. 1974. *How Democracies Vote*. London: Faber and Faber.

Lancaster, Thomas D., and W.D. Patterson. 1990. "Comparative Pork Barrel Politics Perceptions from the West-German-Bundestag." *Comparative Political Studies* 22(4): 458–477.

Landman, Todd. 2000. *Issues and Methods in Comparative Politics*. London: Routledge. Chapter 2.

Lane, Jan-Erik, and Svante Ersson. 1990. "Macro and micro understanding in political science: What explains electoral participation?" *European Journal of Political Research* 18(4): 457–465.

Lane, Jan-Erik, David McKay, and Kenneth Newton. Eds. 1997. *Political Data Handbook*. 2nd ed. Oxford: Oxford University Press.

Lardeyret, Guy. 1991. "The problem with PR." *Journal of Democracy* 2(3): 30–35.

Laver, Michael, and Kenneth A. Sheplse. 1990. "Coalitions and cabinet government." *American Political Science Review* 84(3): 873–90.

———. 1995. *Making and Breaking Governments: Cabinet Ministers and Parliamentary Government*. New York: Cambridge University Press.

Laver, Michael, and Norman Schofield. 1990. *Multiparty Government*. Oxford: Oxford University Press.

Law Commission of Canada. 2002. *Renewing Democracy: Debating Electoral Reform in Canada*. Discussion Paper JL2–20/2002. Ottowa: Law Commission of Canada.

Lawless, J.L., and R.L. Fox. 2001. "Political participation of the urban poor." *Social Problems* 48(3): 362–385.

Lawson, Kay. 1980. *Political Parties and Linkage: A Comparative Perspective*. New Haven, CT: Yale University Press.

Lawson, Kay, and Peter Merkl. Eds. 1988. *When Parties Fail: Emerging Alternative Organizations*. Princeton, NJ: Princeton University Press.

Lazarsfeld, Paul F., Bernard Berelson, and H. Gaudet. 1948. *The People's Choice*. New York: Columbia University Press.

LeDuc, Lawrence. 1979. "The dynamic properties of party identification: A four nation comparison." *European Journal of Political Research* 9(3): 257–268.

———. 1998. "The Canadian Federal Election of 1997." *Electoral Studies* 17(1): 132–137.

LeDuc, Lawrence, Richard G. Niemi, and Pippa Norris. Eds. 1996. *Comparing Democracies: Elections and Voting in Global Perspective*. Thousand Oaks, CA: Sage.

———. Eds. 2001. *Comparing Democracies 2: Elections and Voting in Global Perspective*. London: Sage.

———. Eds. 2002. *Comparing Democracies 2: New Challenges in the Study of Elections and Voting*. Thousand Oaks, CA: Sage.

Lehoucq, Fabrice Edouard. 1995. "Institutional change and political conflict: Evaluating alternative explanations of electoral reform in Costa Rica." *Electoral Studies* 14(1):23–46.

Lerner, Daniel. 1958. *The Passing of Traditional Society: Modernizing the Middle East*. New York: The Free Press.

Lewis-Beck, Michael S. 1988. *Economics and Elections: The Major Western Democracies*. Ann Arbor, MI: University of Michigan Press.

Lewis-Beck, Michael S., and Andrew Skabalan. 1992. "France." In *Electoral Change: Responses to Evolving Social and Attitudinal Structures in Western Countries*. Eds. Mark Franklin, Tom Mackie, Henry Valen et al. Cambridge, U.K.: Cambridge University Press.

Lewis-Beck, Michael S., and M. Stegmaier. 2000. "Economic determinants of electoral outcomes." *Annual Review of Political Science* 3:183–219.

Liebes, T., and Y. Peri. 1998. "Electronic journalism in segmented societies: Lessons from the 1996 Israeli elections." *Political Communication* 15(1): 27–43.

Lijphart, Arend. 1971. "Comparative politics and comparative method." *American Political Science Review* 65(3): 686.

———. 1979. "Religion vs. linguistic vs. class voting." *American Political Science Review* 73: 442–458.

———. 1980. "Language, Religion, Class, and Party Choice: Belgium, Canada, Switzerland and South Africa Compared." In *Electoral Participation: A Comparative Analysis*. Ed. Richard Rose. Beverly Hills, CA: Sage.

———. 1984. *Democracies: Patterns of Majoritarian and Consensus Government in Twenty-One Countries*. New Haven, CT: Yale University Press.

———. 1986. "Degrees of Proportionality of Proportional Representation Formulas." In *Electoral Laws and Their Political Consequences*. Eds. Bernard Grofman and Arend Lijphart. New York: Agathon Press.

———. 1990. "The political consequences of electoral laws, 1945–85." *American Political Science Review* 84(2): 481–496.

———. 1991. "Constitutional choices for new democracies." *Journal of Democracy* 2(1): 72–84.

———. 1991. "Proportional representation: Double checking the evidence." *Journal of Democracy* 2(2): 42–48.

———. 1994. *Electoral Systems and Party Systems: A Study of Twenty-Seven Democracies, 1945–1990.* New York: Oxford University Press.

———. 1995. "Electoral Systems." In *The Encyclopedia of Democracy.* Ed. S.M. Lipset. Washington, D.C.: Congressional Quarterly Press.

———. 1997. "Unequal participation: Democracy's unresolved dilemma." *American Political Science Review* 91(1): 1–14.

———. 1999. "Australian democracy: Modifying majoritarianism?" *Australian Journal of Political Science* 34 (3): 313–326.

———. 1999. *Patterns of Democracy: Government Forms and Performance in 36 Countries.* New Haven, CT: Yale University Press.

———. Ed. 1992. *Parliamentary versus Presidential Government.* Oxford: Oxford University Press.

Lijphart, Arend, and Carlos H. Waisman. 1996. *Institutional Design in New Democracies.* Boulder, CO: Westview Press.

Lijphart, Arend, and Bernard Grofman. Eds. 1984. *Choosing an Electoral System: Issues and Alternatives.* New York: Praeger.

Lin, J.W. 1999. "Democratization under one-party dominance: Explaining Taiwan's paradoxical transition." *Issues & Studies* 35(6): 1–28.

Linz, Juan J. 1990. "The Perils of Presidentialism." *Journal of Democracy* 1(1): 51–69.

Linz, Juan J., and Alfred C. Stepan. 1996. *Problems of Democratic Transition and Consolidation: Southern Europe, South America and Post-Communist Europe.* Baltimore: The Johns Hopkins University Press.

Linz, Juan J., and Arturo Valenzuela. Eds. 1994. *The Failure of Presidential Democracy.* Baltimore: The Johns Hopkins University Press.

Lippmann, Walter. 1925. *The Phantom Public.* New York: Harcourt Brace.

Lipset, Seymour M. 1959. "Some social requisites of democracy, economic development and political legitimacy." *American Political Science Review* 53(1): 69–105.

——— 1960. *Political Man: The Social Basis of Politics.* New York: Doubleday.

——— 1993. "A comparative analysis of the social requisites of democracy." *International Social Science Journal* 136(2): 155–175.

——— 1994. "The social requisites of democracy revisited." *American Sociological Review* 59(1): 1–22.

Lipset, Seymour Martin, and Stein Rokkan. 1967. *Party Systems and Voter Alignments.* New York: The Free Press.

Lipset, Seymour Martin, R.M. Worcester, and F.C. Turner. 1998. "Opening the Mexican political system: Public opinion and the elections of 1994 and 1997." *Studies in Comparative International Development* 33(3): 70–89.

Listhaug, Ola, B. Aardal, and I. Opheim. 2000. "Institutional Variation and Political Support: CSES Data from 16 Countries." Paper presented at the *International Political Science Association World Congress,* Quebec, August 1–6.

Loewenberg, Gerhard, and Samuel C. Patterson. 1979. *Comparing Legislatures.* Boston: Little, Brown and Company.

Lovenduski, Joni. 2001. "Women and Politics: Minority Representation or Critical Mass?" In *Britain Votes 2001.* Ed. Pippa Norris. Oxford: Oxford University Press.

Lovenduski, Joni, and Pippa Norris. 1994. "Women's Quotas in the Labour Party." In *British Parties and Elections Yearbook, 1994.* Eds. David Broughton et al. London: Frank Cass, pp. 167–181.

————. Eds. 1993. *Gender and Party Politics*. London: Sage.

Lust-Okar, Ellen, and Amaney Jamal. 2002. "Rulers and rules: Reassessing the influence of regime type on electoral law formation." *Comparative Political Studies* 35(3): 337–366.

Lyons, W., and R. Alexander. 2000. "A tale of two electorates: Generational replacement and the decline of voting in presidential elections." *Journal of Politics* 62(4): 1014–1034.

Mackerras, M., and Ian McAllister. 1999. "Compulsory voting, party stability and electoral advantage in Australia." *Electoral Studies* 18(2): 217–233.

Mackie, Thomas J., and Richard Rose. 1991. *The International Almanac of Electoral History*. 3rd edition. Washington, D.C.: Congressional Quarterly Press.

————. 1997. *A Decade of Election Results: Updating the International Almanac*. Glasgow: Centre for the Study of Public Policy, University of Strathclyde.

Magar, E., M.R. Rosenblum, and D. Samuels. 1998. "On the absence of centripetal incentives in double-member districts – The case of Chile." *Comparative Political Studies* 31(6): 714–739.

Maguire, Maria. 1983. "Is There Still Persistence? Electoral Change in Western Europe, 1948–1979." In *Western European Party Systems: Continuity and Change*. Eds. Hans Daalder and Peter Mair. Beverly Hills, CA: Sage Publications.

Mainwaring, Scott. 1988. "Political parties and democratization in Brazil and the Southern Cone." *Comparative Politics* 21(1): 91–120.

————. 1990. "Presidentialism in Latin America." *Latin American Research Review* 25: 157–179.

————. 1997. "Multipartism, robust federalism, and Presidentialism in Brazil." In *Presidentialism and Democracy in Latin America*. Eds. Scott Mainwaring and Matthew Soberg Shugart. New York: Cambridge University Press.

————. 1998. "Electoral volatility in Brazil." *Party Politics* 4(4): 523–545.

Mainwaring, Scott, and Timothy Scully. 1995. *Building Democratic Institutions: Party Systems in Latin America*. Stanford, CA: Stanford University Press.

Mainwaring, Scott, Guillermo O'Donnell, and J. Samuel Valenzuela. 1992. *Issues in Democratic Consolidation: The New South American Democracies in Comparative Perspective*. Notre Dame, IN: University of Notre Dame Press.

Mair, Peter. 1983. "Adaptation and Control: Towards an Understanding of Party and Party System Change." In *Western European Party Systems: Continuity and Change*. Eds. Hans Daalder and Peter Mair. Beverly Hills, CA: Sage Publications.

————. 1986. "Districting Choices under the Single-Transferable Vote." In *Electoral Laws and Their Political Consequences*. Eds. Bernard Grofman and Arend Lijphart. New York: Agathon.

————. 1993. "Myths of electoral change and the survival of traditional parties." *European Journal of Political Research* 24(2): 121–33.

————. 1997. *Party System Change*. Oxford: Oxford University Press.

————. 2001. "In the aggregate: Mass electoral behaviour in Western Europe, 1950–2000." In *Comparative Democracy*. Ed. Hans Keman. London: Sage.

————. 2001. "Party membership in twenty European democracies 1980–2000." *Party Politics* 7(1): 5–22.

Mair, Peter, and C. Mudde. 1998. "The party family and its study." *Annual Review of Political Science* 1: 211–229.

Maley, Michael. 2000. "Absence Voting." In *The International Encyclopedia of Elections*. Ed. Richard Rose. Washington, D.C.: Congressional Quarterly Press.

Mansbridge, Jane. 1999. "Should blacks represent blacks and women represent women? A contingent 'yes.'" *Journal of Politics* 61(3): 628–657.

Manza, Jeff, and Clem Brooks. 1998. "The gender gap in U.S. presidential elections: When? Why? Implications?" *American Journal of Sociology* 103(5): 1235–1266.

———. 1999. *Social Cleavages and Political Change: Voter Alignments and U.S. Party Coalitions*. New York: Oxford University Press.

March, James, and Johan Olsen. 1989. *Rediscovering Institutions: The Organizational Basis of Politics*. New York: The Free Press.

Marquez, M.L., and V. Ramirez. 1998. "The Spanish electoral system: Proportionality and governability." *Annals of Operations Research* 84: 45–59.

Marr, Ted. 1993. "Why minorities rebel? A global analysis of communal mobilization and conflict since 1945." *International Political Science Review* 14(2): 161–201.

Marsh, Alan. 1977. *Protest and Political Consciousness*. Beverly Hills, CA: Sage.

———. 1990. *Political Action in Europe and the USA*. London: Macmillan.

Martinez, M.D., and D. Hill. 1999. "Did motor voter work?" *American Politics Quarterly* 27(3): 296–315.

Massicotte, Louis, and André Blais. 1999. "Mixed electoral systems: A conceptual and empirical survey." *Electoral Studies* 18(3): 341–366.

Mateju, P., and K. Vlachova. 1998. "Values and electoral decisions in the Czech Republic." *Communist and Post-Communist Studies* 31(3): 249–269.

Matland, Richard E. 1993. "Institutional variables affecting female representation in national legislatures: The case of Norway." *Journal of Politics* 55(3): 737–755.

———. 1998. "Enhancing Women's Political Participation: Legislative Recruitment and Electoral Systems." In *Women in Parliament: Beyond Numbers*. Ed. Azza Karam. Stockholm: International IDEA.

———. 1998. "Women's representation in national legislatures: Developed and developing countries." *Legislative Studies Quarterly* 23(1): 109–125.

Matland, Richard E., and Donley Studlar. 1996. "The contagion of women candidates in single member district and proportional representation electoral systems: Canada and Norway." *Journal of Politics* 58(3): 707–733.

———. (In press). "Determinants of legislative turnover: A Cross-national analysis." *British Journal of Political Science*.

Matsuzato, K. 2001. "All Kuchma's men: The reshuffling of Ukrainian governors and the presidential election of 1999." *Post-Soviet Geography and Economics* 42(6): 416–439.

Mattes, Robert B., A. Gouws, and H.J. Kotze. 1995. "The emerging party system in the new South Africa." *Party Politics* 1(3): 381–395.

Mattes, Robert B., and Amanda Gouws. 1999. "Race, Ethnicity and Voting Behavior: Lessons from South Africa." In *Electoral Systems and Conflict in Divided Societies*. Eds. Andrew Reynolds and Ben Reilly. Washington, D.C.: National Academy Press.

Matthews, Donald R. 1985. "Legislative Recruitment and Legislative Careers." In *Handbook of Legislative Research*. Eds. Gerhard Loewenberg, Samuel C. Patterson, and Malcolm E. Jewell. Cambridge, MA: Harvard University Press.

Mayer, Lawrence, and Roland E. Smith. 1985. "Feminism and Religiosity: Female Electoral Behavior in Western Europe." In *Women and Politics in Western Europe.* Ed. Sylvia Bashevkin. London: Frank Cass.

Mayhew, David R. 1986. *Placing Parties in American Politics: Organization, Electoral Settings, and Government Activity in the Twentieth Century.* Princeton, NJ: Princeton University Press.

————. 1991. *Divided We Govern: Party Control, Lawmaking, and Investigations, 1946–1990.* New Haven, CT: Yale University Press.

————. 2002. *Electoral Realignments: A Critique of the American Genre.* New Haven, CT: Yale University Press.

McAllister, Ian. 1986. "Compulsory voting, turnout and party advantage in Australia." *Politics* 21(1): 89–93.

————. 1997. "Australia." In *Passages to Power: Legislative Recruitment in Advanced Democracies.* Ed. Pippa Norris. Cambridge, U.K.: Cambridge University Press.

————. 2001. "Elections without cues: The 1999 Australian republic referendum." *Australian Journal of Political Science* 36(2): 247–269.

McAllister, Ian, and Clive Bean. 2000. "The electoral politics of economic reform in Australia: The 1998 election." *Australian Journal of Political Science* 35(3): 383–399.

McAllister, Ian, and Martin Wattenberg. 1995. "Measuring levels of party – Does question order matter?" *Public Opinion Quarterly* 59(2): 259–268.

McCann, J.A., and Jorge I. Dominguez. 1998. "Mexicans react to electoral fraud and political corruption: an assessment of public opinion and voting behavior." *Electoral Studies* 17(4): 483–503.

McCargo, Duncan. 2002. *Reforming Thai Politics.* Denmark: Nordic Institute for Asian Politics.

McCormick, Peter, Ernest Manning, and Gordon Gibson. 1990. "Regional Representation in Canada." In *Representation and Electoral Systems: Canadian Perspectives.* Eds. J. Paul Johnston and Harvey E. Pasis. Scarborough, Ontario: Prentice-Hall.

McDonald, Michael P., and Samuel L. Popkin. 2000. "The Myth of the Vanishing Voter." Paper presented at the 2000 *American Political Science Convention.* Washington, D.C. August 31–September 3.

McDonald, Ronald H., and J. Mark Ruhl. 1989. *Party Politics and Elections in Latin America.* Boulder, CO: Westview.

McGerr, Michael E. 1986. *The Decline of Popular Politics: The American North, 1865–1928.* New York: Oxford University Press.

McGregor J., S. Fountaine, and M. Comrie. 2000. "From contest to content: The impact of public journalism on New Zealand election campaign coverage." *Political Communication* 17(2): 133–148.

McKean, M., and E. Scheiner. 2000. "Japan's new electoral system: La plus ça change . . ." *Electoral Studies* 19(4): 447–477.

McKenzie, Robert T. 1955. *British Political Parties.* New York: St. Martin's Press.

McLean, Iain. 1998. "Principles of electoral reform." *Party Politics* 4(3): 412–413.

Meie, Petra. 2000. "The evidence of being present: Guarantees of representation and the example of the Belgian case." *Acta Politica* 35(1): 64–85.

Meneguello, R. 1995. "Electoral behaviour in Brazil: The 1994 presidential elections." *International Social Science Journal* 47(4): 627–632.

Merriam, Charles Edward. 1924. *Non-Voting: Causes and Methods of Control.* Chicago: The University of Chicago Press.

Michaels, Robert. [1911] 1962. *Political Parties: A Sociological Study of the Oligarchical Tendencies of Modern Democracy*. New York: The Free Press.

Midtbo, T., and K. Hines. 1998. "The referendum-election nexus: An aggregate analysis of Norwegian voting behaviour." *Electoral Studies* 17(1): 77–94.

Midtbo, T., and K. Stromsnes. 1996. "Voter turnout in Norway. Time, space, and causality." *Scandinavian Political Studies* 19(4): 379–400.

Mihut, L. 1994. "The emergence of political pluralism in Romania." *Communist and Post-Communist Studies* 27(4): 411–422.

Milbrath, Lester, and M.L. Goel. 1977. *Political Participation: How and Why Do People Get Involved in Politics?* 2nd ed. New York: University Press of America.

Miller, Arthur H. 1974a. "Political issues and trust in government, 1964–1970." *American Political Science Review* 68(3): 951–972.

———. 1974b. "Rejoinder to 'Comment' by Jack Citrin: Political discontent or ritualism?" *American Political Science Review* 68(3): 989–1001.

———. 2000. "The development of party identification in post-soviet societies." *American Journal of Political Science* 44(4): 667–686.

Miller, Warren E. 1991. "Party identification, realignment, and party voting: Back to the basics." *American Political Science Review* 85:2:557–568 (June).

Miller, Warren E., and J. Merrill Shanks. 1996. *The New American Voter*. Cambridge, MA: Harvard University Press.

Miller, William L., Stephen White, and Paul Heywood. 1998. *Values and Political Change in Post-communist Europe*. New York: St. Martin's Press.

Milner, Henry. 1997. "Electoral systems, integrated institutions and turnout in local and national elections: Canada in comparative perspective." *Canadian Journal of Political Science-Revue Canadienne de Science Politique* 30(1): 89–106.

———. Ed. 1999. *Making Every Vote Count: Reassessing Canada's Electoral System*. Peterborough, Ontario: Broadview Press.

———. 2002. *Civil Literacy: How Informed Citizens Make Democracy Work*. Hanover, MA: University Press of New England.

Morgenstern, S., and E. Zechmeister. 2001. "Better the devil you know than the saint you don't? Risk propensity and vote choice in Mexico." *Journal of Politics* 63(1): 93–119.

Morlino, Leonardo. 1998. *Democracy between Consolidation and Crisis: Parties, Groups, and Citizens in Southern Europe*. Oxford: Oxford University Press.

Moser, Robert G. 1999. "Electoral systems and the number of parties in post-communist states." *World Politics* 51(3): 359–385.

———. 2001. "The consequences of Russia's Mixed-Member Electoral System." In *Mixed-Member Electoral Systems: The Best of Both Worlds?* Eds. Matthew Soberg Shugart and Martin P. Wattenberg. Oxford: Oxford University Press.

———. 2001. "The effects of electoral systems on women's representation in post-communist states." *Electoral Studies* 20(3): 353–369.

———. 2001. *Unexpected Outcomes: Electoral Systems, Political Parties and Representation in Russia*. Pittsburgh: University of Pittsburgh Press.

Mozaffar, Shaheen. 1997. "Electoral systems and their political effects in Africa: A preliminary analysis." *Representation* 34(3/4): 148–156.

Mozaffar, Shaheen, and Andreas Schedler. 2002. "The comparative study of electoral governance." *International Political Science Review* 23(1): 5–28.

Mueller, Dennis C. 2000. *Constituional Democracy*. Oxford: Oxford University Press.

Mughan, Anthony. 1983. "Accommodation or diffusion in the management of ethnic conflict in Belgium." *Political Studies* 31(3): 431–451.

Munck, G.L., and J. Verkuilen. 2002. "Conceptualizing and measuring democracy – Evaluating alternative indices." *Comparative Political Studies* 35(1): 5–34.

Myerson, Roger. 1993. "Incentives to cultivate favored minorities under alternative election systems." *American Political Science Review* 87(4): 856–869.

Nachmias, David, and Itai Sened. 1998. "The Bias of Pluralism: The Redistributional Effects of the New Electoral Law in Israel's 1996 Election." In *Elections in Israel – 1996*. Eds. Asher Arian and Michal Shamir. Albany, NY: SUNY Press.

Nadeau, Richard, and Michael S. Lewis-Beck. 2001. "National economic voting in U.S. presidential elections." *Journal of Politics* 63(1): 159–181.

Nagler, Jack. 1991. "The effects of registration laws and education on U.S. voter turnout." *American Political Science Review* 85(4): 1393–1405.

Narud, Helga M., and Henry Valen. 1996. "Decline of electoral turnout: The case of Norway." *European Journal of Political Research* 29(2): 235–256.

Nechemias, Carol. 1994. "Democratization and women's access to legislative seats – The Soviet case, 1989–1991." *Women & Politics* 14(3): 1–18.

Neeley, G.W., and L.E. Richardson. 2001. "Who is early voting? An individual level examination." *Social Science Journal* 38(3): 381–392.

Neto, Octavio Amorim, and F. Santos. 2001. "The executive connection: Presidentially defined factions and party discipline in Brazil." *Dados-Revista De Ciencias Sociais* 44 (2): 291–321.

Neto, Octavio Amorim, and Gary Cox. 1997. "Electoral institutions, cleavage structures and the number of parties." *American Journal of Political Science* 41(1): 149–174.

Nevitte, Neil, André Blais, Elisabeth Gidengil, and Richard Nadeau. 2000. *Unsteady State: The 1997 Canadian Federal Election*. Oxford: Oxford University Press.

Nie, Norman, Sidney Verba, and John Petricik. 1976. *The Changing American Voter*. Cambridge, MA: Harvard University Press.

Nielsen, H.J. 1999. "The Danish election 1998." *Scandinavian Political Studies* 22(1): 67–81.

Niemi, Richard G., Guy Whitten, and Mark Franklin. 1992. "Constituency characteristics, individual characteristics and tactical voting in the 1987 British general election." *British Journal of Political Science* 22(Part 2, April): 229–254.

Nieuwbeerta, Paul. 1995. *The Democratic Class Struggle in Twenty Countries 1945–90*. Amsterdam: Thesis Publishers.

Nieuwbeerta, Paul, and H. Flap. 2000. "Crosscutting social circles and political choice – Effects of personal network composition on voting behavior in The Netherlands." *Social Networks* 22(4): 313–335.

Nieuwbeerta, Paul, and Nan Dirk De Graaf. 1999. "Traditional Class Voting in 20 Postwar Societies." In *The End of Class Politics?* Ed. Geoffrey Evans. Oxford: Oxford University Press.

Nohlen, Dieter. 1996. *Elections and Electoral Systems*. Delhi: Macmillan.

Nohlen, Dieter, Florian Grotz, and Christof Hartmann. Eds. 2002. *Elections in Asia and the Pacific: A Data Handbook*. Oxford: Oxford University Press.

Nohlen, Dieter, Michael Krennerich, and Bernhard Thibaut. Eds. 1999. *Elections in Africa: A Data Handbook*. Oxford: Oxford University Press.

Noiret, Serge. Ed. 1990. *Political Strategies and Electoral Reforms: Origins of Voting Systems in Europe in the 19th and 20th Centuries*. Baden-Baden: Nomos Verlagsgesellschaft.

Norpoth, Helmut, Michael S. Lewis-Beck, and Jean-Dominique Lafay. Eds. 1991. *Economics and Politics: The Calculus of Support*. Ann Arbor, MI: University of Michigan Press.

Norris, Pippa. 1985. "Women in European legislative elites." *West European Politics* 8(4): 90–101.

———. 1995. "The politics of electoral reform in Britain." *International Political Science Review* Special Issue on Electoral Reform 16(1): 65–78.

———. 1996. *Electoral Change Since 1945*. Oxford: Blackwell.

———. 1997. "Choosing electoral systems." *International Political Science Review* 18(3): 297–312.

———. 1997. "The puzzle of constituency service." *The Journal of Legislative Studies* 3(2): 29–49.

———. 2000. *A Virtuous Circle: Political Communication in Post-Industrial Democracies*. New York: Cambridge University Press.

———. 2001. "U.S. Campaign 2000: Of pregnant chads, butterfly ballots and partisan vitriol." *Government and Opposition* 35(2): 1–24.

———. 2001. "Women's Power at the Ballot Box." In *IDEA Voter Turnout from 1945 to 2000: A Global Report on Political Participation*. 3rd edition. Stockholm: International IDEA.

———. 2001. *Digital Divide: Civic Engagement, Information Poverty and the Internet Worldwide*. New York: Cambridge University Press.

———. 2002. "The twilight of Westminster? Electoral reform and its consequences." *Political Studies* 49(5): 877–900.

———. 2002. *Democratic Phoenix: Political Activism Worldwide*. New York: Cambridge University Press.

———. Ed. 1998. *Passages to Power*. Cambridge, U.K.: Cambridge University Press.

———. Ed. 1999. *Critical Citizens: Global Support for Democratic Governance*. Oxford: Oxford University Press.

———. Ed. 2001. *Britain Votes 2001*. Oxford: Oxford University Press.

Norris, Pippa, and Ivor Crewe. 1994. "Did the British marginals vanish? Proportionality and exaggeration in the British electoral system revisited." *Electoral Studies* 13(3): 201–221.

Norris, Pippa, and Joni Lovenduski. 1995. *Political Recruitment: Gender, Race and Class in the British Parliament*. Cambridge, U.K.: Cambridge University Press.

Norris, Pippa, and Robert Mattes. 2003. "Does ethnicity determine support for the governing party?" Afrobarometer Working Papers No. 26. Available online at http://www.afrobarometer.org/abseries.html.

Norris, Pippa, Elizabeth Vallance, and Joni Lovenduski. 1992. "Do candidates make a difference? Gender, race, ideology and incumbency." *Parliamentary Affairs* 45(4): 496–517.

North, Douglas C. 1990. *Institutions, Institutional Change, and Economic Performance*. Cambridge, U.K.: Cambridge University Press.

Norton, Philip, and David Wood. 1993. *Back from Westminster: British Members of Parliament and their Constituents*. Lexington, KY: The University Press of Kentucky.

———. 1994. "Do candidates matter? Constituency-specific vote changes for incumbent MPs, 1983–87." *Political Studies* 40(2): 227–238.

O'Donnell, Guillermo, and Phillippe C. Schmitter. 1986. *Transitions from Authoritarian Rule: Tentative Conclusions about Uncertain Transitions.* Baltimore: The Johns Hopkins University Press.

Oppenhuis, Eric. 1995. *Voting Behavior in Europe: A Comparative Analysis of Electoral Participation and Party Choice.* Amsterdam: Het Spinhuis.

Ordeshook, Peter C., and Olga Shvetsova. 1994. "Ethnic heterogeneity, district magnitude and the number of parties." *American Journal of Political Science* 38(1): 100–123.

Pacek, Alexander, and Benjamin Radcliffe. 1995. "Turnout and the left-of-center parties: A cross-national analysis." *British Journal of Political Science* 25(Part 1, January): 137–143.

Pammett, Jon H., and Joan DeBardeleben. Eds. 1998. "Special issue: Voting and elections in post-communist states." *Electoral Studies* 17(2): 143–148.

Panebianco, Angelo. 1988. *Political Parties: Organization and Power.* Cambridge, U.K.: Cambridge University Press.

Pankhurst, D. 2002. "Women and politics in Africa: The case of Uganda." *Parliamentary Affairs* 55(1): 119–125.

Papadakis, E., and Clive Bean. 1995. "Independents and minor parties: The electoral system." *Australian Journal of Political Science* 30(Special Issue): 97–110.

Parry J.A., and T.G. Shields. 2001. "Sex, age, and the implementation of the Motor Voter Act: The 1996 presidential election." *Social Science Quarterly* 82(3): 506–523.

Pastor, Robert A. 1999. "The role of electoral administration in democratic transitions: Implications for policy and research." *Democratization* 6(4): 1–27.

Pattie, Charles, and Ron Johnston. 1999. "Context, conversation and conviction: Social networks and voting at the 1992 British General Election." *Political Studies* 7(5): 877–889.

Pederson, Morgens N. 1979. "The dynamics of European party systems: Changing patterns of electoral volatility." *European Journal of Political Research* 7(1): 1–26.

Pempel, T.J. 1990. *Uncommon Democracies: The One-Party Dominant Regimes.* Ithaca, NY: Cornell University Press.

Percheron, Annick, and M. Kent Jennings. 1981. "Political continuities in French families: A new perspective on an old controversy." *Comparative Politics* 13(4): 421–436.

Perea, Eva. 2002. "Individual characteristics, institutional incentives and electoral abstention in Western Europe." *European Journal of Political Research* 41(5): 643–673.

Peretz, D., and G. Doron. 1996. "Israel's 1996 elections: A second political earthquake?" *Middle East Journal* 50(4): 529–546.

Pérez-Liñán, Aníbal. 2001. "Neo-institutional accounts of voter turnout: Moving beyond industrial democracies." *Electoral Studies* 20(2): 281–297.

Perrigo, Sarah. 1996. "Women and Change in the Labour Party 1979–1995." In *Women in Politics.* Eds. Joni Lovenduski and Pippa Norris. Oxford: Oxford University Press.

Peters, Anne, Robery Seidman, and Ann Seidman. 1999. *Women, Quotas, and Constitutions: A Comparative Study of Affirmative Action for Women under*

American, German and European Community and International Law. The Hague: Kluwer Law International.

Phillips, Anne. 1995. *The Politics of Presence.* Oxford: Clarendon Press.

Pilon, Dennis. 2002. *Renewing Canadian Democracy: Citizen Engagement in Voting System Reform.* Ontario: Law Commission of Canada/Fair Vote Canada.

Pinto-Duschinsky, Michael. 2002. "Overview." In *Handbook on Funding of Parties and Election Campaigns.* Stockholm: International IDEA.

Pitkin, Hanna F. 1967. *The Concept of Representation.* Berkeley: University of California Press.

Polsby, Nelson. 1983. The *Consequences of Party Reform.* Oxford: Oxford University Press.

Pomper, Gerald. 1997. *The Election of 1996.* Chatham, NJ: Chatham House.

Powell, G. Bingham, Jr. 1980. "Voting turnout in thirty democracies: Partisan, legal and socioeconomic influences." In *Electoral Participation: A Comparative Analysis.* Ed. Richard Rose. London: Sage.

———. 1982. *Contemporary Democracies: Participation, Stability, and Violence.* Cambridge, MA: Harvard University Press.

———. 1986. "American voter turnout in comparative perspective." *American Political Science Review* 80(1): 17–43.

———. 1989. "Constitutional design and citizen electoral control." *Journal of Theoretical Politics* 1(2): 107–130.

———. 2000. *Elections as Instruments of Democracy.* New Haven, CT: Yale University Press.

Powell, G. Bingham, Jr., and Georg Vanberg. 2001. "Election laws, disproportionality and median correspondence: Implications for two visions of democracy." *British Journal of Political Science* 30(July): 383–411.

Powell, G. Bingham, Jr., and Guy D. Whitten. 1993. "A cross-national analysis of economic voting: Taking account of the political context." *American Journal of Political Science* 37(2): 391–414.

Power, T.J., and J.T. Roberts. 1995. "Compulsory voting, invalid ballots, and abstention in Brazil." *Political Research Quarterly* 48(4): 795–826.

Powers, D.V., and J.H. Cox. 1997. "Echoes from the past: The relationship between satisfaction with economic reforms and voting behavior in Poland." *American Political Science Review* 91(3): 617–633.

Preiser, S., S. Janas, and R. Theis. 2000. "Political apathy, political support and political participation." *International Journal of Psychology* 35(3): 74–84.

Price, Stuart, and David Sanders. 1995. "Economic expectations and voting intentions in the UK, 1979–87 – A pooled cross-section approach." *Political Studies* 43(3): 451–471.

Przeworski, Adam, and Henry Teune. 1970. *The Logic of Comparative Social Inquiry.* New York: Wiley–Interscience.

Przeworski, Adam, and John Sprague. 1986. *Paper Stones: A History of Electoral Socialism.* Chicago: The University of Chicago Press.

Przeworski, Adam, Michael E. Alvarez, Jose Antonio Cheibub, and Fernando Limongi. 2000. *Democracy and Development.* Cambridge, U.K.: Cambridge University Press.

Przeworski, Adam, Susan C. Stokes, and Bernard Manin. Eds. 1999. *Democracy, Accountability and Representation.* Cambridge, U.K.: Cambridge University Press.

Putnam, Robert. 2000. *Bowling Alone*. New York: Simon & Schuster.

Rabinowitz, G., and S.E. Macdonald. 1989. "A directional theory of issue voting." *American Political Science Review* 83(1): 93–121.

Rae, Douglas W. 1967. *The Political Consequences of Electoral Laws*. New Haven, CT: Yale University Press [2nd edition 1971].

Rahat, G., and M. Sznajder. 1998. "Electoral engineering in Chile: The electoral system and limited democracy." *Electoral Studies* 17(4): 429–442.

Ranney, Austin. 1983. *Channels of Power: The Impact of Television on American Politics*. New York: Basic Books.

Reed, Steven R. 1994. "Democracy and the Personal Vote – A Cautionary Tale from Japan." *Electoral Studies* 13(1): 17–28.

———. 1997. "The 1996 Japanese general election." *Electoral Studies* 16(1): 121–126.

———. 1999. "Strategic voting in the 1996 Japanese general election." *Comparative Political Studies* 32(2): 257–270.

Reeve, Andrew, and Alan Ware. 1992. *Electoral Systems: A Comparative and Theoretical Introduction*. London and New York: Routledge.

Reif, Karl, and Hermann Schmitt. 1980. "Nine national second order elections." *European Journal of Political Research* 8(1): 3–44.

Reilly, Ben. 2001. *Democracy in Divided Societies: Electoral Engineering for Conflict Management*. New York: Cambridge University Press.

Reilly, Ben and Andrew Reynolds. 1998. *Electoral Systems and Conflict in Divided Societies*. Washington, D.C.: National Academy Press.

Reingold, Beth. 2000. *Representing Women: Sex, Gender, and Legislative Behavior in Arizona and California*. Chapel Hill, NC: University of North Carolina Press.

Reynolds, Andrew. 1993. *Voting for a New South Africa*. Cape Town: Maskew Miller Longman.

———. 1995. "The case for proportionality." *Journal of Democracy* 6(4): 117–124.

———. 1999. *Electoral Systems and Democratization in Southern Africa*. Oxford: Oxford University Press.

Reynolds, Andrew, and Ben Reilly. 1999. *Electoral Systems and Conflict in Divided Societies*. Washington, D.C.: National Academy Press.

———. Eds. 1997. *The International IDEA Handbook on Electoral System Design*. Stockholm: IDEA.

Reynolds, Andrew, and Scott Mainwaring. Eds. 2002. *The Architecture of Democracy*. Oxford: Oxford University Press.

Riker, William H. 1962. *The Theory of Political Coalitions*. New Haven, CT: Yale University Press.

———. 1976. "The number of political parties: A reexamination of Duverger's Law." *Comparative Politics* 9(1): 93–106.

———. 1982. "The two-party system and Duverger's Law: An essay on the history of political science." *American Political Science Review* 76(4): 753–766.

———. 1986. "Duverger's Law Revisited." In *Electoral Laws and Their Political Consequences*. Eds. Bernard Grofman and Arend Lijphart. New York: Agathon Press.

Roberts, K.M., and M. Arce. 1998. "Neoliberalism and lower-class voting behavior in Peru." *Comparative Political Studies* 31(2): 217–246.

Roberts, Nigel. 1997. "New Zealand: A Long Established Westminster Democracy Switches to PR." In *The International IDEA Handbook of Electoral System Design.* Eds. Andrew Reynolds and Ben Reilly. Stockholm: International IDEA.

Rohrschneider, Robert. 2002. "Mobilizing versus chasing: How do parties target voters in election campaigns?" *Electoral Studies* 21(3): 367–382.

Rokkan, Stein. 1970. *Citizens, Elections, Parties: Approaches to the Comparative Study of the Processes of Development.* New York: McKay.

Rose, Richard. 1982. *The Territorial Dimension in Politics.* Chatham, NJ: Chatham House.

———. 1997. "Voter turnout: A global survey." In *IDEA Voter Turnout from 1945 to 1997: A Global Report on Political Participation.* 2nd ed. Stockholm: International IDEA.

———. Ed. 1974. *Electoral Behavior: A Comparative Handbook.* New York: The Free Press.

———. Ed. 1980. *Electoral Participation: A Comparative Analysis.* London: Sage.

———. Ed. 2000. *The International Encyclopedia of Elections.* Washington, DC: Congressional Quarterly Press.

Rose, Richard, and Derek W. Urwin. 1969. "Social cohesion, political parties and strains in regime." *Comparative Political Studies* 2(3): 7–67.

Rose, Richard, and Derek W. Urwin. 1970. "Persistence and change in Western party systems since 1945." *Political Studies* 18(3): 287–319.

Rose, Richard, and Ian McAllister. 1986. *Voters Begin to Choose.* London: Sage.

Rose, Richard, and Neil Munro. 2002. *Elections without Order: Russia's Challenge to Vladimir Putin.* New York: Cambridge University Press.

Rose, Richard, Neil Munro, and Tom Mackie. 1998. *Elections in Central and Eastern Europe Since 1990.* Glasgow, Scotland: Center for the Study of Public Policy.

Rosenstone, Stephen, R.L. Behr, and E.H. Lazarus. 1996. *Third Parties in America.* Princeton, NJ: Princeton University Press.

Rossiter, David, Ron Johnston, Charles Pattie, Danny F.L. Dorling, Ian MacAllister, and H. Tunstall. 1999. "Changing biases in the operation of the U.K.'s electoral system, 1950–97." *British Journal of Politics and International Relations* 1(2): 133–164.

Rostow, Walt W. 1952. *The Process of Economic Growth.* New York: Norton.

Rudig, Wolfgang. 1991. "Green Party Politics around the World." *Environment* 33(8): 7–9, 25–31.

———. Ed. 1990. *Green Politics One, 1990.* Edinburgh: Edinburgh University Press.

Rudig, Wolfgang, and Mark N. Franklin. 1992. "Green Prospects: The Future of Green Politics, in Germany, France, and Britain." In *Green Politics Two, 1991.* Ed. Wolfgang Rudig. Edinburgh: Edinburgh University Press.

Rueschemeyer, Dietrich, Marilyn Rueschemeyer, and Bjorn Wittrock. Eds. 1998. *Participation and Democracy, East and West: Comparisons and Interpretations.* Armonk, NY: M.E. Sharpe.

Rule, Wilma. 1987. "Electoral Systems, Contextual factors and women's opportunity for election to parliament in twenty-three democracies." *Western Political Quarterly* 40(3): 477–486.

———. 1994. "Women's under-representation and electoral systems." *PS: Political Science and Politics* 27(4): 689–692.

————. 2000. "Women's Enfranchisement." In *International Encyclopedia of Elections*. Ed. Richard Rose. Washington, D.C.: Congressional Quarterly Press.

Rule, Wilma, and Joseph F. Zimmerman. Eds. 1992. *United States Electoral Systems: Their Impact on Women and Minorities*. New York: Greenwood Press.

————. Eds. 1994. *Electoral Systems in Comparative Perspective: Their Impact on Women and Minorities*. Westport, CT: Greenwood Press.

Russell, Meg. 2000. *Women's Representation in U.K. Politics: What Can Be Done within the Law?* London: The Constitution Unit Report. University College.

————. 2001. *The Women's Representation Bill: Making it Happen*. London: The Constitution Unit Report. University College.

Saideman, S.M., D.J. Lanoue, M. Campenni, and S. Stanton. 2002. "Democratization, political institutions, and ethnic conflict – A pooled time-series analysis, 1985–1998." *Comparative Political Studies* 35(1): 103–129.

Sakamoto, T. 1999. "Explaining electoral reform – Japan versus Italy and New Zealand." *Party Politics* 5(4): 419–438.

Samuels, David J. 2000. "Concurrent elections, discordant results: Presidentialism, federalism, and governance in Brazil." *Comparative Politics* 33(1): 1–20.

————. 2001. "Incumbents and challengers on a level playing field: Assessing the impact of campaign finance in Brazil." *Journal of Politics* 63(2): 569–584.

————. 2001. "Money, elections, and democracy in Brazil." *Latin American Politics and Society* 43(2): 27–48.

————. 2002. *Ambition, Federalism and Legislative Politics in Brazil*. New York: Cambridge University Press.

Sarlvik, Bo, and Ivor Crewe. 1983. *Decade of Dealignment: The Conservative Victory of 1979 and Electoral Trends in the 1970s*. Cambridge, U.K.: Cambridge University Press.

Sartori, Giovanni. 1976. *Parties and Party Systems: A Framework for Analysis*. New York: Cambridge University Press.

————. 1994. *Comparative Constitutional Engineering: An Inquiry into Structures, Incentives, and Outcomes*. New York: Columbia University Press.

Sawer, Marian. Ed. 2001. *Elections: Full, Free and Fair*. Sydney: The Federation Press.

Schattschneider, E.E. 1942. *Party Government*. New York: Farrar and Rinehart.

Scheepers P., H. Schmeets, and A. Felling. 1997. "Fortress Holland? Support for ethnocentric policies among the 1994 electorate of The Netherlands." *Ethnic and Racial Studies* 20(1): 145–159.

Schickler E., and D.P. Green. 1997. "The stability of party identification in western democracies – Results from eight panel surveys." *Comparative Political Studies* 30(4): 450–483.

Schmitt, Hermann, and Sören Holmberg. 1995. "Political Parties in Decline?" In *Citizens and the State*. Eds. Hans-Dieter Klingemann and Dieter Fuchs. Oxford: Oxford University Press.

Schmitt-Beck, R. 1996. "Mass media, the electorate, and the bandwagon. A study of communication effects on vote choice in Germany." *International Journal of Public Opinion Research* 8(3): 266–291.

Schumpeter, Joseph A. 1952. *Capitalism, Socialism and Democracy*. 4th edition. London: George Allen & Unwin.

Searing, Donald. 1994. *Westminster's World: Understanding Political Roles*. Cambridge, MA: Harvard University Press.

Selle, Per. 1991. "Membership in party organizations and the problems of decline of parties." *Comparative Political Studies* 23(4): 459–477.

Semetko, Holli A., Jay G. Blumer, Michael Gurevitch, and David H. Weaver. 1991. *The Formation of Campaign Agendas: A Comparative Analysis of Party and Media Roles in Recent American and British Elections*. Hillsdale, NJ: Lawrence Erlbaum Associates.

Sen, Amartya. 1999. *Development as Freedom*. New York: Anchor Books.

Shamir, M., and Asher Arian. 1999. "Collective identity and electoral competition in Israel." *American Political Science Review* 93(2): 265–277.

Shelley, F.A. 2002. "The Electoral College and the election of 2000." *Political Geography* 21(1): 79–83.

Sholdan, B. 2000. "Democratisation and electoral engineering in post-ethnic conflict societies." *Javnost-The Public* 7(1): 25–40.

Shugart, Matthew Soberg. 2001. "Electoral 'efficiency' and the move to mixed-member systems." *Electoral Studies* 20(2): 173–193.

———. 2001. "'Extreme' electoral systems and the appeal of the mixed-member alternative." In *Mixed-Member Electoral Systems: The Best of Both Worlds?* Eds. Matthew Soberg Shugart and Martin P. Wattenberg. New York: Oxford University Press.

Shugart, Matthew Soberg, and John M. Carey. 1992. *Presidents and Assemblies: Constitutional Design and Electoral Dynamics*. Cambridge, U.K.: Cambridge University Press.

Shugart, Matthew Soberg, and Martin P. Wattenberg. Eds. 2001. *Mixed-Member Electoral Systems: The Best of Both Worlds?* New York: Oxford University Press.

Shvetsova, Olga. 1999. "A survey of post-communist electoral institutions: 1990–1998." *Electoral Studies* 18(3): 397–409.

Siaroff, Alan. 2000. "Women's representation in legislatures and cabinets in industrial democracies." *International Political Science Review* 21(2): 197–215.

Simon, Janos. 1997. "Electoral systems and democracy in Central Europe, 1990–1994." *International Political Science Review* 18(4): 361–379.

Sineau, Mariette. 2002. "La Parité in Politics: From a Radical Idea to a Consensual Reform." In *Beyond French Feminisms: Debates on Women, Politics and Culture in France: 1980–2001*. Ed. Isabelle de Courtivron. New York: Palgrave.

Sisk, Timothy D., and Andrew Reynolds. Eds. 1998. *Elections and Conflict Management in Africa*. Washington, DC: U.S. Institute of Peace Press.

Sniderman, Paul M., R.A. Brody, and P.E. Tetlock. 1991. *Reasoning and Choice*. Cambridge, U.K.: Cambridge University Press.

Somit, Albert. Ed. 1994. *The Victorious Incumbent: A Threat to Democracy?* Aldershot, U.K.: Dartmouth.

Sorauf, Frank J. 1976. *Party Politics in America*. 3rd ed. Boston: Little, Brown.

Southwell, Patricia L. 1997. "Fairness, governability, and legitimacy: The debate over electoral systems in France." *Journal of Political and Military Sociology* 25(2): 163–185.

Steed, Michael. 1985. "The Constituency." In *Representatives of the People: Parliamentarians and Constituents in Western Democracies*. Ed. Vernon Bogdanor. Aldershot, Hants, U.K.: Gower.

Stratmann T., and M. Baur. 2002. "Plurality rule, proportional representation, and the German bundestag: How incentives to pork-barrel differ across electoral systems." *American Journal of Political Science* 46(3): 506–514.

Strøm, Kaare. 1990. *Minority Government and Majority Rule.* New York: Cambridge University Press.

———. 2000. "Delegation and accountability in parliamentary democracies." *European Journal of Political Research* 37(3): 261–289.

Studlar, Donley T., and Ian McAllister. 1996. "Constituency activity and representational roles among Australian legislators." *Journal of Politics* 58(1): 69–90.

Sundquist, James L. 1988. "Needed: A political theory for the new era of coalition government in the United States." *Political Science Quarterly* 103(4): 613–635.

Swank, O.H., and R. Eisinga. 1999. "Economic outcomes and voting behaviour in a multi-party system: An application to the Netherlands." *Public Choice* 101(3–4): 195–213.

Swatos, W.H., and K.J. Christiano. 2001. "Secularization theory: The course of a concept." *Sociology of Religion* 60(3): 209–228.

Swers, Michele. 1998. "Are women more likely to vote for women's issue bills than their male colleagues?" *Legislative Studies Quarterly* 23(3): 435–448.

———. 2002. "Understanding the policy impact of electing women: Evidence from research on congress and state legislature." *PS: Political Science and Society* 34(2): 217–220.

Swindle, S.M. 2002. "The supply and demand of the personal vote – Theoretical considerations and empirical implications of collective electoral incentives." *Party Politics* 8(3): 279–300.

Taagepera, Rein. 1994. "Beating the Law of Minority Attrition." In *Electoral Systems in Comparative Perspectives.* Eds. Wilma Rule and Joseph Zimmerman. Westport, CT: Greenwood Press.

———. 1998. "How electoral systems matter for democratization." *Democratization* 5(3): 68–91.

———. 1999. "The number of parties as a function of heterogeneity and electoral system." *Comparative Political Studies* 32(5): 531–548.

———. 2002. "Nationwide threshold of representation." *Electoral Studies* 21(3): 383–401.

Taagepera, Rein, and Bernard Grofman. 1985. "Rethinking Duverger's Law: Predicting the effective number of parties in plurality and PR systems – Parties minus issues equals one." *European Journal of Political Research* 13(4): 341–352.

Taagepera, Rein, and Matthew Soberg Shugart. 1989. *Seats and Votes: The Effects and Determinants of Electoral Systems.* New Haven, CT: Yale University Press.

Tan, A.C., and T.C. Yu. 2000. "The December 1998 elections in Taiwan." *Electoral Studies* 19(4): 621–628.

Tan, A.C., K. Ho, K.T. Kang, and T.C. Yu. 2000. "What if we don't party? Political partisanship in Taiwan and Korea in the 1990s." *Journal of Asian and African Studies* 35(1): 67–84.

Taras, Raymond, and Rajat Ganguly. 1998. *Understanding Ethnic Conflict.* New York: Longman.

Taylor, L. 2000. "Patterns of electoral corruption in Peru: The April 2000 general election." *Crime Law and Social Change* 34(4): 391–415.

Thomassen, Jacques. 1976. "Party identification as a cross-national concept: Its meaning in the Netherlands." In *Party Identification and Beyond*. Eds. Ian Budge, Ivor Crewe, and Dennis Farlie. London: John Wiley.

———. 1994. "The intellectual history of election studies." *European Journal of Political Research* 25(3): 239–245.

Thomsen, S.R. 1998. "Impact of national politics on local elections in Scandinavia." *Scandinavian Political Studies* 21(4): 325–345.

Thomson, R. 2001. "The programme to policy linkage: The fulfillment of election pledges on socio-economic policy in the Netherlands, 1986–1998." *European Journal of Political Research* 40(2): 171–197.

Tingsten, Herbert. 1937. *Political Behavior: Studies in Election Statistics*. Reprinted 1963. Totowa, NJ: Bedminister Press.

Tolbert, C.J., J.A. Grummel, and D.A. Smith. 2001. "The effects of ballot initiatives on voter turnout in the American states." *American Politics Research* 29(6): 625–648.

Topf, Richard. 1995. "Electoral Participation." In *Citizens and the State*. Hans-Dieter Klingemann and Dieter Fuchs. Eds. Oxford: Oxford University Press. Pp. 43–45.

Torgovnik, E. 2000. "Strategies under a new electoral system. The Labor Party in the 1996 Israeli elections." *Party Politics* 6(1): 95–106.

Trechsel, Alexander H., and P. Sciarini. 1998. "Direct democracy in Switzerland: Do elites matter?" *European Journal of Political Research* 33(1): 99–124.

Tremblay, Manon. 1998. "Do female MPs substantively represent women?" *Canadian Journal of Political Science* 31(3): 435–465.

Tremblay, Manon, and R. Pelletier. 2000. "More feminists or more women? Descriptive and substantive representations of women in the 1997 Canadian federal elections." *International Political Science Review* 21(4): 381–405.

Tsebelis, George. 1990. "Elite interaction and constitution building in consociational democracies." *Journal of Theoretical Politics* 2(1): 5–29.

Tsfati, Y. 2001. "Why do people trust media pre-election polls? Evidence from the Israeli 1996 elections." *International Journal of Public Opinion Research* 13(4): 433–441.

Tucker, J.A. 2002. "The first decade of post-communist elections and voting: What have we studied, and how have we studied it?" *Annual Review of Political Science* 5: 271–304.

Tully, James. 1995. *Strange Multiplicity: Constitutionalism in an Age of Diversity*. Cambridge, U.K.: Cambridge University Press.

United Nations Development Programme. 2002. *Human Development Report 2002*. New York: Oxford University Press.

van Deemen, A.M.A., and N.P. Vergunst. 1998. "Empirical evidence of paradoxes of voting in Dutch elections." *Public Choice* 97(3): 475–490.

van der Brug, W. 1999. "'Voters' perceptions and party dynamics." *Party Politics* 5(2): 147–169.

van der Eijk, Cees, and Kees Niemoller. 1994. "Election studies in the Netherlands: Pluralism and accommodation." *European Journal of Political Research* 25(3): 323–342.

van der Eijk, Cees, and Mark Franklin. 1996. *Choosing Europe? The European Electorate and National Politics in the Face of the Union*. Ann Arbor, MI: University of Michigan Press.

van der Eijk, Cees, Mark Franklin, and Michael Marsh. 1996. "What voters teach us about Europe-wide elections: What Europe-wide elections tell us about voters." *Electoral Studies* 15(2): 149–166.

Van Egmond M., N.D. De Graaf, and Cees van der Eijk. 1998. "Electoral participation in the Netherlands: Individual and contextual influences." *European Journal of Political Research* 34(2): 281–300.

Vengroff, Richard. 1994. "The impact of electoral systems on the transition to democracy in Africa: The case of Mali." *Electoral Studies* 13(1): 29–37.

Verba, Sidney, Kay Schlozman, and Henry Brady. 1995. *Voice and Equality: Civic Volunteerism in American Politics*. Cambridge, MA: Harvard University Press.

Verba, Sidney, Norman Nie, and Kae-on-Kim. 1978. *Participation and Political Equality: A Seven-Nation Comparison*. New York: Cambridge University Press.

Vowles, Jack. 1995. "The politics of electoral reform in New Zealand." *International Political Science Review* 16(1): 95–116.

———. 2000. "Research note: The New Zealand Election Study." *Political Science* 52(2): 150–157.

———. 2002. "Offsetting the PR effect? Party mobilization and turnout decline in New Zealand, 1966–99." *Party Politics* 8(5): 587–605.

Vowles, Jack, Peter Aimer, Susan Banducci, and Jeffrey Karp. 1998. *Voters' Victory? New Zealand's First Election under Proportional Representation*. Auckland: Auckland University Press.

Voye, L. 1999. "Secularization in a context of advanced modernity." *Sociology of Religion* 60(3): 275–288.

Wald, K., and S. Shye. 1995. "Religious influence in electoral-behavior – The role of institutional and social forces in Israel." *Journal of Politics* 57(2): 495–507.

Wang, Y.L. 1996. "The political consequences of the electoral system: Single nontransferable voting in Taiwan." *Issues & Studies* 32(8): 85–104.

Ware, Alan. 1985. *The Breakdown of Democratic Party Organization, 1940–1960*. New York: Oxford University Press.

Wattenberg, Martin P. 1991. *The Rise of Candidate Centered Politics*. Cambridge, MA: Harvard University Press.

———. 1998. *The Decline of American Political Parties 1952–1996*. Cambridge, MA: Harvard University Press.

———. 2002. *Where Have All the Voters Gone?* Cambridge, MA: Harvard University Press.

Wessels, Bernhard. 1997. "Germany." In *Passages to Power: Legislative Recruitment in Advanced Democracies*. Ed. Pippa Norris. Cambridge, U.K.: Cambridge University Press.

———. 1999. "Whom to Represent? The Role Orientations of Legislators in Europe." In *Political Representation and Legitimacy in the European Union*. Oxford: Oxford University Press.

Western, Bruce. 1994. "Institutionalized mechanisms for unionization in 16 OECD countries: An analysis of social survey data." *Social Forces* 73(2): 497–519.

———. 1998. "Causal heterogeneity in comparative research: A Bayesian hierarchical modeling approach." *American Journal of Political Science* 42(4): 1233–1259.

Western, Mark, and Bruce Tranter. 2001. "Postmaterialist and economic voting in Australia, 1990–98." *Australian Journal of Political Science* 36(3): 439–458.

Weyland, K. 2002. "Limitations of rational-choice institutionalism for the study of Latin American politics." *Studies in Comparative International Development* 37(1): 57–85.

White, Stephen, Richard Rose, and Ian McAllister. 1996. *How Russia Votes*. Chatham, NJ: Chatham House.

Whitefield, S. 2002. "Political cleavages and post-communist politics." *Annual Review of Political Science* 5: 181–200.

Whitten G.D., and H.D. Palmer. 1996. "Heightening comparativists' concern for model choice: Voting behavior in Great Britain and the Netherlands." *American Journal of Political Science* 40(1): 231–260.

Wilson, James Q. 1973. *Political Organizations*. New York: Basic Books.

Wilson, President Woodrow. (1884). "Committee or cabinet government?" *Overland Monthly* 2(3): 17–33.

Wlezien, Christopher, and Mark N. Franklin. Eds. 2002. "The future of election studies." Special issue of *Electoral Studies* 21(2): 157–160.

Wolfinger, Ray, and Steven Rosenstone. 1980. *Who Votes?* New Haven, CT: Yale University Press.

Wolfinger, Ray, David P. Glass, and Peverill Squire. 1990. "Predictors of electoral turnout: An international comparison." *Policy Studies Review* 9(3): 551–574.

Wolintz, Steven B. 1979. "The transformation of Western European party systems revisited." *West European Politics* 2:7–8.

———. 1988. *Parties and Party Systems in Liberal Democracies*. London: Routledge.

Wood, David M., and G. Young. 1997. "Comparing constituency activity by junior legislators in Great Britain and Ireland." *Legislative Studies Quarterly* 22(2): 217–232.

Wust, A.M. 2000. "New citizens – New voters? Political preferences and voting intentions of naturalized Germans: A case study in progress." *International Migration Review* 34(2): 560–567.

Zaller, John. 1992. *The Nature and Origins of Mass Opinion*. New York: Cambridge University Press.

Zarycki, T., and A. Nowak. 2000. "Hidden dimensions: The stability and structure of regional political cleavages in Poland." *Communist and Post-Communist Studies* 33(3): 331–354.

Zielinski, Jakub. 2002. "Translating social cleavages into party systems: The significance of new democracies." *World Politics* 54(2): 184–211.

Zielonka, Jan. Ed. 2001. *Democratic Consolidation in Eastern Europe. Volume 1: Institutional Engineering*. Oxford: Oxford University Press.

Zuckerman, A.S., N.A. Valentino, and E.W. Zuckerman. 1994. "A structural theory of vote choice – Social and political networks and electoral flows in Britain and the United-States." *Journal of Politics* 56(4): 1008–1033.

Notes

Chapter 1: Do Rules Matter? Structure versus Culture

1. For one of the clearest arguments for this thesis see Amartya Sen. 1999. *Development as Freedom*. New York: Anchor Books.
2. See Thomas Carothers. 1999. *Aiding Democracy Abroad: The Learning Curve*. Washington, D.C.: Carnegie Endowment.
3. For an annual assessment of the state of democracy and changes worldwide see Freedom House. *Freedom in the World. The Annual Survey of Political Rights and Civil Liberties*. Available online at www.freedomhouse.org.
4. See, for example, the other procedural requirements discussed by Robert Dahl. 1971. *Polyarchy: Participation and Opposition*. New Haven, CT: Yale University Press. See also the discussion in Robert A. Pastor. 1999. "The role of electoral administration in democratic transitions: Implications for policy and research." *Democratization* 6(4): 1–27; Shaheen Mozaffar and Andreas Schedler. 2002. "The comparative study of electoral governance." *International Political Science Review* 23(1): 5–28.
5. See Thomas Carothers. 1999. *Aiding Democracy Abroad: The Learning Curve*. Washington, D.C.: Carnegie Endowment. Chapter 6. Giovanni Sartori suggests the idea that these reforms could be understood as "constitutional engineering." 1994. *Comparative Constitutional Engineering: An Inquiry into Structures, Incentives, and Outcomes*. New York: Columbia University Press.
6. Matthew Soberg Shugart and Martin P. Wattenberg. Eds. 2001. *Mixed-Member Electoral Systems: The Best of Both Worlds?* New York: Oxford University Press.
7. Andrew McLaren Carstairs. 1980. *A Short History of Electoral Systems in Western Europe*. London: George Allen and Unwin; Stefano Bartolini and Peter Mair. 1990. *Identity, Competition and Electoral Availability*. Cambridge, U.K.: Cambridge University Press. Pp.154–155; Serge Noiret. Ed. 1990. *Political Strategies and Electoral Reforms: Origins of Voting Systems in Europe in the 19th and 20th Centuries*. Baden-Baden: Nomos Verlagsgesellschaft; C. Boix. 1999. "Setting the rules of the game: The choice of electoral systems in advanced democracies." *American Political Science Review* 93(3): 609–624.
8. U.K. reforms include the introduction of the Additional Member system for the Scottish Parliament, the Welsh Assembly, and the London Assembly; the

Supplementary Vote for the London Mayor; the Regional Party List system for European elections; and the Single Transferable Vote for the Northern Ireland Assembly. For details see Robin Blackburn. 1995. *The Electoral System in Britain.* New York: St. Martin's Press; Patrick Dunleavy and Helen Margetts. 1995. "Understanding the dynamics of electoral reform." *International Political Science Review* 16(1): 9–30; Patrick Dunleavy and Helen Margetts. 2001. "From majoritarian to pluralist democracy? Electoral reform in Britain since 1997." *Journal of Theoretical Politics* 13(3): 295–319. For updates see also The Electoral Reform Society. Available online at www.electoral-reform.org.uk.

9. R. Mulgan. 1995. "The democratic failure of single-party government: The New Zealand experience." *Australian Journal of Political Science* 30: 82–96; Jonathan Boston, Stephen Levine, Elizabeth McLeay, and Nigel S. Roberts. 1996. *New Zealand under MMP: A New Politics?* Auckland: Auckland University Press; Jack Vowles, Peter Aimer, Susan Banducci, and Jeffrey Karp. 1998. *Voters' Victory? New Zealand's First Election under Proportional Representation.* Auckland: Auckland University Press; Michael Gallagher. 1998. "The political impact of electoral system change in Japan and New Zealand, 1996." *Party Politics* 4(2): 203–228; Keith Jackson and Alan McRobie. 1998. *New Zealand Adopts Proportional Representation.* Aldershot, U.K.: Ashgate.

10. Abraham Diskin and Hanna Diskin. 1995. "The politics of electoral reform in Israel." *International Political Science Review* 16(1): 31–46; Reuven Y. Hazan. 1996. "Presidential parliamentarism: Direct popular election of the Prime Minister, Israel's new electoral and political system." *Electoral Studies* 15(1): 21–37; Yossi Beilin. 1996. "An Accident Named the Direct Election to Prime Minister." In Gideon Doron. Ed. *The Electoral Revolution.* Tel Aviv: Hakibutz Hameuchad Publishing House (in Hebrew); David Nachmias and Itai Sened. 1998. "The Bias of Pluralism: The Redistributional Effects of the New Electoral Law in Israel's 1996 Election." In Asher Arian and Michal Shamir. Eds. *Elections in Israel – 1996.* Albany, NY: SUNY Press; Reuven Y. Hazan and Abraham Diskin. 2000. "The 1999 Knesset and prime ministerial elections in Israel." *Electoral Studies* 19(4): 628–637; Asher Arian and Michael Shamir. 2001. "Candidates, parties and blocs: Israel in the 1990s." *Party Politics* 7(6): 689–710.

11. Mark Donovan. 1995. "The politics of electoral reform in Italy." *International Political Science Review* 16(1): 47–64; Richard S. Katz. 1996. "Electoral reform and the transformation of party politics in Italy." *Party Politics* 2: 31–53; Richard S. Katz. 2001. "Reforming the Italian Electoral Law, 1993." In Matthew Soberg Shugart and Martin P. Wattenberg. Eds. 2002. *Mixed-Member Electoral Systems: The Best of Both Worlds?* Oxford: Oxford University Press.

12. S. Ellner. 1993. "The deepening of democracy in a crisis setting: Political reform and the electoral process in Venezuela." *Journal of Interamerican Studies and World Affairs* 35(4): 1–42; Brian F. Crisp and Juan Carlos Rey. 2000. "The Sources of Electoral Reform in Venezuela." In Matthew Soberg Shugart and Martin P. Wattenberg. Eds. 2002. *Mixed-Member Electoral Systems: The Best of Both Worlds?* Oxford: Oxford University Press.

13. T. Sakamoto. 1999. "Explaining electoral reform – Japan versus Italy and New Zealand." *Party Politics* 5(4): 419–438; David W.F. Huang. 1996. "Electoral reform is no panacea: An assessment of Japan's electoral system after the 1994 reform." *Issues & Studies* 32(10): 109–139; Gary W. Cox, F.M. Rosenbluth,

and M.F. Thies. 1999. "Electoral reform and the fate of factions: The case of Japan's Liberal Democratic Party." *British Journal of Political Science.* 29(1): 33–56; Otake Hideo. Ed. 1998. *How Electoral Reform Boomeranged: Continuity in Japanese Campaigning Style.* Tokyo: Japan Center for International Exchange; Margaret McKean and Ethan Scheiner. 2000. "Japan's new electoral system: La plus ça change..." *Electoral Studies* 19(4): 447–477.

14. For more details see the Administration and Cost of Elections Project (ACE). Available online at www.aceproject.org.

15. The original distinction between the "mechanical" and "psychological" effects of electoral systems was made by Maurice Duverger. 1954. *Political Parties: Their Organization and Activity in the Modern State.* New York: Wiley.

16. Anthony Downs. 1957. *An Economic Theory of Democracy.* New York: Harper and Row.

17. We put aside, for the moment, any consideration concerning "informal" electoral rules, which can be understood as those widely shared, tacit social norms and conventions governing electoral behavior within any particular culture, enforced by social sanction. These are more properly understood, as discussed later, within cultural modernization theories, as social norms rather than informal institutions. This definition also excludes more ambiguous cases, such as party rulebooks that are enforced by internal committees within particular party organizations rather than by court of law, although there is a gray dividing line as these cases may be relevant for legal redress. For a discussion of the meaning of "rules" see J.M. Carey. "Parchment, equilibria, and institutions." *Comparative Political Studies* 33(6–7): 735–761.

18. Adam Przeworski and John Sprague. 1986. *Paper Stones: A History of Electoral Socialism.* Chicago: The University of Chicago Press; Herbert Kitschelt. 1994. *The Transformation of European Social Democracy.* Cambridge, U.K.: Cambridge University Press; Herbert Kitschelt. 1995. *The Radical Right in Western Europe.* Ann Arbor, MI: The University of Michigan Press; Herbert Kitschelt. 1993. "Class-structure and Social-Democratic Party strategy." *British Journal of Political Science* 23(3): 299–337; Herbert Kitschelt. 2000. "Linkages between citizens and politicians in democratic polities." *Comparative Political Studies* 33(6–7): 845–879. See also Thomas Koelble. 1992. "Recasting social democracy in Europe: A nested games explanation for strategic adjustment in political parties." *Politics and Society* 20(1): 51–70.

19. The distinction between bridging and bonding parties is derived from the literature on social capital, as originally applied to social groups and associations. See Robert D. Putnam. *Democracies in Flux.* New York: Oxford University Press. P.11. The term *bridging party* is similar to the use of the term *catch-all* developed by Kirchheimer, except that these concepts carry different normative baggage. See Otto Kirchheimer. 1966. "The Transformation of Western European Party Systems." In *Political Parties and Political Development.* Eds. J. La Palombara and M. Weiner. Princeton, NJ: Princeton University Press.

The electoral system may also prove important for the development of "cartel" parties, but this debate about party financing and organization is not addressed centrally in this study. See, however, Richard S. Katz and Peter Mair. 1995. "Changing Models of Party Organization and Party Democracy: The emergence of the cartel party." *Party Politics* 1(1): 5–28; Richard S. Katz and

Peter Mair. 1996. "Cadre, catch-all or cartel? A rejoinder." *Party Politics* 2(4): 525–534.

20. Gary W. Cox. 1990. "Centripetal and centrifugal incentives in electoral systems." *American Journal of Political Science* 34(4): 903–935.

21. Gary W. Cox. 1990. "Centripetal and centrifugal incentives in electoral systems." *American Journal of Political Science* 34(4): 903–935.

22. Pippa Norris. 1995. "May's Law of Curvilinearity revisited: Leaders, officers, members and voters in British political parties." *Party Politics* 1(1): 29–47.

23. For a discussion see John Carey and Matthew Soberg Shugart. 1995. "Incentive to cultivate a personal vote: A rank-ordering of electoral formulas." *Electoral Studies* 14(4): 417–440.

24. See the discussion in Bruce E. Cain, John A. Ferejohn, and Morris P. Fiorina. 1987. *The Personal Vote: Constituency Service and Electoral Independence.* Cambridge, MA: Harvard University Press.

25. John Carey and Matthew Soberg Shugart. 1995. "Incentive to cultivate a personal vote: A rank-ordering of electoral formulas." *Electoral Studies* 14(4): 417–440.

26. Pippa Norris. 1997. "The puzzle of constituency service." *The Journal of Legislative Studies* 3(2): 29–49; Vernon Bogdanor. Ed. 1985. *Representatives of the People? Parliamentarians and Constituents in Western Democracies.* Aldershot, Hants, U.K.: Gower.

27. See the discussion in Robert Rohrschneider. 2002. "Mobilizing versus chasing: How do parties target voters in election campaigns?" *Electoral Studies* 21(3): 367–382.

28. Michael Pinto-Duschinsky. 2002. "Overview." *Handbook on Funding of Parties and Election Campaigns.* Stockholm: International IDEA.

29. B. Scholdan. 2000. "Democratisation and electoral engineering in post-ethnic conflict societies." *Javnost-The Public* 7(1): 25–40.

30. See Arend Lijphart, 1994. *Electoral Systems and Party Systems.* Oxford: Oxford University Press. Appendix B.

31. David J. Samuels. 2002. *Ambition, Federalism and Legislative Politics in Brazil.* New York: Cambridge University Press.

32. Stephen Knack. 2001. "Election-day registration: The second wave." *American Politics Research* 29(1): 65–78; M.D. Martinez and D. Hill. 1999. "Did motor voter work?" *American Politics Quarterly* 27(3): 296–315.

33. For a more detailed treatment of modernization theory see Ronald Inglehart and Pippa Norris. 2003. *Rising Tide: Gender Equality and Cultural Change Around the World.* New York: Cambridge University Press.

34. Daniel Lerner. 1958. *The Passing of Traditional Society: Modernizing the Middle East.* New York: Free Press; Seymour Martin Lipset. 1959. "Some social requisites of democracy: Economic development and political legitimacy." *American Political Science Review* 53(1): 69–105; Seymour Martin Lipset. 1960. *Political Man: The Social Basis of Politics.* New York: Doubleday; Walt W. Rostow. 1952. *The Process of Economic Growth.* New York: Norton; Walt W. Rostow. 1960. *The Stages of Economic Growth.* Cambridge, U.K.: Cambridge University Press; Karl W. Deutsch. 1964. "Social mobilization and political development." *American Political Science Review* 55(3): 493–514; Daniel Bell. 1999. *The Coming of Post-Industrial Society: A Venture in Social Forecasting.* New York: Basic

Books [1st edition 1973]; Seymour Martin Lipset, Kyoung-Ryung Seong, and John Charles Torres. 1993. "A comparative analysis of the social requisites of democracy." *International Social Science Journal* 45(2): 154–175.

35. Daniel Bell. 1999. *The Coming of Post-Industrial Society: A Venture in Social Fore-casting.* New York: Basic Books [1st edition 1973].

36. For the key texts see Ronald Inglehart. 1977. *The Silent Revolution: Changing Values and Political Styles Among Western Publics.* Princeton, NJ: Princeton University Press; Ronald Inglehart. 1990. *Culture Shift in Advanced Industrial Society.* Princeton, NJ: Princeton University Press; Ronald Inglehart. 1997. *Modernization and Postmodernization: Cultural, Economic and Political Change in 43 Societies.* Princeton, NJ: Princeton University Press; Ronald Inglehart and Pippa Norris. 2003. *Rising Tide: Gender Equality and Cultural Change Around the World.* Cambridge, U.K.: Cambridge University Press.

37. For an extended argument along these lines, see Russell Dalton. 2002. *Citizen Politics.* 3rd edition. New York: Chatham House.

38. Shaun Bowler and Bernard Grofman. Eds. 2000. *Elections in Australia, Ireland and Malta under the Single Transferable Vote: Reflections on an Embedded Institution.* Ann Arbor, MI: University of Michigan Press.

39. For social psychological accounts of leadership see, for example, Alexander L. George. 1998. *Presidential Personality and Performance.* Boulder, CO: Westview Press; James David Barber. 1992. *The Presidential Character.* Englewood Cliffs, NJ: Prentice Hall; Stanley Renshon. 1996. *The Psychological Assessment of Presidential Candidates.* New York: New York University Press; Donald Searing. 1994. *Westminster's World: Understanding Political Roles.* Cambridge, MA: Harvard University Press.

40. Angus Campbell, Philip Converse, Warren E. Miller, and Donald E. Stokes. 1960. *The American Voter.* New York: John Wiley & Sons, Inc. For recent work in the tradition of the Michigan school see Warren Miller and J. Merrill Shanks. 1996. *The New American Voter.* Cambridge, MA: Harvard University Press.

41. Carol Christy. 1987. *Sex Differences in Political Participation: Processes of Change in Fourteen Nations.* New York: Praeger.

42. Douglas C. North. 1990. *Institutions, Institutional Change, and Economic Performance.* Cambridge, U.K.: Cambridge University Press; S. Whitefield. 2002. "Political cleavages and post-communist politics." *Annual Review of Political Science* 5: 181–200.

43. K. Weyland. 2002. "Limitations of rational-choice institutionalism for the study of Latin American politics." *Studies in Comparative International Development* 37(1): 57–85; see also V. Bunce. 2000. "Comparative democratization – Big and bounded generalizations." *Comparative Political Studies* 33(6–7): 703–734.

44. Maurice Duverger. [Orig. 1954] 1964. *Political Parties.* London: Methuen; Douglas Rae. 1967. *The Political Consequences of Electoral Laws* [1971 revised edition]. New Haven, CT: Yale University Press.

45. See, for example, Enid Lakeman. 1974. *How Democracies Vote.* London: Faber and Faber; Dieter Nohlen. 1996. *Elections and Electoral Systems.* Delhi: Macmillan; Vernon Bogdanor and David Butler. Eds. 1983. *Democracy and Elections.* Cambridge, U.K.: Cambridge University Press; Bernard Grofman and Arend Lijphart. Eds. 1986. *Electoral Laws and Their Political Consequences.* New York: Agathon Press; Rein Taagepera and Matthew S. Shugart. 1989. *Seats and*

Votes: The Effects and Determinants of Electoral Systems. New Haven, CT: Yale University Press; Andrew Reeve and Alan Ware. 1992. *Electoral Systems: A Comparative and Theoretical Introduction.* London and New York: Routledge; Pippa Norris. 1997. "Choosing electoral systems." *International Political Science Review* 18(3): 297–312; David Farrell. 1997. *Comparing Electoral Systems.* London: Prentice Hall/Harvester Wheatsheaf; Gary W. Cox. 1997. *Making Votes Count: Strategic Coordination in the World's Electoral Systems.* Cambridge, U.K.: Cambridge University Press; Richard Katz. 1997. *Democracy and Elections.* Oxford: Oxford University Press; Andrew Reynolds and Ben Reilly. 1997. *The International IDEA Handbook of Electoral System Design.* Stockholm: International IDEA.

46. In the United States this originated with the Progressive Movement in the early twentieth century, and PR was eventually adopted by two-dozen cities, including Boulder, Colorado; Cincinnati, Ohio; and Cambridge, Massachusetts, before being abandoned everywhere except for Cambridge, Massachusetts. See Douglas J. Amy. 1996. "The forgotten history of the Single Transferable Vote in the United States." *Representation* 34(1): 13–20. For Western Europe, see Andrew McLaren Carstairs. 1980. *A Short History of Electoral Systems in Western Europe.* London: George Allen and Unwin; Dennis Pilon. 2002. *Renewing Canadian Democracy: Citizen Engagement in Voting System Reform.* Ontario: Law Commission of Canada/Fair Vote Canada.

47. The French adopted PR in 1945, moving back to the majoritarian Second Ballot system to avoid party fragmentation in 1958 under de Gaulle's Fifth French Republic. In 1986, in a bid to split the right, President François Mitterrand moved the adoption of PR nationally. Two years later parliament voted to return to the country's traditional majoritarian double ballot. See Andrew Knapp. 1987. "Proportional but bipolar: France's electoral system in 1986." *West European Politics* 10(1): 89–114; Byron Criddle. 1992. "Electoral systems in France." *Parliamentary Affairs* 45(1): 108–116; Patricia L. Southwell. 1997. "Fairness, governability, and legitimacy: The debate over electoral systems in France." *Journal of Political and Military Sociology* 25(2): 163–185.

48. On electoral reform, for Britain see Lord Jenkins. 1998. *The Report of the Independent Commission on the Voting System.* London: Stationery Office. Cm 4090–1; Pippa Norris. 1995. "The politics of electoral reform in Britain." *International Political Science Review* 16(1): 65–78; Ron Johnston and Charles Pattie. 2002. "Campaigning and split-ticket voting in new electoral systems: The first MMP elections in New Zealand, Scotland and Wales." *Electoral Studies* 21(4): 583–600. For New Zealand see Jonathan Boston, Stephen Levine, Elizabeth McLeay, and Nigel S. Roberts. 1996. *New Zealand under MMP: A New Politics?* Auckland: Auckland University Press; Jack Vowles, Peter Aimer, Susan Banducci, and Jeffrey Karp. 1998. *Voters' Victory? New Zealand's First Election under Proportional Representation.* Auckland: Auckland University Press. For Israel see Reuven Y. Hazan. 1996. "Presidential parliamentarism: Direct popular election of the Prime Minister, Israel's new electoral and political system." *Electoral Studies* 15(1): 21–37. For Japan see Otake Hideo. Ed. 1998. *How Electoral Reform Boomeranged: Continuity in Japanese Campaigning Style.* Tokyo: Japan Center for International Exchange; Takayuki Sakamoto. 1999. "Explaining electoral reform: Japan versus Italy and New Zealand." *Party Politics* 5(4): 419–438.

49. Maurice Duverger. 1954. *Political Parties: Their Organization and Activity in the Modern State*. New York: Wiley.

50. Pippa Norris. 1985. "Women in European legislative elites." *West European Politics* 8(4): 90–101; Wilma Rule. 1987. "Electoral systems, contextual factors and women's opportunity for election to parliament in twenty-three democracies." *Western Political Quarterly* 40(3): 477–486; Wilma Rule. 1994. "Women's underrepresentation and electoral systems." *PS: Political Science and Politics* 27(4): 689–692; Richard Matland. 1998. "Enhancing women's political participation: Legislative recruitment and electoral systems. In *Women in Parliament: Beyond Numbers*. Azza Karam. Ed. Stockholm: International IDEA.

51. For overviews see Kathleen Knight and Michael Marsh. 2002. "Varieties of election studies." *Electoral Studies* 21(2): 161–168; Jacques Thomassen. 1994. "The intellectual history of election studies." *European Journal of Political Research* 25(3): 239–245.

52. John Curtice. 2002. "The state of election studies: Mid-life crisis or new youth?" *Electoral Studies* 21(2): 161–168.

53. This approach is exemplified by Mark Franklin, Tom Mackie, Henry Valen, et al. Eds. 1992. *Electoral Change: Responses to Evolving Social and Attitudinal Structures in Western Countries*. Cambridge, U.K.: Cambridge University Press; Russell J. Dalton and Martin Wattenberg. Eds. 2001. *Parties without Partisans*. New York: Oxford University Press.

54. See, for example, the Appendix in Ivor Crewe and Anthony Fox. 1995. *The British Electorate 1963–92*. Cambridge, U.K.: Cambridge University Press.

55. For an example of this approach, examining trends in the British Election Study 1964–1997, see Geoffrey Evans and Pippa Norris. Eds. 1999. *Critical Elections*. London: Sage. Yet there are often major inconsistencies in the starting and ending dates for analyzing trends; for example, using the available series of national election studies that start in 1952 in the United States, but three decades later in Iceland, Russell Dalton uses regression models to compare trends in partisan identification in many OECD nations See Table 2.1 in Russell J. Dalton. 2002. "The Decline of Party Identification." In Russell J. Dalton and Martin P. Wattenberg. Eds. *Parties without Partisans*. New York: Oxford University Press.

56. See, for example, Jack Vowles. 2002. "Offsetting the PR effect? Party mobilization and turnout decline in New Zealand, 1996–99." *Party Politics* 8(5): 587–605.

57. Note that the CSES dataset includes election surveys in Hong Kong, but these were dropped to facilitate consistent comparison across independent nation-states. The dataset used in this study is based on the July 31, 2002 release of Module 1. The dataset also merged two separate election studies for Belgium-Walloon and Belgium-Flemish, and these were merged for analysis. Full details are available online at www.umich.edu/~nes/cses.

58. Matthis Bogaards. 2000. "The uneasy relationship between empirical and normative types in consociational theory." *Journal of Theoretical Politics* 12(4): 395–423.

59. For a discussion of these alternative approaches see Todd Landman. 2000. *Issues and Methods in Comparative Politics*. London: Routledge. Chapter 2.

60. Although Thomas Carothers suggests that even the use of the term *transitional democracies* is misleading as it can suggest a teleological view of democratic

progress for many countries that have elections but that have experienced lit-
tle substantial political change during the last decade beyond these contests.
See Thomas Carothers. 2002. "The end of the transition paradigm." *Journal of
Democracy* 13(1): 5–21.

61. For a discussion of these alternative indices see G.L. Munck and J. Verkuilen.
2002. "Conceptualizing and measuring democracy – Evaluating alternative indices." *Comparative Political Studies* 35(1): 5–34. See also David Beetham. Ed.
1994. *Defining and Measuring Democracy*. London: Sage; David Beetham. 2001.
International IDEA Handbook of Democracy Assessment. New York: Kluwer.

62. Samuel P. Huntington. 1993. *The Third Wave*. Norman, OK: University of
Oklahoma Press.

63. For a discussion of these issues see Matthew Soberg Shugart and John Carey.
1992. *Presidents and Assemblies: Constitutional Design and Electoral Dynamics*.
Cambridge, U.K.: Cambridge University Press.

64. See, for example, Gary C. Jacobson. 2001. *The Politics of Congressional Elections*.
New York: Longman.

65. D.J. Samuels. 2000. "Concurrent elections, discordant results: Presidentialism,
federalism, and governance in Brazil." *Comparative Politics* 33(1): 1–20; D. J.
Samuels. 2000. "The gubernatorial coattails effect: Federalism and congres-
sional elections in Brazil." *Journal of Politics* 62(1): 240–253; Scott Mainwar-
ing. 1997. "Multipartism, robust federalism, and presidentialism in Brazil." In
Presidentialism and Democracy in Latin America. Scott Mainwaring and Matthew
Soberg Shugart. Eds. New York: Cambridge University Press; Barry Ames. 2001.
The Deadlock of Democracy in Brazil. Ann Arbor, MI: University of Michigan
Press.

66. Douglas C. North. 1990. *Institutions, Institutional Change, and Economic Perfor-
mance*. Cambridge, U.K.: Cambridge University Press; James March and Johan
Olsen. 1989. *Rediscovering Institutions: The Organizational Basis of Politics*. New
York: Free Press.

67. Alternative sources of time-series and cross-national survey data that are avail-
able include the American National Election Study, the World Values Survey
(WVS), the International Social Survey Programme (ISSP), and the 15-nation
Eurobarometer.

68. Maurice Duverger. 1954. *Political Parties, Their Organization and Activity in the
Modern State*. New York: Wiley. Pp.217, 239.

69. Douglas W. Rae. 1967. *The Political Consequences of Electoral Laws*. New Haven,
CT: Yale University Press [1971 revised edition]; William H. Riker. 1976. "The
number of political parties: A reexamination of Duverger's Law." *Comparative Politics* 9(1): 93–106; William H. Riker. 1982. "The two-party system and
Duverger's Law: An essay on the history of political science." *American Political Science Review* 76(4): 753–766; William H. Riker. 1986. "Duverger's Law
Revisited." In *Electoral Laws and Their Political Consequences*. Bernard Grofman
and Arend Lijphart. Eds. New York: Agathon Press; Maurice Duverger. 1986.
"Duverger's Law: Forty Years Later." In *Electoral Laws and Their Political Consequences*. Bernard Grofman and Arend Lijphart. Eds. New York: Agathon Press;
Arend Lijphart. 1994. *Electoral Systems and Party Systems*. Oxford: Oxford University Press.

70. Mark Franklin, Tom Mackie, Henry Valen, et al. Eds. 1992. *Electoral Change: Responses to Evolving Social and Attitudinal Structures in Western Countries.* Cambridge, U.K.: Cambridge University Press. See, however, Geoffrey Evans. Ed. 1999. *The Decline of Class Politics?* Oxford: Oxford University Press.
71. Ivor Crewe and David Denver. Eds. 1985. *Electoral Change in Western Democracies: Patterns and Sources of Electoral Volatility.* New York: St. Martin's Press; Russell J. Dalton, Scott C. Flanagan, Paul A. Beck, and James E. Alt. Eds. 1984. *Electoral Change in Advanced Industrial Democracies: Realignment or Dealignment?* Princeton, NJ: Princeton University Press; see also Russell J. Dalton and Martin P. Wattenberg. Eds. 2001. *Parties without Partisans.* New York: Oxford University Press.
72. G. Bingham Powell, Jr. 1986. "American voter turnout in comparative perspective." *American Political Science Review* 80(1): 17–43; Robert W. Jackman. 1987. "Political institutions and voter turnout in industrialized democracies." *American Political Science Review* 81(2): 405–23; Robert W. Jackman and Ross A. Miller. 1995. "Voter turnout in industrial democracies during the 1980s." *Comparative Political Studies* 27(4): 467–492. André Blais and Agnieszka Dobrzynska. 1998. "Turnout in electoral democracies." *European Journal of Political Research.* 33(2): 239–261; A. Ladner and H. Milner. 1999. "Do voters turn out more under proportional than majoritarian systems? The evidence from Swiss communal elections." *Electoral Studies* 18(2): 235–250.
73. See the discussion in André Blais and Agnieszka Dobrzynska. 1998. "Turnout in electoral democracies." *European Journal of Political Research* 33(2): 239–261.
74. Pippa Norris. 1985. "Women in European legislative elites." *West European Politics* 8(4): 90–101; Wilma Rule. 1987. "Electoral systems, contextual factors and women's opportunity for election to parliament in twenty-three democracies." *Western Political Quarterly* 40(3): 477–486; Wilma Rule. 1994. "Women's underrepresentation and electoral systems." *PS: Political Science and Politics* 27(4): 689–692; Wilma Rule and Joseph Zimmerman. Eds. 1994. *Electoral Systems in Comparative Perspective: Their Impact on Women and Minorities.* Westport, CT: Greenwood Press.
75. Arend Lijphart and Bernard Grofman. Eds. 1984. *Choosing an Electoral System: Issues and Alternatives.* New York: Praeger; Arend Lijphart. 1984. *Democracies.* New Haven, CT: Yale University Press; Arend Lijphart. 1986. "Degrees of Proportionality of Proportional Representation Formulas." In *Electoral Laws and Their Political Consequences.* Bernard Grofman and Arend Lijphart. Eds. New York: Agathon Press; Arend Lijphart. 1991. "Constitutional choices for new democracies." *Journal of Democracy* 2(1): 72–84; Arend Lijphart. 1991. "Proportional representation: Double checking the evidence." *Journal of Democracy* 2(3): 42–48; Arend Lijphart. 1994. *Electoral Systems and Party Systems: A Study of Twenty-Seven Democracies, 1945–1990.* New York: Oxford University Press; Arend Lijphart. 1995. "Electoral Systems." In *The Encyclopedia of Democracy.* Seymour Martin Lipset. Ed. Washington, D.C.: Congressional Quarterly Press; Arend Lijphart. 1999. *Patterns of Democracy: Government Forms and Performance in 36 Countries.* New Haven, CT: Yale University Press.
76. Donald L. Horowitz. 1991. *A Democratic South Africa? Constitutional Engineering in a Divided Society.* Berkeley: University of California Press; Ben Reilly. 2001.

Democracy in Divided Societies: Electoral Engineering for Conflict Management.
New York: Cambridge University Press.

77. See, for example, Bernard Grofman, Sung-Chull Lee, Edwin A. Winckler, and Brian Woodall. Eds. 1997. *Elections in Japan, Korea and Taiwan under the Single Non-Transferable Vote: The Comparative Study of an Embedded Institution.* Ann Arbor, MI: University of Michigan Press.

Chapter 2: Classifying Electoral Systems

1. For comparative overviews of constitutional structures and issues of constitutional design see Samuel E. Finer. 1995. *Comparing Constitutions.* Revised edition. Oxford: Oxford University Press; Arend Lijphart. 1999. *Patterns of Democracy.* New Haven, CT: Yale University Press; Dennis C. Mueller. 2000. *Constitutional Democracy.* Oxford: Oxford University Press; Matthew Soberg Shugart and John M. Carey. 1992. *Presidents and Assemblies: Constitutional Design and Electoral Dynamics.* Cambridge, U.K.: Cambridge University Press; Joachim Jens Hesse. Ed. 1995. *Constitutional Policy and Change in Europe.* Oxford: Oxford University Press; Andrew Reynolds and Scott Mainwaring. Eds. 2002. *The Architecture of Democracy.* Oxford: Oxford University Press.

2. Maurice Duverger. 1954. *Political Parties, Their Organization and Activity in the Modern State.* New York: Wiley; Douglas W. Rae. 1967. *The Political Consequences of Electoral Laws.* New Haven, CT: Yale University Press. Useful summaries are provided by André Blais and Louis Massicote. 1997. "Electoral formulas: A macroscopic perspective." *European Journal of Political Research* 32(1): 107–129; André Blais and Louis Massicotte. 2002. "Electoral Systems." In *Comparing Democracies 2: Elections and Voting in Global Perspective.* Lawrence LeDuc, Richard G. Niemi, and Pippa Norris. Eds. London: Sage.

3. It can be argued that a further distinction needs to be drawn between majority and plurality elections, given the higher effective electoral threshold used in the former. The contrast is evident, for example, between First-Past-the-Post (FPTP) used in Canadian parliamentary elections, which requires a plurality of votes (winning at least one more vote than any other candidate) to gain office and the Second-Ballot system used in the Russian presidential elections, which requires an absolute majority to win office. Nevertheless, the classification used in this study is more parsimonious, the ballot structure used for plurality and majoritarian elections is similar (casting a vote for a single candidate), and it is the standard typology used in the literature.

4. In a few countries using plurality presidential elections, such as Costa Rica and Argentina, there is a minimum threshold requirement; otherwise, a runoff is held.

5. Maurice Duverger. 1954. *Political Parties, Their Organization and Activity in the Modern State.* New York: Wiley. Pp.217, 239.

6. Douglas W. Rae. 1967. *The Political Consequences of Electoral Laws.* New Haven, CT: Yale University Press; William H. Riker. 1976. "The number of political parties: A reexamination of Duverger's Law." *Comparative Politics* 9(1): 93–106; William H. Riker. 1982. "The two-party system and Duverger's Law: An essay on the history of political science." *American Political Science Review* 76: 753–766;

William H. Riker. 1986. "Duverger's Law Revisited." In Bernard Grofman and Arend Lijphart. Eds. *Electoral Laws and Their Political Consequences*. New York: Agathon Press; Maurice Duverger. 1986. "Duverger's Law: Forty Years Later." In *Electoral Laws and Their Political Consequences*. Bernard Grofman and Arend Lijphart. Eds. New York: Agathon Press; Arend Lijphart, 1994. *Electoral Systems and Party Systems*. Oxford: Oxford University Press.

7. See, for example, Ron Johnston, Charles Pattie, Danny F.L. Dorling, and David Rossiter. 2001. *From Votes to Seats: The Operation of the UK Electoral System since 1945*. Manchester, U.K.: Manchester University Press.

8. For details see M.J. Hinich, M.C. Munger, and S. De Marchi. 1998. "Ideology and the construction of nationality: The Canadian elections of 1993." *Public Choice* 97(3): 401–428.

9. Wilma Rule and Joseph Zimmerman. 1992. *United States Electoral Systems: Their Impact on Women and Minorities*. New York: Praeger.

10. For details of these elections see Pippa Norris. 1997. "Anatomy of a Labour landslide." In *Britain Votes 1997*. Pippa Norris and Neil Gavin. Eds. Oxford: Oxford University Press. Pp.1–24; Geoffrey Evans and Pippa Norris. Eds. 1999. *Critical Elections: British Parties and Voters in Long-term Perspective*. London: Sage; Gerald Pomper. 1997. *The Election of 1996*. Chatham, NJ: Chatham House.

11. For a discussion see Pippa Norris. 2002. "The twilight of Westminster? Electoral reform and its consequences." *Political Studies* 49(5): 877–900.

12. John Curtice. 2001. "The Electoral System: Biased to Blair." In *Britain Votes, 2001*. Pippa Norris. Ed. Oxford: Oxford University Press; David Rossiter, Ron Johnston, Charles Pattie, Danny F.L. Dorling, Ian MacAllister and H. Tunstall. 1999. "Changing biases in the operation of the U.K.'s electoral system, 1950–97." *British Journal of Politics and International Relations* 1(2): 133–164.

13. See Lawrence LeDuc. 1998. "The Canadian federal election of 1997." *Electoral Studies* 17(1): 132–137; Neil Nevitte, André Blais, Elisabeth Gidengil, and Richard Nadeau. 2000. *Unsteady State: The 1997 Canadian Federal Election*. Oxford: Oxford University Press.

14. For the debate about electoral reform in Canada see the Law Commission of Canada. 2002. *Renewing Democracy: Debating Electoral Reform in Canada*. Discussion Paper. JL2–20/2002. Ottawa: Law Commission of Canada.

15. Bernard Grofman, Sung-Chull Lee, Edwin A. Winckler, and Brian Woodall. Eds. 1997. *Elections in Japan, Korea and Taiwan under the Single Non-Transferable Vote: The Comparative Study of an Embedded Institution*. Ann Arbor, MI: University of Michigan Press.

16. Marian Sawer. Ed. 2001. *Elections: Full, Free and Fair*. Sydney: The Federation Press. For details of the 1996 Australian election see Clive Bean, Scott Bennett, Marian Simms, and John Warhurst. Eds. 1997. *The Politics of Retribution: The 1996 Australian Federal Election*. Sydney: Allen and Unwin; Clive Bean. 1997. "Australia's experience with the alternative vote." *Representation* 34(2): 103–10.

17. Clive Bean. 1996. "The 1996 Australian federal election." *Electoral Studies* 15(3): 422–424.

18. For details of these elections see Richard Rose, Neil Munro, and Tom Mackie. 1998. *Elections in Central and Eastern Europe since 1990*. Glasgow, Scotland:

Center for the Study of Public Policy; Dennis Deletant and Peter Saini-Davies. 1998. "The Romanian elections of November 1996." *Representation* 35(2/3): 155–167; David Nachmias and Itai Sened. 1998. "The Bias of Pluralism: The Redistributional Effects of the New Electoral Law in Israel's 1996 Election." In Asher Arian and Michal Shamir. Eds. *Elections in Israel – 1996.* Albany, NY: SUNY Press; Reuven Y. Hazan. 1996. "Presidential parliamentarism: Direct popular election of the prime minister, Israel's new electoral and political system." *Electoral Studies* 15(1): 21–37; Reuven Y. Hazan. 1997. "Three levels of election in Israel: The 1996 party, parliamentary and prime ministerial elections." *Representation* 34(3/4): 240–249.

19. Shaun Bowler and Bernard Grofman. Eds. 2000. *Elections in Australia, Ireland and Malta under the Single Transferable Vote: Reflections on an Embedded Institution.* Ann Arbor, MI: University of Michigan Press.

20. See, for example, the arguments of Enid Lakeman. 1974. *How Democracies Vote.* London: Faber and Faber.

21. For a discussion and classification of "mixed systems" see Louis Massicotte and André Blais. 1999. "Mixed electoral systems: A conceptual and empirical survey." *Electoral Studies* 18(3): 341–366; Matthew Soberg Shugart and Martin P. Wattenberg. Eds. 2001. *Mixed-Member Electoral Systems: The Best of Both Worlds?* New York: Oxford University Press. Combined systems are also sometimes known as "mixed," "mixed-member," or "hybrid."

22. See Jonathan Boston, Stephen Levine, Elizabeth McLeay, and Nigel S. Roberts. 1996. *New Zealand Under MMP: A New Politics?* Auckland: Auckland University Press; Jack Vowles, Peter Aimer, Susan Banducci, and Jeffrey Karp. 1998. *Voters' Victory? New Zealand's First Election under Proportional Representation.* Auckland: Auckland University Press.

23. For a discussion see Louis Massicotte and André Blais. 1999. "Mixed electoral systems: A conceptual and empirical survey." *Electoral Studies* 18(3): 341–366.

24. John Fuh-Sheng Hsieh and Emerson M.S. Niou. 1996. "Taiwan's March 1996 Elections." *Electoral Studies* 15(4): 545–550; Bernard Grofman. 1997. "SNTV, STV, and Single-Member District Systems: Theoretical Comparisons and Contrasts." In *Elections in Japan, Korea and Taiwan under the Single Non-Transferable Vote: The Comparative Study of an Embedded Institution.* Bernard Grofman, Sung-Chull Lee, Edwin A. Winckler, and Brian Woodall. Eds. Ann Arbor, MI: University of Michigan Press.

25. Sarah Birch. 1997. "Ukraine: The Perils of Majoritarianism in a New Democracy." In *The International IDEA Handbook of Electoral System Design.* Andrew Reynolds and Ben Reilly. Eds. Stockholm: International IDEA; Sarah Birch and Andrew Wilson. 1999. "The Ukrainian parliamentary elections of 1998." *Electoral Studies* 18(2): 276–282; Sarah Birch. 1998. "Electoral reform in Ukraine: The 1988 parliamentary elections." *Representation* 35(2/3): 146–154.

26. Sarah Birch and Andrew Wilson. 1999. "The Ukrainian parliamentary elections of 1998." *Electoral Studies* 18(2): 276–282.

27. For a worldwide comparison see André Blais, Louis Massicotte, and Agnieszka Dobrzynska. 1997. "Direct presidential elections: A world summary." *Electoral Studies* 16(4): 441–455. For their consequences see also Mark P. Jones. 1995. *Electoral Laws and the Survival of Presidential Democracies.* Notre Dame, IN: University of Notre Dame Press.

28. Stephen White, Richard Rose, and Ian McAllister. 1996. *How Russia Votes.* Chatham, NJ: Chatham House.
29. F.A. Shelley. 2002. "The Electoral College and the election of 2000." *Political Geography* 21(1): 79–83.
30. George Tsebelis. 1990. "Elite interaction and constitution building in consociational democracies." *Journal of Theoretical Politics* 2(1): 5–29.

Chapter 3: Evaluating Electoral Systems

1. See Patrick Dunleavy and Helen Margetts. 1995. "Understanding the dynamics of electoral reform." *International Political Science Review* 16(1): 9–30.
2. See G. Bingham Powell, Jr. 2000. *Elections as Instruments of Democracy.* New Haven, CT: Yale University Press. Chapter 1.
3. See, for example, the discussion in Andrew Reynolds and Ben Reilly. 1997. *The International IDEA Handbook of Electoral System Design.* Stockholm: International IDEA.
4. See, for example, Douglas J. Amy. 2000. *Behind the Ballot Box: A Citizen's Guide to Electoral Systems.* Westport, CT: Praeger.
5. Richard Katz provides the most comprehensive overview of classic debates in the history of political thought, although some of the considerations in democratic theory are rather remote from the practical arguments commonly heard in policy debates, as well as from the operation of actual electoral systems. See Richard Katz. 1997. *Democracy and Elections.* Oxford: Oxford University Press.
6. Arend Lijphart. 1999. *Patterns of Democracy: Government Forms and Performance in 36 Countries.* New Haven, CT: Yale University Press.
7. Pippa Norris. 2002. "The twilight of Westminster? Electoral reform and its consequences." *Political Studies* 49(5): 877–900.
8. See G. Bingham Powell, Jr. 2000. *Elections as Instruments of Democracy.* New Haven, CT: Yale University Press.
9. For a discussion of the typology see Matthew Soberg Shugart and John M. Carey. 1992. *Presidents and Assemblies: Constitutional Design and Electoral Dynamics.* New York: Cambridge University Press.
10. Samuel E. Finer. Ed. 1975. *Adversary Politics and Electoral Reform.* London: Anthony Wigram. It should be noted that Lijphart uses the term consensus democracy, not consensual, but it seems preferable to refer to this by the ideal mode of operation as a democratic process, rather than by its ideal end state.
11. Walter Lippmann. 1925. *The Phantom Public.* New York: Harcourt, Brace. P.126.
12. David Austen-Smith and Jeffrey S. Banks. 1988. "Elections, coalitions, and legislative outcomes." *American Political Science Review* 82(2): 405–422; David Austen-Smith and Jeffrey S. Banks. 1990. "Stable governments and the allocation of policy portfolios." *American Political Science Review* 84(3): 891–906; Kaare Strøm. 1990. *Minority Government and Majority Rule.* New York: Cambridge University Press; Kaare Strøm. 2000. "Delegation and accountability in parliamentary democracies." *European Journal of Political Research* 37(3): 261–289.
13. John M. Carey and Matthew S. Shugart. 1995. "Incentives to cultivate a personal vote: A rank ordering of electoral formulas." *Electoral Studies* 14(4): 417–440.

14. See Pippa Norris. Ed. 1998. *Passages to Power*. Cambridge, U.K.: Cambridge University Press.

15. Although it should be noted that open list PR, where voters can cast a preference vote among individual candidates, is also believed to strengthen the incentive to cultivate a personal vote. See the discussion in Vernon Bogdanor. Ed. 1985. *Representatives of the People? Parliamentarians and Constituents in Western Democracies*. Aldershot, Hants, U.K.: Gower; Bruce E. Cain, John A. Ferejohn, and Morris P. Fiorina. 1987. *The Personal Vote: Constituency Service and Electoral Independence*. Cambridge, MA: Harvard University Press; Richard Katz. 1999. "Role Orientations." Richard S. Katz and Bernhard Wessels. Eds. In *The European Parliament, the National Parliaments, and European Integration*. Oxford: Oxford University Press; John M. Carey and Matthew S. Shugart. 1995. "Incentives to cultivate a personal vote: A rank ordering of electoral formulas." *Electoral Studies* 14(4): 417–440.

16. For a discussion see Kaare Strøm. 1990. *Minority Government and Majority Rule*. New York: Cambridge University Press; Michael Laver and Kenneth Schepsle. 1995. *Making and Breaking Governments*. New York: Cambridge University Press.

17. For a discussion see Jon Elster. Ed. 1998. *Deliberative Democracy*. Cambridge, U.K.: Cambridge University Press; John S. Dryzak. 2000. *Deliberative Democracy and Beyond: Liberals, Critics, Contestations*. Oxford: Oxford University Press.

18. G. Bingham Powell, Jr. 1986. "American voter turnout in comparative perspective." *American Political Science Review* 80(1): 17–43; Robert W. Jackman. 1987. "Political institutions and voter turnout in industrialized democracies." *American Political Science Review* 81(2): 405–423; Robert W. Jackman and Ross A. Miller. 1995. "Voter turnout in industrial democracies during the 1980s." *Comparative Political Studies* 27(4): 467–492. André Blais and Agnieszka Dobrzynska. 1998. "Turnout in electoral democracies." *European Journal of Political Research* 33(2): 239–261; A. Ladner and H. Milner. 1999. "Do voters turn out more under proportional than majoritarian systems? The evidence from Swiss communal elections." *Electoral Studies* 18(2): 235–250; Pippa Norris. 2002. *Democratic Phoenix: Reinventing Political Activism*. New York: Cambridge University Press. Chapter 4.

19. Pippa Norris. 1985. "Women in European legislative elites." *West European Politics* 8(4): 90–101; Wilma Rule. 1987. "Electoral systems, contextual factors and women's opportunity for election to parliament in twenty-three democracies." *Western Political Quarterly* 40(3): 477–486; Wilma Rule. 1994. "Women's underrepresentation and electoral systems." *PS: Political Science and Politics* 27(4): 689–692; Richard Matland. 1998. "Enhancing Women's Political Participation: Legislative Recruitment and Electoral Systems." In *Women in Parliament: Beyond Numbers*. Azza Karam. Ed. Stockholm: International IDEA; Inter-Parliamentary Union. 2002. *Women in National Parliaments*. www.ipu.org.

20. Drude Dahlerup. 1998. "Using Quotas to Increase Women's Political Representation." In *Women in Parliament: Beyond Numbers*. Azza Karam. Ed. Stockholm: International IDEA; Miki Caul. 2001. "Political parties and the adoption of candidate gender quotas: A cross-national analysis." *Journal of Politics* 63(4): 1214–1229.

21. Jane Mansbridge. 1999. "Should blacks represent blacks and women represent women? A contingent 'yes.'" *Journal of Politics* 61(3): 628–657; Anne Phillips.

1995. *The Politics of Presence.* Oxford: Clarendon Press; Sue Thomas. 1994. *How Women Legislate.* Oxford: Oxford University Press; Susan J. Carroll. 2001. Ed. *The Impact of Women in Public Office.* Bloomington, IN: University of Indiana Press.

22. Arend Lijphart. 1994. "Democracies – forms, performance, and constitutional engineering." *European Journal of Political Research* 25(1): 1–17; Arend Lijphart. 1999. *Patterns of Democracy: Government Forms and Performance in 36 Countries.* New Haven, CT: Yale University Press.

Chapter 4: Party Systems

1. Russell J. Dalton and Martin P. Wattenberg. 2001. *Parties without Partisans: Political Change in Advanced Industrial Democracies.* Oxford: Oxford University Press.
2. Maurice Duverger. 1954. *Political Parties, Their Organization and Activity in the Modern State.* New York: Wiley.
3. Maurice Duverger. 1986. "Duverger's Law: Forty Years Later." In *Electoral Laws and their Political Consequences.* Bernard Grofman and Arend Lijphart. Eds. New York: Agathon Press.
4. Douglas W. Rae. 1967. *The Political Consequences of Electoral Laws.* New Haven, CT: Yale University Press [1971 revised edition]; William H. Riker. 1976. "The number of political parties: A reexamination of Duverger's Law." *Comparative Politics* 9(1): 93–106; William H. Riker. 1982. "The two-party system and Duverger's Law: An essay on the history of political science." *American Political Science Review* 76(4): 753–766; William H. Riker. 1986. "Duverger's Law Revisited." In *Electoral Laws and Their Political Consequences.* Bernard Grofman and Arend Lijphart. Eds. New York: Agathon Press; Arend Lijphart. 1994. *Electoral Systems and Party Systems.* Oxford: Oxford University Press.
5. See André Blais and R. Kenneth Carty. 1991. "The psychological impact of electoral laws – measuring Duverger's elusive factor." *British Journal of Political Science* 21(1): 79–93; Ken Benoit. 2002. "The endogeneity problem in electoral studies: A critical re-examination of Duverger's mechanical effect." *Electoral Studies* 21(1): 35–46.
6. Peter C. Ordeshook and Olga Shvetsova. 1994. "Ethnic heterogeneity, district magnitude and the number of parties." *American Journal of Political Science* 38(1): 100–123; Octavio Amorim Neto and Gary W. Cox. 1997. "Electoral institutions, cleavage structures and the number of parties." *American Journal of Political Science* 41(1): 149–174. See also, however, the discussion in Ken Benoit. 2002. "The endogeneity problem in electoral studies: A critical re-examination of Duverger's mechanical effect." *Electoral Studies* 21(1): 35–46.
7. M. Laakso and Rein Taagepera. 1979. "Effective number of parties: A measure with application to Western Europe." *Comparative Political Studies.* 12(1): 3–27.
8. Arend Lijphart. 1994. *Electoral Systems and Party Systems: A Study of Twenty-Seven Democracies, 1945–1990.* New York: Oxford University Press.
9. Richard Katz. 1997. *Democracy and Elections.* Oxford: Oxford University Press.
10. Election results were compared based on the data contained in *Elections Around the World.* Available online at www.agora.stm.it/elections/alllinks.htm. Where election results were missing from this source alternatives were used, including

Electoral Studies and the *International Foundation for Electoral Systems* (IFES). Available online at http://www.ifes.org/eguide/elecguide.htm. The total analysis compared elections held from 1995 to 2000 for the lower house of parliament in 143 nations where results were available, including the share of votes and seats held by 1,244 electoral parties.

11. Similar patterns are found if the analysis is confined to the 37 nations classified worldwide by the Freedom House Gastil Index as "older" or "newer" democracies. In these countries, the mean number of parliamentary parties was 7.4 in majoritarian systems and 10.22 in PR systems. The mean effective number of relevant parties was 3.0 in majoritarian systems and 5.5 in PR systems.

12. Robert Moser. 2001. "The consequences of Russia's Mixed-Member Electoral System." In *Mixed-Member Electoral Systems: The Best of Both Worlds?* Matthew Soberg Shugart and Martin P. Wattenberg. Eds. Oxford: Oxford University Press.

13. Arend Lijphart. 1994. *Electoral Systems and Party Systems: A Study of Twenty-Seven Democracies, 1945–1990.* New York: Oxford University Press.

14. Arend Lijphart. 1994. *Electoral Systems and Party Systems: A Study of Twenty-Seven Democracies, 1945–1990.* New York: Oxford University Press.

15. Ken Benoit. 2002. "The endogeneity problem in electoral studies: A critical re-examination of Duverger's mechanical effect." *Electoral Studies* 21(1): 35–46.

Chapter 5: Social Cleavages

1. Seymour Martin Lipset and Stein Rokkan. 1967. *Party Systems and Voter Alignments.* New York: The Free Press. See also Robert R. Alford. 1967. "Class Voting in the Anglo-American Political Systems." In *Party Systems and Voter Alignments: Cross National Perspectives.* Seymour M. Lipset and Stein Rokkan. Eds. New York: The Free Press; Richard Rose and Derek W. Urwin. 1970. "Persistence and change in Western party systems since 1945." *Political Studies* 18(3): 287–319; Richard Rose. Ed. 1974. *Electoral Behavior: A Comparative Handbook.* New York: The Free Press.

2. For Britain see David Butler and Donald Stokes. 1974. *Political Change in Britain.* London: Macmillan. On France see Michael Lewis-Beck and Andrew Skalaban. 1992. "France." In *Electoral Change: Responses to Evolving Social and Attitudinal Structures in Western Countries.* Mark Franklin, Tom Mackie, Henry Valen, et al. Eds. Cambridge, U.K.: Cambridge University Press. On Belgium see Anthony Mughan. 1983. "Accommodation or diffusion in the management of ethnic conflict in Belgium." *Political Studies* 31(3): 431–51.

3. For a more recent argument that these stable patterns have persisted with considerable continuity displayed within the major "left" and "right" blocks, see Stefano Bartolini and Peter Mair. 1990. *Identity, Competition, and Electoral Availability: The Stabilization of European Electorates, 1885–1985.* Cambridge, U.K.: Cambridge University Press.

4. Hans Daalder and Peter Mair. Eds. 1985. *Western European Party Systems.* London: Sage; Morgens N. Pederson. 1979. "The dynamics of European party systems: Changing patterns of electoral volatility." *European Journal of Political Research* 7(1): 1–26.

5. Ivor Crewe, Jim Alt, and Bo Sarlvik. 1977. "Partisan dealignment in Britain 1964–1974." *British Journal of Political Science* 7(April): 129–190; Norman Nie, Sidney Verba, and John Petrocik. 1976. *The Changing American Voter.* Cambridge, MA: Harvard University Press; Ivor Crewe and David Denver. Eds. 1985. *Electoral Change in Western Democracies: Patterns and Sources of Electoral Volatility.* New York: St. Martin's Press; Mark Franklin, Tom Mackie, Henry Valen, et al. Eds. 1992. *Electoral Change: Responses to Evolving Social and Attitudinal Structures in Western Countries.* Cambridge, U.K.: Cambridge University Press; Russell J. Dalton, Scott Flanagan, and Paul Allen Beck, Eds. 1984. *Electoral Change in Advanced Industrial Democracies: Realignment or Dealignment?* Princeton, NJ: Princeton University Press; Mark Franklin. 1985. *The Decline of Class Voting in Britain: Changes in the Basis of Electoral Choice, 1964–1983.* Oxford: Clarendon Press; Jeff Manza and Clem Brooks. 1999. *Social Cleavages and Political Change: Voter Alignments and U.S. Party Coalitions.* New York: Oxford University Press; Terry Nichols Clark and Seymour Martin Lipset. Eds. 2001. *The Breakdown of Class Politics.* Baltimore, MD: The Johns Hopkins University Press.

6. The term *catch-all* was first developed by Kirchheimer to describe the transformation of the German SDP when they abandoned their radical Marxist roots in the late 1950s. See Otto Kirchheimer. 1966. "The Transformation of Western European Party Systems." In *Political Parties and Political Development.* J. La Palombara and M. Weiner. Eds. Princeton, NJ: Princeton University Press.

7. Adam Przeworski and John Sprague. 1986. *Paper Stones: A History of Electoral Socialism.* Chicago: The University of Chicago Press.

8. Herbert Kitschelt. 1994. *The Transformation of European Social Democracy.* Cambridge, U.K.: Cambridge University Press; Herbert Kitschelt. 1995. *The Radical Right in Western Europe.* Ann Arbor, MI: The University of Michigan Press; Herbert Kitschelt. 1993. "Class-structure and Social-Democratic Party strategy." *British Journal of Political Science* 23(3): 299–337; Herbert Kitschelt. 2000. "Linkages between citizens and politicians in democratic polities." *Comparative Political Studies* 33(6–7): 845–879. See also Thomas Koelble. 1992. "Recasting social democracy in Europe: A nested games explanation for strategic adjustment in political parties." *Politics and Society* 20(1): 51–70.

9. See also Robert T. McKenzie. 1955. *British Political Parties.* New York: St. Martin's Press; Angelo Panebianco. 1988. *Political Parties: Organization and Power.* Cambridge, U.K.: Cambridge University Press.

10. Maurice Duverger. 1954. *Political Parties, Their Organization and Activity in the Modern State.* New York: Wiley; Richard S. Katz and Peter Mair. Eds. 1994. *How Parties Organize: Change and Adaptation in Party Organizations in Western Democracies.* London: Sage.

11. For details of the success of the Labour strategy in the 1997 and 2001 U.K. elections see Geoffrey Evans and Pippa Norris. Eds. 1999. *Critical Elections: British Parties and Voters in Long-term Perspective.* London: Sage; Pippa Norris. Ed. 2001. *Britain Votes 2001.* Oxford: Oxford University Press; Anthony F. Heath, Roger M. Jowell, and John K. Curtice. 2001. *The Rise of New Labour: Party Policies and Voter Choices.* Oxford: Oxford University Press.

12. Anthony F. Heath, Roger M. Jowell, and John K. Curtice. 2001. *The Rise of New Labour: Party Policies and Voter Choices.* Oxford: Oxford University Press.

13. Donald L. Horowitz. 1991. *A Democratic South Africa? Constitutional Engineering in a Divided Society.* Berkeley: University of California Press.
14. Ben Reilly. 2001. *Democracy in Divided Societies: Electoral Engineering for Conflict Management.* New York: Cambridge University Press.
15. See Russell J. Dalton. 2002. *Citizen Politics.* 3rd edition. Chatham, NJ: Chatham House.
16. Daniel Lerner. 1958. *The Passing of Traditional Society: Modernizing the Middle East.* New York: The Free Press; Seymour Martin Lipset. 1959. "Some social requisites of democracy: Economic development and political legitimacy." *American Political Science Review* 53(1): 69–105; Seymour Martin Lipset. 1960. *Political Man: The Social Basis of Politics.* New York: Doubleday; Walt W. Rostow. 1952. *The Process of Economic Growth.* New York: Norton; Walt W. Rostow. 1960. *The Stages of Economic Growth.* Cambridge, U.K.: Cambridge University Press; Karl W. Deutsch. 1964. "Social mobilization and political development." *American Political Science Review* 55(3): 493–514; Daniel Bell. 1999. *The Coming of Post-Industrial Society: A Venture in Social Forecasting.* New York: Basic Books; Seymour Martin Lipset, Kyoung-Ryung Seong, and John Charles Torres. 1993. "A comparative analysis of the social requisites of democracy." *International Social Science Journal* 45(2): 154–175.
17. See Ronald Inglehart. 1977. *The Silent Revolution: Changing Values and Political Styles Among Western Publics.* Princeton, NJ: Princeton University Press; Ronald Inglehart. 1990. *Culture Shift in Advanced Industrial Society.* Princeton, NJ: Princeton University Press; Ronald Inglehart. 1997. *Modernization and Postmodernization: Cultural, Economic and Political Change in 43 Societies.* Princeton, NJ: Princeton University Press; Russell J. Dalton. 2002. *Citizen Politics.* 3rd edition. Chatham, NJ: Chatham House.
18. Daniel Bell. 1999. *The Coming of Post-Industrial Society: A Venture in Social Forecasting.* New York: Basic Books [1st edition 1973].
19. For a discussion see Ronald Inglehart. 1997. *Modernization and Postmodernization: Cultural, Economic and Political Change in 43 Societies.* Princeton, NJ: Princeton University Press; Ronald Inglehart and Pippa Norris. 2003. *Rising Tide: Gender Equality and Cultural Change Around the World.* Cambridge, U.K.: Cambridge University Press.
20. Pippa Norris. 2000. *A Virtuous Circle.* Cambridge, U.K.: Cambridge University Press.
21. On secularization see Steve Bruce. Ed. 1992. *Religion and Modernization.* Oxford: Oxford University Press; O. Tschannen. 1991. "The secularization paradigm." *Journal for the Scientific Study of Religion* 30(4): 395–415; W.H. Swatos and K.J. Christiano. 2001. "Secularization theory: The course of a concept." *Sociology of Religion* 60(3): 209–228; Steve Bruce. 1996. *Religion in the Modern World: From Cathedrals to Cults.* Oxford: Oxford University Press; Sheena Ashford and Noel Timms. 1992. *What Europe Thinks: A Study of Western European Values.* Aldershot, U.K.: Dartmouth; Wolfgang Jagodzinski and Karel Dobbelaere. 1995. "Secularization and Church Religiosity." In *The Impact of Values.* Jan W. van Deth and Elinor Scarbrough. Eds. Oxford: Oxford University Press; L. Voye. 1999. "Secularization in a context of advanced modernity." *Sociology of Religion* 60(3): 275–288; Ted Gerard Jelen and Clyde Wilcox. Eds. 2002. *Religion and Politics in Comparative Perspective.* New York: Cambridge University Press;

Pippa Norris. 2002. *Democratic Phoenix*. New York: Cambridge University Press. Chapter 9.

22. Bernhard Ebbinghaus and Jelle Visser. 1999. "When institutions matter: Union growth and decline in Western Europe, 1950–1995." *European Sociological Review* 15(2): 135–158 and also Sabine Blashke. 2000. "Union density and European integration: Diverging convergence." *European Journal of Industrial Relations* 6(2): 217–236; Bruce Western. 1994. "Institutionalized mechanisms for unionization in 16 OECD countries: An analysis of social survey data." *Social Forces* 73(2): 497–519.

23. For example, in some cases regional parties such as the Bloc Québécois or the Scottish National Party are to the left, and in other cases parties are to the right, of the political spectrum, so it seemed preferable to exclude these rather than coding them on a more arbitrary basis. The excluded parties all attracted relatively few voters in any country so their exclusion did not have a major effect on the interpretation of the results.

24. Missing data in some countries means that caution should be exercised in interpreting the results, but, nevertheless, it seemed important to include the full range of indicators of socioeconomic status, given debates about the most appropriate measures. Other regression models were run alternatively excluding social class, linguistic minorities, and left–right position, as well as using different indicators of religiosity. Although this slightly altered the strength of the coefficients, as expected, this did not have a major impact on their significance or direction. Hence, for example, including income but not class in the models strengthened the coefficients for income but did not change their significance. All regression models were also checked for potential problems of multicollinearity using tolerance statistics and were found to be unaffected by this.

25. Anthony Heath, Roger Jowell, and John Curtice. 1985. *How Britain Votes*. Oxford: Pergamon Press; Anthony Heath, Roger Jowell, John Curtice, Geoffrey Evans, Julia Field, and Sharon Witherspoon. 1991. *Understanding Political Change: The British Voter 1964–1987*. Oxford: Pergamon Press; Anthony Heath, Roger Jowell, and John Curtice, with Bridget Taylor. Eds. 1994. *Labour's Last Chance? The 1992 Election and Beyond*. Aldershot, U.K.: Dartmouth; Anthony Heath, Geoffrey Evans, and Clive Payne. 1995. "Modeling the class/party relationship in Britain, 1964–92." *Journal of the Royal Statistical Society, Series A*, 158(Part 3): 563–574; Geoffrey Evans. 1999. *The Decline of Class Politics?* Oxford: Oxford University Press; Geoffrey Evans. 2000. "The continued significance of class voting." *Annual Review of Political Science* 3: 401–417; Russell J. Dalton and Martin Wattenberg. Eds. 2001. *Parties without Partisans*. New York: Oxford University Press.

26. Paul Nieuwbeerta. 1995. *The Democratic Class Struggle in Twenty Countries 1945–90*. Amsterdam: Thesis Publishers; Paul Nieuwbeerta and Nan Dirk De Graaf. 1999. "Traditional Class Voting in 20 Postwar Societies." In *The End of Class Politics?* Geoffrey Evans. Ed. Oxford: Oxford University Press.

27. Geoffrey Evans, Anthony Heath, and Clive Payne. 1999. "Class: Labour as a Catch-All Party?" In *Critical Elections: British Parties and Voters in Long-term Perspective*. Geoffrey Evans and Pippa Norris. Eds. London: Sage.

28. See, for example, discussions and alternative measurements in John Goldthorpe. 1987. *Social Mobility and the Class Structure in Modern Britain*. Oxford: Clarendon

Press; Anthony Heath, Roger Jowell, and John Curtice. 1985. *How Britain Votes*. Oxford: Pergamon Press; Anthony Heath, Roger Jowell, John Curtice, Geoffrey Evans, Julia Field, and Sharon Witherspoon. 1991. *Understanding Political Change: The British Voter 1964–1987*. Oxford: Pergamon Press; Richard Rose and Ian McAllister. 1986. *Voters Begin to Choose*. London: Sage.

29. Cramer's $V = 0.14$ Sig. p.000.
30. Pippa Norris. 2002. *Democratic Phoenix*. Cambridge, U.K.: Cambridge University Press. Chapter 9.
31. Ronald Inglehart and Pippa Norris. 2003. *Rising Tide: Gender Equality and Cultural Change Around the World*. Cambridge, U.K.: Cambridge University Press.
32. Ted Gerard Jelen and Clyde Wilcox. Eds. 2002. *Religion and Politics in Comparative Perspective*. New York: Cambridge University Press.
33. Ronald Inglehart. 1997. *Modernization and Postmodernization: Cultural, Economic and Political Change in 43 Societies*. Princeton, NJ: Princeton University Press.
34. For more details see Samuel Barnes and Janos Simon. Eds. 1998. *The Post-Communist Citizen*. Budapest, Hungary: Erasmus Foundation; William L. Miller, Stephen White, and Paul Heywood. 1998. *Values and Political Change in Postcommunist Europe*. New York: St. Martin's Press; R.E. Bohrer, A.C. Pacek, and B. Radcliff. 2000. "Electoral participation, ideology, and party politics in postcommunist Europe." *Journal of Politics* 62(4): 1161–1172; Herbert Kitschelt, Zdenka Mansfeldova, Radoslaw Markowski, and Gabor Toka. 1999. *Post-Communist Party Systems*. Cambridge, U.K.: Cambridge University Press.
35. Gabriel A. Almond and Sidney Verba. 1963. *The Civic Culture: Political Attitudes and Democracy in Five Nations*. Princeton, NJ: Princeton University Press. P.325; Seymour M. Lipset. 1960. *Political Man: The Social Bases of Politics*. Garden City, NY: Doubleday. P.260; Jean Blondel. 1970. *Votes, Parties and Leaders*. London: Penguin. Pp.55–56.
36. Lawrence Mayer and Roland E. Smith. 1985. "Feminism and Religiosity: Female Electoral Behavior in Western Europe." In Sylvia Bashevkin. Ed. *Women and Politics in Western Europe*. London: Frank Cass; David DeVaus and Ian McAllister. 1989. "The changing politics of women: Gender and political alignments in 11 nations." *European Journal of Political Research* 17(3): 241–262.
37. Jeff Manza and Clem Brooks. 1998. "The gender gap in U.S. presidential elections: When? Why? Implications?" *American Journal of Sociology* 103(5): 1235–1266.
38. Ronald Inglehart and Pippa Norris. 2003. *Rising Tide: Gender Equality and Cultural Change Around the World*. Cambridge, U.K.: Cambridge University Press.
39. Hans-Dieter Klingemann. 1979. "Measuring Ideological Conceptualizations." In *Political Action*. Samuel Barnes and Max Kaase, et al. Eds. Beverley Hills, CA: Sage; Dieter Fuchs and Hans-Dieter Klingemann. 1989. "The Left-Right Schema." In *Continuities in Political Action*. M. Kent Jennings and Jan van Deth. Eds. Berlin: de Gruyter.
40. John Fuh-Sheng Hsieh. 2002. "Continuity and Change in Taiwan's Electoral Politics." In *How Asia Votes*. John Fuh-Sheng Hsieh and David Newman. Eds. New York: Chatham House.
41. Philip Converse. 1969. "Of time and partisan stability." *Comparative Political Studies* 2(2): 139–171.

42. Mark Franklin, Tom Mackie, Henry Valen, et al. 1992. Eds. *Electoral Change: Responses to Evolving Social and Attitudinal Structures in Western Countries.* Cambridge, U.K.: Cambridge University Press. Figure 19.2. P.394.

Chapter 6: Party Loyalties

1. Angus Campbell, Philip Converse, Warren E. Miller, and Donald E. Stokes. 1960. *The American Voter.* New York: John Wiley & Sons, Inc. For the latest work from the Michigan school see Warren Miller and J. Merrill Shanks. 1996. *The New American Voter.* Cambridge, MA: Harvard University Press.
2. Philip Converse. 1969. "Of time and partisan stability." *Comparative Political Studies* 2(2): 139–171.
3. Philip Converse. 1969. "Of time and partisan stability." *Comparative Political Studies.* 2: 139–171.
4. For Britain see David Butler and Donald Stokes. 1974. *Political Change in Britain.* Revised edition. London: Macmillan. For Norway see Angus Campbell and Henry Valen. 1961. "Party identification in Norway and the United States." *Public Opinion Quarterly* 22(4): 505–525. For France see Philip E. Converse and Georges Dupeux. 1962. "Politicization of the electorate in France and the United States." *Public Opinion Quarterly* 26(1): 1–23; Philip E. Converse and Roy Pierce. 1986. *Political Representation in France.* Cambridge, MA: Harvard University Press.
5. David Butler and Donald Stokes. 1974. *Political Change in Britain.* Revised edition. London: Macmillan.
6. Jacques Thomassen. 1976. "Party identification as a cross-national concept: Its meaning in the Netherlands." In *Party Identification and Beyond.* Ian Budge, Ivor Crewe, and Dennis Farlie. Eds. London: John Wiley; Lawrence LeDuc. 1979. "The dynamic properties of party identification: A four nation comparison." *European Journal of Political Research* 9(3): 257–268; Richard A. Brody and Lawrence S. Rothenberg. 1988. "The instability of party identification: An analysis of the 1980 presidential election." *British Journal of Political Science* 18(Part 4, October): 445–465; Sören Holmberg. 1994. "Party identification compared across the Atlantic." In *Elections at Home and Abroad.* M. Kent Jennings and Thomas Mann. Eds. Ann Arbor, MI: University of Michigan Press; I. Kabashima and Y. Ishio. 1998. "The instability of party identification among eligible Japanese voters – A seven-wave panel study, 1993–6." *Party Politics* 4(2): 151–176; E. Schickler and D.P. Green. 1997. "The stability of party identification in Western democracies – Results from eight panel surveys." *Comparative Political Studies* 30(4): 450–483; M. Brynin and David Sanders. 1997. "Party identification, political preferences, and material conditions – Evidence from the British Household Panel Survey, 1991–2." *Party Politics* 3(1): 53–77.
7. Morris Fiorina. 1981. *Retrospective Voting in American National Elections.* New Haven, CT: Yale University Press; Christopher Achen. 1992. "Social psychology, demographic variables, and linear regression: Breaking the iron triangles in voting research." *Political Behavior* 14(3): 195–211; John Bartle. 2001. "The measurement of party identification in Britain: Where do we stand now?" In

British Elections and Parties Review: 11. Jonathan Tonge, Lynn Bennie, David Denver, and Lisa Harrison. Eds. London: Frank Cass.

8. Morris Fiorina. 1981. *Retrospective Voting in American National Elections.* New Haven, CT: Yale University Press.

9. Russell J. Dalton and Martin Wattenberg. Eds. 2001. *Parties without Partisans.* New York: Oxford University Press.

10. Ivor Crewe and David Denver. Eds. 1985. *Electoral Change in Western Democracies: Patterns and Sources of Electoral Volatility.* New York: St. Martin's Press; Russell J. Dalton, Scott C. Flanagan, Paul A. Beck, and James E. Alt. Eds. 1984. *Electoral Change in Advanced Industrial Democracies: Realignment or Dealignment?* Princeton, NJ: Princeton University Press.

11. See Herbert Kitschelt, Zdenka Mansfeldova, Radoslaw Markowski and Gabor Toka. 1999. *Post-Communist Party Systems.* Cambridge, U.K.: Cambridge University Press; Stephen White, Richard Rose, and Ian McAllister. 1996. *How Russia Votes.* Chatham, NJ: Chatham House; Arthur H. Miller. 2000. "The development of party identification in post-soviet societies." *American Journal of Political Science* 44(4): 667–686; Richard Rose and Neil Munro. 2002. *Elections without Order: Russia's Challenge to Vladimir Putin.* New York: Cambridge University Press.

12. Herman Schmitt and Sören Holmberg. 1995. "Political Parties in Decline?" In *Citizens and the State.* Hans-Dieter Klingemann and Dieter Fuchs. Eds. Oxford: Oxford University Press.

13. Russell J. Dalton. 2001. "The Decline of Party Identification." In *Parties without Partisans.* Russell J. Dalton and Martin Wattenberg. Eds. New York: Oxford University Press.

14. This school arises from Anthony Downs. 1957. *An Economic Theory of Democracy.* New York: Harper. See Morris P. Fiorina. 1981. *Retrospective Voting in American National Elections.* New Haven, CT: Yale University Press.

15. Herman Schmitt and Sören Holmberg. 1995. "Political Parties in Decline?" In *Citizens and the State.* Hans-Dieter Klingemann and Dieter Fuchs. Eds. Oxford: Oxford University Press.

16. John M. Carey and Matthew S. Shugart. 1995. "Incentives to cultivate a personal vote: A rank ordering of electoral formulas." *Electoral Studies* 14(4): 417–440.

17. Philip E. Converse and Roy Pierce. 1985. "Measuring partisanship." *Political Methodology* 11:143–166; Anthony Heath and Roy Pierce. 1992. "It was party identification all along – Question order effects on reports of party identification in Britain." *Electoral Studies* 11(2): 93–105; Ron J. Johnston and Charles J. Pattie. 1996. "The strength of party identification among the British electorate: An exploration." *Electoral Studies* 15(3): 295–309; Ian McAllister and Martin Wattenberg. 1995. "Measuring levels of party identification – Does question order matter?" *Public Opinion Quarterly* 59(2): 259–268; André Blais, Elizabeth Gidengil, Richard Nadeau, and Neil Nevitte. 2001. "Measuring party identification: Britain, Canada, and the United States." *Political Behavior* 23(1): 5–22.

18. By contrast, the standard question on the direction and strength of partisanship carried since 1952 in the American National Election Study asks: *"Generally speaking, do you usually think of yourself as a Republican, a Democrat, an*

Independent, or what?" (IF REPUBLICAN OR DEMOCRAT) *"Would you call yourself a strong* (REPUBLICAN/DEMOCRAT) *or a not very strong* (REPUB-LICAN/DEMOCRAT)?" (IF INDEPENDENT, OTHER, [1966 and later]: OR NO PREFERENCE]) *"Do you think of yourself as closer to the Republican or Democratic party?"* The same item, with the inclusion of cues for the Conservative, Labour, and Liberal Democratic parties, has been included in the series of British Election Studies since 1964. The inclusion of the standard cued item in the Australian and the Belgian election survey in the CSES dataset generated far higher levels of partisanship, and, as a result, these elections were dropped from the analysis in this chapter.

19. Philip Converse. 1969. "Of time and partisan stability." *Comparative Political Studies* 2(2): 139–171.
20. See Herbert Kitschelt, Zdenka Mansfeldova, Radoslaw Markowski, and Gabor Toka. 1999. *Post-Communist Party Systems*. Cambridge, U.K.: Cambridge University Press; Sten Berglund and Jan A. Dellenbrant. 1994. *The New Democracies in Eastern Europe: Party Systems and Political Cleavages*. Aldershot, U.K.: Edward Elgar.
21. See, for example, Bernard Grofman, Sung-Chull Lee, Edwin A. Winckler, and Brian Woodall. Eds. 1997. *Elections in Japan, Korea and Taiwan under the Single Non-Transferable Vote: The Comparative Study of an Embedded Institution*. Ann Arbor, MI: University of Michigan Press.
22. See Moshe M. Czudnowski. 1975. "Political Recruitment." In *Handbook of Political Science, Volume 2: Micro-Political Theory*. Reading, MA: Addison-Wesley; Donald R. Matthews. 1985. "Legislative Recruitment and Legislative Careers." In *Handbook of Legislative Research*. Gerhard Loewenberg, Samuel C. Patterson, and Malcolm E. Jewell. Eds. Cambridge, MA: Harvard University Press. Pp.17–55; Gerhard Loewenberg and Samuel C. Patterson. 1979. *Comparing Legislatures*. Boston: Little, Brown and Company; Michael Gallagher and Michael Marsh. Eds. 1988. *Candidate Selection in Comparative Perspective*. London: Sage; Pippa Norris and Joni Lovenduski. 1995. *Political Recruitment: Gender, Race and Class in British Parliament*. Cambridge, U.K.: Cambridge University Press; Pippa Norris. Ed. 1997. *Passages to Power: Legislative Recruitment in Advanced Democracies*. Cambridge, U.K.: Cambridge University Press; Reuven Hazan. 2002. "Candidate Selection." In *Comparing Democracies*. 2nd edition. Lawrence LeDuc, Richard G. Neimi, and Pippa Norris. Eds. London: Sage.
23. Pippa Norris. Ed. 1997. *Passages to Power: Legislative Recruitment in Advanced Democracies*. Cambridge, U.K.: Cambridge University Press.
24. For a discussion see Anthony King. 1999. *Running Scared: Why America's Politicians Campaign Too Much and Govern Too Little*. New York: The Free Press.
25. Russell J. Dalton. 2001. "The Decline of Party Identification." In *Parties without Partisans*. Russell J. Dalton and Martin Wattenberg. Eds. New York: Oxford University Press.
26. Warren Miller and J. Merrill Shanks. 1996. *The New American Voter*. Cambridge, MA: Harvard University Press.
27. Pippa Norris. 2002. *Democratic Phoenix*. New York: Cambridge University Press. Chapter 6.

Chapter 7: Turnout

1. Martin P. Wattenberg. 2002. *Where Have All the Voters Gone?* Cambridge, MA: Harvard University Press; Thomas Patterson. 2002. *The Vanishing Voter.* New York: Alfred A. Knopf Publishers.

2. Charles Edward Merriam. 1924. *Non-Voting: Causes and Methods of Control.* Chicago: The University of Chicago Press; Harold Foote Gosnell. 1930. *Why Europe Votes.* Chicago: The University of Chicago Press; Herbert Tingsten. 1937. *Political Behavior: Studies in Election Statistics* [reprinted 1963]. Totowa, NJ: Bedminster Press.

3. G. Bingham Powell, Jr. 1980. "Voting Turnout in Thirty Democracies: Partisan, Legal and Socioeconomic Influences." In *Electoral Participation: A Comparative Analysis.* Richard Rose. Ed. London: Sage; G. Bingham Powell, Jr. 1982. *Contemporary Democracies: Participation, Stability and Violence.* Cambridge, MA: Harvard University Press; G. Bingham Powell, Jr. 1986. "American voter turnout in comparative perspective." *American Political Science Review* 80(1): 17–43.

4. Robert W. Jackman and Ross A. Miller. 1995. "Voter turnout in the industrial democracies during the 1980s." *Comparative Political Studies* 27(4): 467–492. See also Richard Katz. 1997. *Democracy and Elections.* Oxford: Oxford University Press.

5. André Blais and Agnieska Dobrzynska. 1998. "Turnout in electoral democracies." *European Journal of Political Research* 33(2): 239–261.

6. Mark Franklin. 2003. *The Dynamics of Voter Turnout in Established Democracies Since 1945.* New York: Cambridge University Press.

7. Raymond Wolfinger and Steven Rosenstone. 1980. *Who Votes?* New Haven, CT: Yale University Press; M.D. Martinez and D. Hill. 1999. "Did motor voter work?" *American Politics Quarterly* 27(3): 296–315.

8. Daniel Bell. 1999. *The Coming of Post-Industrial Society: A Venture in Social Forecasting.* New York: Basic Books; Russell Dalton. 2002. *Citizen Politics: Public Opinion and Political Parties in Advanced Industrialized Democracies.* 3rd edition. Chatham, NJ: Chatham House; Ronald Inglehart. 1997. *Modernizations and Postmodernization.* Princeton, NJ: Princeton University Press.

9. Pippa Norris. 2002. *Democratic Phoenix: Reinventing Political Activism.* New York: Cambridge University Press.

10. See, for example, Sidney Verba, Kay Schlozman, and Henry E. Brady. 1995. *Voice and Equality: Civic Voluntarism in American Politics.* Cambridge, MA: Harvard University Press.

11. Anthony Downs. 1957. *An Economic Theory of Democracy.* New York: Harper Row.

12. Carol Christy. 1987. *Sex Differences in Political Participation: Processes of Change in Fourteen Nations.* New York: Praeger.

13. Henry Milner. 2002. *Civic Literacy: How Informed Citizens Make Democracy Work.* Hanover, MA: University Press of New England.

14. Gabriel Almond and Sidney Verba. 1963. *The Civic Culture: Political Attitudes and Democracy in Five Nations.* Princeton, NJ: Princeton University Press.

15. Gabriel Almond and Sidney Verba. 1963. *The Civic Culture: Political Attitudes and Democracy in Five Nations.* Princeton, NJ: Princeton University Press; Sidney Verba, Norman Nie, and Jae-on Kim. 1978. *Participation and Political Equality: A*

Seven-Nation Comparison. New York: Cambridge University Press; Samuel Barnes and Max Kaase. 1979. *Political Action: Mass Participation in Five Western Democracies.* Beverley Hills, CA: Sage; Sidney Verba, Kay Schlozman, and Henry E. Brady. 1995. *Voice and Equality: Civic Voluntarism in American Politics.* Cambridge, MA: Harvard University Press; Nancy Burns, Kay Lehman Schlozman, and Sidney Verba. 2001. *The Private Roots of Public Action.* Cambridge, MA: Harvard University Press.

16. See the debate in Arthur H. Miller. 1974a. "Political issues and trust in government, 1964–1970." *American Political Science Review* 68(3): 951–972; Jack Citrin. 1974. "Comment: The political relevance of trust in government." *American Political Science Review* 68(3): 973–988; Arthur H. Miller. 1974b. "Rejoinder to 'Comment' by Jack Citrin: political discontent or ritualism?" *American Political Science Review* 68(3): 989–1001; Pippa Norris. Ed. 1998. *Critical Citizens: Global Support for Democratic Governance.* Oxford: Oxford University Press.

17. Ray Wolfinger and Steven Rosenstone. 1980. *Who Votes?* New Haven, CT: Yale University Press.

18. Warren E. Miller and J. Merrill Shanks. 1996. *The New American Voter.* Cambridge, MA: Harvard University Press. P.41.

19. Robert Putnam. 2000. *Bowling Alone.* New York: Simon & Schuster.

20. Mark Franklin. 2003. *The Dynamics of Voter Turnout in Established Democracies Since 1945.* New York: Cambridge University Press.

21. For a discussion of the role of mobilizing agencies such as union membership and church attendance see Pippa Norris. 2002. *Democratic Phoenix: Reinventing Political Activism.* New York: Cambridge University Press. Chapter 5. For a detailed discussion of the role of the news media and civic engagement see Pippa Norris. 2001. *A Virtuous Circle.* New York: Cambridge University Press.

22. Daniel Bell. 1999. *The Coming of Post-Industrial Society: A Venture in Social Forecasting.* New York: Basic Books; Russell Dalton. 2002. *Citizen Politics: Public Opinion and Political Parties in Advanced Industrialized Democracies.* 3rd edition. Chatham, NJ: Chatham House; Ronald Inglehart. 1997. *Modernization and Postmodernization: Cultural, Economic and Political Change in 43 Societies.* Princeton, NJ: Princeton University Press.

23. Pippa Norris. 2002. *Democratic Phoenix: Reinventing Political Activism.* New York: Cambridge University Press.

24. See, for example, Sidney Verba, Kay Schlozman, and Henry E. Brady. 1995. *Voice and Equality: Civic Voluntarism in American Politics.* Cambridge, MA: Harvard University Press.

25. For more details see Pippa Norris. 2002. *Democratic Phoenix: Reinventing Political Activism.* New York: Cambridge University Press.

26. G. Bingham Powell, Jr. 1986. "American voter turnout in comparative perspective." *American Political Science Review* 80(1): 17–43; Robert W. Jackman. 1987. "Political institutions and voter turnout in industrialized democracies." *American Political Science Review* 81(2): 405–423; Robert W. Jackman and Ross A. Miller. 1995. "Voter turnout in industrial democracies during the 1980s." *Comparative Political Studies* 27(4): 467–492. André Blais and Agnieszka Dobrzynska. 1998. "Turnout in electoral democracies." *European Journal of Political Research.* 33(2): 239–261; A. Ladner and H. Milner. 1999. "Do voters turn out more under

proportional than majoritarian systems? The evidence from Swiss communal elections." *Electoral Studies* 18(2): 235–250.

27. See the discussion in André Blais and Agnieszka Dobrzynska. 1998. "Turnout in electoral democracies." *European Journal of Political Research*. 33(2): 239–261.

28. For a discussion see Robert Dahl. 1998. *On Democracy*. New Haven, CT: Yale University Press.

29. For a discussion about this in the context of Britain and the United States see Bruce Cain, John Ferejohn, and Morris Fiorina. 1987. *The Personal Vote*. Cambridge, MA: Harvard University Press.

30. See, for example, the discussion of role orientations of Members of the European Parliament (MEPs) and MPs in different electoral systems in Richard S. Katz. 1999. "Role Orientations in Parliament." In *The European Parliament, the National Parliaments, and European Integration*. Richard S. Katz and Bernhard Wessels. Eds. Oxford: Oxford University Press.

31. Karl Reif and Hermann Schmitt. 1980. "Nine national second order elections." *European Journal of Political Research* 8(1): 3–44.

32. For a fuller discussion of the nature of presidential systems see Arend Lijphart. Ed. 1992. *Parliamentary versus Presidential Government*. Oxford: Oxford University Press.

33. Mark Franklin, Cess van der Eijk, and Erik Oppenhuis. 1996. "The Institutional Context: Turnout." In *Choosing Europe? The European Electorate and National Politics in the Face of Union*. Cees van der Eijk and Mark Franklin. Eds. Ann Arbor, MI: University of Michigan Press.

34. Mark Franklin. 2001. "Electoral Participation." In *Comparing Democracies 2: Elections and Voting in Global Perspective*. Lawrence LeDuc, Richard G. Niemi, and Pippa Norris. Eds. London: Sage; Arend Lijphart. 2000. "Turnout." In the *International Encyclopedia of Elections*. Richard Rose. Ed. Washington, D.C.: Congressional Quarterly Press.

35. Anthony King. 1999. *Running Scared*. New York: The Free Press. P.157.

36. Maurice Duverger. 1954. *Political Parties*. London: Methuen.

37. See also Arend Lijphart. 1999. *Patterns of Democracy*. New Haven, CT: Yale University Press. Pp.168–170.

38. Sarah Birch. 1997. "Ukraine: the Perils of Majoritarianism in a New Democracy." In *The International IDEA Handbook of Electoral System Design*. Andrew Reynolds and Ben Reilly. Eds. Stockholm: International IDEA; Sarah Birch and Andrew Wilson. 1999. "The Ukrainian parliamentary elections of 1998."*Electoral Studies* 18(2): 276–282; Sarah Birch. 1998. "Electoral reform in Ukraine: The 1988 parliamentary elections." *Representation*. 35(2/3): 146–154.

39. André Blais and R. Kenneth Carty. 1990. "Does proportional representation foster voter turnout?" *European Journal of Political Research* 18(2): 167–181.

40. J.M. Colomer. 1991. "Benefits and costs of voting." *Electoral Studies*. 10(4): 313–325.

41. André Blais and R. Kenneth Carty. 1990. "Does proportional representation foster voter turnout?" *European Journal of Political Research* 18(2): 167–181.

42. Robert W. Jackman. 1987. "Political institutions and voter turnout in industrialized democracies." *American Political Science Review* 81(2): 405–424.

43. Pippa Norris. 2002. *Democratic Phoenix: Reinventing Political Activism*. New York: Cambridge University Press. Figure 4.2.

44. Wolfgang Hirczy. 1994. "The impact of mandatory voting laws on turnout: A quasi experimental approach." *Electoral Studies* 13(1): 64–76; Arend Lijphart. 1997. "Unequal participation: Democracy's unresolved dilemma." *American Political Science Review* 91(1): 1–14; Mark Franklin. 1999. "Electoral engineering and cross-national turnout differences: What role for compulsory voting?" *British Journal of Political Science* 29(1): 205–216; Wolfgang Hirczy. 2000. "Compulsory Voting." In *The International Encyclopedia of Elections*. Richard Rose. Ed. Washington, D.C.: Congressional Quarterly Press.

45. I am most grateful for help received from Gillian Evans, Lisa Hill, Marian Sawer, Ian McAllister, and Wolfgang Hirczy in identifying the countries that use compulsory voting.

46. Ian McAllister. 1986. "Compulsory voting, turnout and party advantage in Australia." *Politics* 21(1): 89–93.

47. One difficulty in analyzing the systematic effects of mandatory voting regulations concerns significant differences among alternative reference sources in the particular countries classified as using these laws. In such cases, the rule was adopted that the use of compulsory voting requirements had to be confirmed in at least three independent sources for classification in this study. These sources included the detailed report provided in a private communication by Gillian Evans and Lisa Hill at the Australian National University; the *International Encyclopedia of Elections*. 2001. Richard Rose. Ed. Washington, D.C.: Congressional Quarterly Press; the Inter-Parliamentary Union *Chronicle of Parliamentary Elections* annual volumes 1995–1999. Geneva: IPU; the list published by the Australian Electoral Commission as provided online by IFES1996 at www.aec.gov.au/voting/compulsory%5Fcountries.htm; the *CIA World Factbook 2000* available online at www.cia.gov/cia/publications/fields/suffrage.html; and the tables provided by Richard Katz. 1997. *Democracy and Elections*. Oxford: Oxford University Press. Table 13.1 and 13.2. Reference was also made to the electoral laws and constitutions compiled by IFES, available online at www.IFES.org.

48. Richard Topf. 1995. "Electoral Participation." *Citizens and the State*. Hans-Dieter Klingemann and Dieter Fuchs. Eds. Oxford: Oxford University Press. Pp.43–45; Warren Miller and Merrill Shanks. 1996. *The Changing American Voter*. Ann Arbor, MI: University of Michigan Press.

49. André Blais and Agnieszka Dobrzynska. 1998. "Turnout in electoral democracies." *European Journal of Political Research* 33(2): 239–261.

50. Florian Grotz. 2000. "Age of Voting." In the *International Encyclopedia of Elections*. Richard Rose. Ed. Washington, D.C.: Congressional Quarterly Press.

51. See Pippa Norris. 2002. *Democratic Phoenix: Reinventing Political Activism*. New York: Cambridge University Press.

52. André Blais, Louis Massicotte, and A. Yoshinaka. 2001. "Deciding who has the right to vote: A comparative analysis of election laws." *Electoral Studies* 20(1): 41–62. See also Richard S. Katz. 1997. *Democracy and Elections*. Oxford: Oxford University Press.

53. See Michael P. McDonald and Samuel L. Popkin. 2000. "The Myth of the Vanishing Voter." Paper presented at the 2000 *American Political Science Convention*, Washington, D.C., August 31–September 3.

54. For details see Wilma Rule. "Women's Enfranchisement" and also Stefano Bartolini. "Franchise Expansion." 2000. Both are in the *International Encyclopedia of Elections*. Richard Rose. Ed. Washington, D.C.: Congressional Quarterly Press.

55. Pippa Norris. 2001. "Women's Turnout." In *Voter Participation from 1945 to 2000*. Stockholm: International IDEA.

56. See Pippa Norris. 2002. *Democratic Phoenix: Reinventing Political Activism*. New York: Cambridge University Press.

57. Ivor Crewe. "Electoral Participation." In *Democracy at the Polls*. Austin Ranney and David Butler. Eds. Washington, D.C.: AEI Press; G. Bingham Powell, Jr. 1986. "American voter turnout in comparative perspective." *American Political Science Review*. 80(1): 17–43; Robert W. Jackman. 1987. "Political institutions and voter turnout in industrialized democracies." *American Political Science Review* 81(2): 405–423; Robert W. Jackman and Ross A. Miller. 1995. "Voter turnout in industrial democracies during the 1980s." *Comparative Political Studies* 27(4): 467–492. André Blais and Agnieszka Dobrzynska. 1998. "Turnout in electoral democracies." *European Journal of Political Research* 33(2): 239–261; Mark Franklin, Cess van der Eijk, and Erik Oppenhuis. 1996. "The Institutional Context: Turnout." In *Choosing Europe? The European Electorate and National Politics in the Face of Union*. Cees van der Eijk and Mark Franklin. Eds. Ann Arbor, MI: University of Michigan Press; Arend Lijphart. 1997. "Unequal participation: Democracy's unresolved dilemma." *American Political Science Review* 91(1): 1–14.

58. Pippa Norris. 2001. "U.S. campaign 2000: Of pregnant chads, butterfly ballots and partisan vitriol." *Government and Opposition* January 35(2): 1–24.

59. Richard Katz. 1997. *Democracy and Elections*. New York: Oxford University Press. Table 13.2.

60. Raymond E. Wolfinger and Steven J. Rosenstone. 1980. *Who Votes?* New Haven, CT: Yale University Press. For a more recent study see Mark J. Fenster. 1994. "The impact of allowing day of registration voting on turnout in U.S. elections from 1960 to 1992." *American Politics Quarterly* 22(1): 74–87.

61. Stephen Knack. 1995. "Does 'motor voter' work? Evidence from state-level data." *Journal of Politics* 57(3): 796–811; M.D. Martinez and D. Hill. 1999. "Did motor voter work?" *American Politics Quarterly* 27(3): 296–315.

62. Craig Leonard Brians and Bernard Grofman. 1999. "When registration barriers fall, who votes? An empirical test of a rational choice model." *Public Choice* 99(1–2): 161–176.

63. Raymond E. Wolfinger, David P. Glass, and Peverill Squire. 1990. "Predictors of electoral turnout: An international comparison." *Policy Studies Review*. 9(3): 551–574.

64. Richard S. Katz. 1997. *Democracy and Elections*. Oxford: Oxford University Press. Tables 13.1 and 13.2.

65. See Pippa Norris. 2002. *Democratic Phoenix: Reinventing Political Activism*. New York: Cambridge University Press. The mean Vote/VAP in the 1990s was the same (72%) in the countries classified by Katz as using automatic and in those using application registration procedures, and the mean Vote/Reg in the 1990s was slightly higher (78.1%) in countries with application procedures than in those with automatic processes (75.1%).

66. The best discussion of the administrative arrangements for registration and balloting found around the world is available online at www.ACE.org; the site was developed by International IDEA and IFES. For further details see Michael Maley. 2000. "Absentee Voting." In *The International Encyclopedia of Elections*. Richard Rose. Ed. Washington, D.C.: Congressional Quarterly Press. See also entry by André Blais and Louis Massicotte. "Day of Election."

67. Mark Franklin. 2001. "Electoral Participation." In *Comparing Democracies 2: Elections and Voting in Global Perspective*. Lawrence LeDuc, Richard G. Niemi, and Pippa Norris. Eds. London: Sage.

68. See Pippa Norris. 2002. *Democratic Phoenix: Reinventing Political Activism*. New York: Cambridge University Press.

69. See Pippa Norris. 2002. *Democratic Phoenix: Reinventing Political Activism*. New York: Cambridge University Press. P.57.

70. See Pippa Norris. "Will new technology boost turnout?" Paper presented at *the Annual Meeting of the APSA*, Philadelphia, August.

Chapter 8: Women's Representation

1. Hanna Pitkin. 1967. *The Concept of Representation*. Berkeley: University of California Press; Anne Phillips. 1995. *The Politics of Presence*. Oxford: Clarendon Press; Anne Phillips. Ed. 1998. *Feminism and Politics*. Oxford: Oxford University Press; Jane Mansbridge. 1999. "Should blacks represent blacks and women represent women? A contingent 'yes.'" *Journal of Politics* 61(3): 628–657.

2. There is a growing and substantial literature on this topic. See, for example, Manon Tremblay. 1998. "Do female MPs substantively represent women?" *Canadian Journal of Political Science* 31(3): 435–465; Manon Tremblay and R. Pelletier. 2000. "More feminists or more women? Descriptive and substantive representations of women in the 1997 Canadian federal elections." *International Political Science Review* 21(4): 381–405; Michele Swers. 2001. "Understanding the policy impact of electing women: Evidence from research on congress and state legislatures." *PS: Political Science and Society* 34(2): 217–220; Michele Swers. 1998. "Are women more likely to vote for women's issue bills than their male colleagues?" *Legislative Studies Quarterly* 23(3): 435–448; Beth Reingold. 2000. *Representing Women: Sex, Gender, and Legislative Behavior in Arizona and California*. Chapel Hill, NC: University of North Carolina Press; Lauri Karvonnen and Per Selle. 1995. *Women in Nordic Politics*. Aldershot, U.K.: Dartmouth; J. Dolan. 1997. "Support for women's interests in the 103rd Congress: The distinct impact of congressional women." *Women & Politics* 18(4): 81–94; Georgina Duerst-Lahti and Rita May Kelly. Eds. 1995. *Gender, Power, Leadership and Governance*. Ann Arbor, MI: University of Michigan Press; Susan Carroll. 2001. Ed. *The Impact of Women in Public Office*. Bloomington, IN: University of Indiana Press.

3. Ronald Inglehart and Pippa Norris. 2003. *Rising Tide: Gender Equality and Cultural Change Around the World*. New York: Cambridge University Press.

4. United Nations. *The Beijing Declaration 1995. Section 13*. Available online at www.unifem.undp.org/beijing+5.

5. United Nations Development Programme. 2002. *Human Development Report 2002*. New York: Oxford University Press. Table 27. "Women's political participation."

6. Inter-Parliamentary Union. 2000. *Women in National Parliaments.* Geneva: IPU. Available online at www.ipu.org.

7. For details see Christina Bergqvist, A. Borchorst, A. Christensen, V. Ramstedt-Silén, N.C. Raaum and A. Styrkársdóttir. Eds. 1999. *Equal Democracies? Gender and Politics in the Nordic Countries.* Olso: Scandinavian University Press.

8. For overviews of the literature see Azza Karam. Ed. 1998. *Women in Politics Beyond Numbers.* Stockholm: International IDEA. http://www.int-idea.se/women/; Andrew Reynolds. 1999. "Women in the legislatures and executives of the world: Knocking at the highest glass ceiling." *World Politics* 51(4): 547–572; Lane Kenworthy and Melissa Malami. 1999. "Gender inequality in political representation: A worldwide comparative analysis." *Social Forces* 78(1): 235–269; Alan Siaroff. 2000. "Women's representation in legislatures and cabinets in industrial democracies." *International Political Science Review* 21(2): 197–215.

9. Michael Gallagher and Michael Marsh. Eds. 1988. *Candidate Selection in Comparative Perspective.* London: Sage; Joni Lovenduski and Pippa Norris. Eds. 1993. *Gender and Party Politics.* London: Sage; Pippa Norris and Joni Lovenduski. 1995. *Political Recruitment: Gender, Race and Class in the British Parliament.* Cambridge, U.K.: Cambridge University Press; Pippa Norris. Ed. 1998. *Passages to Power.* Cambridge, U.K.: Cambridge University Press; Miki Caul. 1999. "Women's representation in parliament – The role of political parties." *Party Politics* 5(1): 79–98.

10. There is good evidence that electability is the primary consideration, at least in Britain, when party selectors are asked what qualities they seek in parliamentary candidates. See Pippa Norris and Joni Lovenduski. 1995. *Political Recruitment: Gender, Race and Class in the British Parliament.* Cambridge, U.K.: Cambridge University Press.

11. For a discussion see Reuven Y. Hazan. 2002. "Candidate Selection." In *Comparing Democracies 2: Elections and Voting in Global Perspective.* Lawrence LeDuc, Richard Neimi, and Pippa Norris. Eds. London: Sage.

12. Ronald Inglehart and Pippa Norris. 2003. *Rising Tide: Gender Equality and Cultural Change.* New York: Cambridge University Press. Chapter 6.

13. It should be noted that alternative regression models entered the Rose Index of Proportionality, instead of the type of electoral system, as an alternative indicator. The results of this process replicated the results of the analysis reported in Table 8.1. This suggests that the results are robust and not just dependent upon the measurement and classification of the type of electoral system.

14. See, for example, Miki Caul. 2001. "Political parties and the adoption of candidate gender quotas: A cross–national analysis." *Journal of Politics* 63(4): 1214–1229.

15. Pippa Norris. 1985. "Women in European legislative elites." *West European Politics* 8(4): 90–101; Wilma Rule and Joseph Zimmerman. Eds. 1992. *United States Electoral Systems: Their Impact on Women and Minorities.* New York: Praeger; Arend Lijphart. 1994. *Electoral Systems and Party Systems: A Study of Twenty-Seven Democracies, 1945–1990.* New York: Oxford University Press; Richard Matland. 1998. "Women's representation in national legislatures: Developed and developing countries." *Legislative Studies Quarterly* 23(1): 109–125; Andrew Reynolds. 1999. "Women in the legislatures and executives of the world: Knocking at the highest glass ceiling." *World Politics* 51(4): 547–572; Lane Kenworthy

and Melissa Malami. 1999. "Gender inequality in political representation: A worldwide comparative analysis." *Social Forces* 78(1): 235–269; Alan Siaroff. 2000. "Women's representation in legislatures and cabinets in industrial democracies." *International Political Science Review* 21(2): 197–215. For the argument that these patterns do not hold in post-Communist states, however, see Robert G. Moser. 2001. "The effects of electoral systems on women's representation in post–communist states." *Electoral Studies* 20(3): 353–369.

16. Joni Lovenduski and Pippa Norris. 1993. *Gender and Party Politics*. London: Sage; Pippa Norris. 1998. *Passages to Power*. Cambridge, U.K.: Cambridge University Press.

17. Pippa Norris and Joni Lovenduski. 1995. *Political Recruitment: Gender, Race and Class in the British Parliament*. Cambridge, U.K.: Cambridge University Press.

18. Albert Somit, Rudolf Wildenmann, Berhnard Boll, and Andrea Rommele. Eds. 1994. *The Victorious Incumbent: A Threat to Democracy?* Aldershot, U.K.: Dartmouth.

19. Richard E. Matland and Donley Studlar. (In press). "Determinants of legislative turnover: A cross-national analysis." *British Journal of Political Science*. Table 1.

20. Richard E. Matland and Donley Studlar. (In press). "Determinants of legislative turnover: A cross-national analysis." *British Journal of Political Science*. See also Albert Somit. Ed. 1994. *The Victorious Incumbent: A Threat to Democracy?* Aldershot, U.K.: Dartmouth.

21. Susan J. Carroll and K. Jenkins. 2001. "Unrealized opportunity? Term limits and the representation of women in state legislatures." *Women & Politics* 23(4): 1–30; A.N. Caress. 1999. "The influence of term limits on the electoral success of women." *Women & Politics*. 20(3): 45–63.

22. It should be noted that the use of reserved seats for women in Bangladesh is currently under review, (at the time of writing [October 2002]), with debate about the appropriate level and whether there should be direct elections. For details see the election commission, available online at http://www.bd-ec.org. Reserved seats for women have also been used in the past in Eritrea, but parliament is currently suspended in this country.

23. D. Pankhurst. 2002. "Women and politics in Africa: The case of Uganda." *Parliamentary Affairs* 55(1): 119–125.

24. Cathryn Hoskins and Shirin Rai. 1998. "Gender, class and representation: India and the European Union." *European Journal of Women's Studies* 5(3–4): 345–355.

25. Council of Europe. 2000. *Positive Action in the Field of Equality Between Women and Men: Final Report of the Group of Specialists on Positive Action in the Field of Equality between Women and Men (EG-S-PA)*. Strasbourg, France. Available online at: www.humanrights.coe.int/equality/Eng/WordDocs/Document%20list.htm; Anne Peters, Robert Seidman, and Ann Seidman. 1999. *Women, Quotas, and Constitutions: A Comparative Study of Affirmative Action for Women under American, German and European Community and International Law*. The Hague: Kluwer Law International.

26. Petra Meie. 2000. "The evidence of being present: Guarantees of representation and the example of the Belgian case." *Acta Politica* 35(1): 64–85; A. Carton. 2001. "The general elections in Belgium in June 1999: A real breakthrough for women politicians?" *European Journal of Women's Studies* 8(1): 127–135.

27. Karen Bird. 2002. "Who Are the Women? Where Are the Women? and What Difference Can They Make? The Effects of Gender Parity in French Municipal Elections." Paper presented at the *Annual Meeting of the American Political Science Association.* August 28–September 1; Janine Mossuz-Lavau. 1998. *Femmes/hommes. Pour la parité.* Paris: Presses de sciences po; Mariette Sineau. 2002. "La parite in politics: From a radical idea to a consensual reform." In *Beyond French Feminisms: Debates on Women, Politics and Culture in France, 1980–2001.* Isabelle de Courtivron. Ed. New York: Palgrave.

28. The Italian articles included law 277\93 for elections at the House of Representatives, law 81\93 for local elections, and law 43\95 for regional elections. For details see *Women in Decision-making: European Database.* Available online at www.db-decision.de.

29. Mark Jones. 1996. "Increasing women's representation via gender quotas: The Argentine Ley de Cupos." *Women & Politics* 16(4): 75–98; Mark Jones. 1998. "Gender quotas, electoral laws, and the election of women – Lessons from the Argentine provinces." *Comparative Political Studies* 31(1): 3–21; Mark Jones. 1999. "Assessing the effectiveness of gender quotas in open-list proportional representation electoral systems." *Social Science Quarterly* 80(2): 341–355; Mala Htun and Mark Jones. 2002. "Engendering the Right to Participate in Decision-Making: Electoral Quotas and Women's Leadership in Latin America." In *Gender and the Politics of Rights and Democracy in Latin America*, Eds. Nikki Craske and Maxine Molyneux. London: Palgrave; Mala Htun. Forthcoming. "Women and Political Power in Latin America." In *Women in Parliament. Beyond Numbers.* Latin America edition. Stockholm: International IDEA.

30. Joni Lovenduski and Pippa Norris. 1993. *Gender and Party Politics.* London: Sage; Drude Dahlerup. 1998. "Using Quotas to Increase Women's Political Representation." In *Women in Parliament: Beyond Numbers.* Azza Karam. Ed. Stockholm: International IDEA; Council of Europe. 2000. *Positive Action in the Field of Equality between Women and Men.* EG-S-PA (2000) 7. Strasbourg: Council of Europe.

31. International IDEA. 2003. *Global Database of Quotas for Women.* Available online at http://www.idea.int/quota/index.cfm.

32. Meg Russell. 2000. *Women's Representation in U.K. Politics: What Can Be Done within the Law?* London: The Constitution Unit Report. University College. See also Meg Russell. 2001. *The Women's Representation Bill: Making it Happen.* London: The Constitution Unit Report. University College.

33. Richard E. Matland. 1993. "Institutional Variables Affecting Female Representation in National Legislatures: The Case of Norway." *Journal of Politics* 55(3): 737–755.

34. Lauri Karvonen and Per Selle. Eds. 1995. *Women in Nordic Politics.* Aldershot, U.K.: Dartmouth.

35. Joni Lovenduski and Pippa Norris. 1994. "Women's Quotas in the Labour Party." In *British Parties and Elections Yearbook, 1994.* David Broughton, et al. Eds. London: Frank Cass. Pp.167–181; Maria Eagle and Joni Lovenduski. 1998. *High Time or High Tide for Labour Women?* London: Fabian Society.

36. Joni Lovenduski. 2001. "Women and Politics: Minority Representation or Critical Mass?" In *Britain Votes 2001.* Pippa Norris. Ed. Oxford: Oxford University Press; Sarah Perrigo. 1996. "Women and Change in the Labour Party

1979–1995." In *Women in Politics*. Joni Lovenduski and Pippa Norris. Eds. Oxford: Oxford University Press; Pippa Norris. 2001. "Breaking the Barriers: British Labour Party Quotas for Women." In *Has Liberalism Failed Women? Assuring Equal Representation in Europe and the United States*. Jyette Klausen and Charles S. Maier. Eds. New York: Palgrave. Pp.89–110.

37. *Socialist International Women*. April 2002. Available online at www. socintwomen.org.uk/Quota.

38. Inter-Parliamentary Union. 1992. *Women and Political Power*. Geneva: Inter-Parliamentary Union. For a more recent discussion see Drude Dahlerup. 1998. "Using Quotas to Increase Women's Political Representation." In *IDEA: Women in Politics Beyond Numbers*. Azza Karam. Ed. Stockholm: International IDEA.

39. Carol Nechemias. 1994. "Democratization and women's access to legislative seats – The Soviet case, 1989–1991." *Women & Politics* 14(3): 1–18; Robert G. Moser. 2001. "The effects of electoral systems on women's representation in post-communist states." *Electoral Studies* 20(3): 353–369.

40. Ronald Inglehart and Pippa Norris. 2003. *Rising Tide: Gender Equality and Cultural Change*. New York: Cambridge University Press. Chapter 6.

41. Ronald Inglehart and Pippa Norris. 2003. *Rising Tide: Gender Equality and Cultural Change*. New York: Cambridge University Press. Chapter 6.

42. Maurice Duverger. 1955. *The Political Role of Women*. Paris: UNESCO.

43. See chapters in Pippa Norris. Ed. 1998. *Passages to Power*. Cambridge, U.K.: Cambridge University Press; Pippa Norris and Joni Lovenduski. 1995. *Political Recruitment: Gender, Race and Class in the British Parliament*. Cambridge, U.K.: Cambridge University Press.

44. Inter-Parliamentary Union. 2000. *Politics: Women's Insight*. IPU Reports and Documents No. 36. Geneva: IPU.

45. Lauri Karvonen and Per Selle. 1995. *Women in Nordic Politics*. Aldershot, U.K.: Dartmouth.

46. This patterns holds despite including the elections as prime minister of Benazir Bhutto in Pakistan, Tansu Ciller in Turkey, and Begum Khaleda Zia and Sheikh Hasina Wajed in Bangladesh. Gehan Abu-Zayd. 1998. "In Search of Political Power: Women in Parliament in Egypt, Jordan and Lebanon." In *Women in Parliament: Beyond Numbers*. Azza Karam. Ed. Stockholm: International IDEA.

47. Wilma Rule. 1987. "Electoral systems, contextual factors and women's opportunities for parliament in 23 democracies." *Western Political Quarterly* 40(3): 477–498.

48. Margaret Inglehart. 1979. "Political interest in West European women." *Comparative Political Studies* 14: 229–336.

49. Andrew Reynolds. 1999. "Women in the legislatures and executives of the world: Knocking at the highest glass ceiling." *World Politics* 51(4): 547–572.

50. For details see Ronald Inglehart and Pippa Norris. 2003. *Rising Tide: Gender Equality and Cultural Change*. New York: Cambridge University Press. Chapter 6.

51. Andrew Reynolds. 1999. "Women in the legislatures and executives of the world: Knocking at the highest glass ceiling." *World Politics* 51(4): 547–572.

52. See Ronald Inglehart and Pippa Norris. 2003. *Rising Tide: Gender Equality and Cultural Change*. New York: Cambridge University Press. Chapter 6.

Chapter 9: Ethnic Minorities

1. For a discussion of the concepts of ethnic and national identity, and ethnic conflict, see, for example, Benedict Anderson. 1996. *Imagined Communities: Reflections on the Origin and Spread of Nationalism*. London: Verso; Michael Billig. 1995. *Banal Nationalism*. London: Sage; Earnest Gellner. 1983. *Nations and Nationalism*. Oxford: Blackwell; Michael Brown, Owen Cote, Sean M. Lynn-Jones, and Steven E. Miller. 1997. *Nationalism and Ethnic Conflict*. Cambridge, MA: The MIT Press; Raymond Taras and Rajat Ganguly. 1998. *Understanding Ethnic Conflict*. New York: Longman.

2. Arend Lijphart and Bernard Grofman. Eds. 1984. *Choosing an Electoral System: Issues and Alternatives*. New York: Praeger; Arend Lijphart. 1984. *Democracies*. New Haven, CT: Yale University Press; Arend Lijphart. 1986. "Degrees of Proportionality of Proportional Representation Formulas." In *Electoral Laws and Their Political Consequences*. Bernard Grofman and Arend Lijphart. Eds. New York: Agathon Press; Arend Lijphart. 1991. "Constitutional choices for new democracies." *Journal of Democracy* 2(1): 72–84; Arend Lijphart. 1991. "Proportional representation: Double checking the evidence." *Journal of Democracy* 2(2): 42–48; Arend Lijphart. 1994. *Electoral Systems and Party Systems: A Study of Twenty-Seven Democracies, 1945–1990*. New York: Oxford University Press; Arend Lijphart. 1995. "Electoral Systems." In *The Encyclopedia of Democracy*. Seymour Martin Lipset. Ed. Washington, D.C.: Congressional Quarterly Press; Arend Lijphart. 1999. *Patterns of Democracy: Government Forms and Performance in 36 Countries*. New Haven, CT: Yale University Press.

3. See Giovanni Sartori. 1994. *Comparative Constitutional Engineering: An Inquiry into Structures, Incentives, and Outcomes*. New York: Columbia University Press; Arend Lijphart and Carlos Waisman. 1996. *Institutional Design in New Democracies*. Boulder, CO: Westview.

4. See, for example, Gary W. Cox. 1997. *Making Votes Count*. Cambridge, U.K.: Cambridge University Press; Richard Katz. 1997. *Democracy and Elections*. Oxford: Oxford University Press.

5. Arend Lijphart. 1999. *Patterns of Democracy*. New Haven, CT: Yale University Press. Table 8.2. P.162.

6. Arend Lijphart. 1999. *Patterns of Democracy*. New Haven, CT: Yale University Press. Other secondary factors influencing this process include the basic electoral formula translating votes into seats (whether majoritarian, mixed, or proportional); the assembly size (the total number of seats in a legislature); linked lists or apparentement provisions; the ballot structure; malapportionment (the size and distribution of the electorate within each constituency); and the difference between parliamentary and presidential systems.

7. Arend Lijphart. 1999. *Patterns of Democracy*. New Haven, CT: Yale University Press. Figure 8.2. P.168.

8. Richard Katz. 1997. *Democracy and Elections*. Oxford: Oxford University Press. Pp.144–160.

9. Arend Lijphart. 1999. *Patterns of Democracy*. New Haven, CT: Yale University Press. P.33.

10. Lijphart 1999, *op. cit.*, 280–282; see also Rein Taagepera (1994), who adopts a similar strategy. "Beating the Law of Minority Attrition." In Wilma Rule and

Joseph Zimmerman. Eds. *Electoral Systems in Comparative Perspective*. Westport, CT: Greenwood Press.

11. Pippa Norris. 1985. "Women in European legislative elites." *West European Politics* 8(4): 90–101; Wilma Rule. 1994. "Women's Under-representation and electoral systems." *PS: Political Science and Politics* 27(4): 689–692; Pippa Norris. 2000. "Women's Representation and Electoral Systems." In *The International Encyclopedia of Elections*. Richard Rose. Ed. Washington, D.C.: Congressional Quarterly Press.

12. Pippa Norris and Joni Lovenduski. 1995. *Political Recruitment: Gender, Race and Class in the British Parliament*. Cambridge, U.K.: Cambridge University Press; Pippa Norris. Ed. 1997. *Passages to Power: Legislative Recruitment in Advanced Democracies*. Cambridge, U.K.: Cambridge University Press; Pippa Norris. 1997. "Equality Strategies in the U.K." In *Sex Equality Policy in Western Europe*. Frances Gardiner. Ed. London: Routledge. Pp.46–59.

13. See, however, Pippa Norris and Robert Mattes. 2003. "Does ethnicity determine support for the governing party?" Afrobarometer Working Papers 26. Available online at http://www.afrobarometer.org/abseries.html.

14. The Gastil Index for these countries estimates that Malaysia can be classified as Partly Free (4.5/7) and that Lebanon is Not Free (5.5/7). See the Freedom House Index of Freedom. Available online at www.freedomhouse.org.

15. Timothy D. Sisk and Andrew Reynolds. 1998. *Electoral Systems and Conflict Management in Africa*. Washington, D.C.: U.S. Institute of Peace Press. See also Ben Reilly and Andrew Reynolds. 1998. *Electoral Systems and Conflict in Divided Societies*. Washington, D.C.: National Academy Press.

16. S.M. Saideman, D.J. Lanoue, M. Campenni, and S. Stanton. 2002. "Democratization, political institutions, and ethnic conflict – A pooled time-series analysis, 1985–1998." *Comparative Political Studies* 35(1): 103–129.

17. See George Tsebelis. 1990. "Elite interaction and constitution building in consociational democracies." *Journal of Theoretical Politics* 2(1): 5–29.

18. Joel Barkan. 1998. "Rethinking the Applicability of Proportional Representation for Africa." In *Electoral Systems and Conflict Management in Africa*. Timothy D. Sisk and Andrew Reynolds. Eds. Washington, D.C.: U.S. Institute of Peace Press.

19. Rein Taagepera. 1998. "How electoral systems matter for democratization." *Democratization* 5(3): 68–91.

20. See Pippa Norris. 1995. "The politics of electoral reform." *International Political Science Review* Special Issue on Electoral Reform. 16(1): 65–78.

21. Arend Lijphart. 1984. *Democracies*. New Haven, CT: Yale University Press. Pp.22–23.

22. Donald L. Horowitz. 1991. *A Democratic South Africa? Constitutional Engineering in a Divided Society*. Berkeley: University of California Press; Donald L. Horowitz. 1993. "Democracy in divided societies." *Journal of Democracy* 4(4): 18–38.

23. André Blais and R. Kenneth Carty. 1990. "Does proportional representation foster voting turnout?" *European Journal of Political Research* 18(2): 167–181.

24. Robert B. Mattes and Amanda Gouws. 1999. "Race, Ethnicity and Voting Behavior: Lessons from South Africa." In *Electoral Systems and Conflict in Divided*

Societies. Andrew Reynolds and Ben Reilly. Eds. Washington, D.C.: National Academy Press. See also Ted Marr. 1993. "Why minorities rebel – A Global analysis of communal mobilization and conflict since 1945." *International Political Science Review* 14(2): 161–201.

25. Christopher J. Anderson and Christine A. Guillory. 1997. "Political institutions and satisfaction with democracy." *American Political Science Review* 91(1): 66–81.

26. Pippa Norris. 1999. "Institutional Explanations for Political Support." In Pippa Norris. Ed. *Critical Citizens: Global Support for Democratic Governance.* Oxford: Oxford University Press. Table 11.3. The social controls included age, gender, socioeconomic status, and education.

27. Susan A. Banducci, Todd Donovan, and Jeffrey A. Karp. 1999. "Proportional representation and attitudes about politics: Results from New Zealand." *Electoral Studies* 18(4): 533–555.

28. Pippa Norris. Ed. 1999. *Critical Citizens: Global Support for Democratic Governance.* Oxford: Oxford University Press.

29. Pippa Norris. Ed. 1999. *Critical Citizens: Global Support for Democratic Governance.* Oxford: Oxford University Press.

30. Martin Bulmer. 1986. "Race & Ethnicity." In *Key Variables in Social Investigation.* Robert G. Burgess. Ed. London: Routledge & Kegan Paul. In contrast, "race," based on how members of society perceive group physical differences such as skin color, can be regarded as a sub-set of broader ethnic identities.

31. It is unfortunate that the merged NES data does not appear to define the Hispanic population in the United States.

32. Peter C. Ordeshook and Olga Shvetsova. 1994. "Ethnic heterogeneity, district magnitude and the number of parties." *American Journal of Political Science* 38(1): 100–123. See also Donald Horowitz. 1991. *A Democratic South Africa?* Cambridge, U.K.: Cambridge University Press.

33. See Ian Budge, et al. 1997. *The Politics of the New Europe.* London: Longmans. Pp.106–107.

34. Pippa Norris and Ivor Crewe. 1994. "Did the British marginals vanish? Proportionality and exaggeration in the British electoral system revisited." *Electoral Studies* 13(3): 201–221.

35. Wilma Rule and Joseph Zimmerman. Eds. 1994. *Electoral Systems in Comparative Perspective: Their Impact on Women and Minorities.* Westport, CT: Greenwood.

36. Arend Lijphart. 1999. *Patterns of Democracy.* New Haven, CT: Yale University Press. P.58.

37. For a comparison of regional parties and their electoral strength in EU member states see Derek J. Hearl, Ian Budge, and Bernard Pearson. 1996. "Distinctiveness of regional voting: A comparative analysis across the European community (1979–1993)." *Electoral Studies* 15(2): 167–182.

38. See, for example, the measure of the "effective number of ethnic groups" used by Peter C. Ordeshook and Olga Shvetsova. 1994. "Ethnic heterogeneity, district magnitude, and the number of parties." *American Journal of Political Science* 38(1): 100–123. See also Octavia Amorim Neto and Gary W. Cox. 1997. "Electoral institutions, cleavage structures and the number of parties." *American Journal of Political Science* 41(1): 149–174.

39. Andrew Reynolds and Ben Reilly. Eds. 1997. *The International IDEA Handbook on Electoral System Design.* Stockholm: International IDEA.

40. Bernard Grofman and Chandler Davidson. Eds. 1992. *Controversies in Minority Voting*. Washington, D.C.: Brookings Institute; Amy, Douglas. 1993. *Real Choices: New Voices: The Case for PR Elections in the United States*. New York: Columbia University Press.

41. Joni Lovenduski and Pippa Norris. Eds. 1993. *Gender and Party Politics*. London: Sage; Pippa Norris. Ed. 1997. *Passages to Power: Legislative Recruitment in Advanced Democracies*. Cambridge, U.K.: Cambridge University Press.

42. Arend Lijphart. 1994. *Electoral Systems and Party Systems: A Study of Twenty-Seven Democracies, 1945–1990*. New York: Oxford University Press. P.140.

Chapter 10: Constituency Service

1. John M. Carey and Matthew Soberg Shugart. 1995. "Incentive to cultivate a personal vote: A rank-ordering of electoral formulas." *Electoral Studies* 14(4): 417–440.

2. For a discussion see John M. Carey and Matthew Soberg Shugart. 1995. "Incentive to cultivate a personal vote: A rank-ordering of electoral formulas." *Electoral Studies* 14(4): 417–440.

3. See, for example, Bernard Grofman, Sung-Chull Lee, Edwin A. Winckler, and Brian Woodall. Eds. 1997. *Elections in Japan, Korea and Taiwan under the Single Non-Transferable Vote: The Comparative Study of an Embedded Institution*. Ann Arbor, MI: University of Michigan Press.

4. Pippa Norris and Joni Lovenduski. 1995. *Political Recruitment: Gender, Race and Class in the British Parliament*. Cambridge, U.K.: Cambridge University Press; Pippa Norris. 1996. "Candidate Recruitment." In *Comparing Democracies*. Lawrence LeDuc, Richard Niemi, and Pippa Norris. Eds. Thousand Oaks, CA: Sage; Reuven Y. Hazan. 2002. "Candidate Recruitment." In *Comparing Democracies 2*. Lawrence LeDuc, Richard Niemi, and Pippa Norris. Eds. London: Sage. It should be noted that the use of term limitations preventing politicians from standing for re-election, such as those used in Brazil, can also be expected to curtail the power of electoral incentives that might otherwise operate in preference-ballots, although this is also beyond the scope of this study.

5. Bruce E. Cain, John A. Ferejohn, and Morris P. Fiorina. 1987. *The Personal Vote: Constituency Service and Electoral Independence*. Cambridge, MA: Harvard University Press; Pippa Norris. 1997. "The puzzle of constituency service." *The Journal of Legislative Studies* 3(2): 29–49; Donley T. Studlar and Ian McAllister. 1996. "Constituency activity and representational roles among Australian legislators." *Journal of Politics* 58(1): 69–90; Richard E. Matland and Donley Studlar. (In press). "Determinants of legislative turnover: A Cross-national Analysis." *British Journal of Political Science*. See also Albert Somit. Ed. 1994. *The Victorious Incumbent: A Threat to Democracy?* Aldershot, U.K.: Dartmouth.

6. For a useful review of the U.S. bias in the literature see Gerald Gamm and John Huber. 2002. "Legislatures as Political Institutions: Beyond the Contemporary Congress." In *Political Science: State of the Discipline*. Ira Katznelson and Helen V. Milner. Eds. New York: W.W. Norton.

7. Bernhard Wessels. 1999. "Whom to Represent? The Role Orientations of Legislators in Europe." In *Political Representation and Legitimacy in the European*

Union. Hermann Schmidt and Jacques Thomassen. Eds. Oxford: Oxford University Press.

8. John Curtice and Phil Shively. 2000. "Who Represents Us Best? One Member or Many?" Paper presented at the *International Political Science Association World Congress*, Quebec, August 1–5.

9. Bruce E. Cain, John A. Ferejohn, and Morris P. Fiorina. 1987. *The Personal Vote: Constituency Service and Electoral Independence*. Cambridge, MA: Harvard University Press; Ian McAllister. 1997. "Australia." In *Passages to Power: Legislative Recruitment in Advanced Democracies*. Pippa Norris. Ed. Cambridge, U.K.: Cambridge University Press; Donley T. Studlar and Ian McAllister. 1996. "Constituency activity and representational roles among Australian legislators." *Journal of Politics* 58(1): 69–90.

10. Pippa Norris and Joni Lovenduski. 1995. *Political Recruitment: Gender, Race and Class in the British Parliament*. Cambridge, U.K.: Cambridge University Press.

11. Philip Norton and David Wood. 1993. *Back from Westminster: British Members of Parliament and Their Constituents*. Lexington, KY: The University Press of Kentucky; Philip Norton and David Wood. 1994. "Do candidates matter? Constituency-specific vote changes for incumbent MPs, 1983–87." *Political Studies* 40(2): 227–238.

12. Data is derived from the series of surveys of more than 1,000 parliamentary candidates and MPs conducted every election by Pippa Norris and Joni Lovenduski. *The British Representation Study, 1992–2001*. Available online at www.pippanorris.com.

13. Pippa Norris. 1997. "The puzzle of constituency service." *The Journal of Legislative Studies* 3(2): 29–49; John Curtice and Michael Steed. 2001. "Appendix 2: The Results Analyzed." Table A2.8. In David Butler and Dennis Kavanagh. *The British General Election of 2001*. London: Palgrave. Curtice and Steed estimate that the personal vote made a difference in the performance of all parties, especially for the minor parties, in the 2001 general election.

14. B.J. Gaines. 1998. "The impersonal vote? Constituency service and incumbency advantage in British elections, 1950–92." *Legislative Studies Quarterly* 23 (2): 167–195.

15. Michael Gallager, Michael Laver, and Peter Mair. 1995. *Representative Government in Modern Europe*. New York: McGraw Hill; David M. Wood and G. Young. 1997. "Comparing constituency activity by junior legislators in Great Britain and Ireland." *Legislative Studies Quarterly* 22(2): 217–232; S.M. Swindle. 2002. "The supply and demand of the personal vote – Theoretical considerations and empirical implications of collective electoral incentives." *Party Politics* 8(3): 279–300.

16. John M. Carey and Matthew Soberg Shugart. 1995. "Incentive to cultivate a personal vote: A rank-ordering of electoral formulas." *Electoral Studies* 14(4): 417–440.

17. R.E. Ingall and Brian Crisp. 2001. "Determinants of home style: The many incentives for going home in Colombia." *Legislative Studies Quarterly* 26(3): 487–512; Brian Crisp and R.E. Ingall. 2002. "Institutional engineering and the nature of representation: Mapping the effects of electoral reform in Colombia."

American Journal of Political Science 46(4): 733–748; Barry Ames. 1995. "Electoral strategy under open-list proportional representation." *American Journal of Political Science* 39(2): 406–433; Robert H. Dix. 1984. "Incumbency and electoral turnover in Latin America." *Journal of InterAmerican Studies and World Affairs* 26(4): 435–448.

18. D.J. Samuels. 2002. "Pork barreling is not credit claiming or advertising: Campaign finance and the sources of the personal vote in Brazil." *Journal of Politics* 64(3): 845–863.

19. Bernhard Wessels. 1997. "Germany." In *Passages to Power: Legislative Recruitment in Advanced Democracies*. Pippa Norris. Ed. Cambridge, U.K.: Cambridge University Press. See also Bernhard Wessels. 1999. "Whom to Represent? The Role Orientations of Legislators in Europe." In *Political Representation and Legitimacy in the European Union*. Oxford: Oxford University Press.

20. T. Stratmann and M. Baur. 2002. "Plurality rule, proportional representation, and the German bundestag: How incentives to pork-barrel differ across electoral systems." *American Journal of Political Science* 46(3): 506–514. See also Thomas Lancaster and William Patterson. 1990. "Comparative pork barrel politics: perceptions from the West-German-Bundestag." *Comparative Political Studies* 22(4): 458–477.

21. E.S. Herron. 2002. "Electoral influences on legislative behavior in mixed-member systems: Evidence from Ukraine's Verkhovna Rada." *Legislative Studies Quarterly* 27(3): 361–382.

22. Vernon Bogdanor. Ed. 1985. *Representatives of the People? Parliamentarians and Constituents in Western Democracies*. Aldershot, Hants, U.K.: Gower.

23. See, for example, Ron J. Johnston and Charles J. Pattie. 2002. "Campaigning and split-ticket voting in new electoral systems: The first MMP elections in New Zealand, Scotland and Wales." *Electoral Studies* 21(4): 583–600.

24. R. Mulgan. 1995. "The democratic failure of single-party government: The New Zealand experience." *Australian Journal of Political Science* 30(Special Issue): 82–96; Jonathan Boston, Stephen Levine, Elizabeth McLeay, and Nigel S. Roberts. 1996. *New Zealand under MMP: A New Politics?* Auckland: Auckland University Press; Jack Vowles, Peter Aimer, Susan Banducci, and Jeffrey Karp. 1998. *Voters' Victory? New Zealand's First Election under Proportional Representation*. Auckland: Auckland University Press; Michael Gallagher. 1998. "The political impact of electoral system change in Japan and New Zealand, 1996." *Party Politics* 4(2): 203–228.

25. Sidney Verba, Kay Schlozman, and Henry Brady. 1995. *Voice and Equality: Civic Volunteerism in American Politics*. Cambridge, MA: Harvard University Press.

26. Adam Przeworski, Susan C. Stokes, and Bernard Manin. Eds. 1999. *Democracy, Accountability and Representation*. Cambridge, U.K.: Cambridge University Press.

27. Bruce E. Cain, John A. Ferejohn, and Morris P. Fiorina. 1987. *The Personal Vote: Constituency Service and Electoral Independence*. Cambridge, MA: Harvard University Press; Pippa Norris. 1997. "The Puzzle of Constituency Service." *The Journal of Legislative Studies* 3(2): 29–49; Donley T. Studlar and Ian McAllister.

1996. "Constituency activity and representational roles among Australian legislators." *Journal of Politics* 58(1): 69–90; Richard E. Matland and Donley T. Studlar. (In press). "Determinants of legislative turnover: A Cross-national analysis." *British Journal of Political Science*. X(X): XX–XX. See also Albert Somit. Ed. 1994. *The Victorious Incumbent: A Threat to Democracy?* Aldershot: Dartmouth.

28. Lord Jenkins. 1998. *The Report of the Independent Commission on the Voting System*. London: Stationery Office. Cm 4090–1; see also Vernon Bogdanor. Ed. 2003. *The British Constitution in the Twentieth Century*. Oxford: Oxford University Press. The Jenkins report concluded that the vast majority of MPs in Britain should continue to be elected on an individual constituency basis by the Alternative Vote, with the remainder elected on a corrective top-up basis based on preferential ballots in small multimember constituencies formed from county or city boundaries.

Chapter 11: The Impact of Electoral Engineering

1. Arend Lijphart. 1994. *Electoral Systems and Party Systems: A Study of Twenty-Seven Democracies, 1945–1990*. New York: Oxford University Press.

2. Stefano Bartolini and Peter Mair. 1990. *Identity, Competition, and Electoral Availability*. Cambridge, U.K.: Cambridge University Press. Pp. 154–155.

3. See Pippa Norris. 1995. "The Politics of Electoral Reform in Britain." *International Political Science Review*. Special Issue on Electoral Reform 16(1): 65–78.

4. See Richard Katz. 1997. *Democracy and Elections*. Oxford: Oxford University Press.

5. Michael Pinto-Duschinsky. 2002. "Overview." In *Handbook on Funding of Parties and Election Campaigns*. Stockholm: International IDEA.

6. See Arend Lijphart. 1994. *Electoral Systems and Party Systems*. Oxford: Oxford University Press. Appendix B.

7. The alliterative phrase "quota queen" was first used in a *Wall Street Journal* op-ed (4/30/93) by Clint Bolick but was quickly picked up by other news media, despite the fact that Lani Guinier advocated PR in multimember districts, not racial quotas. For her argument, see Lani Guinier. 1994. *The Tyranny of the Majority: Fundamental Fairness in Representative Democracy*. New York: The Free Press.

8. Wilma Rule and Joseph Zimmerman. 1992. *United States Electoral Systems: Their Impact on Women and Minorities*. New York: Greenwood Press; Lani Guinier. 1994. *The Tyranny of the Majority: Fundamental Fairness in Representative Democracy*. New York: The Free Press; Douglas J. Amy. 1996. *Real Choices/New Voices: The Case for Proportional Representation Elections in the United States*. New York: Columbia University Press; Douglas J. Amy. 2000. *Behind the Ballot Box: A Citizen's Guide to Electoral Systems*. Westport, CT: Praeger; Pippa Norris. 2001. "U.S. campaign 2000: Of pregnant chads, butterfly ballots and partisan vitriol." *Government and Opposition* 35(2): 1–24; Gerald Ford. 2002. *To Assure Pride and Confidence in the Electoral Process: Report of the National Commission on Federal Election Reform*. Washington, D.C.: Brookings Institute.

9. Andreas Auer and Alexander H. Trechsel. 2001. *Voter par Internet? Le projet e-voting dans le canton de Geneve dans une perspective socio-politique et juridique.* Available online at www.helbing.ch.

10. "May elections to trial online voting." Press release February 5, 2002. U.K. Department of Transport, Local Government, and Regions.

11. Andreas Auer and Alexander H. Trechsel. 2001. *Voter par Internet? Le projet e-voting dans le canton de Geneve dans une perspective socio-politique et juridique.* Available online at www.helbing.ch.

12. *Report of the National Workshop on Internet Voting.* March 2001. Internet Policy Institute for the National Science Foundation. Available online at http://www.internetpolicy.org/research/e_voting_report.pdf; The Independent Commission on Alternative Voting Methods. *Elections in the 21st Century: From Paper-Ballot to e-voting.* Electoral Reform Society. January 2002. Available online at www.electoral-reform.org.uk.

13. Pippa Norris. 2001. *Digital Divide: Civic engagement, information poverty, and the Internet worldwide.* New York: Cambridge University Press.

14. Available online at http://www.umich.edu/~nes/cses/studyres/module2/module2.htm.

15. Russell J. Dalton and Martin P. Wattenberg. 2001. *Parties without Partisans: Political Change in Advanced Industrial Democracies.* Oxford: Oxford University Press.

16. Anthony Heath, Roger Jowell, and John Curtice. 2001. *The Rise of New Labour.* Oxford: Oxford University Press; Herbert Kitschelt. 1994. *The Transformation of European Social Democracy.* Cambridge, U.K.: Cambridge University Press.

17. Pippa Norris. 2002. *Democratic Phoenix: Reinventing Political Activism.* New York: Cambridge University Press.

18. For further work on this see Pippa Norris and Robert Mattes. 2003. "Does Ethnicity Determine Support for the Governing Party?" Afrobarometer Working Paper 26. Available online at http://www.afrobarometer.org/abseries.html.

19. See Giovanni Sartori. 1994. *Comparative Constitutional Engineering: An Inquiry into Structures, Incentives, and Outcomes.* New York: Columbia University Press; Arend Lijphart and Carlos Waisman. 1996. *Institutional Design in New Democracies.* Boulder, CO: Westview.

20. Olga Shvetsova. 1999. "A survey of post-communist electoral institutions: 1990–1998." *Electoral Studies* 18(3): 397–409.

21. See, for example, the ACE project, available online at www.idea.int.

Index